Philosophers in **Exile**

*Studies in Phenomenology and
Existential Philosophy*

Philosophers in **Exile**

*The Correspondence of Alfred Schutz and
Aron Gurwitsch, 1939–1959*

Edited by Richard Grathoff
Translated by J. Claude Evans
Foreword by Maurice Natanson

INDIANA UNIVERSITY PRESS ❖ BLOOMINGTON AND INDIANAPOLIS

© 1989 by Indiana University Press

The German edition of this correspondence was published as *Alfred Schütz, Aron Gurwitsch: Briefwechsel, 1939–1959,* © 1985 Wilhelm Fink Verlag

Manufactured in the United States of America

Library of Congress Cataloging-in-Publication Data
Schutz, Alfred, 1899–1959.
[Alfred Schütz, Aron Gurwitsch. English]
Philosophers in exile : the correspondence of Alfred Schutz and Aron Gurwitsch, 1939–1959 / edited by Richard Grathoff ; translated by J. Claude Evans ; foreword by Maurice Natanson.
p.   cm.—(Studies in phenomenology and existential philosophy)
Translation of : Alfred Schütz, Aron Gurwitsch.
Bibliography: p.
Includes index.
ISBN 0-253-32627-3
1. Schutz, Alfred, 1899–1959—Correspondence. 2. Gurwitsch, Aron—Correspondence. 3. Husserl, Edmund, 1859–1938. 4. Phenomenology. 5. Philosophers—United States—Biography.   I. Gurwitsch, Aron.   II. Grathoff, Richard.   III. Title.   IV. Series.
B945.S354A4   1989
193—dc19
88-46037
CIP

[B]

1 2 3 4 5 93 92 91 90 89

C O N T E N T S

Foreword

MAURICE NATANSON

This book presents the remarkable correspondence between Alfred Schutz and Aron Gurwitsch, both European Jews born at the turn of the century, both philosophers deeply influenced by Edmund Husserl, both exiled more than once (the two first met in Paris in the mid-thirties, at the suggestion of Husserl), both ultimately seminal figures in the establishment of phenomenology in the United States. The dates of the Schutz-Gurwitsch correspondence—1939–1959—provide a focus for but not an explanation of the scope of this exchange.

The correspondents were strongly entrenched in the history of their times, but their intellectual and cultural roots were defined humanistically by the classical gymnasia that they attended, by the Continental universities at which they studied, by their immersion in philosophy (Edmund Husserl's phenomenology, in particular), and by their comprehension of the grounding of the social as well as the natural sciences in a logic whose terms relate profoundly to the world of daily life—the ambience of human experience as it is lived in immediacy by all of us.

But more than being intellectual products of a certain European tradition, Schutz and Gurwitsch were historically located at a savage juncture of world events: they were Europeans compelled to leave their cultural homes to become exiles not only from their lands but also from the European tradition itself—a tradition which, far from ridding itself of what it deemed undesirable "elements," splintered into the shards of irrationalism, genocide, and historical disgrace. A central part of what makes this correspondence remarkable is that Schutz and Gurwitsch understood the chaos of the events of their times and yet in the midst of their own personal losses comprehended the loss of that European humanism which wounded itself beyond recovery. These refugees did not escape the Europe that made them possible; that Europe no longer existed.

What remained was the world that Schutz and Gurwitsch constituted in their correspondence and personal meetings—perhaps above all through the philosophical papers which they wrote, sent to each other faithfully, and discussed with the deepest critical care and philosophical urgency—as well as in the no less important personal concern that they showed for each other, for their families, and for their friends. Paradoxically, theirs was not a private but a universal world. What, then, makes this correspondence "remarkable"?

To the reasonable question: What, essentially, is the Schutz-Gurwitsch correspondence about? no simple response is possible. It is correct to say that the entire correspondence is, *au fond*, a reflection of the relationship between two extraordinary individuals— that the correspondence is essentially a human document. But being correct is not always enough. In this instance, it must also be said that though the correspondence is a mirror of a transcendent friendship and of a world shared by exceptional relations and friends, it is at the same time a philosophical venture by Schutz and Gurwitsch to work out their ideas through and with each other, to determine whether their fundamentally resonant but more than occasionally divergent views could achieve clarity and resolution. The image used by the correspondents is that of a "tunnel" that they are digging from different ends and which may or may not "meet." The tunnel is being dug "together"; whether the diggers finally "meet" is of vital importance to them; but the image has its limits. The phenomenological theme of the correspondence is the practice of philosophy: the nature of that practice, its implications for the practitioners, and the transformation of both self and world in the course of what might be called a genuine philosophical existence. In a way, the correspondence is about itself, for both partners are self-consciously and overtly aware of the activity of philosophy which is engendered by their reports to each other, their exchanges, their arguments, and their reliance on each other for the expert understanding and unqualified honesty in theoretical as well as practical matters which are so rarely found in combination.

From a different vantage point, one may say with confidence that, depending on where one samples these letters, a variety of themes provides legitimate (if partial) answers to the question of what this correspondence is about. A strong part of the book is concerned with problems of what has come to be known as the subject of "refugee scholars" in the United States in the 1930s and 1940s. What is different about the Schutz-Gurwitsch exchange when viewed under the rubric of "refugee scholars" is the internal—or better, *interior*—character of a sustained discussion between such scholars themselves rather than by their observers in the literature devoted to what is now a "research" subject. Ironically, perhaps, Max Weber's notion of the actor's interpretation of the meaning of his own act—the "subjective interpretation of meaning"—so well known to Schutz and Gurwitsch, became particularized in the actuality of the lives of the correspondents. They were refugee scholars who not only knew their sociological placement but who were also concerned with its philosophical implications. We have a doubling effect: refugee scholars who were professionally concerned with some of the most fundamental aspects of the situation of which they are prime examples. But the meaning of the "refugee scholar" would be lost in its deepest aspect with regard to Schutz and Gurwitsch if it were not recognized that for them the "refugee" problem had its own history, its own "sedimentation of meaning" (to use Husserl's language), for the "problem" is closer to Socrates than to Hitler. The force of events in 1939 cannot be wished away by invoking the ancient history of the "refugee"; neither can the historical scene of 1939 be comprehended fully without access to what lies so anciently behind it—not in a causal but in a humanistic sense. What identifies the essence of humanism in this context is the recognition that "history" is primarily not what happened but what keeps happening. The last historical event looks back to its origins not out of nostalgia but by virtue of an integral philosophic effort which human beings may make to grasp the meaning they bear in a "preinterpreted" world.

Still another feature of the correspondence is the intensive discussion of phenomenology—of a considerable number of phenomenological problems, to be more precise—which for the two men was a fire fed by the exchange of their writings. This discussion will be precious to the reader acquainted with philosophy in general and phenomenology in particular; approached in the wrong way, it may very well lead the reader who is not especially interested in phenomenology to conclude that *whatever* the problems at issue are, they are intended only for readers of Husserl. What possible change in approach can alter this circumstance? What would an approach "in the right way" mean? What is at issue in the discussions of phenomenological problems in the correspondence between Schutz and Gurwitsch is not textual in character; that is, neither correspondent is primarily concerned with what Husserl meant by a particular point made in a particular passage. The task of the correspondence is not the explication or the exegesis of the writings of Edmund Husserl.

Early in the exchange, Schutz (in his letter of August 19, 1939) wrote: "As you know, for me the question concerning the 'correct,' namely orthodox, Husserl interpretation is always secondary to the question concerning the true states of affairs." Of course, the proper understanding of Husserl and his texts was of major importance to the friends. Of much greater significance was what Husserl sought: an immensely thorough—philosophically stubborn—description, analysis, and comprehension of "the true states of affairs," the "things themselves." Still, more than a rigorous discussion of phenomenological problems, the correspondence shows itself to be a sophisticated but, in a powerful way, raw specimen of philosophizing of the most searching order regarding the meaning of perception, action, intersubjectivity, objectivity, the ego, consciousness, knowledge of the Other, the proper station of social science, and the limits of symbol, relevance, and even "limit" itself in "lived experience": the place of transcendence (to paraphrase one of Wolfgang Köhler's titles) in a world of finitude.

To say that a considerable part of the correspondence consists in the discussion of philosophical problems is, once again, the "wrong" way of reading this book. The statement is true but banal. Rather, the discussion of philosophical problems by Schutz and Gurwitsch is perhaps the most incisive exchange of views in the course of a twenty-year correspondence in recent philosophy. If the number of members of the class of outstanding philosophers who have sustained a twenty-year intellectual correspondence is small, it is all the more important testimony to the unusual character of this book and all the more clarification of what "remarkable" means here: The correspondence is alive with the swift current of deeply consonant and yet strongly independent and sometimes antagonistic views; these pages present philosophical thinking in process and in the presence of another mind at once profoundly congenial and committed only to the truth that philosophers have traditionally heralded but seldom lived by.

Yet the philosophical correspondence cannot be taken at surface value. It *is* extremely telling that the discussion between Schutz and Gurwitsch deepens our understanding of phenomenology in quite specific ways. For example, take the different interpretations and emphases that the two men gave to Husserl's conceptions of the noetic and the noematic polarities of intentional experience; that is, the way in which consciousness builds up the unities of meaning and those unities taken as accomplished, as presented to the perceiver—in phenomenological terms, "as meant." Schutz has been called a "noetic" phenomenologist and Gurwitsch has been termed a "noematic" phenomenologist. What the correspondence reveals, however, is that both sides of the perceptual process, the "subjective" and the "objective" sides, are issues which are very far from being phenomenologically settled; to the contrary, they remained for the two writers "problem children" as well as "problem adults" in the house of phenomenology. For both parties to the discussion, it was not enough to think through or to argue out what Husserl meant by these fundamental concepts; the still deeper demand they made of each other was the achievement of full clarity about the philosophical grounds of phenomenological issues. In this correspondence, phenomenology is philosophy in process, not philosophy become but philosophy becoming.

A still further way of taking the "right approach" to the distinctively phenomenological discussions in this book is to recognize as soon as possible what is revealed as the years of the correspondence pass: that the philosophizing together of Schutz and Gurwitsch is unthinkable without Husserl but is distorted if their letters are regarded as restricted either to Husserl, to Husserl's phenomenology, or to matters which are somehow all derivative from Husserlian thought. The two thinkers were thoroughly acquainted with the history of philosophy from Sextus Empiricus (Carneades) to work done in recent times. Both men shared a profound interest in the thought of Leibniz; both men could justifiably take for granted a detailed grasp of Plato and Aristotle; both men had read their Kant; and perhaps most important of all, they had unequal backgrounds in certain domains: Gurwitsch had devoted himself deeply to the study of Gestalt psychology; Schutz was saturated with the literature of the social sciences. Gurwitsch taught mathematics and physics; Schutz had an impressive knowledge of musicology as well as of the philosophical problems relating to music. For work on the foundations of arithmetic, one turns to Gurwitsch; for an essay such as "Mozart and the Philosophers," one turns to Schutz.

Their differences are as important as their similarities in coming to terms with what

Schutz and Gurwitsch contribute to this book. But the range of their discussion is not confined to philosophy in a purely academic sense. Philosophy provided, for them, the matrix in which basic problems of history, claims of cultural relativism (whether anthropological, linguistic, or generated in specific form by such disciplines as the "sociology of knowledge"), and the complexities of signs and symbols found their placement, if not resolution. Whether the issue being discussed was nihilism or transcendence, the correspondents shared a communality of understanding which, in considerable degree, was a function of their grasp of all realms of knowledge, art, and science as inwardly related, not merely interconnected. They were integral minds, not guardians of specialties or preserve-keepers of the intellect. Such integrity is more than the result of a classical education; it is the discipline and freedom of the philosophical life.

The correspondence does not merely go on; it develops. Preliminary probing of phenomenological issues soon reveals the differences between the two men. Schutz and Gurwitsch, for different reasons, were critical of transcendental phenomenology. Schutz never accepted Husserl's argument in the Fifth of his *Cartesian Meditations* concerning the Other. Gurwitsch developed his own particular sense of the transcendental. Indeed, in the latter part of the correspondence (November 30, 1954) Gurwitsch wrote: "I believe that I have made the discovery that there is no transcendental consciousness, but rather only a constitutive function of consciousness." By the end of their writing to each other, Schutz came to question almost every major concept in phenomenology. This is not as surprising as it might appear, for at least two reasons: first, Schutz from the outset of his study of Husserl's thought—long before the correspondence began—had strong reservations about transcendental phenomenology's intrinsic capacity to solve the problem of intersubjectivity and he recognized, early on, that without such a resolution the relevance of transcendental phenomenology to mundane experience would be, at best, highly problematic; second, when Schutz questioned practically the entire vital range of the vocabulary of phenomenology, it must be understood that he was writing to Gurwitsch, not just to anyone—whether knowledgeable about Husserl or not.

In different terms, it must be recognized that the external formulation carries an internal signification: it was only on the grounds of a mastery of and a profound involvement with phenomenology that Schutz could raise the far-reaching criticisms of Husserl which appear in the later part of this book. To take these remarks as Schutz's repudiation of phenomenology would be to betray Schutz's meaning and, even worse, to misgauge the level at which this correspondence was being carried on. Finally, the "internal" meaning of the criticism of phenomenology by both Gurwitsch and Schutz must be understood as an exercise in philosophical freedom. If phenomenology can be understood only from "within," then it may be said that the criticisms of Husserl's thought which are to be found in these letters are comprehensible only in phenomenological terms. As Schutz writes (April 20, 1952), "You know very well that my goal in all of my works . . . is a phenomenological analysis."

By the end of the correspondence there was considerable agreement between Schutz and Gurwitsch about the philosophical matters which had occupied them for twenty years. Without the slightest lessening of the intellectual or personal intensity of their exchange of letters, a final tribute to their friendship asserted itself. At the outset—in 1939 and the years immediately following—Schutz, by virtue of his professional position, which permitted him to join the New York City office of the firm with which he had been associated in Europe, was in a relatively strong set of circumstances in contrast to Gurwitsch, whose first need was to escape with his wife from the advance of the Nazi occupation of France and whose need, once that was accomplished, was to find appropriate academic employment in the United States. The struggle, detailed by the correspondence, was terrifically difficult on both counts. In different forms, the struggle continued for many years, now transformed, now disguised, but always disheartening, if occasionally lifted and relieved by a change for the better in circumstances. What remained constant was being a refugee, a Jew, and a representative of a school of philosophy that was largely unknown in the United States in the 1930s and 1940s and that was widely misunderstood where it was known. In contrast, Schutz had not only a solid professional position but had started what was to become his teaching career at the Graduate Faculty of the New School for Social Research. At the time of his arrival in the United States and for a number of years following, Gurwitsch's "star" was obscure, his situation precarious, his surroundings alien in a variety of senses. By the end of the correspondence, the situations of the two men were curiously altered in a number of ways. Gurwitsch had found an academic niche for himself in the United States, had had a major work published, had had a great success in a year's stay in the academic world of Europe, had been offered a professorship at the University of Berlin, and if he had not fully "arrived" had at least made his presence known and respected. Schutz rejoiced in his friend's recognition and successes—rejoiced in a way which may be understood only by the reader who has followed the correspondence to the end, to the period of Schutz's final illness. Their situations were in certain ways quite different at the end of the letters but the victory of the correspondence lies in the ultimate dignity and love of the two friends, for whom the accomplishment of either was the delight of the other.

The Schutz-Gurwitsch correspondence is a major achievement in its revelation of a world constituted in intimacy by two philosophers of brilliance, in its phenomenological depth of exploration and productive debate, in its celebration of a shared reality. Gurwitsch (in his letter of February 17, 1952) cites Goethe: "One is always indebted to others for what one is." What is celebrated in the other as well as with the other is the sense of coherence a life may possess when it is in alliance with the Good, willing to stand alone if necessary in the face of evil, and free in its coincidence with Spirit.

Acknowledgments

At the very moment
when man admits
that he knows less than ever
about himself . . .
there seems to have arisen
a new courage of truthfulness . . .
he is developing
a new kind of self-consciousness . . .

—Max Scheler, from the Preface to *Man's Place in Nature*

The publication of the correspondence between Alfred Schutz and Aron Gurwitsch is the result of a generous and courageous decision by their wives. They became convinced that over and above the indisputable scholarly significance of this correspondence, the personal experiences of being cast out of Europe and of life in American exile is of public interest. Schutz and Gurwitsch now belong to the classical figures of their discipline. Thus, their pointed observations, including their sometimes rather hard judgments about a post-war generation of philosophers from which they are separated "only" by their emigration, should meet with a critical understanding on the part of the reader. In any case, here we find documents which give voice to a scholarly milieu at a specific point in time, documents which are distinguished by the "courage of truthfulness" of a generation which exhibited new forms of self-awareness and self-understanding.

The editor thanks Alice Gurwitsch and Ilse Schutz for entrusting the correspondence to him. But above all, I would like to thank them for their patience. They have accompanied and aided every step of the long path toward publication. They now allow the reader a look into their personal world, the fate of their own emigration, and for this courageous step they have earned our deepest thanks and respect. May reader as well as critic, while concentrating on the text, respect the lives which come into view here!

The work on the publication of this correspondence began in 1977, when Gordon Turpin (M.A., Constance, 1973), supported by a research grant from the Fritz Thyssen Foundation, began transcribing the mostly hand-written letters, which were then typed by Gisela Huson (Bielefeld). This text of more than one thousand typewritten pages was the basis for a colloquium, "Phenomenology and Social Science," June 16–20, 1981, at the Center for Interdisciplinary Research of the University of Bielefeld, West Germany. Many footnotes in this volume are based on information provided by the participants. The contributions to the colloquium were published in *Sozialität und Intersubjektivität: Phänomenologische Perspektiven der Sozialwissenschaften im Umkreis von Aron Gurwitsch und Alfred Schütz*, edited by Richard Grathoff and Bernhard Waldenfels (Munich: Fink Verlag, 1983). The editors hope that the publication of these two volumes will bring new life into the sometimes somewhat quiet field between phenomenology and the social sciences.

The editor hopes that his choice of chapter titles and footnotes, the extensive index, and the prefaces will not distract the reader from the actual text of this correspondence.

The letters speak a clear and extraordinarily lively language, and do not really need any commentary.

Oerlinghausen, West Germany   Richard Grathoff

The English edition is largely identical with the German edition: *Alfred Schütz, Aron Gurwitsch: Briefwechsel 1939–1959,* edited by Richard Grathoff (Munich: Wilhelm Fink Verlag, 1985). A few letters have been reedited, some of the editorial footnotes have been corrected or enlarged, and some notes have been added. A complete list of letters and a detailed statement of editorial principles can be found in the German edition. English translations of Ludwig Landgrebe's Introduction and Richard Grathoff's Afterword to the German edition will be published elsewhere.

The translator wishes to thank Herbert Spiegelberg, Lester Embree, Maurice Natanson, Steven S. Schwarzschild, and Bernhard Waldenfels for information and advice concerning editing and translation. Above all, I would like to thank Richard Grathoff for his fine editing and his aid in the process of translating.

St. Louis   J. Claude Evans

Introduction

RICHARD GRATHOFF

The correspondence between Alfred Schutz (1899–1959) and Aron Gurwitsch (1901–1973) is, in spite of the great interest of the philosophical themes addressed, above all the document of a friendship in exile. It began with their encounter with Edmund Husserl and grew with the common effort to address the question of the relationship between life-world and science, which led Schutz and Gurwitsch deep into the thicket of the philosophy, methodology, and epistemology of the social sciences. "Myself digging a tunnel," as Gurwitsch describes their common project after he reading Schutz's "Multiple Realities" (S1945c), "I hear the knocking which announces the worker on the other side" (GS 9.3.45).[1] The metaphor of this shared labor on a tunnel, which confronts the phenomenology of everyday action (Schutz) with the problems of the theory of perception and science (Gurwitsch), becomes the guiding thread of their letters and discussions.

In the first letters the reader is introduced to the temporary exile in Paris, where Schutz and Gurwitsch met shortly before the outbreak of the Second World War. Husserl, as Alice (Raja) Gurwitsch recalls, had called Aron's attention to Schutz: "There is a young man in Vienna who spends his days at the bank and is a phenomenologist by night." And on January 12, 1948, Schutz writes to Kurt Riezler, then dean of the New School for Social Research,

> It was Edmund Husserl who in 1935 urged me to meet during my forthcoming trip to Paris Aron Gurwitsch, whom he considered to be one of his most promising students. I was immediately fascinated by his personality, his erudition, and the originality of his philosophical thought.

Nothing more is known about their first meeting in 1935. We know that Schutz was in Paris on a business trip for the Viennese bank, Reitler & Co., for which he worked from 1929 until the end of his life.[2] Gurwitsch, who had emigrated from Germany with his wife in 1933, taught at the Institut d'Histoire des Sciences at the Sorbonne, occupying one of twelve positions for emigrants which were financed with the aid of American donations. This aid for refugee German scientists had a certain similarity to the University in Exile (which later became the Graduate Faculty of the New School for Social Research) which was established in New York in the same year, and where Alfred Schutz and, following Schutz's death, Aron Gurwitsch later taught.

The correspondence begins in early 1938.[3] It was a cold and wet summer in Paris. Schutz, who had to leave Austria with his family following the *Anschluß*, was now, following a one-year stay in Paris, in New York. He wrote during a "day of the greatest anxiety and agitation" for the friends who remain in Paris (SG 8.19.39). The occasion for these first letters is the contributions which Schutz and Gurwitsch wrote for the Husserl volume planned by Marvin Farber, which was published in 1940 by the Harvard University Press and which was to make Husserl's phenomenology known to a broader public in America.

Edmund Husserl had died on April 26, 1938 in Freiburg. His philosophy was persecuted just like "degenerate art," and his papers were smuggled as diplomatic mail from

Freiburg to Louvain, where the Franciscan Father Hermann Leo Van Breda hid them, allowing work on them in the protection of a cloister even during the war years and offering many refugees protection and work.[4] Husserl's relationship to his successor at the chair for philosophy in Freiburg, Martin Heidegger, was at an end following Heidegger's election as Rector of the university in May of 1933.[5] Only one thing, which must have hurt Husserl deeply, need be mentioned here: Heidegger's inaugural speech as Rector, entitled "The Self-Assertion of the German University," celebrated the unique value of German science, the setting-forth for new horizons. It wasted not a single word on the "Law for the Restitution of Professional Civil Servants" which had been passed six weeks earlier (April 11, 1933) and which was to exclude Husserl (and, had they been there at the time, Gurwitsch and Schutz) along with all "non-Aryans" from the university. In a more conciliatory mood, one might follow Hannah Arendt in speaking of a short-lived "error" on Heidegger's part,[6] as long as one is prepared to overlook the elective affinity between decision-oriented models of everyday action and the highly stylized authenticity of the *Führer*–state which defined its own norms.[7]

But neither confessions of individual guilt nor the general ascription of motives can sound the depths of the conflict which after 1933 led to the destruction of the European social scientific milieu that had grown up between Berlin and Strasbourg, between Vienna, Prague, and Cracow since the turn of the century. An extensive literature, much of which was written in emigration, can inform the reader.[8] But the conflict has rarely been grasped more sharply than in the discourse between Schutz and Gurwitsch concerning the characteristics of their exile, which runs through the correspondence and becomes especially poignant in the last two years of the war.

The contemporary refugee (the *"refugié,"* as Gurwitsch wrote on July 16, 1944) "in one sense comes out of the void, in another sense out of a 3000-year past." Gurwitsch saw the gaping rupture of anarchy, of a nihilism which clothes itself as renewal, proclaiming the radical departure from history in the to-and-fro of gnostic, ideological, or utopian adventure. The void of nothingness, on the one hand completely bound to the concrete, on the other hand gains its orienting power from the formalisms of social systems. Out of the cynicism of the systems—regardless of which political color—nihilism offers its alternatives, consuming friend and foe without distinction. "We haven't broken with this world of ours," wrote Gurwitsch;

> on the contrary, it has been shattered. If we have brought anything with us, then [it is] precisely the historical forces which have made us what we are. We didn't want to break with our past, we didn't want to leave the world in which we grew up. The forces which drove us out were the enemies of Europe. When it was no longer possible to live in Europe as a European, at precisely that moment we had to leave in order to save our bare lives. (GS 7.16.44)

Alfred Schutz followed this motif of nihilism into the heart of the modern understanding of science, going far beyond Husserl's diagnosis, which saw the source of the "crisis of European humanity" in the radical formalization and indirect mathematization of the very qualities of life, in the course of which Galilean science robbed itself of its ground in the life-world. For Schutz the problem lay at the threshold of his own discipline: social philosophers and theorists of society fan the conflict, often blind to the consequences of their own actions. But can one, as Gurwitsch did in his nihilism essay (G1945), "ascribe to all sociology nihilistic tendencies which, e.g., the most modern sociology of knowledge without doubt exhibits?" With this question Schutz defined his own realm of work:

> As soon as sociology claims to explain the riddle of the world, to deal with the essence of man, to trace epistemological categories back to social existence, etc., it has already fallen prey to the nihilistic devil. But there is an intermediate sphere—that of the relatively natural

Weltanschauung—for whose description and analysis philosophical categories are just as inadequate as sociological categories for the explanation of the most modest philosophical problem. (SG 6.11.1945)

The nihilism of modernity has and is above all a method: On the surface, the radical formalization and mathematization leads to forgetting the ground of scientific research in the life-world and thus to the "liquidation of philosophy."[9] But when one probes beneath the surface one encounters an unlimited carelessness, which dissolves all boundaries delimiting the possibility of empirical research among those sociologies and behavioristic philosophies which, ignoring these limits, try to penetrate the riddle of man and world. Whereas Gurwitsch attempted an epistemological definition of nihilism, Schutz, working from the point of view of the sociology of action, discovered its essence in the refusal of a life-worldly, i.e., mundane, foundation for the transcendences of everyday life.[10]

Only the analysis of action leads into the "intermediate sphere" and uncovers the relative naturalness of that which is only apparently so self-evidently natural. "Nature" is accessible for everyday understanding and thus also for scientific investigation only within the limits of its relative worldliness, and the same holds for "society." The investigation of the "intermediate sphere" cannot deal with the immediate structure of a society, but rather with the more pregnant, narrower question of an interpretive construction of a social life-world which constitutes both a "nature" and "society." That is the central theme of Schutz's first (and only) book (S1932). From this perspective his demand that it is "high time that action be made the theme of philosophy" becomes comprehensible. What is new in this demand?

Action had become the theme of social science, indeed the basic theme of sociology, in the work of Max Weber. But his radical foundation broke through the ground of nihilism and leads sociology to claim an ultimate self-grounding. Society is equated with Being, which is Nothing if the transcendences of everyday experience and its life-worldly symbolism are forgotten. This rapprochement between Being and Nothingness, which Heidegger and Sartre pursued, was broken off by Schutz.

Both Schutz and Gurwitsch were less concerned with defending the theoretical positions of a school than with the special processes of human understanding in substantive, problem-oriented research. The Schutzian thesis, that in the "intermediate sphere" of the everyday and the life-world there is a fruitful and legitimate field for scientific description and analysis, was not merely shared by Gurwitsch, who had himself contributed to the Schelerian provenance of such investigations.[11] On the contrary, with the establishment of sociology there had developed a new understanding of scientific investigation which had spurred the discussion of the methodology of the social sciences since the turn of the century (Georg Simmel, Wilhelm Dilthey, Max Weber, etc.) and which received great stimulus from Husserlian phenomenology.[12] The programmatic development of phenomenological research in the strict sense can be followed in the publications in Husserl's *Jahrbuch für Philosophie und phänomenologische Forschung,* a development which began in 1913 with Husserl's *Ideas I* and ended in roughly 1928 (with Landgrebe's dissertation on Dilthey).[13] In the early 1930s the epistemological approaches to phenomenological research were scattered. Circles and research centers of European scope had been established: Vienna had become a center for the social sciences, competing with Göttingen, the Mecca of the natural sciences; in Paris, Alexandre Koyré and others started the *Recherches Philosophiques* in 1931;[14] Frederick J. J. Buytendijk was working in Groningen (later with Helmut Plessner), Van Breda in Louvain; the *Cercle philosophique de Prague,* started by Emil Utitz and J. B. Kozak, developed further.[15] This very active field has not yet been systematically investigated.

So Schutz, working in Vienna, and Gurwitsch, working in Frankfurt (as well as Göttingen and Berlin), were by no means isolated. Schutz's path (analyzing, from within the sociology of action, the meaningful construction of social reality) and Gurwitsch's

Alfred Schutz in the Austrian Military Service, 1916–1918.

path (analyzing, within cognitive psychology, human encounters in the social world) were intimately related to one another, as a glance at their earlier works confirms. Their relationship to Edmund Husserl deserves special attention. Both, as the Husserl expert will see immediately, pursued their work at a great distance from and at times sharply rejecting Husserl, whose experience with scientific research came only from mathematics and psychology. The reader of the correspondence will gain a deep insight into these decisive differences in phenomenological approach. Schutz and Gurwitsch developed their approaches to a phenomenologically motivated investigation in the social sciences at first in complete independence from one another and at times in contradictory fashion. The certainty of the common "digging the tunnel" develops only after 1945.

Schutz (born on April 13, 1889; originally Schütz) came from a middle-class though by no means wealthy Viennese family. Following his military service and studies of law in Vienna (1918–1921: he received his Doctor of Laws degree from the University of Vienna), he went into finance. This profession was to assure him independence for his unusually varied interests.[16] His days spent at the bank and his nights devoted to phenomenology have often been called a "double life." But that doesn't do justice to Schutz the musician (who worked with the historian of music Emanuel Winternitz),[17] the economic consultant to the American government, the philosopher of history, and the thinker whom Eric Voegelin remembered as "one of the keenest philosophical minds of our time."[18] And his family, for whom Schutz lived, should not be forgotten: in 1926 he married the art historian Ilse Heim; daughter Evelyn and son George were born in Vienna. The perspectives of Viennese friendships (in addition to Winternitz and Voegelin, above all with Felix Kaufmann) were supplemented in exile by an extraordinarily broad and intensive correspondence[19] which is often mentioned in the correspondence with Gurwitsch. In this respect it may help to recall Schutz's basic theme: The multiplicity of the provinces of meaning of everyday life as well as of science stands at the center of Schutz's never exclusively epistemological interest in the world. But if one wants a typology, his study of the "Well-Informed Citizen" (S1946) describes Schutz best: the politically active and carefully informed citizen whose expertise is not adequate to safeguard his everyday life, and who nevertheless as a layman, as a "man on the street," must trust the expertise of others.

The development of typological analyses of social action from the Weberian theory of ideal types into a general theory of typification of the life-world is one of Schutz's most important achievements. His Viennese teachers Hans Kelsen (rather distant) and Ludwig von Mises (his mentor and friend) followed his imaginative transformation of the Weberian analyses of action in phenomenological investigations, which above all Fritz Machlup then applied in economics: "I regard the work of Alfred Schutz as one of the most original, significant, and illuminating contributions to the methodology of the social sciences."[20] Sociology (for example Talcott Parsons, with whom Schutz carried on a sharp controversy concerning Weber's theory of rationalization in 1939–40[21]) recognized his achievement only much later.

If Schutz was a dialogical man given to long nighttime discussions, Gurwitsch was more of a loner. A brief letter from Alexandre Koyré drove him to long, restless walks through the Cambridge night (GS 12.17.50). The metaphor of the tunneler ("the knocking which announces the worker on the other side") is from Gurwitsch. Schutz calls him "Philalethes," the friend of the truth, whose fear that in his isolation he will end up a dilettante runs through the correspondence. Schutz encourages him with proverbs and quotations. Gurwitsch returns the favor and is teased in return: "The fact that you like your book doesn't surprise me at all, since you do have a very healthy power of judgment. Why don't you trust mine?" (SG 11.18.56).

Aron Gurwitsch was born on January 17, 1901 in Vilna,[22] where his father traded in lumber.[23] After the pogroms of 1905–6, he moved his family to Danzig, where Aron attended the *Gymnasium*. When inflation ruined his business, the father left his family and emigrated via Paris to New York, where his son later found him living among Russian emigrants in the Bronx. Aron Gurwitsch followed the same "passological" paths of Eastern European Jewish emigrants: from Vilna and Danzig through Berlin, Frankfurt, and Göttingen to Paris and finally to the United States of America. At every stop he encountered the already "established" generations of emigrants, which gave him insight into the variety of worlds of Jewish exile.

An individual who lives exclusively for and through scholarship chooses a precarious course. In Berlin Gurwitsch began to study mathematics and physics in 1919, then transferred to the newly opened university in Frankfurt, where the unification of already established educational institutions (academies for economics, medical clinics, etc.) and the founding of new institutes (Academy of Labor, Institute for Social Research) quickly created a superb milieu for research. In Kurt Riezler the Prussian Culture Ministry in Berlin had chosen an excellent and experienced official as Chancellor of the new university.[24] Here Gurwitsch attended the seminars of the psychologist Adhemar Gelb, who with Kurt Goldstein investigated veterans with head wounds. Their now classical studies of perceptual and orientational pathologies led to investigations of the amnesia of color names, with which Gestalt theory could establish itself in the field of psychopathology. Here Gurwitsch, as he later wrote (GS 9.4.51), received the decisive stimulus which led him to deal with Gestalt psychological problems using the methods of the phenomenology of perception. Gelb introduced him to Max Wertheimer, the famous Gestalt psychologist, whom Gurwitsch met again in New York exile. He began work on his dissertation, on a field theory of perception: against the "phenomenology of the pure ego" (Husserl's *Ideas*), Gurwitsch developed a "phenomenology of thematics" which later found a marked parallel in Sartre's non-egological theory and which was to have a decisive influence above all on Merleau-Ponty. Gurwitsch had wanted to do his Ph.D. under Max Scheler, who had accepted a position at Frankfurt but who suddenly died. Karl Mannheim, who took over the chair, was not a suitable alternative: thus Gurwitsch went to Moritz Geiger in Göttingen,[25] for whom he worked as an assistant for one year. Gurwitsch's lecture on "Existence and Knowledge"[26] before the famous Göttingen Kant Society demonstrated the level of achievement and recognition of the young scholar.

Dr. Aron Gurwitsch and Alice Stern (from Fulda)[27] married in 1929 and went to Berlin with a Prussian habilitation grant: there Gurwitsch worked on his *Human Encounters in the Social World* (G1976 and G1979), an investigation of typical styles of socialization in everyday life starting from the anonymity of social roles through partnership to intimate relationships, oriented above all towards Max Scheler. "The studies were concerned with a phenomenological clarification of some of Weber's basic concepts and the phenomenon of human living with one another" (GS 11.9.48). Methodologically Gurwitsch attempted to apply the theme-field analyses of the dissertation to empirical problems in the investigation of everyday action. The work was submitted to Max Dessoir in late 1931, but the habilitation remained incomplete. Political motives seem to have played a decisive role: the Gurwitsches were already talking with their friends Siegfried and Lilli Kracauer about emigrating to France. Gurwitsch mentions the habilitation thesis only once (GS 11.9.48); the theme is not mentioned in this correspondence in spite of (or perhaps because of) its closeness to Schutz's *Sinnhafte Aufbau*.[28]

Alice and Aron Gurwitsch left for Paris on April 1, 1933, as the first organized boycott of Jewish businesses began in Germany. They had no position in Paris, no funds; there was contact with Alexandre Koyré, whom Gurwitsch knew from the Göttinger circle of phenomenologists and with whom he had spoken at the International University Weeks in Davos. Koyré too was a Russian emigrant who came to Husserl about 1910 from Rostow on the Don, and who was then teaching, along with Emmanuel Levinas and Georges Gurvitsch, in Paris.[29] Initially, Alice worked in the office of the "League of Human Rights" (an organization for the aid of emigrants established by Gerlach and led

Aron and Alice Gurwitsch in Paris.

by Prof. Gumbel), which aided in the searches for apartments and jobs, in getting passports and papers. The power of the bureaucrats over passport, living permit, and visa became a fateful matter: whether one received a passport for Germans[30] (like Kracauer's) or a foreigner's passport (like Gurwitsch's, who was from Vilna, thus a Lithuanian), was later to decide whether one was interned or could leave.

Gurwitsch found an academic position in the first year: Sylvain Lévi (a sinologist at the Sorbonne) had established a Committee for the Aid of Emigrants and had received money from America (H.I.A.S. Fund) for some twelve instructor positions which were integrated into the Sorbonne. Gurwitsch taught along with Eric Weil (Hegelian philosophy), Paul-Ludwig Landsberg (Max Scheler expert), Fritz London (physicist from Bonn), David Nachmansohn (later at Columbia; biology), Paul Schrecker (Leibniz expert from Vienna), and others. Gurwitsch taught above all Gestalt psychology and phenomenology; Merleau-Ponty began attending Gurwitsch's lectures very early and later came to the Gurwitsch home for discussions every other week.

Two circles in which Gurwitsch moved in Paris between 1933 and 1940, though his participation varied, can be named in addition to this circle of emigrant scholars: the political circle and that of Jewish emigrants. The political emigrants were split into enemy camps of communists and socialists; through the League for Human Rights Alice Gurwitsch was active in this circle too. In Jewish emigrant circles (here especially the families Gurwitsch and Schutz, the Schönberg student pianist Erich Kahn and his parents, Hannah Arendt and Günter Stern, Siegfried and Lilli Kracauer) there was already at a very early date a center of Zionist immigration, above all for young refugees and children, for whom Hannah Arendt worked during this period. This led to her acquaintance with Alice Gurwitsch, who had worked in a kibbutz during the 1920s.

These circles were totally dependent upon their contacts and relations with the "natives" and "settlers" in Paris. Lucien Goldmann, Raymond Aron, Gaston Berger, and Alexandre Koyré belonged to the French horizon. The teaching position at the Sorbonne opened some doors, e.g., through a friend (Monique Picard, who studied with Gurwitsch) to Gabriel Marcel and Hélène Metzger (niece of Lucien Lévy-Bruhl, the famous anthropologist). As Schutz later remarked, "France is the land of cousins" (SG 11.10.52). Even the war didn't change this.

Schutz had long-time professional contacts and friendships in Paris (e.g., with Raymond Aron).[31] He had become acquainted with the emigrant milieu, but had hardly lived in it. The German invasion of Austria on March 13, 1938, caught Schutz on a business trip in Paris. He wanted to return to his family, but the Gurwitsches, experienced with the Nazi machinery, kept him in Paris. Ilse Schutz (in Vienna with her two children) sold their possessions and applied for legal immigration[32] in order to make later visits easier. But for Schutz Paris was only a stopping-off point: the invasion of Prague a year later (which forced Ludwig Landgrebe and his wife to leave Prague and accept Van Breda's invitation to Louvain) only made Schutz's decision to go to the U.S.A. more firm. Many, including the Gurwitsches, owed their chance to flee to the United States and thus their lives to this decision and above all to Schutz's careful planning and economic common sense. He found berths for his family on the "New Amsterdam," and they left for New York on July 14, 1939. Schutz's boxes of books began their bizarre trip from Paris through Casablanca to New York (the "Casablanca lift" of the correspondence), where they, along with the earthly goods of the Gurwitsches, arrived only after the end of the war.

In contrast to almost all emigrants who made it to New York, Schutz already had a secure position there. His activity at the banking house gave him access to financial aid which made possible the immigration of friends still in France. Following the Gurwitsches, who arrived in May 1940, the Kahn and Kracauer families were able to come in April 1941, and Schutz's parents in October 1941. In addition to the costs (fare, fees, higher and higher security: cf. especially SG 8.20.40) one had to secure an affidavit

The Graduate Faculty of the New School for Social Research, New York, 1945–1946. Clockwise around the table from the left: Julie Meyer, Horace Kallen, Felix Kaufmann, Frieda Wunderlich, Erich Hula, Alvin Johnson, Klara Mayer, Hans Staudinger, Arnold Brecht, Kurt Riezler, President Hovde, Albert Salomon, Leo Strauss, Salomon Ash, Hans Neisser, Mary Henle, Aba Lerner, Adolf Löwe, Carl Mayer, Dean Eduard Heimann.

(guarantee of support) as well as the professional requirements for a "non-quota visa":[33] for scholars, e.g., a position at an American college or university for at least one year was required, or an official exemption from the State Department. It was this work of aiding refugees, and not academic interests, that brought Schutz into contact with the New School for Social Research, the only emigrant graduate school with a full program of courses in the United States. As an institution which offered positions to immigrants it was of course long since over-staffed, but it offered important contacts to other universities, academic groups, and—last but not least—to aid organizations such as the Emergency Committee in Aid of Displaced Foreign Scholars, which was established by Stephen Duggan[34] and had a personal connection to the New School through Else Staudinger (Executive Secretary of the Emergency Committee).[35]

The New School for Social Research was established in New York in 1919 as the first university for adult education in the social sciences. The economist Alvin Johnson (editor of *The New Republic* and associate editor of the classic *Encyclopedia of the Social Sciences*) and the philosopher Horace M. Kallen were among the founders; later John Dewey taught there, and also William Isaac Thomas for some years. In the 1920s it was a center of progressive activity. To this day, the New School has an extraordinarily colorful and manifold program, from courses in art and languages to a philosophical workshop and a forum for political discussions. This framework is important for understanding the incorporation of the Graduate Faculty within the New School: Johnson wanted to create a model in order to preserve the German university in a living, institutional form of academic teaching. Carl Mayer, who in the 1950s was a member of the Sociology Department along with Alfred Schutz and Albert Salomon, formulated the idea in this way:

> It was established not so much with a view to offering shelter and a haven to German refugee scholars, but primarily in order to preserve an institution or rather the idea of which this institution had for a long time been the embodiment. With the advent of barbarism in Germany, the German university as it had developed in a long tradition had, together with many another institution of freedom, disappeared overnight.[36]

Some information concerning the history of the establishment of the Graduate Faculty can cast light on the correspondence. The idea of establishing a "University in Exile" within the New School came from Alvin Johnson, who during Schutz's lifetime bore the entire burden of arranging the financial affairs of the university, which depended on gifts and tuition. On April 14, 1933, Alvin Johnson wrote a letter to Professor Seligmann (Columbia University) with the request that he collect money for the scholars who were fleeing Germany. He had a concrete plan:

> Merely vocal protest will help these men little if at all. I therefore propose a protest which will arrest the attention of every person interested in scholarship, namely the prompt establishment of an institution to be known as 'The University in Exile.' Because everything turns on prompt action, if the protest is really to count, I propose to confine it to the social sciences—broadly interpreted—a field which is also the center of the battle. I have asked the Board of the New School to grant me the authority to set up such an institution in the New School, and have their enthusiastic support.

This letter led to the establishment of the "Graduate Faculty of Political and Social Sciences" in 1933, which is recalled by Arnold Brecht, a member of the original faculty:

> Three days after my arrival I participated in a faculty meeting of the Graduate Faculty for the first time, along with Max Ascoli. We were the tenth and eleventh members. The others were Emil Lederer, from the University of Berlin, earlier from Heidelberg, our first Dean; Arthur

Feiler from the University of Königsberg, earlier business editor of the *Frankfurter Zeitung;* Max Wertheimer, creator of Gestalt psychology, of the University of Frankfurt; Eduard Heimann, economist and sociologist from the University of Hamburg; Frieda Wunderlich, sociologist and member of parliament; Karl Brandt (Agricultural College of Berlin) and Hans Speier (Hochschule für Politik, Berlin); in addition the sociologist of music von Hornbostel (University of Berlin), who was in the hospital and died a few months later.

The twelfth member of the original faculty was not yet in New York: Albert Salomon, co-editor of the Berlin weekly *Die Gesellschaft.* Emil Lederer and Alvin Johnson first invited Karl Mannheim to come to the New School. Mannheim, a friend of Salomon's from their student years in Heidelberg, wanted to remain in London and suggested Albert Salomon, who had lost his chair in Cologne and was in a Cologne hospital suffering from polio.[37] These twelve emigrants constituted the original faculty, and were joined in the following years by Adolf Löwe and Hans Neisser, the Italian sociologist of law Nino Levi, Fernando de los Rios (Madrid), Leo Strauss (Berlin), Erich Hula (Vienna), and many others. The list of emigrants who were supported by the New School in the form of teaching positions of one kind or another comprises 176 scholars.[38]

The proud refusal which illuminates Carl Mayer's and Alvin Johnson's words, and completely dominates the autobiographical account of Arnold Brecht, is overshadowed by the horrible realities of the German occupation in France. In this gloom Gurwitsch recognized the abyss of nihilism. If a metaphor is allowable in such contexts, one might compare a note by Schutz with a poem by Arnold Brecht, who, looking back, summarized his experiences as Prussian Under-Secretary of State in the Berlin of 1933: "I do not want to argue, you are much too dumb to say. When monkeys ride on asses, the wise man turns away."[39] The pride of the Prussian emigrant did not yet grasp the nihilistic abyss which was to follow the German invasions of Vienna, Prague, and Paris. Schutz, closer to events and to the suffering of the Jews, grasped the horror much more clearly: everything is now "secondary to the question whether the beast to which power is given will once again force kings to bow before him" (SG 8.19.39). The classical idea of exile and emigration became a mere historical memory in the face of total war and the holocaust.

In this sense Schutz and Gurwitsch speak in the correspondence about the "passology," the science of passports and permits, of exile. The historical course is well known: The emigrants who had to leave Germany in 1933 had managed to establish themselves one way or another in Vienna, Prague, Cracow, or Paris, only to be overtaken by German troops and forced to flee all over again. The situation in Paris, which was hopelessly overcrowded before the outbreak of war, became chaotic and insane; with the outbreak of war those who had been seeking asylum became enemy aliens (in the United States they were later classified as "enemy aliens in the technical sense"; GS 7.16.44) and were interned, most of them in Gurs in southern France.[40] Following the German attack on Belgium and Holland (beginning on May 10, 1940) and the occupation of Paris (June 14), Vichy France remained unoccupied for the time being. Those emigrants who had fled to the south had one last chance if they could get on a ship from Marseilles or Lisbon. In 1942 southern France too was occupied by German troops; most of those who had been interned were taken to Bergen-Belsen, Dachau, Auschwitz, or some other concentration camp. Paul-Ludwig Landsberg was one of them. Maurice Halbwachs died in Buchenwald. The mother of Aron Gurwitsch, the parents and relatives of Albert Salomon: there was not a single emigrant who did not lose relatives or friends in the holocaust.

The Gurwitsches were able to flee on May 19, 1940, as German troops approached Paris. At the last moment they received a visa for the United States[41] and berths on the "Champlain" from Le Havre to New York: the last crossing, for on its return the ship was struck by German torpedos. The Kahns and Kracauers fled to the south and escaped through Lisbon to New York. Bureaucratic accidents, bribery, and fraud determined life or death. Most did not survive.[42]

In the United States, as the correspondence tells, the position at Johns Hopkins was renewed once for one year, financed by a donation from the Rothschild family through the mediation of an aunt in Baltimore (GS 1.26.41; SG 2.9.53). The dependence and uncertainty weighed heavily on Aron Gurwitsch—as it did in each such situation, be it at Harvard, where he received a temporary position teaching physics from 1943 to 1946, or at Brandeis University, whose establishment he followed with great interest and where he taught from 1948 to 1959, until Schutz's death, and where he suffered under faculty politics, personal intrigues, and scholarly mediocrity. Schutz continually wrote letters of recommendation and requests in order to help his friend get a grant, money to pay printing costs, or a new position. The times—also in the post-war years—were not exactly favorable for the phenomenologists.

Schutz himself was invited to be a Visiting Professor at the Graduate Faculty beginning in 1943–44. Only after the death of Felix Kaufmann did he take over a full professorship, later becoming chairman of the Department of Sociology, simultaneously building up the Philosophy Department and ruining his health with his professional double life. "My head is a suitcase," as he writes Gurwitsch on December 20, 1953, "which won't close." In May 1959, Gurwitsch had accepted an invitation from Ludwig Landgrebe to be guest professor in Cologne; there he received the news of the death of his friend, along with the urgent request from Hans Staudinger, now Dean, to come to the New School.

The correspondence between Alfred Schutz and Aron Gurwitsch stretches over the twenty years during which phenomenology became established in America (1939–59). The foundation was laid above all by a Husserl student, Marvin Farber (1901–80).[43] Schutz had met Farber during his first visit to America in 1937, again on the basis of a recommendation by Husserl, and immediately recognized Farber's organizational talent in clearing the grounds for phenomenology in the United States. A crucial element was the excellent cooperation between Farber and Schutz. In spite of all later substantive differences and Farber's sharp encounters with Aron Gurwitsch and Helmut Kuhn (SG 2.4.48), Schutz always appreciated Farber's efforts and attempted to mediate.

Farber's *The Foundation of Phenomenology* (Harvard University Press, 1942) symbolizes the first phase (up to roughly 1948) of the establishment of phenomenological research in America. This phase is characterized by Farber's unreserved substantive and personal engagement—and by his offer to the emigrants to work for Husserl's cause and that of phenomenological research. Based at the University of Buffalo, Farber indefatigably worked on three projects. The first was editing the first Husserl Memorial Volume (*Philosophical Essays in Memory of Edmund Husserl*, Harvard University Press, 1940). When one thinks of the difficulties Gurwitsch had later with this university press, which demanded such radical revision of his *Field of Consciousness* that he finally withdrew it, one can get some idea of just how shrewdly Farber must have proceeded. At the same time he was working on two other projects: on the one hand he established an International Phenomenological Society, working (by means of Schutz through Gurwitsch in Paris: SG 11.10.39) to win Van Breda and Landgrebe in Louvain as well as Gaston Berger, Raymond Aron, and Jean-Paul Sartre in France as founding members. This society was headquartered in Buffalo and published a journal whose first number appeared in 1940: *Philosophy and Phenomenological Research (PPR)*. Farber invited a carefully selected group of Americans (Gordon Allport, Dorion Cairns, V. J. McGill, and John Wild) and Europeans (Aron Gurwitsch, Gerhard Husserl, Felix Kaufmann, Fritz Kaufmann, Helmut Kuhn, Alfred Schutz, and Herbert Spiegelberg) to be members of the editorial board. Their work was restricted to evaluating texts and reviews; the main work was done by Farber himself. "Foreign editors" (Léon Brunschvicg, Antonio Banfi, Gaston Berger,

Eugen Fink, Jean Hering, Ludwig Landgrebe, and Francisco Romero) were to function as advisors. They were all in Europe, but in this way a connection was established which could be taken up again at once following the war.

In the beginning Schutz was much more pessimistic than Gurwitsch concerning their chances to continue their work, writing in April 1941: "Are you still enough of an optimist to believe that phenomenology will save itself out of the ruins of this world—as *philosophica aere perennius*? I simply don't believe that any more. The Bushmen will surely first have to become acquainted with National Socialist ideas" (SG 4.26.41). Marvin Farber too, though for very different reasons, was skeptical concerning a common project of phenomenological research.

Farber took up the Husserl critique which begins to appear in "his" (SG 10.4.50) journal after the war from the pens of Schutz and Gurwitsch, among others, turning it into a very sharp rejection whose philosophical background is to be found in his conscious turn to materialistic theories. A collection, *Philosophy of the Future: The Quest for Modern Materialism,*[44] was the culmination of this personal transformation, which Herbert Spiegelberg has carefully traced. The International Phenomenological Society continued to publish Farber's journal and became an almost exclusively American society which continued to function until about 1950 and was then supplanted by national organizations for phenomenological research in the United States and in various European countries.[45] A series of international symposia (Brussels 1951, Krefeld 1956, Royaumont 1957) accompanied this "coming of age in phenomenology," as one might call this process of maturation and institutionalization. The Husserl Archive in Louvain, not Buffalo, became the center of international phenomenological research.[46]

Schutz and Gurwitsch had more and more, Farber less and less, to do with the second phase of establishing phenomenology in America. Schutz returned to Europe on a business trip in 1946 (SG 10.18.46), saw his Parisian friends (Raymond Aron, Gaston Berger, Alexandre Koyré), met Maurice Merleau-Ponty, and visited Hermann L. Van Breda and Walter Biemel in Louvain. Alice and Aron Gurwitsch returned to Paris for the first time in 1949. The search for a secure teaching position (Gurwitsch received an offer to return to Paris) and his disputes with Farber were central moments in the first postwar years.

After years away from teaching philosophy (Gurwitsch taught mathematics and physics, and Schutz was only occasionally a lecturer at the New School) and with the reestablishment of their European ties, their phase of intensive academic teaching finally began. At the New School Felix Kaufmann died and Schutz became a member of the Sociology Department.[47] Gurwitsch went to Brandeis. He began his systematic work, *The Field of Consciousness.* In 1951 he offered the manuscript to the Harvard University Press, which rejected it. A French translation appeared in 1957,[48] the American version only in 1964, after Schutz's death. A German translation appeared posthumously in 1975.

Schutz did not live to finish another book.[49] His double life sapped his health. The manuscripts of his lectures and essays were written on weekends, generally dictated and then typed by Ilse Schutz. Among the many works of the 1950s are three major essays which Schutz first presented at colloquia and discussed at length with Gurwitsch in the correspondence: *Princeton 1953:* "Common Sense and Scientific Interpretation of Human Action" (S1953c), an investigation of the characteristics of analyses in the sociology of action, set off against the neopositivistic positions of Nagel and Hempel—as well as against Felix Kaufmann, to which Schutz studies up to now have paid little attention; *Harvard 1955:* "Symbol, Reality and Society" (S1955), his study dealing with the problem of meaning, which develops the "finite provinces of meaning" into a theory of signs and symbols; *Royaumont 1957:* "The Problem of Transcendental Intersubjectivity in Husserl" (S1957c), a final distancing from Husserl, culminating in his "theory of mundane intersubjectivity."

The publication of this correspondence is an immense step forward for research on both Schutz and Gurwitsch: one can follow the discussion of these already classic essays between author and friend, who reciprocally and without false overtones address each other as the only competent critic. But the reader will find agreement less often than clear and often sharp distance: in what sense can one speak of a commonality, consensus, or intersubjectivity in the process of investigation? The answer is sketched in the metaphor of the digging of a tunnel and is quite simple: it rests on the willingness of each to read the text of the other, to take up its creative moments, and to probe experimentally and imaginatively the issues of one's own research within the tunnel of the other.[50]

Many readers might find it helpful to know the major markers which can guide one through the tunnels and which allow one to locate Schutz and Gurwitsch at their changing work places. Four figures run through all particular themes of the correspondence: Edmund Husserl, Max Weber, William James, and—perhaps more than any other— Gottfried Wilhelm Leibniz. The reader might make himself or herself familiar with at least one of these figures if he or she wishes to recognize clearly the ways in which problems and solutions in the field between philosophy and the social sciences are often given a fundamentally new formulation. Schutz and Gurwitsch attack this "mountain" of problems by extending their "tunnels": the reader is challenged to start his or her own labor, and is offered access to the passageways, paths, and signposts of the two scouts.

Edmund Husserl is, of course, the first marker of this correspondence: phenomenology is a radical inquiry into the interplay between theory construction, methods of investigation, and ways of posing problems in a given historical situation. Under the slogan "to the things themselves," Husserlian phenomenology searches for a new understanding of the empirical for every kind of empirical research. In addition to this fundamental agreement, the reader will observe the developing critique (in which the two often differ quite radically) and at times sharp rejection of Husserl by Schutz and Gurwitsch. This critique is determined above all by problems in the sociological studies of actions, which of course were not Husserl's concern.[51] As problems of the typologizing grasp of action and cognition, these questions must be posed anew, taking the structure of action as point of departure (so Schutz). New—this means two things: a transcendental path to the foundation of intersubjective understanding, of the kind first established by Kant and Neo-Kantianism in their theory of knowledge and then transformed by Husserl's phenomenological approach, is no longer available when dealing with these problems. *Doxa* and *episteme,* the classical poles of human action and cognition, are to be founded in the life-world.

This thesis was ultimately confirmed by the publication of Husserl's *Crisis of the European Sciences* (edited by Walter Biemel, 1954).[52] Schutz and Gurwitsch read and discussed this last work of Husserl, and wrote reviews of this and other books by Husserl in which their distance from Husserl solidifies, but without either of them abandoning the phenomenological motifs originally sounded by Husserl. This abandonment happened, as they noted with dismay, in the French and German phenomenological scene in which they participated following the end of the war and in the 1950s. There the Husserlian impetus to phenomenological investigations, which for Schutz and Gurwitsch remained a guiding thread as well as an object of their critique, oscillated uncertainly between hermeneutics, the analysis of *Dasein,* and existentialism. The sense of a common labor grew in these years—but also the recognition of the loneliness of their endeavor: digging the tunnel became the metaphor in terms of which their reciprocal understanding and orientation reaches its high point.

Max Weber's crucial significance for Schutz and Gurwitsch could easily be overlooked on a quick reading of the correspondence. A glance back at their early work immediately corrects this impression. Schutz, who had started studying economic and legal sociology in Vienna, concentrated on Weber's analysis of action. Weber's construction of ideal types for penetrating the meaningful structures of actors in historical situations was considerably refined by Schutz and grounded in the typologies of everyday understanding. Thus, Schutz was able to further Weber's goal of a science of human action which takes into account the intended meaning of the action and explains its objective meaning.[53]

Gurwitsch was of course familiar with these Weberian works, but with a somewhat different orientation. The Weberian themes of church, sect, and charisma occupied him, and he discussed them with his later colleague Carl Mayer in 1928 at the University Weeks in Davos.[54] He followed Weber's thesis concerning the Protestant ethic in Bernard Groethuysen's investigation of the bourgeois world view in France (G1933a) and worked systematically on problems in the sociology of organizations in his habilitation thesis (1931, published G1976), a study of the modes of encounter and styles of socialization in everyday milieus. The Weberian influence can be followed even into the very language he uses. All theories, writes Gurwitsch,

> that are not oriented toward the moments constitutive for a consociation [*Verband*], but instead are oriented toward feelings and sentiments which the members foster toward one another without asking about the 'place' of these feelings and sentiments within the present social structure, (G1976, 206; G1979, 143)

are unacceptable.

It would be just as unacceptable to interpret this thesis as expressing a reservation or even objections to sensations and structures of sentiment, since Weber as well as Schutz and Gurwitsch (and above all Max Scheler) put them into the center of interest for all investigation of action. All social facts have their horizons of feelings and sentiments. Perceptions and perceptual judgments are tied to the context of the world and of the experiencing subject by sentiments. Their "reality," that which is held to be real in action and thus defines the motives and goals of action as well as the reality of the consequences of the action, becomes the first theme of a philosophy of human action.[55]

Given this field of interest, it is not immediately clear why William James (whom Gurwitsch had already discussed extensively in his dissertation on the phenomenology of horizons and marginal consciousness: G1929) became the third signpost of the correspondence between Schutz and Gurwitsch. Henri Bergson, whom both had discussed in their early work, would have been the more obvious figure. Bergson and James had sharpened the problem of reality into the quest for the experiential character of the real. Charles S. Peirce, whose work neither Schutz nor Gurwitsch knew in any detail, would have induced them to pursue the pragmatist premises more deeply.[56] But the presence of phenomenological themes was much more obvious in James (S1941), and his theory of consciousness (G1943 and G1947) provided a mode of access to Schutz's theory of "multiple realities" (S1945c), the manifold realities and their finite provinces of meaning (S1955). Instrumental acts and communicative action, dreaming as well as play, theory construction and meditation are not to be left to separate disciplines and their specific understanding of reality: human action does not care for the lines drawn by traditional sciences, and constantly crosses their boundaries.

But for just this reason, every radical thematization of social action makes its scientific study an urgent problem. Schutz and Gurwitsch chose two ways of proceeding: Schutz followed the constitution of action itself as a meaning-instituting and meaning-interpreting process within the diversity of everyday behavior. The problem of meaning stands at the entrance to his tunnel. Gurwitsch singled out scientific study, the historical traces of the *raison universelle,* as the guiding thread for every understanding of action within the field of consciousness founded in the life-world. The problem of context was Gurwitsch's entrance to the tunnel. Both marked their entrances in terms of a common point of reference: Leibniz.

We need not go into the multiple references to Leibniz here. The reader will find them even in the first letters exchanged between Paris and New York shortly before the beginning of the war. One particular episode provides a good sense of the importance of

Leibniz. The two friends discuss their contributions to the Husserl Memorial Volume which was being prepared by Marvin Farber. Schutz recalls Leibniz's *New Essays on the Human Understanding,* the dialogue between Philalethes (the friend of truth) and Theophilus (the friend of God): Schutz addresses Gurwitsch as "Dear Friend Philalethes," and gives us a perfect characterization of writer as well as addressee in his refusal to sign the letter as "Theophilus." Schutz, with wit and irony, designates himself as Voltaire's "Pangloss."

The correspondence has been divided chronologically into nine parts. The choice of the parts, and of the titles and themes which precede each letter, are merely aids to the reader provided by the editor; it is hoped that they will not disturb the expert. Each part is headed by one of the "tunnel themes" in terms of which the development of the correspondence can be articulated. They stem from each of the correspondents in turn. Their choice is briefly discussed in a short editor's note at the beginning of each part. These notes also contain additional biographical information which fills in the "landscape" of the correspondence a bit more than this introduction is able to do.

The first two parts cover the letters from the war years, the flight from France to the American exile, the difficult years as "enemy aliens in the technical sense," the establishment of a new existence, the beginning of an unusual scholarly cooperation. The tunnel themes begin in the third part. Each theme gives information about the direction and progress of the other's work to date. Their mutual understanding, i.e., their coming to agreement about the proper way of posing problems and attacking their solution, is by no means a simple presupposition of their "discourse," but rather a daily workload leading to results symbolized by their "tunnels" of shared theory formations. Their certainty of a mutual project reaches its high point—and its abrupt end—in the final part.

Part 1: "The Riders of the Apocalypse" (1939–41). A Gurwitsch metaphor describing the hopeless situation of their friends who were still in France and his own despair concerning the possibility of future work. Details of the flight from Europe to America as well as the situation of the emigrants in America. The first topic of their discussion is the Husserlian concept of consciousness, which Schutz criticizes along with the non-egological variants developed by Sartre and Gurwitsch.[57] Schutz presents his analyses of action.

Part 2: "The Strange and the Stranger" (1941–44). A Schutzian theme, arising from the experience of exile but investigated on a fundamental level: between the modes of familiarity with the world and its typicality, the stranger necessarily misses the mode of everyday acquaintance in terms of which the known and the unknown can be distinguished. In a sharp argument the disagreement is traced back to the tension between *episteme* and *doxa: doxa versus episteme* in the search for the *raison universelle,* that is Gurwitsch's approach; *doxa and episteme,* a clarification of the cognitive styles of the lived experience of action, that is the Schutzian approach, which he leads on to analyses of the life-world.

Part 3: "Context as a Problem of Order" (1945–50). The central Gurwitsch theme: the problem of thematization makes the context of theme and thematic field accessible; formalization and mathematization, especially in the Platonic tradition, are criticized. Schutz discusses it in terms of the contrast between "relevance" and "pertinence" (as he calls the narrower concept of relevance in Gurwitsch) and criticizes Gurwitsch's narrow tunnel entrance, which (like Husserl and Merleau-Ponty) remains tied to a phenomenology of perception. The question concerning the constitution and reconstitution of any order is posed as a problem of context. Is order an organization of the field of consciousness (Gurwitsch)? To what extent is it a social problem?[58]

Part 4: "Oh, Holy Mannheim!" (1950–51). The suggestion that the eidos might be relative to situations elicits this cry from Schutz. The connection between type and eidos, which appear as closely related in Schutz's last essay (S1959b), makes its first appearance in a brief discussion of the phenomenology of space (GS 7.27.50)—and in a variety of problems which are discussed in this chapter. Schutz follows the theme into the contrast between types as constructs of the first (everyday) and second (scientific) order. Gurwitsch addresses the problem in terms of the contrast between concrete and abstract thinking: where their difference is blurred or negated, he sees a source of nihilistic thought and action.

Part 5: "The Field of Consciousness" (1951-52). Once the book manuscript is finished Gurwitsch began a period of suffering as it made its way through the hands of publishers and readers: Schutz comments with indignation and encouragement. More important: their discussion of specific themes from the text makes visible a whole series of their tunnel differences. Gurwitsch's solution to the problem of the phenomenological reduction, by means of which he wants to avoid a transcendental approach, stands in the center: the abandonment of the constancy hypothesis opens up a sufficiently reduced access to the field of consciousness. This thesis is embedded in his theory of the *trois dimensions du réel* [three orders of being] which is touched on in the last part of *The Field of Consciousness* (G1964a, 414ff.) and which he planned to develop in detail elsewhere (now part of the Gurwitsch archive). The difficulties are substantial and clearly visible on both sides: the difference from Schutz's "finite provinces of meaning," which is only mentioned in the book, is broadened in the course of their discussion by Schutz, who counters with his own version of the problematic of the reduction:[59] working it out requires substantial additional studies in the theory of symbols, signs, and systems.

Part 6: "From the Theory of Action to the Theory of Science" (1952–53). This discussion, which begins with Schutz's "Princeton paper" (S1953c), brings the closest points of contact between the two positions: we repeatedly hear that "the tunnels meet." The positions they oppose have also been clearly worked out. "It's enough to drive you crazy," Schutz complains with reference to Hempel, Nagel, "and Co.," and: "Don't you want to see your friend cast to the wild animals?" (SG 4.9.53). Gurwitsch develops the main idea that concept formation in the social sciences is to be based on the structures of action: the verification of scientific hypotheses is itself a process of social action.

Part 7: "Concepts of the Life-World" (1953–56). Another high point of the correspondence: Gurwitsch returned from a lecture tour in Europe, where to his great surprise he was met with great interest at German universities (Cologne, Frankfurt, Munich, Berlin—he received an offer of a chair in Berlin, but declined). They agree that there cannot be a transcendental foundation for the life-world: Gurwitsch is much closer to Husserl's concept of the life-world as a critical tool for gaining a human distance to the formalizing and mathematizing sciences. Schutz leaps far into the "*bathos* of the life-world" and formulates the problem of a mundane intersubjectivity as pivot for the problematic of the life-world, which is to be opened up by means of an analysis of symbols within social action.[60] A secondary theme is a Voegelin discussion concerning the historical dimensions of the life-world, which the two insist they neither oppose nor neglect.

Part 8: "Investigation of the Life-World vs. Transcendental Constitutional Analysis" (1956–57). Schutz prepares his lecture for the phenomenology congress in Royaumont, France (S1957b), his most detailed critical discussion of Husserl, which leads to substantial theoretical differences but never to disregard. He is bothered by the fashion, above all in France, of Heidegger and an existentialism which no longer knows (or never became acquainted with) Husserl. Schutz insists on the original impetus to a phenomenologically oriented investigation which has the task of awakening in all sciences a sense for the openness of the problems concerning the life-world.

Part 9: "Parting" (1957–59). The last two years pass in the shadow of Schutz's illness, but are still an extraordinarily active phase of work and publication. Especially in Schutz's letters it becomes clear how he wants to understand the differences and agreements in their tunnel-work. The Gurwitsch problem, as he calls it, lies in the context of the constitution of types and typification. The Schutz problem: where does intersubjectivity and socialization begin? But such a summary is perhaps only "a slave rebellion on the part of a consciousness which the Cartesian devil has banned into the dungeons of solipsism" (SG 12.7.57).

One last summer in Europe: the Schutz family in the Steiermark, Alice (Raja) and Aron Gurwitsch in upper Engadin; their last meeting was during the World Philosophy Congress in September 1958 in Venice. Gurwitsch accepted Ludwig Landgrebe's invitation to be guest professor for one year in Cologne and Schutz returned to New York, where he prepared to take a leave of absence. Gurwitsch was to be his temporary replacement. His last letter, on May 16, 1959, deals with these arrangements, four days before the death of Alfred Schutz.

NOTES

1. Bibliographical references for Schutz (here: S1945c) or Gurwitsch (e.g., G1945) refer to the bibliography at the end of this volume. References to letters (e.g., GS 9.3.45) name the writer and then the recipient (here: Gurwitsch to Schutz), and then the date (September 3, 1945).

2. Not much is known to date about Schutz's "daytime life," as he called his professional life at the bank. The brief characterization which Ilse Schutz sent to the editor (3.29.1984) is all the more important:

> His first position (starting in 1920) was as secretary of the Vereinigung Öster-
> reichischer Mittelbanken [Union of Austrian Banks]. In 1929 he began his activity at
> the banking house of Reitler & Co. in Vienna, where he was the advisor for all legal
> problems, not only for Austria, Hungary, and Czechoslovakia but also for their foreign
> connections in France, Holland, and other countries. In this function he also worked
> for the banking house Dreyfus in Paris, but only in connection with his position with
> Reitler. He worked for the same group in America.

See also Helmut Wagner, *Alfred Schutz: An Intellectual Biography* (Chicago: University of Chicago Press, 1983).

3. Two short letters preceding those published here (SG 4.16.38 and GS 1.23.39, with references to even earlier letters which have been lost) have not been printed. Concerning the editorial principles see the introductory remarks to the complete list of letters in the German edition of the correspondence.

4. For example, Stephan Strasser, who edited the German edition of Husserl's *Cartesian Meditations,* was there. Cf. H. L. Van Breda's presentation "Die Rettung des Husserl-Nachlaß und die Gründung des Husserl-Archivs" in *Husserl und das Denken der Neuzeit,* ed. Van Breda and Taminiaux (The Hague: Martinus Nijhoff, 1959). Van Breda had come to Freiburg in search of material for his dissertation (cf. Herbert Spiegelberg, *The Phenomenological Movement* [The Hague: Martinus Nijhoff, rev. third ed. 1982], 433).

5. Ludwig Landgrebe, then Husserl's assistant in Freiburg, remarks in this context (in a personal letter to the editor):

> "The relationship between Husserl and Heidegger had cooled off since the fall of 1930,
> a development strengthened by Heidegger's wife, an officer's daughter with anti-
> semitic attitudes. Heidegger's period as Rector brought the low point with Husserl's
> being forbidden to enter his old departmental rooms. The document to this effect from

the office of the rector bore Heidegger's signature in a facsimile stamp. Husserl was appalled by Heidegger's inaugural speech as Rector."

6. Cf. Walter Biemel, *Heidegger*, tr. J. L. Mehta (New York: Harcourt Brace Jovanovich, 1976), xii.
7. Cf. Helmuth Plessner, *Die Verspätete Nation* (Stuttgart, 1959, first ed. 1935) and his student Christian Graf von Krockow, *Die Entscheidung: Eine Untersuchung über Ernst Jünger, Carl Schmitt, Martin Heidegger* (Stuttgart, 1958).
8. A selection: Eduard Heimann, *Freedom and Order: Lessons from the War* (New York, 1947); Hans Speier, *Social Order and the Risks of War* (Cambridge, 1952); Alvin Johnson, *Pioneer's Progress* (New York, 1952); Arnold Brecht, *Mit der Kraft des Geistes,* vol. 2 of his memoirs *Lebenserinnerungen* (Stuttgart, 1967).
    Research into migration: B. Bailyn and D. Fleming, *The Intellectual Migration: Europe and America 1930–1960* (New York, 1968); Stuart Hughes, *The Sea Change: The Migration of Social Thought 1930–1965* (New York, 1975); Rainer Lepsius, *Die Entwicklung der Soziologie nach dem 2. Weltkrieg,* a special volume of the *Kölner Zeitschrift für Soziologie,* 1979; Herbert Strauss, *Jewish Immigrants of the Nazi Period in the U.S.A.,* 2 vols. (New York, 1981); J. Jackmann and D. Borden, *The Muses Flee Hitler* (Washington: Smithsonian Press, 1983).
    Concerning the New School: Monika Plessner, "Die deutsche 'University in Exile,' " *Frankfurter Hefte* 19 (1964): 181–186; Charles Lachman, "The University in Exile," *Discourse* (Stony Brook) 2 (1976): 25–37; Walter Sprondel, "Erzwungene Diffusion," in *Geschichte der Soziologie,* ed. W. Lepenies (Frankfurt, 1982); Benita Luckmann, "A. Schütz and A. Gurwitsch an der 'New School,' " in *Sozialität und Intersubjektivität,* ed. R. Grathoff and B. Waldenfels (Munich: Wilhelm Fink Verlag, 1983).
9. Roman Ingarden, "L'Essai logistique d'une refonte de la philosophie," *Revue Philosophique de la France et l'Etranger* 60 (1935): 137–159.
10. Most sharply of course in Sartre: cf. Schutz's critique in S1948. A systematic study of these nihilistic motifs in Heidegger and Sartre from the perspective of the sociology of action would be fascinating. Cf. in this context Sartre's essay "Descartes and Freedom" (1948), which is motivated by the interplay between Cartesian method and nihilism.
11. Cf. his habilitation thesis from 1931 concerning Scheler's milieu theory (G1979, English translation G1976).
12. An example of the indirect effects of this elective affinity between phenomenology and sociology is Norbert Elias's demand for "research into the human" [*Menschenforschung*], in which the diffusion of phenomenological motives (especially as mediated through Karl Mannheim) could easily be demonstrated. Similarly for Carl Grünberg's program of the Frankfurt Institute for Social Research, but equally for the Vienna research project on "the Unemployed from Marienthal," which made Paul Lazarsfeld known.
13. Ludwig Landgrebe, "Wilhelm Diltheys Theorie der Geisteswissenschaften, Analyse ihrer Grundbegriffe," *Jahrbuch für Philosophie und phänomenologische Forschung* 9 (1928).
14. Cf. B. Waldenfels, *Phänomenologie in Frankreich* (Frankfurt: Suhrkamp, 1983), 39f.
15. Details are added by Prof. Landgrebe, whom Husserl in 1933 sent to Prague to habilitate under Oskar Kraus: "That wasn't possible anywhere else at that time." Phenomenology was strongly represented in Prague by Thomas Masaryk, himself a student of Franz Brentano. In 1934 Emil Utitz, who came from an old Prague family, was called from Halle to Prague. Along with J. B. Kozak, he founded the Cercle Philosophique, whose secretary was Jan Patocka; the Rockefeller Foundation supported the institute.

Landgrebe received a Rockefeller grant to prepare Husserl's *Experience and Judgment* for publication (Prague, 1938). In November 1935 Husserl gave his last public lectures in Prague. Kozak went to the U.S.A. Van Breda brought the two Husserl assistants Landgrebe and Eugen Fink to Louvain as "scribes": they could read, and thus teach to the institute, the (Austrian) Gabelsberg stenography which Husserl used exclusively.

16. Concerning biography, cf. R. Grathoff, "Alfred Schütz," in *Klassiker des soziologischen Denkens,* ed. D. Käsler, vol. 2 (Munich, 1978).

Ilja Srubar, director of the *Sozialwissenschaftliches Archiv* at the University of Constance, adds:

> The matter of Schutz's studies is difficult. To the extent that the records which we have in the archives can be reconstructed, he studied law from the winter semester of 1918–1919 to the summer semester of 1921, passing his final oral examinations in 1921. Following this he studied political science [*Staatswissenschaften*] in the winter semesters of 1921–22 and 1922–23.

17. Cf. Winternitz's study "The Role of Music in Leonardo's 'Paragone,' " *Phenomenology and Social Reality,* ed. M. Natanson (The Hague: Nijhoff, 1970).

18. Eric Voegelin, "In Memoriam Alfred Schutz," *The Philosophy of Order,* ed. Peter S. Opitz and Gregor Sebba (Stuttgart: Klett-Cotta, 1981), 465.

19. To date only his correspondence with Talcott Parsons (S1977 and S1978) has been published. Of the very large and intensive correspondence with Eric Voegelin, only one letter from Schutz concerning Voegelin's *New Science of Politics* (cf. Opitz and Sebba, eds. 434–448) and three letters from Voegelin, one concerning Husserl's philosophy of history in the *Crisis* (German only, cf. E. Voegelin, *Anamnesis* [Munich: R. Piper & Co. Verlag, 1966], 21–36), and two letters answering Schutz's letter concerning the *New Science* (cf. Opitz and Sebba, eds., 449–462), have been published. In his Schutz biography, Helmut Wagner has given a sketch of the entire Schutz correspondence. Cf. also Helmut Wagner, "Agreement in Discord: Alfred Schutz and Eric Voegelin," in Opitz and Sebba (eds.), 74–90.

20. Fritz Machlup, "Homo Oeconomicus and his Class Mates," in M. Natanson, ed. 131.

21. *The Theory of Social Action: The Correspondence of Alfred Schutz and Talcott Parsons,* ed. Richard Grathoff (Bloomington and London: Indiana University Press, 1978).

22. Mrs. Gurwitsch writes the editor: "His father and his mother came from long lines of Jewish scholars which go back into the fifteenth century. Under the influence of the Gaon of Vilna, there developed a tradition which included science in its study of the Talmud." Concerning Gurwitsch's biography, cf. also Lester Embree, "Nachruf auf Aron Gurwitsch," *Zeitschrift für allgemeine Wissenschaftstheorie* 5 (1974): 1–8.

23. Arthur Koestler reports that the lumber trade was almost a Jewish monopoly in Poland (and Lithuania): *The Thirteenth Tribe: The Khazar Empire and its Heritage* (London, 1978), 137.

24. Kurt Riezler worked for the foreign service even prior to the First World War. Cf. Arnold Brecht's memoirs: *Aus nächster Nähe: Lebenserinnerungen 1884–1927* (Stuttgart: Deutsche Verlaganstalt, 1966); English translation ("condensed and rewritten") in *The Political Education of Arnold Brecht* (Princeton: Princeton University Press, 1970), vol. 1, pp. 325–327. Following the Russian February revolution of 1917 Riezler had the delicate task of accompanying Lenin through German territory on his train trip from Switzerland through Sweden to Russia. Riezler's later activity in Frankfurt was supported above all by Adolf Grimme, who was the Prussian Minister of Culture in 1930–32. Ludwig Landgrebe remarks: "Grimme sought Husserl's advice whenever a position in philosophy was to be filled. I had the task of typing these letters of recommendation." It is well known that Riezler and Grimme, when they brought Karl Mannheim to Frankfurt, created the first chair for sociology in Prussia (the Prussian Ministry of Science

was located in Berlin; Prussia was one of the states in the federal Weimar Republic) which was not "stolen" from a neighboring discipline.

25. There is no reference to Moritz Geiger in the works Gurwitsch himself published, although he did his doctorate under Geiger *summa cum laude*. (But cf. Gurwitsch's habilitations thesis: G1979). This is astonishing, since 1) Geiger's interest in the phenomenology of objects and acts lay very close to Gurwitsch's own interests, and 2) he was the first Husserl student to go to America: in 1907 he visited William James and Josiah Royce at Harvard, and in 1933 he emigrated to the U.S.A., where he taught at Vassar College. Geiger died in 1937. (Cf. Spiegelberg, 200–212.)

26. Unpublished (Göttingen, 1933): Along with copies of the other Gurwitsch papers, the manuscript is in the *Sozialwissenschaftliches Archiv Konstanz* and in the Gurwitsch archive at Duquesne University.

27. Alice (called "Raja") was engaged in Zionist youth work ("first the *Wandervogel*, then blue-white") in Frankfurt, where she met Aron. Concerning the history of this Jewish youth movement, cf. the survey by Hermann Meier-Cronemeyer in *Germanica Judaica* 8 (1969): 78–86 and the contributions by Chanoch Rinott and Dietrich Goldschmidt in *Neue Sammlung* 17 (1977): 102–107. (I am indebted to Prof. Dietrich Goldschmidt for these references.)

28. Only in 1976 was the work edited posthumously by A. Métraux. Claude Evans found a carbon copy of the manuscript in the library of the philosophy department at the Ruhr-University Bochum, West Germany. It had probably been purchased in East Germany in the late 1960s.

29. Cf. Waldenfels, 34–42. A small episode reported by Alice Gurwitsch signals the distance between the "old" and the "new" emigration: "We originally lived very close to Georges Gurvitch, so that the mailman from time to time mixed up our letters. One day Gurvitch stormed up waving a letter for Aron in his hand: '*Voilà une lettre pour vous. Mais Gurvitch: C'est moi!*' "

30. The special passport for German refugees was introduced under the socialist government of Léon Blum (1936–37). Gurwitsch was able to ward this off and received a foreigner's passport (information from Alice Gurwitsch). The "Récépissé" was useless for leaving the country, being merely a kind of official receipt for travel documents when registering refugees. Schutz avoided this pseudo-passport with the help of his Parisian friends (information from Ilse Schutz.)

31. Raymond Aron, who was a friend of Schutz, agreed to write the introduction to this volume. On September 8, 1983, shortly before his death, he wrote the editor:

> Bien entendu, je me souviens parfaitement d'Alfred Schütz, j'avais étudié attentivement son premier livre que j'avais d'ailleurs cité dans ma thèse. Pendant son séjour à Paris, je l'ai rencontré plus d'une fois et nos relations amicales se sont poursuivies bien au'delà de la guerre. Chaque fois qu'il venait à Paris, il me faisait signe et bien souvent, quand je passais par New York, j'allais le voir. J'écrirai donc volontiers l'introduction que vous souhaitez, mais je ne sais trop comment le faire. J'évoquerais volontiers sa personnalité, une visite avec lui au *Metropolitan Museum*, nous avons quelquefois discuté de problèmes philosophiques, il avait lu avec intérêt ma thèse d'Introduction à la philosophie de l'Histoire.

32. "A *Reichsfluchtsteuer* [a tax levied on refugees by the Nazi government] was not applicable because the family's income was too low" (Ilse Schutz to the editor on November 4, 1977, in New York).

33. The American immigration laws (especially those from 1924) determined the quotas for the different countries in terms of countries of origin of the American population. This "quota-immigration" favored the classical emigration countries (Germany, Italy, Ireland, etc.). But by 1939–40 their quotas were long since exhausted, so that generally a visa could be obtained only by means of a very liberal interpretation of the

"non-quota immigration." Since Mexico and the other American countries did not fall under "quota immigration," many emigrants attempted to "buy" one of their citizenships in order to reach the U.S.A. through these countries.

34. Stephen Duggan, *The Rescue of Science and Learning* (New York: Macmillan, 1948); Norman Bentwich, *The Rescue and Achievement of Refugee Scholars 1933–1952* (The Hague: Martinus Nijhoff, 1953).

35. Hans Staudinger, along with Kurt Riezler, Hans Simons, and Arnold Brecht, belonged to that group of political emigrants at the New School who had been forced out of the Prussian civil service after 1933 and had entered the academic world (cf. the *Lebenserinnerungen* of Arnold Brecht).

36. *Carl Mayer 1902–1974,* ed. *Sozialwissenschaftliches Archiv* (Constance, 1974), 11. Cf. also Carl Mayer, "On the Intellectual Origins of National Socialism," *Social Research* 9 (1942): 225–247, and "The Crisis of German Protestantism," *Social Research* 12 (1945): 397–432.

37. According to autobiographical notes by Albert Salomon; cf. the Salomon edition being prepared by Ulf Mathiesen, forthcoming, in the series *"Übergänge"* (Fink-Verlag, Munich).

38. See studies on the "University in Exile" by Charles Lachman, Benita Luckmann, Monika Plessner (a list of these 176 names is in the archives in Constance).

39. Arnold Brecht, *Lyrisches Vermächtnis* (privately published in New York, 1974), 54.

40. One example: Ludwig Landgrebe and Eugen Fink were arrested in Louvain on May 10, 1940. They were taken to the internment camp near Elne, south of Perpignan. Following the agreement with the Vichy government they were brought back to Louvain. Landgrebe, whose wife gave birth to their second child in Brussels, received "returning emigrants document of the N.S.D.A.P." (recognition as a "privileged mixed marriage") and train tickets to Reinbek near Hamburg. He worked in the office of a Hamburg iron export firm which by that time no longer exported iron but only salt for the herring industry in Norway. His father-in-law Goldschmidt was arrested in 1942 and deported to Theresienstadt. He survived the concentration camp and returned to Hamburg after the end of the war. Ludwig Landgrebe was appointed *Dozent* at the newly reopened university in Hamburg on August 1, 1945.

Gurs is now part of the town of Navarrenx (west of Pau/Pyrennées). It was originally built for Spanish refugees of the Civil War; after 1940 it was a camp for 12,000 Jewish and other political refugees, mostly from Germany. Cf. H. Schramm and B. Vormeier, *Vivre à Gurs: Une camp de concentration française* (Paris: Maspero, 1979). (Information from the *Bertelsmann Auskunftdienst.)*

41. Alice and Aron Gurwitsch received their visas on the basis of an official letter of invitation for a one-year lectureship at the Johns Hopkins University. But the American Consulate doubted the authenticity of the letter and demanded that the envelope too be submitted. According to Alice Gurwitsch, Aron had the habit of saving envelopes: an envelope as life-saver, an empirical detail from a world turning nihilistic.

42. It is impossible to write about those who were able to leave France without mentioning those whose despair drove them to suicide. Raoul Hoffmann (DS 12.18.1983):

> Many see no way out. They let themselves be driven like sheep to camps which the French have erected 'just in case' . . . . These events drive many writers to suicide, since many thought that they had escaped the Nazis—and now they are at the gates of Paris. The writer Carl Einstein cuts his arteries in an internment camp in July 1940 as the Germans approach. In the same year Walter Benjamin commits suicide at the Spanish-French border. Walter Hasenclever poisons himself in a camp. Ernst Weiß takes poison in his hotel room after the Germans enter Paris, lies down in the bathtub and cuts his arteries. Even writers who have already arrived at their new exile give up: Ernst Toller

hangs himself in the summer of 1939 in his New York hotel; Stefan Zweig commits
suicide in South America.

Cf. in this context Paul-Ludwig Landsberg, *The Experience of Death: The Moral Problem of
Suicide,* tr. Cynthia Rowland (New York: Arno Press, 1977).

43. Farber is the central figure among American phenomenologists in this phase. In
1919 he studied in Vienna (cf. his correspondence with Karl Kautsky in the Amsterdam
Archive for Social History), studied in Freiburg under Husserl, and received his Ph.D. in
1928 at Harvard (dissertation on "Phenomenology as a Method and as a Philosophical
Discipline"). See Herbert Spiegelberg, 663, and Helmut Wagner, 181–184.

44. Ed. R. W. Sellars, V. J. McGill, and M. Farber (New York, 1949).

45. The correspondence notes various stages (Hunter College, etc.). SPEP (Society
for Phenomenology and Existential Philosophy) was founded in 1962 with Gurwitsch's
help. In the early 1970s the Deutsche Gesellschaft für phänomenologische Forschung
was founded, thanks in part to the strong support from Gerd Brand (publication:
Phänomenologische Forschung, published by the Alber Verlag in Freiburg). The British
Society for Phenomenology began publishing its journal, *JBSP,* in 1969. Concerning
Holland, Poland, Japan, and other countries, see the "Forschungsberichte" in R.
Grathoff and B. Waldenfels (eds.), *Sozialität und Intersubjektivität* (Munich: Wilhelm
Fink Verlag, 1983).

46. Here too, the financial side was decisive. See Gurwitsch's lament over "Farber's
failure to interest the foundations" (GS 10.16.1951), whereas Van Breda was able to tap
international sources of money for work on Husserl. One effect is noted in the German
edition of the *Crisis:* "Ouvrage préparé sous les auspices du Conseil international de la
Philosophie et des Sciences Humaines et de la Fédération internationale des Sociétes de
Philosophie avec l'aide de L'U.N.E.S.C.O." When one considers the fact that in the
beginning UNESCO worked almost exclusively with American financial support, and
that in addition the Rockefeller Foundation financed the first Husserl research in Prague,
the "American tragedy" of which Gurwitsch speaks becomes understandable.

47. When Schutz began teaching at the New School, Alvin Johnson warned him:
"But do not teach my children phenomenology. They will not swallow that stuff." (SG
9.27.1955)

48. Translated by M. Butor, now a famous French writer (information from W. Biemel).

49. He began working on *The Structures of the Life-World* (S1973 and S1984) in the
summer of 1958: concerning the history of the two-volume work, cf. especially the
appendix with the remarks by editor Thomas Luckmann (vol. 2, 215ff.).

50. A certain sort of "critical" understanding took up a contrary alternative attitude:
texts were read, if at all, only "against the grain" until one had worked out an opposing
position; further reading was unnecessary once this position was clear. Vulnerable moments were noted and refuted by means of one's own research data (in case one works
empirically). Since every understanding, including this one, had to be intersubjectively
grounded, although this "critical understanding" was not intersubjectively constituted in
terms of the research process, it was dependent on ideological premises such as some
formal "logic of scientific discovery" or other. These "alternatives" were criticized above
all by Gurwitsch (cf. GS 5.15.1953).

51. Husserl's first-hand knowledge of the sciences came from mathematics and psychology, disciplines in which he had research experience: he was assistant to the founder
of the theory of functions, Karl Weierstrass, in Berlin, where he received an important
impetus for the procedure of eidetic variation; Franz Brentano in Vienna and his student
Carl Stumpf in Halle (where Husserl did his habilitation) introduced Husserl to psychological analyses. His logical investigations and work in the philosophy of science were
predetermined by this research experience.

52. Husserl's posthumous work, the *Crisis*, has to be located differently in the history of theoretical discussions in German social philosophy: Husserl only slowly began to be taken into account again and introduced to the post-war generation (by Jürgen Habermas, Hermann Lübbe, Niklas Luhmann, etc.). It is understandable that this first reception was very superficial. As Hermann Lübbe (*Kant-Studien* 49, 1957–58) put it, with the *Crisis* Husserl "breaks out of . . . the circle of problems" in which he had been caught, problems which Heidegger appeared to have left behind long ago. The differences between Heidegger, Husserl, and Schutz are covered over in Habermas' *Logik der Sozialwissenschaften* (1967), similarly in Luhmann's *Vertrauen* (1968). To be sure, Husserl's *Crisis* immediately demanded to be taken into account, but until quite recently there has been no serious critical discussion. This *Crisis* reception has been investigated by Landgrebe, in his Luhmann critique *Der Streit um die philosophischen Grundlagen der Gesellschaftstheorie* (Cologne: Westdeutscher Verlag, n.d.), and Ulf Matthiesen, in his Habermas critique *Das Dickicht der Lebenswelt und die Theorie des kommunikativen Handelns* (Munich: Wilhelm Fink Verlag, 1983).

53. The first and fifth sections of the *Sinnhafte Aufbau* (S1932a, English translation S1967) contain a careful Weber critique, which has hardly been noticed by the Weberians.

54. Cf. *Carl Mayer: 1902–1974* (Sozialwissenschaftliches Archiv Konstanz), 10. In addition: "Sekte und Kirche: ein religionssoziologischer Versuch" (Carl Mayer's dissertation in Heidelberg, 1933).

55. This formulation refers to Schutz's demand that action "be made the theme of philosophy" (SG 8.19.39). The sociologist will recognize in this theme references to fundamental theoretical aspects of his discipline: Emile Durkheim's "*fait social*," William Isaac Thomas's "definition of the situation," Florian Znaniecki's "humanistic coefficient," and Max Weber's "*Wirklichkeitswissenschaft*" pursue from various perspectives this task of grasping the "reality" of action. Schutz takes the decisive further step: "*Realität*" and "*Aktualität*" of action are themselves thematized in an effort to separate fictional and non-fictional aspects of action. The English texts of Schutz as well as of Gurwitsch translate both *Realität* and *Wirklichkeit* as "reality." (Cf. R. Grathoff, "Ansätze zu einer Theorie sozialen Handelns bei A. Schütz," *Neue Hefte für Philosophie* 9 (1976): 115–133.)

56. A comparison with Peirce's theory of firstness, secondness, and thirdness would be interesting.

57. Cf. B. Waldenfels, "Das umstrittene Ich: Ichloses und ichhaftes Bewußtsein bei A. Gurwitsch und A. Schütz," in R. Grathoff and B. Waldenfels (eds.), *Sozialität und Intersubjektivität*.

58. Cf. the study by Eduard Heimann, also a member of the early New School faculty: *Freedom and Order: Lessons from the War* (New York, 1947).

59. Cf. Schutz's hints concerning the "theory of the modified epoché" (SG 1.25.1952, ftn. 14). Future research will have to deal above all with this problem of the reduction. Gurwitsch's and Schutz's conceptions seem to converge here.

60. Cf. an extensive presentation by R. Grathoff: "Das Problem der Intersubjektivität bei Aron Gurwitsch und Alfred Schütz," in Grathoff and Waldenfels, eds.

Philosophers in **Exile**

1
The Riders of the Apocalypse
(August 5, 1939–October 9, 1941)

The hope that Schutz would return to Paris from New York in September was not fulfilled. Following the German attack on Poland, France declared war. The Gurwitsch, Kahn, and Kracauer families left the city for the Paris suburb of Gif-sur-Yvette. Recalling these days, Mrs. Gurwitsch wrote:

> Gif-sur-Yvette! These memories remain unforgettable, against the background of the coming catastrophe, bound together by humanity and comedy in the house of the Gagets, who are now dead and who took us, four couples, into their large house, into a society of nine prize-winning dogs, all kinds of poultry, some cats and a donkey. . . . The Gagets, childless, owned, in addition to a large piece of land with vegetables and fruit, their own forest, towards which in the first days of the declaration of war a procession moved: a cart on which Madame was enthroned, pulled by the nine harnessed dogs, followed by the Kracauers, Kahns, the parents of Kahns, and us. At the end Monsieur, who always wobbled along slightly tipsy, and at the very end the donkey. In the forest we had to play cricket with the Gagets, and we were in general a gift from heaven for them. And then all the neighbors came to the forest to greet the 'enemy aliens.' (letter of May 21, 1984 to the editor)

> The police appeared once in order to get information from Kracauer. He came down, with his Offenbach book under his arm, very fearful, but was able to convince the *gendarme* of his peaceful intentions. He: good books make their way. (conversation with Mrs. Gurwitsch on September 2, 1979)

> Later Aron was the only man left in the house, the others had to go to camps; he had to console the women and write petitions," (from the letter mentioned above)

Refugees with German passports, such as Kahn and Kracauer, were interned. From New York, Schutz aided the immigration of these friends following the occupation of France. "The riders of the Apocalypse" occupied one country after another: "All the terrors of the past years repeat themselves again and again, but on a continually growing scale and on a continually broadened basis" (GS 4.20.41).

Schutz was working in New York, Gurwitsch at Johns Hopkins University in Baltimore. Their contributions to the Husserl Memorial Volume edited by Marvin Farber and their essays on the theories of consciousness of James and Sartre constitute the focus of this first chapter. Above all Gurwitsch, after his experiences with anti-Semitism in German universities, was very sensitive to the prejudices of American colleagues.

2

Gurwitsch: *I hope to see you again in September in Paris*
             (Paris, August 5, 1939)

Dear Friend,

You have now been gone a bit more than three weeks. But we have the
feeling that it has been an eternity since you left, although nothing special has
happened in this period, at any rate nothing which would fall out of the *cadre*
which we have gotten used to in these fine times *tant bien que mal,* but especially
mal. We hope that your trip went well in spite of all of the complications it
involves because of your baby. I can well imagine his indignation at the constant
changes in his environment. I hope that you arrived well and in good health and
are beginning to settle down in New York. We can't wait to hear what you will
report about yourselves and also about the country. But make good use of the
time which places you at least at a spatial distance from the sources of unrest.

Nothing special has happened here. We are getting ready to go on vacation,
but are not sure just where. We shall probably go to the Midi because of the cold
and rain. It is possible that we will remain there until the end of September, since
we have an offer to take a French boy along, and the offer covers two months. If
this works out, I shall begin to work there in September.

This letter is so "inflationary" because it contains the product of my English
efforts from July. The copies for Farber are going into the mail along with this
letter. I really owe you a two-fold thanks for the article, not only because you
provoked and arranged the invitation from Farber,[1] but above all because the
discussions with you have brought my opposition to a head. In a sense, the
article is a continuation of these discussions. I am hoping for your opposition,
for further discussions, and thus for still more stimulation and encouragement.
What a pleasure it would be to get into wild phenomenological discussions with
you, far from all the things which make life so little worth living.

I am sending all of the copies (except those for Farber) to you, and leave it up
to you to do with them as you see fit. You will know best what to do. At any
rate, many thanks for your willingness and for all of your efforts.

I would very much like to know what you think about the content of the
Farber essay as well as about its English. I don't have many illusions concerning
the latter point, but since Farber requested that I write in English and volun-
teered to correct it, I have sent him this *English-made-in-Europe*.[2]

I hope to see you all in September/October in Paris, in good health and in
"peace." I would be very happy to hear from you about how you are getting
along.

With best wishes for both of you and the children *par procuration*.

                                        Yours very truly,
                                        Aron Gurwitsch

1. Marvin Farber's invitation to contribute to *Philosophical Essays in Memory of Edmund Husserl,* ed. Marvin Farber (Cambridge: Harvard University Press, 1940).

2. Phrases in English (in the original German letters) are in Italics.

Appendix: Excerpts from Aron Gurwitsch's contribution to the Husserl Memorial Volume edited by Marvin Farber (G1940b).

On the Intentionality of Consciousness

The intentionality of consciousness may be defined as a relation which all, or at least certain, acts bear to an object. In this manner, Brentano introduced the notion into contemporary philosophy. Seeking to account for the difference between what he calls "physical phenomena" and what he calls "psychical phenomena" Brentano found, among other characteristics, that the latter are distinguished by a relation to, or a direction toward, an object. . . .

. . . [Husserl] agrees with Brentano in acknowledging the existence of a highly important class of mental facts—for which Husserl reserves the title of acts—which have the peculiarity of presenting the subject with an object. Experiencing an act, the subject is aware of an object, so that the act may be characterized, as Husserl does, as a *consciousness* of an object whether real or ideal, whether existent or imaginary.

This peculiarity, however, ought not to be considered as a real quality or as a real property of acts, such, for example, as intensity, which is held by many psychologists to be a real property common to all sense data. In fact, to ascribe to an act, under the heading of intentionality, a real quality which makes it transcend itself to seize an object belonging, as is the case in the perception of a real thing, to a universe external to the sphere of consciousness, to which the act, though endowed with the transcending quality, remains tied nevertheless—this would be to bestow on the act a magic or at least mysterious power. . . .

Out of these we choose the most elementary, but as we think, at the same time the most fundamental one. *To be aware of an object means that, in the present experience, one is aware of the object as being the same as that which one was aware of in the past experience, and as the same as that which one may expect to be aware of in a future experience, as the same as that which, generally speaking, one may be aware of in an indefinite number of presentative acts.* Identity in this sense is, no doubt, constitutive of objectivity [*Gegenständlichkeit*]. But, even if considered on the most elementary level, the identity of objects, inasmuch as it is a conscious fact—and it is only for this reason that we have any knowledge of it and may talk of it—turns out to be an insoluble problem for the traditional conception of consciousness. We shall go on to show, if possible, that the treatment of this problem leads to a new conception of consciousness that is radically opposed to the traditional one. . . .

Husserl's noesis-noema doctrine . . . is simply a descriptive statement of an objectivating mental state, i.e., of a mental state through which the experiencing subject is confronted with an object. Every mental state of this kind must then be accounted for in terms of identity as well as of temporality. The traditional conception of consciousness, in which emphasis is placed upon temporality, the succession of acts and the variations each act undergoes by its duration, is certainly not false, since the fact emphasized is a real fact of consciousness. But this conception is incomplete and unilateral. No mental state is to be conceived only and exclusively as a real and temporal event in the stream of consciousness, without any reference to a sense . . . *Identity is to be acknowledged as a fact irreducible to any other; it turns out to be a fact of consciousness, no less authentic and no less fundamental than temporality is.* Thus we are led to a duality.

Aron Gurwitsch in his study, 2 Square du Port Royal, Paris, 1938–1939.

Schutz: *It is high time that action be made the theme of philosophy*
           (NEW YORK, AUGUST 19, 1939)

Dear Friend Philalethes[1]!

Many thanks for your very kind letter and for the enclosed copies of your essay. Although the days since its arrival have not been precisely conducive to reflective contemplation (and—it's a crying shame—will be even less so when you have these lines in your hands), I have now read your work attentively three times and would like to make a few remarks today concerning matters of principle, with an eye to the course of our later discussions, which I still want to believe in. To begin with, my sincere congratulations for a truly excellent piece of work—excellent as to both content and form. With regard to the linguistic side, I am—in English—unfortunately not at all competent, and my judgment wouldn't carry much weight. For my part, however, I should be delighted if I could write such English. After these preliminaries, let's get down to business:

As you know, for me the question concerning the "correct," namely orthodox, Husserl interpretation is always secondary to the question concerning the true states of affairs. Please keep this attitude of mine in mind in reading what follows. If I refer to Husserl, this is only as an example—although I would also have objections from the point of view of pure Husserl interpretation.

You are right a hundred times over in working out so sharply and clearly the connections between temporality and identity as a basic problem for any theory of consciousness. In principle, I also can't object if one wants to assume that there are in a sense two strata of consciousness, understood as a provisional intermediate solution for a specific way of posing the problem (one can go a long way with it). Purely from the point of view of presentation, such a provisional assumption will often facilitate matters greatly; the intermediate solution is legitimate as a provisional point of departure because it is adequate above all for the monographic study of the noematic-noetic problems. But it seems to me one must always remain aware that it is an intermediate solution and not the final result of exact description. This was my thesis in all of our discussions, and it is even more so after my reading of your essay.

As you know, I claim that the two-sidedness [*Doppelschichtigkeit*] of consciousness is not a demonstrable finding of phenomenological analysis, but rather the linguistic expression for a two-fold possibility of interpreting "the same" phenomena. They are considered on the one hand as the finished result of constitution, as *tout-fait;* on the other hand "interrogated as to their history."

In the first approach the point of departure is the natural attitude, in which for pragmatic reasons (not, of course, in the sense of that naive pragmatism from Bergson, James, and Scheler on down) a world of identical objects is assumed as unquestionable and self-evidently given. If one then penetrates deeper into the analysis of the conscious processes and encounters the problem of temporality, this produces the break in the Humean paradox as you interpret it. (But I fail to understand how you arrive at your final result without a sophism: namely that a consciousness for which there was only change could never attain a representation of time. I think that something is wrong here from the point of view of immanent critique as well, or it should at least be presented more clearly; either I haven't understood or it is false, but that is only an aside.)

In the other case, one doesn't address the problems concerning consciousness using the guiding thread of the "world of pragmatic identities," which is straightforwardly given in the naive attitude; one rather follows the constitutions of the intentional performances in the flow of their temporal course: this leads to the "break" in the difficulty of arriving at the identical thing. I say advisedly at the identical *thing*, not at the identical *sense* or to the identical meaning [*Meinung*]. For I am convinced that both paradoxes of both approaches arise from the fact that there is an incredible equivocation in the term "identity" here.

Sense, meaning [*Sinn, Meinung, Bedeutung*] can be invariant over against the acts of intentionality. This means that this sense can always be produced again as "the same" in reactivation and reproduction: thus, something that is indeed numerically identical. But the tree-thing [*Baumding*] there in front of me manifests its identity with what was just seen and with what will be seen in a completely different manner. Or, more properly, identity means something completely different here: for what is produced or reactivated as identical in this case? I am speaking of the tree-*thing* of the natural attitude, not of the tree-*noema* or the tree-*noematis*. By the way, I think that noema is (not linguistically, of course, but logically) essentially a *plurale tantum*.

Now what happens if one does not distinguish between these two concepts of identity, but rather naively and unreflectively identifies thing-identity and sense-identity? What happens is that one finds only three ways out. Either one comes to the *Hume*an result: Identity is mere appearance, for philosophical thought there cannot be an identical thing, there being such only for the vulgar understanding. Or to the *Husserl*ian result: There is identical sense; this is the constitutive product of intentionality; thus there are as it were identical "thing senses" (the whole problem lies in these words), namely noemata. The third solution—as another Theophilus argued against another Philalethes—is the *principium identitatis indiscernibilium:* if one rigorously applies this to the problem of temporality, as *Leibniz* suggested, then one has—it seems to me—a proper approach to the problem. But more about that another time.

The crux lies much deeper yet. It is a question of nothing less than the difficulty every subjectivistic (to say nothing of transcendentally oriented) philosophy has in coming to terms with the fact of the objective world which it has "put in brackets" or "annihilated."[2] This world, our *life*-world, is after all there, with that sense which is proper to it, a sense which is given over to me for interpretation. With that hubris which phenomenology shares with all transcendental systems I act as if I, the *ego transcendental,* myself produced this sense, if not the world itself. But in all this I don't produce anything at all other than sense and new sense, and with all of my productive intentionalities I don't move one single grain of sand and with all of my kinaesthesias I don't change one single thing in the world of things.

But if the simplest practical performance presupposes "identical" things and "identical" ways of handling things that are repeatable and learnable, are we speaking of "identical sense"? Does the ideality of the "and-so-forth" and the "one-can-always-do-it-again," does the theory of memory and reproduction explain to me the simple phenomenon of the *actio*? The *actio* in the truest, namely most vulgar, sense: e.g., writing these ink marks, not producing what they mean or the sense which their meanings, grasped as symbols in words—in sentences—in letters—can institute in our relationship. And yet I have learned, practiced, and made automatic the motions involved in the act of writing; and don't try to tell me that I have only forgotten or failed to pay attention to the history of its sense. I produce "identical" letters with "identical" motions—but this identity is surely not that of an invariant sense or of something which is "numerically one"? It is high time that action, namely corporeal πραττεῖν in the external world, be made the theme of philosophy.

But it goes without saying that I have nothing against it if one views identity as Husserl did and as in the final analysis you do too, purely as a phenomenon of sense, a phenomenon which has its legitimacy and its primal institution exclusively in productive intentionality. It is true that in this case sense is attributed to all kinds of ideal or irreal [*idealen oder irrealen oder irreellen*] objects (or however you choose to call the realm that of course also includes the noemata), but not to the "things"—those things that fall to the annihilation of the world, among them my mundane ego itself. After all, the things have no sense; their noemata, for me who produces them, are the only "sense" which is attributed to the things. But in the realm of "senses" (and according to this approach identity is after all a predicate only of structures of sense) I remain in the pure temporality of my flowing consciousness, and it is a tremendous problem for Husserl to trace this identity back to the "temporalizing of time."[3] Thus: even the identity of the noema is no great shakes! We have the noetic/noematic modifications of doxic attentionality, positionality, and neutrality; we have the noematic cores and syntheses of recognition and identification and association; we have above all the passive synthesis of prepredicative experience with its syntactic cores, syntagmas, and syntaxes, and behind all that the x of the thing-appearances according to the last paragraphs of the *Ideas*.[4]

But: all things considered, Husserl carried out large portions of these analyses, whose goal it is to disclose the sedimentations in which monothetic and polythetic syntheses lead to the production of the identically-one, and that on the basis of primally instituting experience. In addition, in Husserl we find important suggestions that these evidences do not have the character of specifically ego acts. (Cf., e.g., *Formal and Transcendental Logic*, paragraph 107, especially section C, which I consider to be one of the main sources for our topic.) The fact that Husserl took this path and personally had to do so is an historical-biographical fact. It does not obligate others to take the same detour—though we be found guilty of heresy.

I prefer to take a short-cut by attacking all of these problems directly in terms of temporality, wherever possible within the mundane sphere. The fact that this method is indeed a short-cut is something that I shall have to demonstrate, and I shall be able to do so only by presenting the concrete results. The fact that it is possible—that is, internally free of contradiction and in harmony with the whole of established phenomenological knowledge—is something that must be granted to me right now.

The important thing about a method of this kind is that it disposes of a serious difficulty concerning the theory of noemata which Husserl (at least in his published writings) did not touch on, but which will have to make itself felt for you too sooner or later. On the one hand, Husserl says again and again that this world is one, a unitary life-world for me and you and everyone, a world in which our experience reciprocally confirms and corrects itself. On the other hand, however, my noema remains a component of my solipsistic primordinal sphere. *How is*—even if we accept all syntheses of identification which are to lead to the thing or to the thing-object X (concluding portion of the *Ideas*)—*intersubjective* identification or *identity possible?* How can this problem be solved, especially for you, who introduce a two-fold stratification of consciousness (which for you means much more than a *façon de parler* or a working hypothesis for specific ways of posing problems; as that it proves its worth, and as that I am prepared to accept it)?

Further: the problem of the "hyletic data" became nothing less than a calamity for Husserl (*FTL*, paragraph 107C). It becomes even worse when one enters the world of thought of the Fifth Cartesian Meditation: for the hyletic data would after all have to remain encapsulated in my monadic primordinal [*primordinal*] sphere, regardless of whether other monads mirror and constitute themselves in this sphere. But how can you solve this problem—not merely in terms of intersubjectivity, but primordinally [*primordinal*]? How can you account for the change of hyletic data in temporality? But I seem to recall that you plan to give a critique of hyletic data in your work.

I am now awaiting this work with even more impatience and still greater interest. It should at last explain to me how things stand with the multiple stratifications of conscious life and what kinds of relations obtain between these various strata. Like the reader of a murder mystery, I can't wait to discover whether the solution will be that in fact two different heroes are responsible for all of these deeds or whether only one hero is at work in two masks. And as Theophilus,[5] as whom I write this letter, I am waiting for the harmony of both spheres, wondering whether it will perchance be preestablished.

And so these reflections have filled a day of the greatest anxiety and agitation, and I can only offer you, the cause and stimulus of this the longest letter of my life, a hearty thanks. May it find you and your wife in health and peace, and may it soon be granted to me to discuss all of this with you personally, at length and often. Since my papers are not yet in order, I shall probably return first in the second half of September—if this is still at all possible then.

In early September I shall attend the philosophy congress at Harvard, and shall distribute your copies there and see if there isn't something else I can do for you. The typescript (German) of my Farber essay will be finished soon, and I shall send you a copy at once. As soon as I have your answer to Kaufmann's suggestions—and I hardly think that you will accept them—I shall get in touch with him on your behalf. He is currently in the country.

But all of that is secondary to the question whether the beast to which power is given will again force kings to bow before him.[6] Let us, dear friend Philalethes, use the time which is given us, and let us hope, as best we can, that the barbarian will not disturb our circles. Though I would have liked to sign this letter as Theophilus—I can't bring myself to do it, in spite of the last chapter of the *Theodicy*—I remain with a warm handshake and a kiss on the hand of your dear, dear wife, only

Your

Pangloss[7]

1. Schutz is recalling Leibniz's *Nouveaux essais sur l'entendement humain,* the dialogue between Philalethes (lover of truth) and Theophilus (lover of God). Pangloss is the (Leibnizian) butt of Voltaire's sarcasm in his *Candide.*

2. In *Ideas,* Husserl writes that "while the being of consciousness . . . would indeed be necessarily modified by an annihilation of the world of physical things, its own existence would not be touched." (*Ideen zu einer reinen Phänomenologie und phänomenologischen Philosophie,* vol. 1, ed. Karl Schuhmann. The Hague: Martinus Nijhoff, 1976; English tr. by F. Kersten: *Ideas,* First Book. The Hague: Martinus Nijhoff, 1982. §49.) This is not to be understood as a metaphysical thesis but as a thought experiment concerning the structure of our experience of the world and the world as experienced.

3. Cf. S1932a, 42 (Eng. tr. S1967, 44, where *"Zeitigung"* is (mis)translated as "inner development"). The term probably comes from Heidegger (cf. *Being and Time,* §65). Husserl first used the term in his Foreword to the English translation of his *Ideas* (first published in German in 1930 as an Afterword to the *Ideas,* cf. *Ideen,* vol. 3 [*Husserliana* V] The Hague: Martinus Nijhoff, 1971, 142), and it played an important role in his reflections on time consciousness in the 1930s.

4. E. Husserl, *Ideas,* book one, tr. Fred Kersten (The Hague: Martinus Nijhoff, 1982), §§131ff.

5. See note 1.

6. Cf. Rev. 13:1–9.

7. See note 1.

Appendix: The following text was written (in German) as the first part of Schutz's "Farber essay" (S1940a), but remained unpublished until 1971.[1] It contains a concise statement of his understanding of the relationship between his own mundane phenomenology and Husserl's transcendental phenomenology.

Phenomenology and the Cultural Sciences

Phenomenological philosophy is above all a philosophy of man. As a "rigorous science" it, like all sciences, concerns the existing world [*Seinswelt*] of man, whose sense it has the task of making intelligible. The mathematical natural sciences, in their orientation toward rational objectivism, have forgotten that this life-world is the sense-foundation of all science. The phenomena of productive subjectivity, which alone constitute the life-world, remain closed off to the mathematical/natural-scientific point of view for essential reasons, and the natural scientist forgets that he himself, with his subjectivity which produces science, cannot find an understanding of himself and his action in any objective science. Only recourse to this sphere of productive subjectivity, which is of course made use of by natural science and by psychology which is oriented toward the natural sciences although it is never brought to a self-understanding, can on the one hand free mathematical natural science from the crises concerning its foundations and on the other hand ground a true science of man [*Geisteswissenschaft*].

This way towards an understanding of the sense of the life-world is that of transcendental phenomenology, which is thus alone capable of creating the foundations for all social and cultural sciences. For all appearances with which these sciences deal are phenomena of this our life-world, and transcendental subjectivity, in whose performances this world constitutes itself, is from the beginning related to other subjectivities, in terms of whose performances it "corrects and amends" its own. *The life-world and its sense are thus from the very beginning referred to others:* it is our common life-world, its sense is instituted by our shared performances and given over to us in common for interpretation. . . .

All cultural and social science is in principle mundane; it is not concerned with the transcendental *ego* or the transcendental *alter ego,* but rather with the phenomena of mundane intersubjectivity. These sciences thus do not have anything to do directly with the constitutive phenomena in the phenomenologically reduced sphere, but rather only with corresponding correlates in the natural attitude. Thus, we are pursuing a genuine psychology of intentionality, which in Husserl's words is nothing other than a constitutive phenomenology of the natural attitude. Psychology understood in this manner is not a science of factual states of affairs, but rather a science of essences which asks, e.g., about the invariant and essential structures of a psyche [*Seele*] or of a community of psychic (spiritual) [*seelischen (geistigen)*] life: i.e., about its *a priori.*

Such an eidetic mundane science of the phenomena of the cultural and social world stands at the beginning of all problems concerning the methodology and philosophy of a specific discipline. But in this science (thus in the psychological apperception of the natural attitude), all analyses carried out within the phenomenological reduction essentially retain their validity, and this is the reason for the incredible significance of Husserl's results for the establishment of a theory of the social and cultural sciences. What are these results? . . .

a) Application of Husserl's analysis of time to the problem of the "*structure of social action*" in the sense of Weber and Parsons.

b) Husserl's theory of signs and symbols with its reference to the positing and interpretation of sense.

c) Husserl's theory of sedimented experiences and their significance for the problem of the constitution of the social world.

d) Formal logic and the theory of the ideal type.

e) The theory of ideal objects and ideal sense-contents (objective spirit).

f) Husserl's teleological interpretation of history. . . .

1. The complete text of this section is published in A. Schütz, *Gesammelte Aufsätze,* Band 1: *Das Problem der sozialen Wirklichkeit,* tr. Benita Luckmann and Richard Grathoff (The Hague: Martinus Nijhoff, 1971), 136–139.

Schutz: *To create a center for phenomenological philosophy*
            (NEW YORK, NOVEMBER 10, 1939)

Dear Friend,

I have just received a letter from Prof. Farber, informing me that the answer from Prof. W.—whom I mentioned in my last letter—was unfortunately unfavorable. Farber has nevertheless written to Prof. F.[1] (University of Southern California) concerning this matter. He has sent me a copy of this letter. I cannot repeat the content of this letter here, but I can tell you that the letter is extraordinarily warm and just what you would wish. I hope that I shall soon be able to show you the the small folder of letters which are in my hands. You will see that you do indeed have good friends who can appreciate your qualities. At my request, Farber has written you a letter responding directly to the ideas in your last letter. I am putting it in the mail along with this letter.

Farber has consulted with me concerning the translation of your essay. I have authorized him in your name to make corrections in the English version and in the translation of the technical terms wherever it seems to him appropriate. I merely requested that he stick as closely as possible to Hume's usage in those sections which deal with Hume's philosophy.

Farber is currently very involved in the founding of an International Philosophical Society, with the purpose of using such an organ to create a center for phenomenological philosophy. This society is to publish a philosophical journal in three languages (English, French, and German), which is to appear three times per year. Farber is already corresponding with our friends in Louvain and has given me the task of approaching our philosophical friends in France and winning their cooperation. I am well aware of the fact that times are not exactly favorable for getting this idea off the ground, but I also know that France will never forget that above and beyond all conflicts of this world the realm of spirit must be preserved, and that an international scholarly cooperation simply cannot stray very far from the bright light of French thought.

I am thinking above all of our friend Gaston Berger, President of the Philosophical Society of Marseille, and of Raymond Aron and Paul Sartre. I don't know whether these young men are in the military by now, but I would appreciate it if you would let me know whether you think that I can approach them directly. In addition, I don't know where Jean Hering of Strasbourg and Prof. Koyré are at present.

You will not only be advancing this idea, which—as I know—will be attractive to you, but you will be an extraordinary help to Farber and myself if you would contact those named above and feel out their attitude, and also send me their addresses so that I can correspond with them directly.

Farber hopes to found the American society on the occasion of the philosophy congress which will take place a few days after Christmas in New York. He would be delighted if he could announce on this occasion that he has received a telegram from a group of French scholars in which they declare their willingness in principle to join such an international organization. You will surely understand that one must treat the question as to who will constitute the executive committee of the society with great tact. This whole question should be decided directly by Farber himself; be especially careful with regard to this question. Do you think that we might win Prof. Brehier for this idea? But please don't approach him directly! It is not our intention to restrict the activities of this society to phenomenology, although the phenomenological school is to constitute the core of this organization. But beyond this every true thinker is welcome. It goes without saying that the American positivists, who after all already have a number of organizations, will not be directly invited to participate, but at the moment opinions diverge on this point as well. I hope that your professional life leaves you enough time to tell me your personal views concerning these matters and to give me the information I have requested.

You asked how my personal life is going. I can only tell you that we are trying to settle down here and that this adjustment is not always very easy.

Please give my greetings to Mme. Gurwitsch and the friends in our circle. Do you have any news concerning their families? Many thanks for all of your friendship. Sincerely

Your

Schutz

1. Identities concealed by the editor. This and the following letter were written in French.

Gurwitsch: *It will be a day "we look forward to"*
              (GIF-SUR-YVETTE, APRIL 29, 1940)

Dear Friend,

. . . My affairs are now enough in order that I can count on my departure on about the 15th of May. My most sincere thanks for your offer to intervene for me in Washington through your friend. It seems to me that such a step is no longer necessary, at least with regard to the Consulate in Paris, which in the end did issue me the visa.

As I said, we will leave by ship on about May 15. But we will only know a few days before our departure which harbor we will be departing from. By the same token, I won't know the exact day of our departure until the last moment. Thus, to my great regret, I cannot inform you of our exact arrival date in advance, and must ask you to make a telephone inquiry at the New York agency of the Compagnie Générale Transatlantique. They will surely be able to tell you when the ship which departs on roughly May 15 will arrive in New York.

It is said here that all passengers in third class are automatically sent to Ellis Island; others deny this. Be that as it may, perhaps you would be so kind as to arrange through your friend in Washington that the immigration authorities are informed of my arrival; in this way we can perhaps avoid my career in the United States beginning with a more or less lengthy stay on this as everyone knows so "charming" island; this will also make it easier to deal with the other formalities. I am sorry to put you to more trouble, and I hope that this will be the last.

I saw Gaston Berger this afternoon. He has been in Paris for quite some time, but I didn't know it. He was too busy to get in touch with me and was in fact completely buried in his work. I hope that he will remain in Paris.

How is your daughter? We not only hope that her health is restored, but also that you have all forgotten this shared suffering by the time we land in New York. It is a day, as I would like to say in my new "mother" tongue, "we look forward to."

My regards to your wife. Sincerely

Your

Aron Gurwitsch

Gurwitsch: *They have saved only their bare lives*
            (BALTIMORE, AUGUST 5, 1940)

My Dear Friend,

We were overjoyed to hear that you have received news of your parents, even if the content is not what we would have wished. We can only hope that they have accommodations which will allow their health to improve. By the way, the American Express Co. accepts money orders for France; one of my acquaintances tried this recently with success. Everyone who has had to flee from France laments the loss of all his possessions. I recently received a similar letter from Montauban. Three Austrians fled Paris. They too have saved only their bare lives.

Hasn't Kracauer written something about the Kahns?[1] After all, they lived with their parents for months. I know the following particulars about the Kracauers: Siegfried K., born in Frankfurt-Main in 1889; Lilli K., née Ehrenreich, born in Strasbourg in 1898. Both came to Paris in 1933, living first at 3 Avenue MacMahon, then since September 1939 at Gif-sur-Yvette, Rue de la Fevrie, c/o L. Gaget. Both possess refugee passports, registered at the consulate on October 4, 1939. I am not absolutely sure about the years of birth. My knowledge stems from last fall, when they were interned and I wrote one petition after another in order to secure their release. I will write to them in Marseille that they should send you the particulars.

Nothing from Wertheimer. Go ahead and send me the particulars about R.;[2] then I will have an excuse to write him and in this way to admonish *de façon inaperçu*. W. [Wertheimer] is one of those people who dislike writing and from whom one has to extort correspondence; I actually understand this quite well, since I am a bit that way myself.

Many thanks for the suggestions concerning my mother. I will be in Washington next week anyway, and will speak with H. then.

How are the two of you and the children getting along? To tell the truth, I have a deep desire to see you, and my wife feels the same way. We are very comfortable in my aunt's house. It is actually a rather fantastic story: we were intended for the concentration camp and then for everything that the Nazi invasion brought with it, and instead of that one finds oneself in this roomy house, one sits on the porch and works on Sartre's theory of the ego. One has to "realize" all that. And where might Sartre be? At times I have the feeling that I am working on nothing other than obituary notices, especially as I reviewed Berger's article in the "Internationale."[3]

My most sincere greetings to both of you, including the two children, also from Raja,

Your

Aron Gurwitsch

Does the boy still demand "cents"?[4]

1. Erich Itor Kahn, pianist and composer, student of Schönberg: he later worked in New York.
2. The names of R. here and H. in the next paragraph have been concealed by the editor.
3. Gaston Berger, "Husserl et Hume," *Revue Internationale de Philosophie* 1 (1939): 342–353.
4. George, Schutz's son, asks for his allowance in French money.

Gurwitsch:　*Is the Mexican matter trustworthy?*
　　　　　　(BALTIMORE, AUGUST 17, 1940)

My Dear Friend,

Early today I finally received a letter from Erich Kahn's wife. They are both in a camp;[1] the letter is dated July 4 (air mail)!

In the interest of the Kahns, who want to wait for their quota number in

Mexico, I would like to ask you for a bit of information. The Mexican matter is in the hands of A. C. from New York, with whom I am in contact. Do you know anything about the man? Is he reliable and trustworthy, especially with regard to money, but also in general from the passological point of view? An American woman has deposited 22,000 pesos for Kahn in this matter. Mr. C. wrote me on July 20 that the regulations have been changed: it now requires 60,000 pesos, plus 1,500 pesos landing money. Once the money has been raised, the Kahns can have their visa within 48 hours. Can we trust that? In addition, after a stay of one week in Mexico Mr. Kahn can withdraw 50,000 of the 60,000. I would be very thankful if you would tell me what you know about these points.

The whole matter is complicated a bit by the fact that the woman in question lived in Paris, and I have not heard a single thing about her whereabouts. But her property is in the United States and is being managed by her brother. He in turn is perhaps not that interested in Erich Kahn; perhaps he lives on the moon and lacks the imagination to "realize" what war is and just what the predicament of the Kahns is. At any rate, he has pursued the matter in a dilatory manner, not only last winter but also since things have gotten "serious." I am going to try to approach relatives of Kahn in South Africa; perhaps they will put up the 39,500 pesos which are lacking. But before I do that I must of course know something about the soundness of the plan as well as the persons involved, and thus the renewed nuisance, which you won't hold against me.

I wrote to Mr. H. in Washington more than a week ago requesting an appointment; to date without reply. Perhaps he is on vacation.

For today I remain very brief, since I still have a extensive *courrier* to finish in connection with the Kahn letter, which also concerns another family of friends of ours.

Greetings to both of you, also from my wife

Your
Aron Gurwitsch

1. The name of the camp is unknown. A list of all French internment camps is in Schramm and Vormeier, *Vivre à Gurs* (Paris: Maspero, 1979).

Schutz: *60,000 pesos are required for a Mexican visa*
(NEW YORK, AUGUST 20, 1940)

Dear Friend Gurwitsch,

Misled by your letterhead, my secretary sent my last letter to that address. As you can see from the enclosed envelope, it was returned as undeliverable. You should make arrangements with the university that letters for you be accepted.

With regard to your letter of 8.17.40 concerning Kahn, we know C. very well, but from a unflattering side. However, we have no idea of the extent to which he can arrange something in Mexico. But we know that he demands excessive fees, achieves nothing, and has been withholding a deposited sum from a friend of ours for more than one and a half years. This is of course in confidence for your information.

I myself have arranged Mexican visas in other ways. It is true that 60,000 pesos are required, plus 1,500 landing fee. This sum must be provided so that the person in question, once in the country, can start an industrial or agricultural enterprise. If he fails to do so within the term of one half year, he forfeits the sum of *c.* 3,500 pesos once and for all, and can use of the remainder only with difficulty. Mexico is something for those who are waiting for permission to go on to the U.S.A. As a friend concerned with Kahn's interest, I would most strongly urge against his taking this path. If one has time and such sums are available, it might be possible to arrange something for him, perhaps even in Argentina or in a decent South American country where a musician also has a chance to get ahead.

With regard to Kracauer, I am cooperating with Schapiro[1] and Adorno. I have received very favorable recommendations concerning him from both of them and have had them presented most emphatically in Washington. Unfortunately, 10 days have passed without my receiving an answer.

Please write more about yourself soon. I have been suffering from a bad tooth problem for the last 3 weeks, which keeps me away from everything else.

Sincere greetings

Your

Alfred Schutz

1. Meyer Schapiro, art historian at Columbia University.

Gurwitsch: *We feel very alone, since we are still rooted in another world*
                     (Baltimore, August 23, 1940)

Dear Friend,

Enclosed are copies of two letters to Wertheimer and to Kaufmann. You can see from them what I am trying to do for R. I have given Wertheimer your address so that he can correspond directly with you, which will be simpler. I am naturally still prepared, if it is desired, to act as middleman. At any rate, please keep me up to date on how things are going in this matter.

The "second part" of the letter from R. was indeed of great interest to me. Do you know that Bergery, who is mentioned there, was one of the fathers and founders of the *Front Populaire?* Déat too comes from socialism.[1] This could occasion all kinds of interesting reflections. It would appear that we reactionaries are the better human beings.

Many thanks of course for the information concerning C. and Mexico, although that robs me of an illusion concerning the possibility of helping Kahn. Now it remains to be seen whether we can somehow get him here sooner. Thus, the question which I ask Wertheimer at the end of my letter[2] is also directed at you.

You complain that I write so little or nothing about myself. Actually, I have almost nothing to write concerning myself in the strict sense. We are quite lonely here. And that not merely in the sense that we see so few people here. But even among those whom we see, we feel very alone, since we are still rooted in another world. And that, I think, won't change very much even with time. I will perhaps meet a few people when the university begins. I have a real desire especially to meet old Lovejoy.[3] In a broader sense, though, I write about us every time it is a matter of emigrantology. You will probably understand how occupied [*erfüllen*], if not satisfied [*ausfüllen*], at least in the normal sense of this word, we are by these things. And this brings me to yet another of the reasons for our isolation even in our "being among others." I would be delighted if we could come to New York again. Don't your travels lead you to Washington now and then, and thus through Baltimore?

How is your tooth? We hope it hasn't brought you in contact with the superb American dental medicine, which for all such things has patent methods which are as simple as they are radical. The little bit that I know about medicine makes me thoroughly sceptical about the manner in which this art is normally practiced here.

Have you found a possibility for sending money to France? I am interested in this, since I am trying to drum up some money for the Kahns and others, and one has to deal with the question of how to get it there. Two days ago I saw Mr. H. in Washington. He has never had a case of this kind and cannot give me any reliable information; he thinks, however, that my brother's reservations are not very well founded. For the rest he referred me to the New York office. This opens up the possibility of a trip.

Farber recently sent an article by Binswanger: pure nonsense. I hope that I have blocked its publication. What has happened with the paper by Blumenfeld?

With sincere greetings to you and your wife from the two of us

Your
Aron Gurwitsch

---

1. Marcel Déat was to become the Minister for National Solidarity under Laval in the Vichy government in 1943.

2. A copy of this letter is in the Archives in Constance.
3. Arthur Oncken Lovejoy (1873–1962) taught at Stanford, Washington University in St. Louis, and Johns Hopkins.

Schutz: *We are receiving despairing letters with threats of suicide*
          (New York, November 2, 1940)

Dear Friend Gurwitsch!

Why don't we hear anything from you? Please write how you and your wife are getting along, how you like Baltimore, how your lectures are going, etc.

I have decided to submit a paper for this phenomenological symposium of the American Philosophical Association after all, although there is surely hardly any chance that it will be accepted.[1] But I had various reasons for doing so. You will find a copy enclosed and I think that the topic, with which you are familiar, will interest you. You can well imagine how curious I am about what you will have to say about it (or better: to write against it).

We are receiving despairing letters from Kracauer with threats of suicide—he wants to follow the example of Walter Benjamin. The U.S.A. consulate has issued him an "affidavit in lieu of passport," but Spain accepts only national passports for transit visas. You can see what his mental state is like from the fact that he pleads with us to push through his naturalization and issuance of a passport in Washington as an exception, and that by cable! Through the institute and Schapiro we have asked the Spanish envoy in Washington to intervene with his government.

We are doing well under the circumstances; we are receiving sad reports from our relatives in Europe.

Love to you and your dear wife from the two of us!
Sincerely

Your
Schutz

How did you like the first number of our review? Please give me your private address!

I have a letter from Hering with particulars concerning him and Koyré. The latter has already been accepted by the New School.

1. "William James' Concept of the Stream of Thought Phenomenologically Interpreted" (S1941).

Gurwitsch: *What is incredibly interesting in America is Jewish life*
              (BALTIMORE, NOVEMBER 3, 1940)

Dear Friend,

While we have agreed that we are bad correspondents, that means: bad, but still correspondents. And so I shall hold to our agreement by first saying that I have read the Husserl fragment with great pleasure and inner gain.[1] I can see just how much work was involved in the editing and must congratulate you for what you have achieved. Not merely for the fact that it has become a coherent text which in this form can and must be studied. But this text is also very significant as a first attempt at a constitution of space. More and more it seems to me that Husserl's late work leads us into dimensions of which we had no idea earlier and whose significance, e.g., for the problematic of mathematics and physics, is slowly becoming clear. I am very curious to see the commentary on the fragment which has been announced.[2]

Concerning us personally I can only say that we are getting along better, even incomparably better, than back then. The reason is that we are living in our own walls and are by and large left in peace. May it only please the great Manitou that it remain this way! On the other hand we have met a few people who fortunately belong to a completely different world, also socially, and so life slowly finds its way onto more fruitful paths.

What is incredibly interesting in America is Jewish life. The area we live in is a kind of Bronx. Most of the people we come into contact with are the children, born here, of Russian Jews who came here in the 1880s or after the revolution of 1905. Thus, more or less in my situation. So I often have the impression that I have returned to my origins. That process of liberation and emancipation which began in Russia and which could not be completed under the conditions there, or at least led to serious battles and conflicts, was able to develop smoothly under the free conditions here, and the results are in part very gratifying.

Those persons of my age or younger who have studied at the colleges and universities here and who still have so much in them that comes from "over there," and who in addition live here in almost normal personal circumstances—compact settlements and without artificially invented problems—are almost exemplary for the continual development of a people. Here I find a great deal that I have dreamed about and wished for myself realized in fact: the self-confident Jew, who has made the step to Europe or America—and I don't mean that geographically—and who constitutes a new and necessary stage in the history of the people. I have always viewed my own life in this way, and there is something deeply satisfying in finding it. We both hope that it will always remain possible for us to live in these compact Jewish settlements.

And now you have heard enough about us; I want to inquire about you. How are your wife and your children? And what do you hear from your parents? Since my correspondence with France has become very regular, I assume that

that is also the case for you and that you often get news from over there. Please let us know what you hear, and be a correspondent, if a poor one. With sincere greetings

Your

A. Gurwitsch

1. "Notizen zur Raumkonstitution" (S1940b).
2. No "commentary" was published, but cf. GS 7.27.50.

Gurwitsch: *Not all who rattle their chains are free*
              (BALTIMORE, NOVEMBER 7, 1940)

Dear Friend,

You can well imagine my joy as I recently received your James manuscript,[1] and my even greater joy as I spent the last few days studying it. If your intent was to discover motivational strands which lead from James to phenomenology and to demonstrate that one who moves in Jamesian thoughts is actually already by and large moving in the realm of phenomenology, then you have indeed succeeded.

But I don't think that that is what you want to hear from me. In what follows I shall thus disregard the direct intent of your paper. This latter aspect is probably also responsible for the short length of your paper; and if I indicate several points which I would have liked to see elaborated further, this is only a question concerning the presentation and does not affect the broad agreement between us concerning the first part (pages 1–10).

Aside from points of secondary interest, which I shall disregard, I was happy to see that you too view the Jamesian concept of the object of thought, as opposed to the topic, as a parallel to the noema. In my *Memorial* Essay[2] I hinted at this briefly (on pages 76–77). You elaborate it further. You are completely right that the Jamesian definition[3] "the object of thought is its entire content or deliverance, neither more nor less" is precisely the definition of the noema. You could have gone even farther in this direction, and I assume that it was the necessary limitations of space that prevented you from doing so. If one considers the fact that the psychologist's reality is after all only given to him in the thought's object (in the case in which, as in phenomenology, the phenomenologist is his own psychologist), the problematic of constitution emerges effortlessly from Jamesian thought. Thus, without recurring to external motives (external relative to James), this whole problematic could be reached by means of a consistent development of his approaches. It is commendable that your article tells the Americans that, or at least intimates it. If one continues in this direction, the naive contrast between the thought's object and the psychologist's reality is dissolved internally.

Another commendable point in this part is the way you show on pages 6–7 [p. 5][4] that in the reduction the things are transformed into meanings. Here one could go on to ask: since James's object is nothing other than a meaning (that which is left over in the reduction), mustn't James have practiced something like a reduction here, without formulating it or knowing it? And mustn't that tie in with a descriptive tendency? I.e., won't a strictly descriptive psychology at least partially come to terms with that which the reduction opens up? This connection between reduced consciousness and what results from a strictly descriptive orientation came to my attention in connection with Gestalt theory. And now your article suggests this connection in terms of James. Shouldn't it be possible to cast new light on the reduction from this point of view, and thus get rid of much of the mystery which it sometimes has in many presentations, e.g., in that of Fink? That is an additional point from which I have continued your line of thought, and from which it would be very interesting to see the further development.

One point at which I disagree with you concerns Husserl's theory of the noematic central cores on page 8 [p. 6]. You are obviously referring to *Ideas* I, paragraph 131.[5] I won't go into our differences here, since I cannot accept this theory of Husserl. But in the present context that is of secondary interest. If this theory of Husserl is very important to you I would be glad, if you wish, to send you the relevant section of my manuscript, in which I have elaborated the reasons why I cannot accept this theory, which by the way does not reappear in any of his later writings.[6]

With regard to part 2, which deals with the "fringes," I would like briefly to sketch, relatively independently from your paper, how I view and hopefully will soon expound this Jamesian theory. What is described as "fringes" are indeed references beyond itself on the part of what is given. And that does have something to do with what Husserl calls a horizon. But it seems to me—we have argued about this often enough—that one can't treat the inner horizon and the outer horizon as facts of the same class. It also seems to me that under "fringes" appear both those factors that guarantee the connection of the theme with its field and the coherence of this field and also those in which the continuity of the stream of consciousness manifests itself.

All cases in which James speaks of the way that new thoughts fit into what is being thought about belong to the first class. Whenever he speaks of "felt pertinence" in terms of "fringes," we are dealing with this class. This is the outer horizon. But this is not the unity of the stream of consciousness, but rather the unity of the fields in question. In addition, phenomena which have to do with the unity of the stream of consciousness are termed "fringes." And when, in the discussion of subjective time, you mention the continua of retentions and protentions which belong to every now as being "fringes," then in my opinion you have hit a point where indeed the Jamesian intentions are not merely parallel to those of Husserl, but even identical. I would suggest that the title "fringes" be reserved solely for this class. But that leads back once again to the problem which we have discussed so often, whether one must distinguish so sharply between field and margin as I do.

But James attributes even more to the fringes. He was the first one to have the courage to speak of a feeling of "if" and a feeling of "and."[7] This too is included under the title "fringes." In addition, the fringes are to be responsible for the universal meanings of words, indeed for the phenomenon of meaning itself. When one surveys the examples, one can see that there is a very colorful multiplicity of cases that sail under this flag. Why is this? He wants to give the vague its rightful psychological place again and thus transcend traditional sensualism. Thus, everything which this sensualism has trouble explaining is classified as fringe. And in this way the continuity of the stream, which was lost for classical sensualism, is to be regained.

If one now takes a closer look at James's examples, one makes the following very curious discovery. That which appears as the core and is surrounded by fringes is always precisely the data which classical sensualism accentuated. E.g., in the case of phenomena of meaning, the body of the word appears as a sensuous datum, as the core, and what gives it its stamp of meaning are its fringes. This is even more curious when one takes account of the fact that these fringes are to be "transient." Thus, the pure meaning cannot be seized and objectivated, but the body of the word can. In addition, the fringes serve the move from one substantive part to the next. And these phenomena of transition are to guarantee the unity of the stream. The result is that in the final analysis the unitary nature of the thought structures is lost all over again, namely as the unity of meaning, and that in its place one has the flitting from substantive part to substantive part.

In this context you should take a look at the *Principles of Psychology*, vol. 1, pages 278–283, where you find the assertion of a temporal adumbration of a meaning unity. Once again, the words which come together in the sentence are accentuated in a curious way, and the meaning of the whole, which is after all constantly in focus, is thus to be a fleeting fringe? You won't accept this any more than I do.

I see the reason for all of this in the fact that James did not, as he wished, succeed in ridding himself of this sensualistic and atomistic theory. This is a typical case that not "all who rattle their chains are free." Basically, he leaves the data which sensualism accentuated in their privileged position, and merely adds additional facts. Take, e.g., the role of sensations or images, which always make their appearance at the end of a line of thought, and whose privileged position lies in their function as terms (how completely different the privileged position of perception in Husserl, as the original having of something itself!). The fringes lead to this term; for even purely verbal thought and understanding, even nonintuitive thought counts as fringes, whose core is precisely this term, the word, the sentence, in which the train of thought ends. The fringes can be forgotten; what counts is the goal to which they lead. And the entire "halo of obscurely felt relations" serves once again only to move from one "substantive part" to another.

In this connection, to return to your paper, I cannot agree with you that the fringes might have something to do with monothetic acts. If the prior polythetic syntheses and syntaxes are sedimented in them and their correlates, I do not see what that has to do with the case in which a more or less confused or even not confused train of thought ends in a "substantive" structure, and the path one takes to get there is irrelevant.

With regard to the theory of fringes, what seems to me above all necessary is a classification of all cases which appear under this title. A classification with the goal of eliminating all phenomena which, like those of meanings in general, and specifically of "if," "and," etc., do not belong there. Once this has been done there remain two large classes of cases. The first are those which announce the unity of theme and thematic field, in my jargon; the other class includes the phenomena which in the same jargon are called the data of marginal consciousness.

Then the question of what this unity of the stream actually is can be discussed. I see it in the temporal horizons, but not in the existence of curious data which make it possible to move from substantive stage to substantive stage. I am well aware of the fact that James himself has protested against viewing his fringes as pure filler material, as filler material which lies between the substantive facts. But he has not merely given aid and comfort to such an understanding in the manner in which he deals with the fringes concretely; he has in fact made them by and large filler material—to exaggerate just a bit—in the manner in which he makes use of them.

Of course, this critique does nothing to impinge on his greatness. The first attempt to free oneself from atomism could only be made on the basis of precisely this atomism; and the privileged position of what is sensuously or quasi-sensuously palpable shows just how much James still stands on this ground. I think that the significance of his theory of fringes lies in the fact that it broaches and opens up a problematic, and not in providing a solution for this problematic. But can one say anything better of a philosopher than that he has given us, his students, work to do?

And of course this critique doesn't touch the aim of your essay of showing that what James is working on is *nostra res*. Although it does seem to me that phenomenology has methods which can deal with these problems with more precision, the commonality of the problems themselves remains. And for this reason—to come back to the aim of your paper—it is enormously important that it come to the attention of a broader circle than the one consisting of one element, of your friend, and it should perhaps include a further development of those points which I allowed myself to point out at the beginning.

I am glad to hear that you are doing as well as the circumstances allow. We can say the same of ourselves. In the course of the one month that I have been holding seminars I have settled in at Johns Hopkins much better than I thought possible at first. My relationships with my professor [*Ordinarius*] have already gone beyond the stage of mere correctness. The seminar itself began with one student; after two meetings there were two; after two further, six. Now the fact is that this one student constitutes the entire population of the department in the graduate faculty. All those who showed up later belong to other departments: mathematics and physics. The only student in the psychology department was not available, since he got his Ph.D. last week.

I recently received the *Memorial Volume*. There are good things in it, but also things which are hardly acceptable, e.g., the essay by McGill. I had already read your contribution in manuscript. I enjoyed those by Cairns and Kaufmann and Farber. Just between you and me: are the contributions to be reviewed in the periodical?[8] If so, I would like to have the four just mentioned, and I would wish that mine land in good hands—yours.

It is of course impossible these days to write a letter that does not contain something passological. My efforts on Kahn's behalf have had the effect that his matter has gone from the Emergency Rescue Committee[9] to the President's Advisory Committee in Washington. Some time ago you were friendly enough to offer the possibility of an intervention in Washington for Kahn when the time came. Could you possibly do something along these lines now? The poor fellow has been interned again in the meantime—for the third time—and is in danger of being sent to forced labor according to the decrees which were recently issued.

What you write concerning Kracauer is heart-rending. During the war we were evacuated along with them for a couple of months, and I can imagine how he is reacting.

Please have Mrs. Staudinger of the New School get in touch with Hering[10] for addresses and particulars of additional Frenchmen. I am glad to hear that Koyré has been accepted by the New School. What is happening with R.?

Love and best wishes to both of you. When can we get together again? Sincerely

Your
Aron Gurwitsch

1. S1941.
2. Farber's memorial volume (G1940b).
3. *Principles of Psychology,* vol. 1, 275.
4. The page numbers in [] refer to Schutz's *Collected Papers,* vol. 3.
5. Husserl: The "object" is the "determinable X in the noematic sense" (cf. SG 8.19.39).
6. Cf. *The Field of Consciousness* (G1964), 179f.
7. James, I, 245.
8. *Philosophy and Phenomenological Research* (PPR), ed., Marvin Farber.
9. "Emergency Rescue Committee," established by the American journalist Varian Fry, who organized the emigration of writers and scientists beginning in August 1940. Cf. Varian Fry, *Surrender on Demand* (New York: Random House, 1945).
10. Jean Hering (1890–1966), student and close friend of Husserl from the Göttingen period, taught at the Strasbourg Protestant Theological Faculty; cf. B. Waldenfels, *Phänomenologie in Frankreich* (Frankfurt: Suhrkamp, 1983), 34f.

Schutz: *By night I am a phenomenologist, but by day an executive*
           (NEW YORK, NOVEMBER 9, 1940)

Dear Friend,

As you know, by night I am a phenomenologist, but by day an executive. At the moment my day life is taking over my night life. For this reason, for today just a line in thanks for your very kind long letter of the 7th, which was an infinite pleasure. I hope to answer it around the end of next week in the detail it deserves.

But you must read *Experience and Judgment* [Husserl] as soon as possible; you need it more than you think. More about that in the near future.

I will make inquiries concerning Kahn. But even if we can solve the matter with regard to the U.S.A., he will hardly get through Spain.

Love to you and your wife from both of us

Your
Schutz

Gurwitsch: *This is what happens when you do not yet have intentionality*
              (BALTIMORE, NOVEMBER 11, 1940)

Dear Friend,

Before I receive the letter that your card promises for the end of next week, I must call your attention to the following three works by James:

1) "On Some Omissions of Introspective Psychology" (*Mind* 1884). By and large worked into the *Principles of Psychology* (sometimes word for word), but still worth reading, especially the last part.

2) *Talks to Teachers,* New York 1909, ch. II, "Streams of Consciousness."

3) "Knowing of Things Together," *Psychological Review* 1895.
I read all three in the last few days, thus after posting my letter.

I read the second one early today: Very important and revealing. What is present simultaneously? Perceptions, memories, wishes, feelings, thoughts, etc. Much of it focal, some of it marginal. But: broken down according to act-categories, without reference to the "objective affairs" [*Gegenständliches*]. Not a word is lost on the question whether a co-present feeling is pertinent to the perceived thing. What is going on when I change? (I can always let something marginal become focal and vice versa.) For example: If I am happy about a gift, I live in this joy. Then: I take a closer look at the gift, perception becomes focal— the joy marginal. Is this change of a kind with: I read and follow the train of thought, in the background (co-present) joy over an impending visit. Then: turn to the joy—the train of thought however "still there"?

This is what happens when one does not yet have intentionality. Not all modifications of the field are of a kind. And again: James wants to get rid of atomism and remains bound up with it. It is almost a tragedy how he conducts his attempts to free himself from this very point of view, attempts which cannot succeed, since he has not abandoned the point of view.

I have been studying *Experience and Judgment*[1] for the past few days.

I hope to hear from you soon. Love

Your

A. Gurwitsch

1. Husserl's *Experience and Judgment* was edited by Ludwig Landgrebe from manuscripts. It was published in 1939 by the Academia-Verlag in Prague, since Husserl could no longer publish in Germany. With the exception of 200 copies which were sent to the publisher Allen & Unwin in London, the entire edition was destroyed during the war. Cf. the foreword to the edition of 1948.

Schutz: *James is in a long chain of philosophers, all of whom were already acquainted with intentionality*
(NEW YORK, NOVEMBER 16, 1940)

Dear Friend,

I can now respond to your two kind letters of the 7th and the 11th, and thank you very much for your very detailed examination of my James essay. In the meantime it has been accepted by the A.P.A. [American Philosophical Association] and will be read on the morning of December 27—I hope in your presence. You are completely right in your assumption that it was written solely for a specific occasion. The reading time is 20 minutes, and 3500 words are hardly possible in this period for such an unclear speaker as I. An expansion is thus—at least for purposes of the congress—impossible, and my main difficulty was giving some short, clear information to a public unfamiliar with phenomenology, taking familiar theories as my point of departure. I am happy that you think that this goal has been realized. This modest essay was not written for readers such as Gurwitsch. But the fact that even you found it interesting enough to use it as the occasion for such instructive and important reflections shows me that it must be by and large a success.

You are absolutely right in what you write about the connection between the thought's object and the problematic of constitution, but it is simply impossible to discuss it in such a limited space. Farber, who liked the essay very much, even advised me to cut out the brief reference to the problematic of constitution, since the public wouldn't understand it. You are also right that James unconsciously, or rather silently, carries through many of his descriptions within the reduced sphere. But to the extent that he does so, he is only one link in a long chain of philosophers and psychologists, all of whom were already acquainted with intentionality, even if they did not use the term. With regard to the reduction, I shall wait until our next meeting to whisper many heretical things in your ear.

With regard to the noematic central core, I don't share your opinion that it is mentioned only incidentally in the *Ideas*. You will find the same ideas elaborated in *Experience and Judgment*, the *Cartesian Meditations* speak of them, and the syntaxes and syntagmas of *Formal and Transcendental Logic* refer to them. Substantively, the problem of identity remained just as insoluble for Husserl as was that of the alter ego—and I am of the opinion that the deep-lying reason is the same in both cases.

The fact that James's concept of fringes is a hodgepodge of thoroughly heterogeneous categories is something that my essay, which only distinguishes three categories, tries to demonstrate. "Inner horizon" and "outer horizon" are certainly not parallel concepts, but they are dealt with in a parallel manner by Husserl himself, and it was after all Husserl's work that was to be presented. With regard to the relation of the fringes to your "field theory," I wonder whether in your opinion James's fringe-relations first constitute the unitary field or whether the already constituted unitary field is the presupposition for the felt pertinence. A great deal in your second letter speaks for the second possibility, other things for the first. It would be very welcome if your planned study would have more to say about this question.

The connection you demonstrate between substantive parts (James) and traditional sensualism is very interesting, certainly correct, and became clear to me only through your discussion. On the other hand, I do not agree with you that for James the substantive parts are only the words (*Wörter*, not *Worte!*) in the proposition [*Satz*], whereas the proposition as a whole, or its sense, is a fleeting fringe. We will have to discuss this some time with the texts in front of us. I consider the proposition that is constituted out of syntagmas and syntaxes, with all of its "if" and "and" relations, as a prime example for polythetic sequences of positings of "substantive parts" connected by means of fringes (the fringes refer precisely to the "if" and "and" syntheses, which produce the connections), in contrast to the propositional sense as the monothetic correlate of these polythetic graspings which are built up in time. In my opinion, this is true for James and Husserl.

That does not affect the importance of the theory of fringes for your account of the thematic field and the data of marginal consciousness. Your reference in this context to the temporal horizons is also legitimate, but what makes these horizons salient in the first place and constitutes sense in them is tied to sedimentations which are already preformed (or to preexisting thematic fields, and these in turn to the temporal perspectives of that which is thematic in the actual present/just-has-been/just-will-be), thus to something which already in the stream of thought had the "quality of being a term" [*Terminusqualität*], as I will call it ad hoc—or, in James's language, is a substantive part. This seems to me to be the ground of the ultimate validity of this concept.

Unfortunately, I can only go into your second letter partially, since the more interesting second part is simply unreadable. You will have to read your letter to me sometime soon, since it is precisely the underlined words which are illegible. I am only familiar with the first work by James to the extent that it was taken into the *Principles* and discussed by James; the second I know very well, and I shall read the third as soon as possible following your recommendation.

Mandelbaum[1] referred me to an essay by Dewey on "James' View of the Self," which is supposed to be published in the penultimate number of the *Journal of Philosophy*.[2] I haven't read it yet.

I plan to travel to Philadelphia soon and will write to you as soon as I know what my schedule will be (probably the weekend of November 30). I hope that you can come too. If Frau Raja(h?) comes with you, I will see if Ilse won't match her.

In the meantime, love and best wishes. Write your James essay soon; given what your letter promises, it will be very significant and important.

Sincerely

Your
Schutz

1. Maurice Mandelbaum, Johns Hopkins University, author of *The Problem of Historical Knowledge,* 1938.
2. John Dewey, "The Vanishing Subject in the Psychology of James," *Journal of Philosophy* 37 (1940): 589–599.

Gurwitsch: *We won't wash our dirty linen in front of the congress*
              (BALTIMORE, NOVEMBER 20, 1940)

Dear Friend,

Many thanks for your so detailed anti-critical letter. There are a couple of points which we will have to discuss personally. We can very easily come to terms if a couple of my assertions are understood in the specific and limited sense in which I meant them: e.g., noematic central core. But that is for our next opportunity, i.e., perhaps in one week. First my congratulations for the acceptance by the A.P.A. That is the very least that your work should receive in way of recognition; the "essay in itself" is by no means as modest as its modest author claims.

I shall of course be in Philadelphia for the congress. I plan to speak in the discussion following your talk. We shall have to arrange this very carefully. It would of course make no sense in that situation for me to discuss with you as I do when we are alone. The idea is that I take up the ball and throw it back by elaborating one or two points beyond what you have said, and you then play the ball further with your own additional remarks. We both have the goal of using James to present motives leading to phenomenology to a public which is unfamiliar with phenomenology. But in this case the ball game can only be played on ground which is *Terrain d'entente* for the two of us, i.e., the first part of your paper; because I really do think very differently from you concerning the fringes, and we won't wash our dirty linen in front of the congress. It is also not the point of my intervention to show where James bogs down, but on the contrary to show the point at which his work leads on to phenomenology.

Concerning the rendez-vous in Philadelphia: I shall be delighted to come on November 30th, but unfortunately without my wife. I would gladly make her come, but she is suffering from depressions once again—without any *fundamentum in rebus*. The idea of the Kahns' life and fate persecutes her continually, and also that of the other friends in France. She would really prefer to see no one. I think it would be better if she would come, but I don't press her.

My situation is that I have a rendez-vous with Köhler in Swarthmore, right by Philadelphia, on either Saturday the 30th or on Monday the 2nd. I don't yet know which day Köhler will choose. In either case I will keep Sunday the 1st of December free for us. For our rendez-vous it is irrelevant whether I am already in Philadelphia on Saturday or still in Philadelphia on Monday. I will be staying with Mrs. Cecilia Astin. But please drop me a line whether the rendez-vous is definite or whether something has changed your plans. If I did not have my rendez-vous with Köhler, I would suggest that the two of you travel an hour longer and visit us here. We live pretty comfortably.

Please excuse me for the illegible letter. It was written late at night, and I didn't want to disturb the sleep around me with the rattle of the typewriter. I was reading James, and under the impression of your paper my reflections in my letter to you took on the form of a discussion with you. It seemed to me only natural to give in to this form and let you know what I had to say to you at the moment and indeed was saying in my fantasy. Sadly, the goal was not realized: a case of a communicatively meant utterance which remains stuck in the nighttime-solitary life of the soul.

Bring the letter with you to Philadelphia. And now I have to choose: either to give you lessons in reading my handwriting or restrict myself to using the typewriter. What shall I do—in the second case—if nighttime discussions with you once again occur in your absence?

Until, I hope, the end of next week
Sincerely

Your
A. Gurwitsch

Gurwitsch: *I attempt, following Sartre, to come at things in precisely the opposite*
             manner as you
             (BALTIMORE, DECEMBER 19, 1940)

Dear Friend,

I am sorry to say that we had to change our plans. We will not be able to come to New York before Christmas, as we had planned. I am very sorry. Thus, I won't be able to see you until Philadelphia; but after the congress we shall go to New York for about a week. I shall write you when I will be in Philadelphia. An acquaintance will probably take me along in his car. It is important to me that I see you prior to the congress in order to agree on my intervention in the debate.

Do you have another copy of your paper which you could send to me here? I don't quite have it committed to memory word for word.

Enclosed you will find the copy of a paper[1] which went off to Farber some time ago. The copy is for you and I am not counting, *sauf tout à fait imprévu*, on its return. You know how I love this form of publication. The paper is all Sartre—with the exception of a couple of items which are marked—and all Gurwitsch. I am eager to know what you think about it. We have often discussed the problem, but the answer hardly at all. That something is wrong with the transcendental ego is something we have both known for a long time. But I attempt, following Sartre and also even earlier and independently of him, to come at things in precisely the opposite manner as you. Something must be dropped: in you transcendental, in myself and Sartre ego is the drop-out.

But you will read all that. I would like to say one thing more. This paper has been finished since September. My corrector let me wait for two months and then lost the manuscript. Thus, it was written prior to my work on American neo-realism, and also prior to my intensive study of James. To my surprise I have seen how close these American things can come to phenomenology when a couple of things are eliminated which are themselves intrinsically indefensible. Then it is almost child's play to translate neo-realism into the phenomenological, and both parties gain infinitely with this translation.

I am not looking for parallels at any price, and I know that dogmatic concordances don't themselves prove anything at all. But the part of my mundane ego—and it is the only one I have—that learned its lessons from Leibniz is time and again happy to discover that every honest and sincere philosophical labor has its validity and its legitimate place, though discovering it in its rivalry [with other positions] is not so easy.

We can talk about everything else in Philadelphia. Best greetings to your wife. Will she come too? Mine wants to come, and I will bring her.

Sincerely

Your

Aron Gurwitsch

---

1. "A Non-Egological Conception of Consciousness" (G1941)

Schutz: *I am terribly busy*
          (NEW YORK, DECEMBER 21, 1940)

Dear Friend Gurwitsch,

Many thanks for your letter of the 19th and the enclosed manuscript. I am so terribly busy with various things that I am afraid that I won't be able to read it in peace prior to Philadelphia. I am also very sorry that our planned meeting didn't work out and that you don't plan to come to New York until the congress. I will be terribly busy during this period, since my boss is expected back after an absence of two months and since in addition we are setting up an office. My wife and I will arrive in Philadelphia on Thursday afternoon, and we will stay at the Hotel Philadelphia, Chestnut at 39th Street, Telephone Evergreen 9 0000.

I am looking forward to seeing you and your wife, and hope that we will find time to talk in peace. A copy of my manuscript is enclosed. But I don't think that there will be much opportunity for an extensive discussion between us, since I hear that Prof. Kraushaar, acting for the Association, has arranged for commentators on my paper. By the way, I intend to leave out the last two pages, since I would otherwise have to read very fast.

Sincerely yours

Your
Alfred Schutz

Gurwitsch: *There is still some hope, but the chances are not too good*
             BALTIMORE, JANUARY 26, 1941)

Dear Friend Schutz.

You have often complained that my letters aren't personal enough. You won't be able to make that objection to this letter. It will deal only with personal things, with such, however, as belong in the realm of "existenciology" (a neighboring science to "passology").

I had an interview in New York with the "Committee for Displaced Foreign Scholars"[1] concerning next year. They were in principle prepared to help me, if an application was made by the president of a university. Thus, I wanted to use my (in the meantime very good) position here to have an application made from here. Boas[2] was ready to do anything; he wrote the president a letter which is one of the warmest statements about myself I have ever seen. He then told me personally that they (that is, he) had received me with mistrust and aversion, but that things were entirely different now. He spoke French with me, which he always does when he is being warm. In addition, the following came out:

whereas *all* of the president's communications with me spoke only of *one* year, the official communication with Boas speaks of two years. Could that have something to do with "testing"? After what happened, I almost believe it. In addition, in the letter to the president, which was written in my presence, Boas did not mention the engagement of R., which is also for two years, but rather requested that he approach the foundations.

The oral answer of the president to Boas was: my *engagement* is for two years, so I have to stay here another year. . . .

In two additional cases, one of which is exactly like mine and the other similar, the decision was unfortunately not at all so favorable. One looks very bad, the other has been tabled. There is still some hope, but the chances are not too good. In light of these cases, one must consider the speed with which my case was settled to be an achievement. Perhaps they really wanted to try me out. . . .

How happy I am that I don't have to cause my friends headaches once again! And that the Schutz-ego can restrict itself to thinking the Gurwitsch-thoughts, and not have to feel the Gurwitsch-pain.

Warmest regards to the two of you also in the name of my wife

Your

Gurwitsch

I read the James article by Cerf.[3] Fantastic and at the same time outrageous! I hope you will be able to read it.

---

1. "Emergency Committee in Aid of Displaced Foreign Scholars"; Chairman, Stephan Duggan. Cf. S. Duggan, *The Rescue of Science and Learning* (New York, 1948).

2. George Boas (b. 1891) taught the history of philosophy at Johns Hopkins. His Carus Lectures were published as *The Inquiring Mind* (La Salle, Ill.: Open Court, 1959).

3. Walter Cerf, who immigrated from Germany in the 1930s, is retired from Indiana University. The "James article" was not published in *PPR*. An earlier essay had compared Heidegger and William James: "An Approach to Heidegger's Ontology," *PPR* 1 (1940): 177–190.

Schutz: *You will achieve whatever a Jew can achieve given contemporary circumstances*
        (NEW YORK, FEBRUARY 22, 1941)

Dear Friend Gurwitsch.

It must have been my answer to you, not your letter to me, that got lost. I told you—only briefly, to be sure, but sincerely—immediately after receipt of your kind lines just how happy I was over your success, about which I never had any doubts. I repeat myself when I say how comforting it is to see that genuine quality asserts itself always and anywhere. You will certainly achieve the optimum which a Jew can achieve given contemporary circumstances, if you can now continue your work in peace. That was roughly the content of the letter, but I cannot reproduce its "fringes." I think that I said that you know very well just how much I think of your humanity and your thinking. If the latter were not the case, I wouldn't be so deeply unhappy when we often have decisive theoretical differences. But after all, these presuppose a primal ground of reciprocal understanding and this is perhaps the best that can be realized.

So, this letter did not reach you and had to be "rationally reconstructed." It is kind of you to send your concerned card, still kinder that you called me up today (give me your telephone number too, *if any!*). My wife has told you how I live: devoting my daylight life, which extends into the night, not to the golden calf but to the cow that gives milk. The high divine goddess has withdrawn into her divine solitude for the time being, but I hope to come to a more peaceful life in perhaps three weeks.

You will be interested to hear that a dispatch from Kracauer arrived, on the basis of which it looks like he might leave next week. Unfortunately, the money which Schapiro had sent did not reach him.

I was very happy to hear the news about Kahn.

To you and your dear wife all the best, let us hear from you soon.

Your
Schutz

P.S. Farber requested suggestions for improving the Cerf paper. I told him that you had seen it and like me are *against* its being accepted. Please write him your judgment, since I told him that I feel particularly biased in this case.

Gurwitsch: *Your friendship belongs among the finest things which life has brought me*
                  (BALTIMORE, MARCH 16, 1941)

Dear Friend Schutz,

It is really unfair of me and a shame that I haven't answered your very kind letter of February 22 any sooner. All the more since that letter, which you wrote out of that *tréfonds* which is prior to all difference and agreement, called forth a resonance out of a similar *tréfonds* on my part. Or can we perhaps say that it is "the same" *tréfonds*? In the few years of our acquaintance you have given me such magnificent proofs of your friendship, and that primal ground of our commonality and our concord has manifested itself so often: that primal ground, on the basis of which we then agree or disagree, and are unhappy when we disagree, and yet never completely unhappy, since we have just this *tréfonds*. Believe me, our friendship belongs among the finest things that life has brought me, me, who is "poor as Hamlet." But perhaps, since life brought just this and continues to bring it, "Hamlet" is not as poor as he often believes.

The new number of our journal came yesterday. I am unhappy at the way Kozak made short shrift of your contribution and that of Klein, while, e.g., the contribution by McGill, which in my opinion is completely worthless, was given so much space, even if that was with polemical intent. Since Kozak is an honest man, I can only explain it in terms of his lack of contact with the social sciences. It is not a very good approach to entrust a collection which contains so many and such heterogeneous contributions to *one* reviewer. After all, even the best man cannot be evenly competent in all disciplines. I don't like the idea that your very fine article (what about the publication of the other paper, the one you read at Harvard?[1]) remains buried in the archives in this manner. We will have to see if the reviews in *Philosophy* and in the *Review* don't do more justice it it. If not, we shall have to do something in this respect.

I am thoroughly incensed about the piece by Kraft.[2] You know that I don't have much sympathy for existential philosophy in general and for Heidegger in particular. But concerning this critique I can only only say that a journal which has any self-respect cannot allow a tone like this between its covers. Such a piece may be very appropriate for amusing the auditors of evening classes in adult education, but cannot be allowed in a publication which after all stands under Husserl's name. The thoughtless and purely verbal use of the world "reason" is just as verbalistic as the similar use of other terms. And then the double abuse of Cassirer. It just shows once again that K. has never understood or comprehended a thing. I say that, I who—as you know—under the impact of the critique from Lévy-Bruhl cannot follow Cassirer in the question of mythology, perhaps precisely cannot follow him in this question, by the way, because I am so attracted to so much in his other theories. To be sure, K. believes himself to be a kind of new Lessing, who takes to the field against obscurantism. But in fact he is only an ignorant and thoughtless stylograph. But I am of the opinion that our journal should remain closed to the "would-be," of this color or any other.

How are you? Have you received any news from your parents? And have the waves of your being overworked settled a bit, so that business is again limited to its proper times and tides?

Best greetings to you and your wife as well as to the children from both of us.

Your
Aron Gurwitsch

1. Parsons and Schumpeter had invited Schutz to speak at Harvard on April 13, 1940. Cf. "Rationality and the Structure of the Social World" (S1943).
2. Julius Kraft, "The Philosophy of Existence," *PPR* 1 (1940–41): 339–358.

Gurwitsch: *We belong to a generation which never got its chance*
              (Baltimore, April 20, 1941)

Dear Friend Schutz:

Once again, weeks have gone by without a single line from you. I must thus
assume that you once again have the bad habit of making night day; the other
habit—correlate of the one just mentioned—of making day night is unfortunately not a possibility for you, and how I would wish for you that you could do
so. We would so like to know how things are going and what you hear from
your parents. When will they be able to leave? Kracauer is finally in Lisbon, as I
hear indirectly from France.

Things here are going the way they can go in these days in which the riders
of the apocalypse are again on the loose. All of the terrors of the past years repeat
themselves again and again, but in steadily increasing extent and on an always
broader basis. It is a dreadful consciousness to experience the end of a world and
to live through the final stages again and again. We belong to a generation—as
you once said—that never got its chance; it seems to me that we, fleeing from
our fate, fled into it.

My student from Paris[1] has written; she is in Paris once again, but writes
from the free zone. The poor girl of 24 has gone through a great deal: her father
died three weeks before their flight, then flight with her younger brother, sleeping in fields, bombarded by airplanes, everything they took with them stolen.
Among these things there was a copy of my book which I had left her when I left
France. This image, that of the fleeing girl trying to save my manuscript, says
more about human loyalty than all words. And one is not left with much more
than the awareness that one has meant something to this and that person.

In this manner I have learned that Sartre is in German captivity. He is among
those whom I tried to get included in the Johnson action.[2] Now it was all in
vain.

Dear Schutz, I know how deeply you reject my essay in the last number.[3] For
just this reason I would be infinitely thankful if you would formulate this rejection, not merely in private talks but printed in the journal. If there is anyone who
can point out the problems and failings of my position, then it is you. In this way
a discussion between us would lead into the full dimensions of phenomenology,
in this way casting a new light on it. We could, discussing with one another
publicly, broach new problems and new aspects of old problems, and the gain
would be substantial for each of us. And this alone is important, and not who is
right in the end, if indeed one of us is definitively right. If phenomenology is
sometime to come to new peoples whose time has come—perhaps the bushmen
in Africa, then—I am sure of this—neither my nor your position will be de-
fended in the form in which we hold it. In the meantime the inner enrichment is
all that counts. We have learned so much from each other in private talks; give us
the opportunity to continue to learn from one another in a new form.

It is possible that I will be coming to New York for a couple of days in the course of the next few weeks. That depends on how Morris Cohen, whose acquaintance I want to make, writes. At any rate I hope that we can get together in the near future, since I am planning to spend some time in New York along with my wife during the summer. But how about an excursion to Baltimore? We can always sleep one—now even two—guests. Take advantage of the opportunity.

With most sincere greetings to both of you from my wife too,

Your

Aron Gurwitsch

1. Monique Picard, née Lipmann, taught philosophy at a *Lycée* in Paris.
2. Cf. GS 11.7.40.
3. "A Non-Egological Conception of Consciousness," *PPR* 1 (1941).

Schutz: *To save phenomenology out of the ruins of this world: I just don't believe it*
(NEW YORK, APRIL 26, 1941)

Dear Friend Gurwitsch,

Many thanks for your good and kind letter of the 20th. You are completely right, my daytime life consumes me and doesn't allow me to sleep at night. In these dreadful times all words have received a perverse meaning: Springtime is the code word for offensive, moonlight no longer interests lovers and poets but rather the night bomber, Olympia has become the quintessence of godlessness. Through the old, newly-revived myths of the battle of Thermopylae and the battle of the seven against Thebes the stymphalidic birds now storm, fouling all food and killing all humanity with their wings of steel—τευχη κυνεσσιν, οἰονοῖσι τε δαιτα.

Are you still enough of an optimist to belive that phenomenology will save itself out of the ruins of this world—as *philosophia aere perennius*? I simply don't believe that any more. The bushmen will surely first have to become acquainted with the National Socialist store of ideas. That doesn't stop us from wanting to die as we have lived, and therefore we have to try to create in *our* world that order which we have to do without in our *world*. The whole conflict—including that between our different approaches—lies hidden in the shift of emphasis.

Farber has requested that I write a reply to your article, and I am genuinely touched at the manner in which you have challenged me to do the same. I have already half accepted Farber, but the project requires a lot of reflection and long preparation.[1] If we survive it, I will go to work with great care. I think that it is better that I answer you than that someone else do so, since I want to see the discussion pursued on the high level which the issue deserves. I will probably first write another essay as preparation, one which on the surface has nothing to do with our issue; you will of course understand the connection at once when I tell you that I have offered Farber a short monographic essay on "The Problem of the Alter Ego in Scheler" for the Scheler number. This is of course a direct introduction to our debate.

The Kracauers arrived in good shape on the "Nyassa" yesterday, although I have not yet been able to see them (their address: 48 West 68th St., N.Y.C.). My parents are in Nice, and the American Consul is pursuing his duty in the form of sabotage in the most indecent ways. Aside from that, berths on ships are almost impossible to come by, and I am convinced that the Lisbon door will soon close. I have hardly any hopes left of seeing my parents, if ever, before the end of the war. What about your mother?

It would be wonderful to see you here. I went through Baltimore two weeks ago on my way to Washington, but had to return to New York on the same day.

Love and best wishes to you and your wife. Give me the pleasure of a letter every now and then; even though I am a bad correspondent, it does me good to know that I have friends.

Sincerely

Your

Schutz

P.S. In the introduction to the third edition of *The Feeling of Sympathy* Scheler praises a work by Albert K. Weinberg: *The Phenomenological Method in Its Application in Max Scheler*. Baltimore, April 1924. I can't get hold of the book here. Perhaps you can learn something there concerning the author and work, which, as Scheler says, "skillfully presents my ideas to the North Americans." Perhaps there is something to be learned terminologically.[2]

1. "Scheler's Theory of Intersubjectivity" (S1942) will contain the reply to Gurwitsch-Sartre. Cf. SG 11.24.42.
2. Weinberg's book could not be located.

Gurwitsch: *Our library has been 'disinfected' of German philosophical literature*
(Baltimore, June 10, 1941)

Dear Friend Schutz:

We are indeed two terrible correspondents. I haven't even gotten around to answering your kind letter of April 26. In that letter you asked me about a work by Albert K. Weinberg: *The Phenomenological Method in Its Application in Max Scheler*. The curious thing is that I have reason to think that I once met the wife of the author, but not he himself; if my hunch is right, he is in Princeton. But I haven't been able to learn anything here about the work itself. Our library is "disinfected" with reference to German philosophical literature. And everyone I asked was "sorry." On the assumption that my hunch concerning his where-abouts is correct, the only explanation I can find is that the author broke one of the many taboos or failed to fit into the caste system in some other way. There is a parallel case here—also a philosopher.

I was very happy that your Philadelphia paper[1] has finally appeared (what about the Harvard paper?). I am now getting down to writing my great—in the sense of size—James essay. The preparations have taken a long time. I am driven from horizon to horizon. In order to analyze only the transitive states themselves it turned out to be necessary to take into account not only the *terminus ad quem* (my work on background and horizons, which are to be dealt with in the papers which will follow), but also to draw on the horizon *a quo* of James's entire work as well as a lot of material from his period here as well in England, at least in the form of co-consciousness.

Now I have enough material to write, in addition to the paper, a congress paper on "Phenomenological Examination of James's Radical Empiricism." What do you think about this idea? "Pure experience" becomes the noema, world and I two systems "within the experiential realm" and in a certain sense indeed out of the same stuff—namely noematic stuff. The question of conscious-ness becomes the question of the I in James, and the "stream of experience" is our good old pure consciousness. The moral of the story is not, of course, James = phenomenology, but that a sufficient radicalization of his position leads to phenomenology. If the circumstances (those about which I shall not speak in this letter) allow, I would like to give several lectures on "From James to Husserl" next year. I now have a lot of material for that too.

Why not, once these lectures have been held, collect them, along with some things you would write, into a book (perhaps under the above title and co-authored)? There are some chapters from this topic which cry out for Schutz, e.g., Bergsonism and "anti-intellectualism" and Husserl's late work "Geometry," etc.; but there is still more. That is a serious project, and when I see you, which I hope will be soon, we should have a serious talk about it.

One more request. A friend of my brother's has arrived here from Paris; she was a very well-known lawyer. I know her too, though not very well, but she made a strong impression on me, if only on the basis of a brief encounter. My brother would like to put her in contact with you. Of course, I don't know whether you might be able to help or advise her in any way. But if your day-life leaves something of you left over which can also be consumed by day—it mustn't be allowed to be at the cost of your nights—I would be thankful if you would talk to the woman, who will use my name when she contacts you either in writing or by telephone. Her name is Assia Miror-Gawronsky. I am not entirely sure about the second half of the name; on this point I have been suffering from aphasia since yesterday, which comes from spending too much time on "we try to recall a forgotten name."

I would very much like to hear from you soon. How are your family and your parents?

Sincere greetings also from my wife to both of you.

Sincerely

Your
Aron Gurwitsch

1. "William James' Concept of the Stream of Thought" (S1941). The "Harvard paper": S1943.

Gurwitsch: *One would do well to inform oneself about the passology which is in force on the moon*
(BALTIMORE, JUNE 24, 1941)

Dear Friend Schutz:

Only a couple of short lines. I am coming to New York on Friday, my wife will come one week later for a couple of days. I will give you a call on early Sunday morning in order to arrange things with you. If you have something to communicate to me before I arrive, then write to me at my brother's address, but write rather than calling up, since you know that never works. I hope that I shall arrive in New York before the stymphalidic bird and its earthly escort arrive in Moscow.[1] For the first time, my wife is more optimistic than I, but sad to say I will turn out to be right. And even if those who think differently from me are right, I will still be right; life is going to become such that one would do well to inform oneself about the passology which is in force on the moon.

I am looking forward to seeing you and your dear wife again.

Sincerely

Your
A. Gurwitsch

1. The German surprise attack upon the Soviet Union began on June 22, 1941.

Gurwitsch: *My disqualifications: foreigner, Jew, unbaptized, Jewish wife. That is too much.*
(BALTIMORE, OCTOBER 9, 1941)

Dear Friend Schutz,

It is an eternity since either of us has heard from the other. We are both guilty: we seem to be rivals as to who is the poorer correspondent. And if there were not a special occasion, I wouldn't come close to *throw in the sponge* in this context! But as things stand, I give you the priority of being the poorer correspondent, hoping that once you have won you too will write to me.

The special occasion is the enclosed manuscript.[1] Please keep the copy; it is for you. It first goes to the corrector and is then to be presented to the Program Committee for the Vassar Congress. I can't wait to hear what you have to say about it. I will bear in mind and also take to heart all of your criticisms with the greatest interest—probably not in the lecture, assuming that it is accepted, but in its publication. I plan to offer the manuscript to *Mind,* although enlarged to roughly twice its present size.

We no longer have even the slightest idea of your life, your problems, the situation with your parents and everything else we participated in during the time in Paris. It is fine of me to complain to you, when we too have left you in ignorance of what is happening to us. Well, there isn't much to tell. Life goes on in the usual manner. My second and last year at Hopkins began this week (Descartes, Malebranche, Berkeley, Hume). I am running the Graduate School practically alone; not a single student came to Boas or to the other lecturer (American, blue-blood, and also desirable in other respects). Our department doesn't have any *graduate students* any more, after the last one got his Ph.D. in June, although he plans to continue working here for a while. Well, I was quite surprised when I began with eight students on Tuesday, six of them from mathematics and physics, and I hear that I will end up with twelve. I can't deny that that is a great success.

But what does that, as well as the fact that I use up the publication budget of our department all by myself, have to say when compared to my disqualifications: foreigner, Jew, unbaptized, Jewish wife, etc. *That* is too much. They could tolerate it if someone would buy me a *chair* for $150,000. Then they would take me in the hope, as one of the professors who is humanly closest to me (German, has been here 30 years, very conservative) told me today, that I wouldn't live all too long, such that the successor would be more acceptable in the social sense. But—enough of the bitterness.

Has Kahn gotten in touch with you? He asked for your address. How are the children, and your wife? And last but most important: how are you? Do the days eat up the nights, or has order returned to you, again separating day from night?

Let me hear from you soon! With warm greetings to all of you, also in my wife's name,

Your

A. Gurwitsch

1. The "*Mind* manuscript" (G1947), in contrast to the "essay on fringes" (G1943). Cf. GS 2.1.42.

2

The Strange and the Stranger
(November 8, 1941–July 16, 1944)

Following the attack on Pearl Harbor, Germany and Italy declared war on the United States on December 11, 1941. The "passology of exile" was repeated for the emigrants who had now fled France and were once again considered enemy aliens. But only the Japanese on the West Coast (who were American citizens) were interned.

Gurwitsch did not have a position at Johns Hopkins after the summer of 1942, and his application for a Guggenheim grant was turned down (GS 3.18.42). Requests, recommendations, rejections: finally he received a one-year fellowship for Harvard. Aron and Alice Gurwitsch moved to Boston, where they remained until Gurwitsch went to the New School in New York following Schutz's death.

Schutz was invited to give a lecture at the New School. Albert Salomon was his advocate there. He presented his study of the "stranger" to the "General Seminar" of the Graduate Faculty, probably in the winter of 1942–43. He stirred up a strong controversy: Schutz dared to compare the immigrants with the peasant's son who comes to the university in a strange city, with the groom who becomes part of the bride's family, with the army recruit who is like a new member in a club. Schutz analyzed the everyday structures of knowledge, its relevance structures and degrees of familiarity which the stranger does not have; he experiences them as a shock and has to master them. Above all Arnold Brecht and Wertheimer, it is reported, attacked Schutz most strongly: the unique historical situation, the unique existential situation of the immigrants seemed completely leveled by such sociological perspectives. Schutz's intention of presenting the modes of everyday knowledge was misunderstood.

In the spring of 1943 Schutz gave his first courses at the New School. After 1944 he became Visiting Professor of Sociology at the New School. The President, Alvin Johnson, gave him his contract with the words: "But do not try to teach my children phenomenology. They do not swallow this stuff!" (SG 9.27.55).

Schutz: *The Conference on Methods in Philosophy and the Sciences will meet at the New School*
(NEW YORK, NOVEMBER 8, 1941)

Dear Friend Gurwitsch,

Day-life and night-life place greater and greater demands on me, so it is only today that I finally come to the promised detailed discussion of your very fine essay. I hope that the committee has accepted it in the meantime, since it will make an excellent congress paper.

42

It is very commendable that you present James's theme of psychology from the subjective point of view (this is the way I allow myself to translate James's discussion of *the psychologist's fallacy* into Weber's and my language) so clearly. Subjective is to be understood in a double sense: on the one hand as "the state of mind studied" in opposition to the "objective" interpretation [*Sinngebung*] of the psychologist; but then also as that which belongs to the "single pulse of subjectivity," which is only subjectively determinable and determined. Both are presented most clearly in your discussion.

The expansion which you promise for publication will surely bring a series of welcome expansions. I hope that a critique of historicism will develop out of the study of Lévy-Bruhl's theory; that Max Weber receives his due in the sense indicated above; that you make some basic remarks about child and depth psychology.

What I most regret is the deliberate restriction to cases in which the psychologist studies his own *state of mind*. The problem can first be fully developed when the thou or we is brought in. I hope and wish that the expanded version will have important things to say about this central problem. I would also like to know how in your opinion the *cognitive reference* to an ideal object is distinguished from that to an object in the external world.

One single half-critical remark: Can one say that the things are "fringed"? Is "fringed" not a predicate which is only appropriate to the "thought"? If in view of the admirable precision of your language the sentence "the perceived thing *is* fringed" (instead of "seems to be fringed" or something like that) really is to say what it says, then I have several difficulties here and, until they are cleared up, misgivings. Your language at this point leaves both solutions open. If under "things" you mean only "a thing as it appears," there are no misunderstandings between us: but then only the "appearance" is *fringed*, but not the thing. But after our discussions, it is also conceivable that you want to relate the predicate "fringed" to that entire "set of past or possible perceptions." If one can speak of "fringes" at all here, it would surely have to be possible to explain them intersubjectively.

That is of course not an *immanent* critique, since you have said what you *wanted* to say in *this* essay with complete clarity. But there is a problem behind it which, as far as I see, is thematic for your entire thought. I have often wanted to talk about it with you, and now we have the desired occasion to hear more about it: how the "fringes" come into the objective world.

I would call your attention to the fact that on November 23 the "Conference on Methods in Philosophy and the Sciences" will meet at the New York New School. Theme: James. Speakers: Dewey, Henry James, Horace M. Kallen, Dickinson Miller, Holt. Public discussion. Malinowski will speak in the afternoon. I think you should be sure to come.—I would be very happy to have you here.

I have finished a longer essay on Scheler's theory of intersubjectivity for Farber's Scheler number. My wife is typing it right now. I will send you two parts in the near future. The first polemicizes against you—*non-egological theory*—in a 700-word footnote; the second criticizes the fifth *Méditation Cartésienne*. I will probably have to delete both parts, since the essay is too long.[1]

My parents arrived safely and feel pretty good. Best greetings and wishes for you and your dear wife. I am counting on you for the 23rd.

Sincerely

Your
Schutz

I have heard nothing from the Kahns and am glad that they arrived safely.

1. S1942. The "Sartre footnote" (cf. S1962, 169) contains Schutz's first published critique of Gurwitsch and leads to a sharp discussion (cf. SG 1.3.42). The critique of Husserl's *Cartesian Meditations* (second footnote) was obviously cut by Farber.

Gurwitsch: *My James paper is a motivation to phenomenology*
             (BALTIMORE, NOVEMBER 19, 1941)

Dear Friend Schutz,

Many thanks for your so kind and detailed letter. Very briefly: I will be coming to New York on Sunday. We will see each other at the New School. Please be there early; I will be there early too, since I am coming early in the morning with the special train and returning at 6 o'clock.

We are very happy that your parents are finally there, which takes a load off of "Atlas's" shoulders.

By the way, my *James paper*[1] was not accepted. "Difficulties of fitting it in and the James symposium" were, as Mandelbaum wrote me, the reason. So I will expand it and offer it to *Mind*. Some of your suggestions will be taken into account (Weber), but unfortunately not all. The presentation of the difference in the physiological, the relation to the noema, and a certain development of the last part will take up all available space. I want to leave the paper the character, indeed accentuate the character still more, of being a motivation to phenomenology, working out possible points of departure for a subjectively oriented philosophy.

I hope we will be able to talk about everything on Sunday. For the moment warmest greetings to you and all of yours

Your
Aron Gurwitsch

1. "On the Object of Thought" (the "*Mind* essay"), G1947.

Schutz: *The chief argument of Sartre-Gurwitsch against the egological theory*
         (NEW YORK, NOVEMBER 24, 1941)

Dear Friend Gurwitsch,

I was very sorry that you had to cancel your trip, since I was so looking forward to a *heart-to-heart* talk after so long a time. I hope nothing serious kept you away. You didn't miss all that much, if you were counting on a discussion. The only discussions concerned secondary themes. But the lectures were good and the 86-year-old Dewey—speaking freely for half an hour—amazing.

I would have liked to show you the relevant parts of my Scheler paper. As it is I am enclosing the section. Out of *courtoisie* to Farber I will send you the entire manuscript (if you want) only when Farber has decided who is to be the reader. Please return the enclosed pages to me after reading them. I have informed Farber that I am sending you the chapter. I await your remarks with the greatest interest.

A pity that the Assn. [American Philosophical Association] won't allow your paper to be read; they obviously have "obligations" elsewhere.

Many best greetings and wishes to you and your wife

Your

Schutz

Enclosure: The Sartre-Gurwitsch Footnote (from S1942)

A. Gurwitsch in discussing a theory of Jean-Paul Sartre has dealt with this problem in a paper entitled "A Non-Egological Conception of Consciousness" (*Philosophy and Phenomenological Research,* Vol. I, 1941, pp. 325–338). The chief argument of Sartre-Gurwitsch against the egological theory maintained in the present paper runs as follows:

As long as we do not adopt the attitude of reflection the ego does not appear. By reflection is meant the grasping of an act A by an act B in order to make the former the object of the latter. The act B, however, in its turn is not grasped by a third act and made its object. The grasping act itself is experienced with a non-reflective attitude exactly as in the case of an act bearing on some object other than a mental fact belonging to the same stream of consciousness. To be sure, by an act of reflection the grasped act may acquire a personal structure and a relation to the ego which it did not have before it was grasped. But the grasping act deals with the ego as an object only. It is the ego of the grasped and not of the grasping act. On the other hand, the grasped act has been experienced before it was grasped, and although reflection entails a modification of the acts grasped by it, this means only that all of the act's structure and components are disentangled and rendered explicit but that none of them is given rise to by reflection. Reflection is disclosing, not producing.

x[1]   How, then, may reflection give rise to a new object, namely, the ego, which did not appear before the act A was grasped? The answer offered is that the ego appears *through* rather than *in* the grasped act.

xx   It is the synthetic unity of certain psychic objects as dispositions, actions and
       certain qualities such as virtues, faults, talents, etc.
xxx   These psychic objects have their support in the ego, which may never be appre-
       hended directly but merely in a reflection as appearing behind the dispositions at
       the horizon. The ego exists neither *in* the acts of consciousness nor *behind* these
       acts. It stands to consciousness and *before* consciousness: it is the noematic correlate
       of reflective acts. Hence it follows that no evidence of the ego is apodictic. It is
       open to doubt.

It is not possible to enter here into a thorough discussion of Sartre-Gurwitsch's
argument, which seems to be not at all conclusive. If they admit that the grasping act B
deals with the ego at all (although with the ego of the grasped act as an object only and
not with the ego of the grasping act), then this ego is grasped by act B as performing act
A (or more precisely, as having performed act A, since reflection can only refer to the
past). If a third act C grasps the act B and through it the act A, the ego with which act C
deals is grasped as having performed act B as well as act A, and it is grasped as the same
and identical ego notwithstanding all the modifications it undergoes in and by the flux of
the stream of experience in inner time.

Furthermore, it is not clear why the ego in the reflection may never be apprehended
directly but merely appear behind the dispositions at the horizon. Even the term "horizon" already refers to an egological consciousness to which alone "frame," "horizon,"
"disposition," "act," and other terms used by Sartre and Gurwitsch become meaningful.
The same becomes valid for the examples quoted by Gurwitsch in order to illustrate his
thesis. If he says that there is no egological moment involved if I see my friend in
adversity and help him and that what is given to me is just "my-friend-in-need-of-aid," it
must be stated that any single element of the hyphenated term "my," "friend," "need,"
"aid," already refers to the ego for which alone each of them may exist. [From "Scheler's
Theory of Intersubjectivity and the General Thesis of the Alter Ego": S1942. The original enclosure to this letter could not be found.]

1. The x's are Gurwitsch's marginalia in the margins of this letter. Gurwitsch comments on them in the next letter.

Gurwitsch: *I do not assume that this letter will convince you*
             (BALTIMORE, NOVEMBER 30, 1941)

Dear Friend Schutz.

Many thanks for your kind letter and for the part of your essay which deals
with the Sartre-Gurwitsch argument. I hope that you will be able to make the
entire essay available to me soon. I will read it with great interest and certainly
with great benefit. Many of my positions (including those about which we do
not agree) have developed on the basis of our conversations. To be provoked to
opposition by you is always stimulating, enriching, and makes me productive.

With regard to the footnote, I shall divide my remarks into various classes.

I. Concerns your *statement* of the Gurwitsch-Sartre theory. Here I would request that you take the following three corrections into account in the publication:

a) The question[1] is not posed by Sartre, but by *Gurwitsch to Sartre*. The paragraph[2] begins with "This statement leaves us with some questions" (p. 331f) and closes with the reference to "what I believe to be a gap in Sartre's argumentation" (p. 333). Gurwitsch plans to give the answer in a later work on the field theory of consciousness. It is roughly as follows: that of which there is a marginal co-consciousness in an unreflected act becomes an element of the new thematic field when the act is reflected.[a] *This* can be done by reflection because it is a change in attitude; the attitude, however, has to be described *in terms* of the thematic field. Thus, something marginal enters the field, and here we find the seed of something which, while not the ego, belongs to the constitution of it. (See III b 3)

b) The statement marked xx is a justification of the question. This question is posed with reference to the Husserlian theory of reflection, which Gurwitsch endorses.

c) The place marked with xxx is not Gurwitsch, but *Sartre,* though by and large endorsed by Gurwitsch. These things are not of equal importance for Gurwitsch within the framework of his paper; the most important thing is the conclusion: ego is not accessible to apodictic evidence, is *open to doubt* in the same sense as the things, i.e., every later experience of the ego can annul earlier ones, thus *every* experience is *in need of verification*.

If I ask you to take these remarks into account, this naturally only with regard to the attributions in question and only to the extent that Gurwitsch's relation to Sartre (a, c) is in question.

II. You will understand that I do not find your so brief argument against us satisfying and convincing. After all, you yourself say that you cannot discuss our argument *thoroughly*.

a) When you say: "The grasping of an act *A* by an act *B* . . . reveals the acting subject and his noetical activity leading to the act *A,* as he performed this act *A*," you are appealing to precisely that which we put in question. All that follows concerning the identity of the ego are precisely the things which appear problematic to us. I cannot see that you have thereby done justice to our description of the phenomenological data (see III b), nor that you do justice to the problems to which our description leads us.

b) Why are "frame" and "horizon" only meaningful with reference to an ego? Aren't these and similar *terms* rather to be defined with reference to that which is the theme, referring to an organization in that which is co-given? Bringing together theme with nearness to the ego (as Husserl continually does in *Experience and Judgment*) is problematic. That is either a *façon de parler*, in which case one can describe the data in other terms and exclude every temptation to smuggle in an ego-substance. Or it really does imply an ego-activity, in which case it leads to absurd consequences such as, e.g., the theory of relations (end of ch. III) in which everything exists twice, and one has to ask what the second—equally prepredicative level—brings in that is new and specific over against the first.

c) That "my," "friend," "need," "aid," refer to an ego is in *one* sense correct, but precisely in a non-phenomenological one. It is correct that everything is only on the basis of my experience and past. If one is doing psychology, one must appeal to the ego (but the empirical ego, there isn't any other!). Psychology means here: following out the genetic formation of structures and functions. The question is: Is the genesis of a structure, once it is constituted, in any sense "contained" in the completed structure? What does sedimentation mean? Can one read its history off of the completed structure? Is *mémoire qui répète* in any sense *mémoire*? Is being able to do something on the basis of having learned to do it to be understood in the sense that the learning process is contained in the concrete functioning?

You see the breadths and depths to which this question leads—too broad and too deep to be dealt with in one letter. One more word: Here is a point at which phenomenology and psychology go their separate ways. Not on the basis of classificatory points of view, but on the basis of a very deep *substantive* problem. If I should ever come to the point of making claims concerning the difference between psychology and phenomenology, I should develop everything I have to say in terms of the topic of "learning."

III. What is at issue in the whole question of the ego? Generally and in principle and aside from the two fixed literary utterances:

a) Scientific progress consists in replacing the category of substance with that of function and relation. This is true for the thing and also for the ego. In the classical critics of the concept of substance the things became bundles of sensations, the ego a bundle of experiences. As dissolution of substance, this was progress, but the question arises as to what gives the bundle its coherence. We must speak of systems rather than bundles; then we have the problem, what gives the system its coherence and its system-character? This must be answered for the thing and for the ego. Here it is a matter of the empirical ego, and the entire problem belongs rather to the general theory of science rather than to the specially phenomenological sphere.

b) Phenomenologically: Are the acts egoical [*ichhaft*] in the sense of *coming-out-of* [*Kommens-aus (sic)*]? Sartre-Gurwitsch deny it. What are the phenomenological findings?

1. The living through or self-awareness [*Sich-selber-Wissen*] of the acts. In perception not only the *thing perceived,* but also *the very perceiving* is given. Not an ego, since *the awareness of the present perceiving* is strictly restricted to the present act.

2. Time, duration, and other marginal elements (such as: acts which just were) which are referred to what is thematically not pertinent. This is in a certain sense the germ-cell of the ego; but one really shouldn't call it that, since here there is also no identity, but precisely only that which is marginally there in the given case, or better: only a part of that, since the margin contains much more.

3. In reflection the margin becomes the thematic field. The *grasped* experience finds itself in a new field which consists merely of constituents of the stream of consciousness. If the reflection is carried through ideally in memory, there is a

chain of all acts which have ever been lived through, in the ideal case without any gaps. The ideal case is in principle not realizable. If you want, you can call *that* ego; in my dissertation[3] I called it "pure ego." Here there is identity, since every new act joins the chain, and the chain is only one. This ego, however, is merely that time which is completely remembered. It is impossible to appeal to ego-activity in the case of *this* ego. *This* ego is *not* a source-point, *it does nothing and suffers nothing*. It is the temporally ordered sum total of all experience of the stream, thus the total stream. (The totality is an ideal case, lies at infinity.)

4. If I now reify [*Nehme ich hier Verdinglichungen vor*], I come up with dispositions, etc., thus with the empirical ego. There is no reason not to view this ego as psycho-physical. The result in this case is something constituted. These considerations lead to problem III a.

Dear friend Schutz, I do not assume that this letter has convinced you. But it might provide the basis for further discussions, both private and public.

Please give my regards to your family

With sincere greetings

Your

Aron Gurwitsch

[a]This is the sense in which what you say must be interpreted. In this way the *paradox of reflection* disappears, reflection being only "disclosing" that yet creates something new. Such a paradox doesn't arise for your position: Reflection finds what was already there.

1. Marked with an *x* in the previous letter: "How, then, may reflection give rise to a new object, namely, the ego, which did not appear before the act *A* was grasped?"
2. In "A Non-Egological Conception of Consciousness," G1941.
3. G1929.

Schutz: *Send a copy to Farber*
          (New York, January 28, 1942)

Dear Friend,

I sent the letter in which you made some remarks concerning my Scheler essay to Farber on the 6th, and I have now learned that Farber never received my letter. I would be greatly obliged to you if you would send a copy of your letter directly to Farber, since he is very interested in it.

I hope that you and your dear wife are well and I remain with sincere greetings

Your
Schutz

Gurwitsch: *The copy has disappeared and the manuscript is not to be found*
(BALTIMORE, FEBRUARY 1, 1942)

Dear Friend,

Je suis navré! After receiving your letter I turned my two studies—at home as well as at the university—upside down, I am sorry to say without any result. The copy of the letter in question has disappeared and does not turn up. Also, the part of the manuscript which you sent to me is not to be found. But I assume that I returned the pages to you. If Farber's interest is so great, there is nothing else to do than send the pages back to me and I shall write you a new letter. The ideas will surely be the same in new dress. *Je suis vraiment navré.*

In the next week I shall get to work preparing the article on "The Object of Thought" [G1947] for publication. I am sorry that I can't go beyond the reference to Weber's subjectively and objectively meant sense. It would be beyond the scope of this essay. But it would be even better if someone—e.g., you, dear friend Schutz—would later discuss Weber's theory of the dual rationalization, perhaps with reference to my essay. The things are so fundamental that they demand and deserve a separate and detailed treatment.

There was a discussion yesterday with Engel-Janosi about this and similar things. But he is one of those historians who see only the unrepeatable and unpredictable individual. Something in him resists the attempt even very tentatively to use ideal types to find formal developmental laws [*Ablaufsgesetze*], which appears to me to be the romantic heritage of all these historians.

The essay on fringes is nearing its end.[1] It only deals with the fringes and the unity of consciousness. I plan to start work on a second concerning fringes and "having in view" (*Meinen*) once it is finished. But now I see to my great horror that the first essay alone will be something like 70 pages long, with some 200 to 250 notes, some of them small treatises. The question arises, should I not put the essay in the desk drawer, write the second, and bring out the two as a small book—perhaps 120 pages? I said something to Boas along these lines recently and he said "*mais celà serait magnifique*" (we sometimes speak French). But he hasn't the slightest interest in the matter, or in anything: lack of interest in him appears in the mode of the "in general" [*im Modus des überhaupt*]. So he can hardly be expected to do anything to get the Hopkins Press to publish it. What do you think of the plan? Do you have any idea to whom one can offer something like this, I mean with an eye to financing it?

I hope to hear something soon about you and your well-being as well as that of your family. I don't suppose I have much chance of success if I once again invite you to come down here for a *weekend* sometime; you won't find time for that. But we so long for dear guests.

Best greetings to you and yours.

Your

Aron Gurwitsch

1. "William James' Theory of the Transitive Parts of the Stream of Consciousness" (G1943).

Schutz: *I am gathering material for my essay "The Strange and the Stranger"*
          (NEW YORK, MARCH 1, 1942)

Dear Friend Gurwitsch,

Friend Farber is a curious man: First, his maid mislays important letters one has written him, including your letter to me of November 30, along with a very interesting statement by Cairns. Then one hears nothing from him for months and suddenly page-proofs of the essay arrive accompanied by a note to please correct and return it *within 24 hours*. Along with it a card in which he says:

> I hope you will *not* delete your note re Gurwitsch-Sartre and that you will not make material changes. A few *minor* changes will meet all needs for the present. *Later* a discussion will be all to the good, and it will be conducted on the high level we always try to maintain.

I hope the last clause doesn't refer to the various Kraft and Cerf controversies.[1] Since I must assume that Farber really does envisage a continuation of the discussion at some point, I have not completely eliminated the "note," merely removing the false attributions and making the second paragraph a bit clearer. Substantively nothing has changed.

In the course of putting my Scheler papers in order I found the fragment Ilse has typed of my letter to you of 12.11.41. I told you about it during my stay in N.Y. I am enclosing the pages *for the record,* and you will see that I have retained the note only with a heavy heart.

Many thanks for your kind letter of the 1st. The adventure with the letter, as I have reported above, ended harmlessly. What has happened with the *Mind* essay?[2] Perhaps it would come into consideration for *Ethics*. Please let me look at the enlarged version.

The idea for a small James book is excellent, but the Johns Hopkins Press would of course be first choice as *publisher*. Why not speak very directly with Boas? After all, he can't say more than "no." He doesn't have to show any interest as long as he gives you a free hand.

In the few hours which are left over for my philosophical Sunday excursions I am gathering material for my essay "The Strange and the Stranger,"[3] which is leading me into the strangest realms of sociological literature. I am not yet entirely sure where it is leading me. In addition I am studying Dewey's *Logic*, which I would strongly recommend to you.

Love and best greetings to you and your wife

Your

Schutz

What do you hear from Guggenheim, Morris Cohen, etc? Write soon about yourself.

1. Cf. SG 2.22.41 and GS 3.16.41.
2. Cf. GS 11.19.41. The essay was not published in *Mind* but rather in *PPR* (G1947).
3. Final title: "The Stranger" (S1944).

Enclosure: Fragment of Schutz's letter of 12.11.41

Dear Friend Gurwitsch,

I owe you an answer to your kind letter of November 30th, but the last few days didn't exactly lend themselves to dealing with your arguments with the necessary tranquility. And even today the time is not ripe to do this, and I hope that your presence in New York in the near future will give us the opportunity for a thorough discussion. Only in order to prepare for this discussion, and to inform Farber, to whom I plan to send a copy of your and my letters, about the state of the discussion, am I appending a short discussion of the points you have made:

Ad I. With regard to your remarks concerning the attribution of the various theses, I see that in spite of my best efforts I myself am not clear as to what comes from you and what from Sartre. I told you back then that I haven't read Sartre's work, and thus only know what he says second-hand, namely from you. I have not been able to correct this omission yet. Your most certainly correct remarks make it clear to me for the first time just how unfair it would be to allow my footnote to be published: It would not only be unfair to you, but also to Sartre, and incompatible with literary conscientiousness if I were to make statements directly or indirectly about the state of a discussion with whose genesis I am admittedly insufficiently acquainted. But it would also be unfair to relegate a problem which is of such central importance for you to a footnote in a work with which it is only vaguely connected. I have therefore decided to cut the entire footnote or to close the reference to the work you cite with the additional remark that you defend a radically different point of view than the one which I present in my text as my own.

I need not tell you that this does not mean that your remarks have changed my mind, and this was not, as you yourself say, the point of your letter. And this brings me to *point II:*

It may be that the conciseness which I imposed on myself was not able to express my train of thought very clearly. You don't seem to view my main argument, that while it is correct that the reflexive act uncovers *the ego of the grasped and not the ego of the grasping act,* nonetheless the ego of the *grasped acts* is disclosed precisely as the ego which performed the *grasped act,* as a phenomenologically demonstrable objection, but rather view it as a "use" [*Ansatz*] of precisely that which you put in question. I don't agree that it is simply a matter of appealing to something. I don't really understand at all how you manage to eliminate the noetic egological structures from the *grasped act.* That which is called the *grasped act* here can after all be interrogated as to the *acting* and as to the *actor.* And if I also admit that one is in a sense justified in saying that the ego which is grasped in the *grasping act* is the object of the *grasping act,* it was nonetheless the subject of that act which is reflected upon and legitimates itself as such.

Sartre obviously says the same thing, and you add a consideration of how it happens that the reflection discloses something which was not contained in the act at which it is after all directed. If an act is grasped in reflection, it can only be grasped in this manner if it was experienced prior to the reflexive advertence. You add that this refers both to the noetic and the noematic structures, and it appears that you come to the result that the ego is introduced as a new object, which you take to be a gap in Sartre's argument. Now, surely the ego that experiences itself in its action, although it first becomes visible as an experiential content in reflection, is one and the same. Were it not possible to bring the acting ego into view, which of course can only happen by way of reflection, then it wouldn't make any sense at all to speak of spontaneous performances, or even of the opposition between activity and passivity. After all, where does the acquaintance with these phenomenologically describable fundamental facts come from?

The whole non-egological conception leads to the result that I can only advert to my thinking, but not to my acting. But I can also think myself as acting, and as far as I am concerned, I agree completely with Husserl when he views thinking as an acting, merely one of a certain kind. But even if the concept of acting is only [applied] to a doing, namely to an intervention in the external world ... [Dictation, spoken on tape and transcribed by Mrs. Schutz, obviously broken off.]

Gurwitsch: *The Jew's place is not in the world of the university*
             (BALTIMORE, MARCH 18, 1942)

Dear Friend Schutz,

I had actually planned to go back to the beautiful hours which I experienced with you on Sunday in this letter, and tell you about the lasting impressions which your arguments against (Husserl's) "Fifth Cartesian Meditation" have made on me. I was still inspired by it on the trip back.

But this letter is unfortunately compelled to a different topic. The answer from Guggenheim is negative. I am completely clear about the situation which this produces. Some of my colleagues will write to a series of universities and colleges. I am also writing Schrecker[1] in order to prepare the way with Cassirer, so that he will make the applications to Oberländer. That is perhaps still a faint hope. It is pitiful enough, however you look at it. And with regard to the other attempts, I am anything but confident.

In one year I have learned what it means, "to keep him down in his place." I don't know what the Jew's place is; at any rate it is not in the world of the university, at least not by his nature. I merely want to tell you that this hardly embitters me. It fits in very well with what my observations have shown me. This is not with reference to the answer from Guggenheim. I view this as being defeated in a competition. There are surely better persons than I. And there is naturally no reason to be embittered about that.

With best greetings to you and yours

Your

Aron Gurwitsch

1. Paul Schrecker from Vienna, Leibniz expert; he taught with Gurwitsch in Paris, and taught later at the University of Pennsylvania.

Schutz: *I by no means view your plans as pessimistically as you*
          (NEW YORK, MARCH 28, 1942)

Dear Friend Gurwitsch,

Many thanks for your letter of the 18th. The short time together was a great pleasure for me too.

Your letter distressed me very much, but to tell the truth, it didn't surprise me. I didn't want to discourage you then, but on the basis of attempts of other friends who have applied to Guggenheim, I know how little chance there is for a non-American who works in the humanities to receive a grant. For this reason, in our last talk I mainly showed interest for your other plans. I by no means view them as pessimistically as you, and believe that you will surely succeed in finding a solution to your problem which appeals to you.

I don't know Schrecker and have no idea what your relationship to him is. Do you really need someone to intervene with Cassirer? It might be better if you were to get on the train and go to Yale. This would also give me the opportunity to see you soon, which would be a real pleasure. Please keep me up to date on what happens; you know how interested I am in everything that concerns you.

All loving and good wishes. Sincerely

Your

Schutz

Gurwitsch's condolences for the death of Schutz's father
(Baltimore, May 20, 1942)

My dear friend Schutz,

My wife called your wife early this morning to ask how your father was doing. Unfortunately, your wife had to give her the sad news.

Language fails us poor mortals in the face of this limiting case of life, in which every life terminates. Let us leave it with this failure instead of stammering what we cannot say adequately. Please tell your mother that the thoughts of my wife and myself are very much with her and with you.

As to the two of us, my dear good friend, the feelings of warmth, devotion, friendship which I have for you have in this moment become an infinite tenderness. I wish I could give it a more immediate expression than holding your hand in my fantasy, long and silently, since we two understand one another without words.

Your true
Aron Gurwitsch

Schutz: *It is good to know that one has friends*
(New York, May 22, 1942)

Dear Friend,

Your letter genuinely moved me, and in such moments it is good to know that one has friends. You will understand that I had many reasons for regretting that it was not possible for me to see you during your stay in New York. But I would still like to know how things stand at the moment in your personal matters and what your chances are. Please write to me about them.

Once again, many thanks for your sympathy, also from my wife and my mother. Many loving greetings to you and your wife.

Your
Alfred Schutz

Gurwitsch: *That would allow us to move to New York*
(Baltimore, May 30, 1942)

Dear Friend Schutz,

I would like to tell you once again how sorry I am that we couldn't see each other this time. All the more since the circumstance which hindered our meeting was such a sad one. Please let us know how your mother is doing. We hope she will find the strength to bear this blow.

As to my affairs, there isn't really much to report. Concentrating on the most essential, this is how things look: I have filed an application with the American Philosophical Society for a Grant in Aid of Research for my James studies. The application is strongly supported by the Hopkins people, who suggested it. If that is approved, I hope to receive some additional money from Friess.[1] That would then allow us to move to New York, where I might come into a certain loose connection with Columbia. It is possible that in the coming winter I will already have a course in a special *extension* of Columbia. That isn't certain yet. Friess told me that once I have been associated with Columbia in this fashion for a year, Columbia would later file the applications to the famous *Committees*. Both Friess and Schneider,[2] though I have not seen the latter personally, seem to me to have good intentions. By the way, in the course of my negotiations with Friess, the question was posed for the first time concerning areas in which I work, what I have done and plan to do. That seems to me significant: otherwise *this* question has never been asked.

The conversation with Flexner[3] was satisfactory. As I could see from the letter of introduction that he wrote to his friend, he has understood. He plans to try New York University and to do some other things in cooperation with Friess. This line is based on my book on perception.[4] In addition there are various and sundry other things under way, in which I have no confidence, since they are a matter of more or less regular college things, naturally always with the aid of the *Committee*. I am becoming more and more clear about the fact that I can receive something only in an unusual manner. The reasons for this are a "broad field for future investigations." I have written Kuhn,[5] but haven't received an answer yet.

That is more or less the essentials. All in all the situation seems to me less dismal. Flexner is a man for whom substantive matters and achievement mean something. Since he still has a certain power, or at least a certain influence, although he is 76 years old and has retired from active duty, I put some trust, if not to say hope, in him. Friess too, and the Columbia people in general, seem to me more impartial in orientation than those "club viewpoints" against which I have no chance. The latter have made me pretty bitter recently, since I found myself as if confronted with a wall that constantly gave way, on which one could never get a grip.

I would of course be delighted to move to New York. A stay in New York affects both of us like a refreshing rain on plants which have been burned by the sun. If I can live in New York, I will be able to lecture at the French university.[6] I want to do that, although it isn't useful in terms of any of the normal considerations. But when I am with these people, I already have the feeling of living in and in terms of a familiar world again.

I went back to work as soon as we were back. The various interruptions recently were tiresome. I had a real longing for my desk, which is always a good sign for me. I hope there won't be any disturbances and that I can get the first James essay ready for print, which I am currently doing. It is only an introduction for what follows: first the field theory. It is curious the way various people whom I have told about this pounce on it. Somehow that seems to me like a worn-out shoe, since the essentials are already there in my dissertation. But I must be on to something, since I am finding more and more consequences, which of course I can't publish yet: e.g., a critique of the theory of implications in hypothetical judgments in logical positivism. With regard to logic, I have come up with a new axiom, which I call the "relevance clause." That leads to a deepening of what is said in *Formal and Transcendental Logic* and goes beyond it. I hope we can talk about it during my next stay in New York.

How are you, your wife, your mother, and your children? Please give them all our best greetings, and greetings to you

From your
Aron Gurwitsch

1. Horace L. Friess (1900–1975), Professor of Philosophy, Columbia University.
2. Herbert W. Schneider (1892–1984), Professor of Philosophy, Columbia University.
3. Probably Abraham Flexner (1866–1959), Director of the Institute for Advanced Study, 1930–1939.
4. First mention of *The Field of Consciousness*.
5. Helmut Kuhn taught at the University of North Carolina while in America, and is now Professor Emeritus at the University of Munich. Cf. Helmut Kuhn and Katharine Gilbert, *A History of Esthetics* (Bloomington: Indiana University Press, 1953).
6. "Ecole Libre" in New York.

Gurwitsch: *The eternally wandering Jew*
              (BALTIMORE, JULY 11, 1942)

Dear Friend Schutz,

Your kind letter of June 25th should have been answered a long time ago. We were sorry to hear that your daughter has been sick several times. We only hope that both diphtheria and mumps are over with by now, and that nothing new follows them. I hope the patient as well as your mother will recuperate in Larchmont, and all of your lives return to normalcy.

I didn't want to write until I had something definite to communicate. But only today did it become quasi-definitive. I know unofficially that the American Philosophical Society in Philadelphia has granted me a Research Grant for my James studies—four projected essays. But the sum is not adequate, so they are trying to find some additional money (some $800), which is apparently not very easy. They have been working on this for weeks, still without result. In addition, from there they have contacted Harvard, and Harvard—via Perry[1]—has offered me a "fellowship by courtesy." You know that that doesn't mean anything more than the right to use the library. It is not a connection with Harvard of even the loosest kind. On the other hand, the chance to make contacts is unmistakable. So if everything works out, we will be there next year, and a year later we will rack our brains as to where we should go then—the eternally wandering Jew.

The first of the James essays is finished, and its English is being corrected by friends in New York. It is a text of more than 50 typed pages with the title: "William James's Theory of the Transitive States of the Stream of Consciousness."[2] Focused on the problem of time; James's theories are compared with those of Husserl concerning time, duration, continuity. The essay contains a long critique of Hume's theory of the experience of time. James's achievement is thus presented and assessed against this historical background. "Transitive states" and "Fringes" emerge as: lived experience [*Erleben*] of continuity = time. In addition, the way is prepared for the new problems which arise from James, and this first essay is a *prélude* to the other two.

The one, a rough draft is finished, is the field theory, dealt with completely from the point of view of "relevance." In "relevance," dear friend, discussions with you are still having their effect. In spite of disagreement, and surely precisely in disagreement, I have learned a lot from you. We should write something together sometime, perhaps in the area of the methodology of the social sciences.

Following the tactic you too use, I will have a copy sent to you as soon as it has been submitted to Farber and Farber has chosen the readers.

I am currently working on the "Object of Thought," which will be pretty long: from the physiology of color, via the analysis of musical tones and overtones, Lévy-Bruhl, etc., etc., to Max Weber, a hymn to something of which the "noema" is only a special case.

Let me hear from you sometime. With best greetings

Your

A. Gurwitsch

P.S. Might I call your attention to my review[3] of Fulton in the last number of our journal? Although it is only a review, I attach some importance to this publication.

1. Ralph Barton Perry taught at Harvard. Cf. *The Thought and Character of William James,* 2 vols. (Boston, 1935).
2. Abbreviation: "essay on fringes" (G1943).
3. Review of James Street Fulton, *The Cartesianism of Phenomenology* (G1942).

Gurwitsch: *The result is a fellowship at Harvard*
(BALTIMORE, JULY 19, 1942)

Dear Friend Schutz,

So, at long last I can announce that our problems have found a solution for another year. The American Philosophical Society, which has something of the character and function of an academy of science, though on a private basis, has found the additional money. So we have a Research Grant for the coming year. In addition: My *application* was sent to Perry because of James. And he not only approved it; the result is a "Fellowship by Courtesy" at Harvard! I need not tell you that that means no more than the possibility of using the library and having certain loose connections with the department. We both have no illusions concerning the fact that we will again be confronted with the same problem next year. Neither of us is thinking of a stabilization at Harvard; and just how hard things are even for Harvard people is demonstrated by the example of Cairns. Be that as it may, the connection with Perry is not to be underestimated. And perhaps the name Harvard will give new prestige.

Both of us would much prefer to go to New York. At Columbia they held out the prospect that possibly if I were there for a year Columbia would apply to the *Committees.* And one must live in New York in order to achieve anything there. If the *extension course* at Columbia, which is run by Friess, should still work out, we would go there, since that would be a plausible reason. But as things stand I don't see that I can turn down a *fellowship by courtesy,* even if it doesn't mean a connection of any kind.

Perry is a truly peculiar man. More than half a year ago I wrote him asking whether James knew anything of Ehrenfels'[1] essay on Gestalt qualities. The name Ehrenfels is not mentioned either in James's works or in Perry's very fine book. I never received an answer to the letter. And now at Harvard they offer me the chance to look at the James manuscripts, and Perry writes delightfully nice letters to my friends at Hopkins.

How are things with you personally? My wife is suffering from the heat which set in a couple of days ago with maximum humidity. I am luckily indifferent to the weather, and am working a great deal and well. The one thing necessary in order to live and endure the times. The moment one comes to, the suffering in Europe becomes thematic. The news from France is terrible.[2] And the military situation doesn't make one hopeful either. So field theory and the "Object of Thought" is the only thing left. At times I begin to believe that you are right when you say that science, music, and so forth are a flight into realms in which a sense and order that have completely disappeared in our world still reign.

Let us hear from you. Best greetings to you and yours from

Your

Aron Gurwitsch

1. Christian von Ehrenfels, "Über Gestaltqualitäten," *Vierteljahresheft für wissenschaftliche Philosophie* 14 (1890): 259.
2. In the summer of 1942 German troops marched into the as-yet-unoccupied portions of France.

Schutz: *In these times one cannot think more than a year ahead*
(NEW YORK, JULY 22, 1942)

Dear Friend Gurwitsch,

I was extraordinarily happy at the good news in your letter and congratulate you and your wife sincerely for the beautiful success. In these times one cannot think more than a year ahead, and what you have managed to do so far you will continue to do, especially if you make such fine progress in your works. I would of course like to have you here in New York, but you will have fewer distractions at Harvard and be able to make better connections. I think that a Harvard *fellowship* has a better ring than working for the Columbia *Extension*.[1]

There is nothing special to report about us. My family, including my mother, is in Larchmont. On August 4 my wife and I are going to the mountains in New Hampshire, where I plan to stay for four weeks. It is possible that I will spend the last days of August in Cambridge. Will you already be at Harvard then? Please keep us up to date.

With best wishes to you and your wife

Your

Schutz

1. Columbia University Extension Program.

Gurwitsch: *A fantastic story from Casablanca*
            (Baltimore, August 18, 1942)

Dear Friend Schutz,

I hope that the stay in the mountains will bring you and your wife the necessary relaxation. If you are in Boston at the end of August, we won't be there, but we hope to be in New York in mid-September.

This letter concerns our already almost forgotten *Lift*,[1] which has suddenly reappeared in Casablanca. This is a long, fantastic story, in which the negligence of the shipping company plays the main role. At any rate, the things have been in Casablanca for two years. The shipping company has known that for one and one half years and didn't notify me. The French Customs plans to auction it off on September 15, if the accumulated costs have not been paid by then. We were actually prepared to pay the costs until bit by bit we were informed of the intolerable sum. Now we have decided to have a confidante whom we luckily have in Casablanca buy a few things at auction which are of value for us. Your boxes of books are of course included, since they went as mine. These things can be bought cheaply, since the interest in such things is sure to be minimal in Casablanca. Your silver is another question. I have to give my confidante a *valeur limite*. On the other hand, I hear that silver is very expensive there. How far may my confidante go, dear Schutz? Please let me know immediately, since things have to be done quickly in view of September 15. Now it is a matter of bringing the things that we want to save to safety as soon as possible. Later we can discuss what possibilities, if any, there are of taking action against the shipping company. I made the entire discovery during my last stay in New York, and at that time I unfortunately couldn't see you because of the death of your father.

I will call your office tomorrow in order to get your address in the mountains. It would be good of you if you would answer my questions by telegraph. I will have to cable Casablanca. The sooner I can cable, the better. My private address: 2446 Lakeside Avenue, Baltimore, Md.

Settling accounts with the confidante in Casablanca (Director of the Gallery Lafayette) was to be done through one of my relatives who has bank accounts in the unoccupied territories. The Federal Reserve Bank has given the required *license*. Now my relative's people seem to have suddenly left Marseille and are not to be found. If you should have money in unoccupied France, it would perhaps not be unwelcome to you to change it into dollars by requesting a *license* for the transaction in Casablanca, and I would pay you the equivalent value for my things in dollars here. But we will have to correspond about this, since in the application for the *license* all objects in the *lift* have to count as my property. But for today that is only a question.

We may visit friends in North Carolina for a week in September. I will take this opportunity to introduce myself at Duke as well as in Chapel Hill. That might perhaps be useful with an eye to the problems of the next few years, which I need to begin working on pretty soon. In mid-September we will be in New York for ten days. We shall surely take this occasion to see each other in New York.

Farber wrote recently concerning the financial difficulties of the journal. Will he perhaps reject my first long James essay because of the length? I expect the corrected copy any day. I hope the journal will not be a victim of the war. Jean Wahl is now in New York as well.

With best greetings from house to house

Your
Aron Gurwitsch

1. Furniture transport underway from Paris to New York.

Schutz: *I would rather go to Macy's and buy new things*
           (CHOCORUA, NEW HAMPSHIRE, AUGUST 25, 1942)

Dear Friend Gurwitsch,

Your special delivery letter of the 18th only reached me yesterday, delayed by my moving here and by the weekend. What a story! As you wished, I telegraphed yesterday that I don't wish to make any expenditure at all to buy back my silver at the auction (this is the sense in which I have understood your not entirely clear account). I don't have any French francs in the unoccupied territory, my account in Paris is frozen or confiscated, and I would thus have to allow the Pétain government to get good dollars at a ridiculous official exchange rate in order to have a very questionable chance of getting possession of my silver *loco* Casablanca. After all, just buying them back doesn't get the things to the U.S.A. So I would rather go to Macy's and buy new things for the same price. With regard to the books, here too I don't want to make any very substantial expenditures, especially in view of the fact that I have no idea what is in the box. But you are probably right in saying that there is little demand for these things and that in addition it will be impossible to separate *par distance* your things from mine. So I would suggest that we let things take their course with regard to the books.

At any rate, many thanks for your efforts. We shall return to New York at the end of this week, and I am very much looking forward to seeing you and your wife there soon. Best greetings from both of us

Your
Schutz

P.S. If you go to Chapel Hill, give our best greetings to the Kuhns.

Gurwitsch: *Maimon, the first of us to search for the path from the ghetto to the*
             West
             (Cambridge, November 3, 1942)

Dear Friend Schutz,

A letter to you was due a long time ago, and yet it was to be written first when we had gotten settled and the waves of getting settled had subsided to the point that I could speak to you in peace. That is almost the case now. "Almost," since just this week we are caught up in a superabundance of *social life* which belongs to the beginning stages, but which will hopefully soon be behind us. It doesn't fit in very well with the quiet life that we are used to.

Well, we are both very, very glad that we are here, here in Cambridge and in our home. Both of us, for the first time since Paris, have the feeling that we have a home again and no mere lodging. The—very welcome—difference from Baltimore is doing us good. It is different in every respect, and pleasingly different. Neither Perry nor Hocking can be compared to Boas. I think that Perry is interested in my studies and approves of their direction. Of course, my contact with him is only very casual; he is totally caught up in *war work*.[1] I did have an extended talk with him; it concerned first my James piece; then we talked about Hodgson and Salomon Maimon. I have gotten acquainted with and come to think highly of the former in the course of the last two years.[2] I have been interested in the latter for years, as a philosopher and as a phenomenon: the first of us and our prototype, we who searched for the path from the ghetto to the West and, each in his own way, found it. How strange that a talk with Perry should bring all this back to me, and a couple of days later should call my attention to a curious genealogical line of phenomenology.

I am sure that Husserl knew nothing about either of them. But on the basis of Kant's critique, Maimon demanded that the Leibniz-Hume problem be posed again; and what are we doing if not that? And Hodgson, the friend of James, who described himself: "I am the pupil of Maimon, the only one, though M. was never a teacher and never had a school," anticipated Husserl in very interesting ways. He demanded a systematic investigation of consciousness, and lay down the postulate that the question "what *is* something" be replaced by "what is it known *as?*"

I don't want to start philosophizing in this letter. The things I just mentioned, which I have slipped into *malgré moi*, only go to show that horizons open up to one again here. That is surely the best that one can say about one's surroundings. And I can add that my wife doesn't feel any differently from the way I do. We both have the feeling that in leaving Baltimore we have found air one can breathe. In Baltimore we both suffered from suffocation attacks of a psychic and spiritual kind. This wasn't the fault of Hopkins. I, at least, cannot live in the ghetto.

There are many Europeans here, clustered around Harvard. There is a nice tone and solidarity among them. One is accepted with the matter-of-factness of those who belong. We speak and discuss with one another as we were used to doing. In this way one once again has something of one's world, and in this way one's personal life becomes more meaningful, perhaps only apparently, but at any rate more bearable.

And now to you. I hope that you and yours are well. Does your daytime life leave you a nighttime *margo* or does it illegitimately eat away at periods which do not belong to it? I would wish and I hope that it is satisfied with that which is sacrificed to it anyway. *By the way,* here I have become acquainted with a Mr. Georg Fleischer from Vienna, who knows you from the Kelsen circle or some other context. What kind of man is he? I hope to hear from you soon. For the moment, please greet your family from both of us, with best greetings to you yourself

Your

Aron Gurwitsch

1. Ralph Barton Perry was Chairman of the "American Defense: Harvard Group," along with G. W. Allport, A. M. Schlesinger, and others. Talcott Parsons was responsible for "national morale."

2. Shadworth Holloway Hodgson (1832–1912), English philosopher who influenced William James. His main work, *Time and Space* (London, 1865), has phenomenological motifs. Salomon Maimon (1752–1800), from Lithuania, was an important critic of Kant's theory of space and time.

Schutz: *I have finished the 'Stranger'*
          (New York, November 9, 1942)

Dear Friend Gurwitsch,

Your letter of the 3rd came just on the afternoon of the day on which I had sent your manuscript to Farber with the recommendation that it be published. If I had known your address earlier, I would have come to an understanding with you concerning one or two points, but as it was I of course recommended it to Farber without reservation. I am very happy to hear from your letter that you feel much better in Cambridge than you did in Baltimore. I was convinced that the atmosphere there would be much more pleasing to you. You will also be much more able to work in peace. I consider it a great success that Perry has received you so well. Curiously enough, you don't mention anything about John Wild. I would be very interested to hear whether he accepts you. Dr. Fleischer, who you mention at the end of your letter, I know very well from Vienna. When you see him, give him my greetings. Nevertheless, I would be surprised if you two were to find any points of mutual interest other than purely social ones.

How is your work coming? I myself have finished the "Stranger," and now plan to rewrite for American readers one problem or another out of the ideas from the manuscript "The Social Person,"[1] which I wrote during my last summer vacation in Europe. But I have not yet decided with which of the many problems I shall begin.

I hope that your path will soon lead you to New York. Please give your wife best greetings from both of us. Please let me know how you are doing and what you are up to.

Sincerely your
Schutz

1. "The Problem of the Personality in the Social World." Unpublished manuscript; a copy is in the Archives for the Social Sciences in Constance. Cf. notes 64 and 72 in I. Srubar's "*Einleitung zu Schütz 'Theorie der Lebensformen'* " (S1981).

Gurwitsch: *John Wild is the only living soul in the department*
(CAMBRIDGE, DECEMBER 21, 1942)

Dear Friend Schutz,

To my consternation I see that I have left your letter unanswered, although an answer has been overdue for weeks. My only explanation is that time no longer exists in my existence here, time in various denotations and connotations. We continue to do very well here; and I live in a complete absorption in my work. Hardly "knowing" what is actually happening, the abstract *entia* are almost my only concrete company.

I am spending all of my time working on the second James essay. I am pretty satisfied with the progress. This progress indicates that what was to have been a paper will probably become a book. Not even a third is finished and it is already more than 40 printed pages. I think I will call it "Outline of a Field-Theory of Consciousness" and publish it as a "memoir" with the Philosophical Society, if that should be at all possible. By now it only deals with James to the extent that I again and again take him as point of departure, using him as the occasion to say things that can also be said independently of him. It is my first attempt to publish my field-ideas in the English language. The ramifications go in many directions, and I flatter myself that you too, dear friend, will find something of use for the phenomenology of the concept of relevance.

John Wild is the only living soul among the younger people in the department here. The rest are more or less victims of symbolic logic, a dreadful thing, since it is a caricature of Leibniz's *mathesis universalis*. Wild does everything to escape it, and he finds life in Aristotle. That isn't my way, but I admit that it is a

way. In spite of all of our differences, I believe that I have most in common with
him and he with me. So we get along with one another and have something to
say to each other. He is very engaging personally.

Farber was here for a day recently. We met, if only briefly. He told me,
among other things, that at the moment my essay is with you again. Please let
me know which points you have objections to. I am of course interested anyway.
And it will be possible to take your critique into account if need be, since I am
going to make a couple of changes in the essay before it is printed. The long
footnote on Stout at the end will be written a bit differently and become
stronger, if also a bit longer. In addition, in the archives I have found a couple of
remarks in which James replies to Marty's critique,[1] and I want to take them into
account. These are only a couple of *scraps,* but in my context they seem to me
worthy of publication. In addition, I shall attempt to make an arrangement to
save some space with the notes. As you see, there will be an extensive *final
revision*. So I will have a good possibility of taking your critique into account and
I am very interested in getting it.

I hope that you and yours are doing well in every respect. We will not be
coming to New York this Christmas. But how about your taking a trip to
Boston? We have a nice home with room for you and a great deal of warmth. We
would be delighted to see you here. And it would be so nice if one did not have
to wait for one of the accidents which brings you to this area now and again.

In the hope that our next meeting will be in Cambridge in the near future—it
is so beautiful and quiet, one is less hectic, and that makes it so much more
appropriate for philosophical conversations—in this hope I wish you and yours,
also in the name of my wife, all the best in the coming year, and am with best
greetings

Your

Aron Gurwitsch

1. This probably refers to Anton Marty's review of James's *Principles of Psychology* in
the *Zeitschrift für Psychologie und Physiologie der Sinnesorgane* 3 (1892): 297–333. The
copy found in the James papers at Houghton Library, Harvard, has annotations from the
hand of William James. (Information from Lester Embree.)

Schutz: *I do not feel that your criticism of James is justified*
            (DECEMBER 24, 1942)

Dear Friend:

Today I am writing you in English since my German secretary is not available. I thank you ever so much for your kind letter of December 21st.

I read with the greatest interest of the progress of your work and am happy to learn that you and your wife are well and continue to enjoy your stay in Cambridge.

I am hurrying to inform you that your assumption that your paper was returned to me is obviously a misunderstanding. I never received your paper again after I had sent it back to Farber. However, a few days before his departure Farber told me that he feels the paper should be shortened somewhat and asked me for my opinion. I answered him immediately that I stick to my previous position. This paper should be printed as it is should he be unable to come to an agreement with you. I informed him that you intend to continue your work on the same topic and that you have, therefore, perhaps included material not used in the present paper. Obviously, Farber had no knowledge of this letter when he left Buffalo for Cambridge and found it on his desk when he returned. He answered me the next day that he had talked over this matter with you and found a satisfactory solution.

The remarks I have to make concerning your paper will not surprise you. I do not agree with the conclusions you have drawn in the last part of your paper and I do not feel that your criticism of James is justified; that has nothing to do with the quality of your paper and my editorial judgment, but refers to the difference in the point of view between us, with which you are familiar. It is rather unfortunate that you are not coming to New York this Christmas and that we cannot meet at Yale. I would have liked to discuss this topic with you again. Under my present circumstances it is impossible to take up such a matter by way of correspondence. There is no chance whatsoever that I shall be at Harvard very soon, so I have to wait for the good chance to see you here.

For the coming year, all our good wishes to you and your wife. With kindest regards,

Sincerely yours,
Alfred Schutz

Schutz: *I have always drawn a sharp line separating that from which one lives and that for which one lives*
(NEW YORK, OCTOBER 1, 1943)

Dear Friend Gurwitsch,

I still have to thank you for your kind letter of September 12, which brought me good news from you. I found it especially touching that Bréhier published your work[1] even after the German occupation. I read it with great pleasure and find it to be a valuable supplement to your first Goldstein essay.[2] Many thanks for sending me an off-print.

The other great piece of news in your letter is your teaching physics at Harvard. I confess that I hadn't expected that. I have always pictured you as a mathematics teacher, but I am convinced that you will do an excellent job of teaching physics as well. In any case, it is valuable to have been a teacher at Harvard. When you write that you basically cannot understand that people are paid for doing what they have mastered relatively the least, but are not paid for doing that which they can really do well, I can only tell you that in the course of a twenty-two year professional life I have long since cured myself of my amazement at this. I have always drawn a sharp line separating that from which one lives and that for which one lives. It is a pity that you could not be spared this not-so-pleasant experience, but as Anton Bruckner says: "Writing an adagio is the hardest thing in the world, but one gets used to it!"

I hereby initiate you into the federation of all those who distinguish between daytime life and nighttime life. I only hope that your physics teaching doesn't seriously hinder you from continuing the work on your book, and that like me you will learn to take care of your routine work with a commensurate inner distance.

In addition to my well-known professional activity and to my lectures at the New School, I have received a third *job,* which I told you a bit about in New York. I have been named Senior Consultant of the Board of Economic Warfare.[3] This work takes a lot of time, more than I had expected, since I have to write a series of memoranda for Washington, which require painstaking Researches in libraries. Thus, my really scholarly work has been reduced to the short vacation period of 17 days which I passed most pleasantly in Lake Placid.

During this period I finished an essay and the first draft of another. The former, of which I will send you a copy in the near future, is a lecture which I will hold next week before a group of New York philosophers who know nothing of phenomenology but would like to learn what it is all about.[4] It was stimulating to attempt to present some of the basic ideas in popular, of course very vague, form, in order to see if one can give open, uninformed people, who of course were brought up completely within the American tradition, an idea of at least the methods of phenomenology; obviously it can only be a rough, inexact presentation.

My other work is much more important to me, but it will be months before it is finished. It is an essay which I plan to publish in our journal.[5] Its content will be an analysis of the problem of multiple realities, which James saw very clearly, but in my opinion did not analyze adequately. Although the essay takes off from James's presentation, it will not be an essay on James. Nonetheless, I believe that you will find the basic ideas, which by and large are from the German manuscript[6] that I wrote during my last Austrian vacation, interesting. But it will be a while before I have brought the difficult material into a fitting form.

In the meantime you should have received the off-print of my *Economica* essay, which you of course already know, since it is only a slight modification of my Harvard lecture.[7] Given the current circumstances and the paper shortage, I find it very touching that the people in London have found the time and desire not only to publish the essay, but to translate all American terminology very carefully into English.

I am currently reading Farber's book[8] and am making as much progress as my very thoroughly filled up time allows. I believe that he has done excellent work and I am glad to hear that you have taken over the book for a review. Farber certainly deserves our thanks, since we now have something to which we can refer.

There is not much to report about my family. My wife, my mother, and the children are all healthy and we are all happy at the good political news.

With best greetings to you and your wife, and in the hope of hearing from you soon, I am

Your

Alfred Schutz

1. "La science biologique d'après Kurt Goldstein": G1940a.
2. "Le fonctionnement de l'organisme d'après Kurt Goldstein": G1939.
3. Schutz was a consultant for the Department of Commerce from August 9, 1943, to April 18, 1945. He was mainly concerned with financial matters in this capacity. (Information from Mrs. Schutz.)
4. "Some Leading Concepts of Phenomenology" (S1945b).
5. "On Multiple Realities" (S1945c).
6. "Das Problem der Personalität in der sozialen Welt" (1936–37) is unpublished.
7. "The Problem of Rationality in the Social World" (S1943).
8. *The Foundation of Phenomenology.*

Gurwitsch: *When it was no longer possible to live in Europe as a European, we had to leave in order to save our bare lives*
(CAMBRIDGE, JULY 16, 1944)

Dear Friend Schutz,

I should have and wanted to thank you for the off-print of the "Stranger"[1] long ago; but you know better than anyone how it is for those who live multiple lives. I would have preferred to leave it at a little thank you note, with the promise of a verbal discussion. There is indeed a whole lot to say about your article. That your path will lead you to Boston at some point is something we almost don't dare hope any more; and only the gods know when we will go to New York again. So there is nothing left but the second best: formulating a few remarks concerning your essay.

From the point of view of formal sociology there is nothing to say against it. But it is precisely this point of view that is questionable; and just your essay makes this questionableness visible. Understand me: it goes without saying that I recognize the legitimacy and the necessity of investigations of this sort concerning the structures of everydayness. I know that for certain theoretical reasons such investigations must be pursued in still greater scope than has been the case up to now. But the question is: How far does the field of formal sociology reach, which phenomena are accessible to its methods and concepts, and which are no longer accessible?

According to you, the stranger is every person who changes his surrounding world for certain reasons. Certainly, the immigrant of the old style, who for certain reasons moves to another country and now takes his bearings. If things don't work out, he can go back, just as the city person who moves to the country can if need be return to the city. But the situation of the immigrant of the last ten years is different. He had no choice, he was confronted with the question of bare survival, and that no longer merely individually but nationally. If already the *réfugié*[2] in general cannot be brought under the formal concept of the *stranger*, as it seems to me, then it is all the more clear in the case of the *réfugié* of today, who in one sense comes out of the void, in another sense out of a 3000-year past. And thus he appears enigmatic and paradoxical to the new environment as well. (I need only think of the *"enemy alien" in the technical sense*, with whose mortal enemies we are after all at war.) The specific characteristics of this curious being, dear Schutz, don't allow themselves to be simply formalized, and the crises that this type lives through are incommensurable with those fundamentally harmless problems of adapting which you describe.

The situation becomes still more complicated when we take into account the fact that this involuntary immigrant (thus *réfugié*) sometimes not only *in fact* comes from a specific historical world, but is very much aware of the historical constellation to which he belongs, and of his place in this constellation. In addition: We have not, after all, broken with this world of ours; on the contrary, it has been shattered. If we have brought anything with us, then it is precisely the historical forces which have made us what we are. We didn't want to break with our past, we didn't want to leave the world in which we grew up. The forces which drove us out were the enemies of Europe. When it was no longer possible to live in Europe as a European, at precisely that moment we had to leave in order to save our bare lives. We had to leave Europe precisely because we were Europeans. And it is just this that makes us exiles,—a title which was very respected in earlier times.

And so we find ourselves in new surroundings, and we soon discover that we are on another planet. We thought—I appeal to the philosopher Schutz—that man must be responsible for the world. That is what we learned from our master Husserl and read in Plato (λόγον διδόναι). And now we learn that that is not the point at all, that the point is to have recipes which allow one to deal with things. We wanted to understand the world and now we learn that the only thing that matters is a smooth and effortless operation in which certain results can be produced. Didn't we all grow up with the νομοι ἀγραφοι of Antigone, and now to our astonishment we learn that social convention is the highest norm? Dear Schutz, can this crisis be described with the categories "scheme of orientation," "pattern of behavior," "way of life"? Is this crisis one of those problems of adaptation that in the final analysis are so harmless? Or isn't this rather "crisis" in the etymological sense: decision?

As I said, I don't challenge the relative legitimacy of formal sociological considerations and the categories that such investigations give rise to. When I take the train, I have to act as the ideal type *conductor* expects and must expect; otherwise I must be prepared for unpleasantness. But, dear Schutz, my behavior on the train is after all surely something very different from my attitude toward the complexus of "science." In the one case it is foolishness not to do what the rest of the world does; in the other case the opposition to the *consensus communis* becomes precisely one's intellectual and therefore moral duty. Are both to fall under "pattern of behavior"? And I appeal once more to the philosopher Schutz. We both know what it means to make the *consensus communis* and "public opinion" the highest norm. Is it not precisely the function of the philosopher to investigate the things themselves and not to accept *what they say*. Don't we know that the truth is the unattainable fruit of endless endeavors and not, precisely not, what "one" thinks, knows from hearsay and passes on in verbal form, perhaps making use of advertising and those techniques that psychology puts at our disposal? Isn't original seeing something very different from hearsay and adaptation?

Here we again confront one of those conflicts that, it seems to me, are more than the difficulties of new beginnings. We don't want to forget, dear friend, that our genealogy as philosophers goes back to a fool and a martyr. Back to the martyr Socrates, who, as I learned, made a *nuisance* of himself because he continually contradicted everyone and asked questions about things which public opinion had long since dealt with, and was in addition very *successless*. But concerning the fool Thales they tell the story that, absorbed in deep reflection, he fell into a manure pit and was jeered at by a milkmaid, since he knew his way around with the stars but was incapable of finding his way on the street. The fool seems to have been incapable of dealing with the things.

Once more: Where are the limits of formal sociology and its concepts? If these concepts are to have an unrestricted validity, if categories such as "pattern of behavior" are to be universally applicable, the result is a positively dreadful picture of man. In this case man is an *animal psychologicum et sociale,* trainable, a being with certain reactions which one can modify by using certain techniques. Then all that matters is handling this supposed crown of creation in the correct manner, to reward it, threaten it, to calculate correctly the deep forces of the unconscious.

I know, it is modern and progressive to speak of the "human animal." Didn't we learn something else? We heard that man is an image of God—does God "adjust" himself? We heard of νοῦς and that ψυχή πως πανια ἐστί. We learned from Malebranche that in the exercise of reason, and he specifically meant mathematical reason, man participates in the *raison universelle,* and understood the vision *de toutes choses en Dieu* in this way. Later we learned that the conditions of possibility of reason and of consciousness are the conditions of possibility of all objects, and that man's claim to nobility lies in his reasonableness. Are we to abandon all that for the Evangelium of universal "adjustment"? Can all that be described with the concepts of "way of life," or are we not rather dealing here with a clash between different worlds? And the tragedy is that it is precisely those things that no one wants to hear about here that hell has revolted against in Europe.

Perhaps you will answer that your article is a sociological study, and as such interested in the *average* and not in the specific problems of those few who are so aware. Then I would ask: why do we find such an interest in the *average* in our times and not in substantive issues? Why does one no longer pose the question concerning truth but only the question concerning the *average opinion?* Who has proven that in these matters statistics provides salvation? There is nothing to say against proceeding in this manner when it is a matter of ἀδιαφορα; but aren't there things for man that are not ἀδιαφορα?

I will never accept that for man the important thing is a well-oiled operation, that it is all a matter of making a smooth functioning possible via *adjustment*. In that case I would ask what is the point of the whole operation? And I would continue to ask this question if the entire world around me were to believe in the new Evangelium of the "human animal." In this situation three thousand years of European history rise up in me; and I stand by this power, not by "pattern of behavior."

Let us hear how you and yours are getting along. Here everything is fine. I ceased being an army teacher about four months ago, and now have to do with the regular functions of the college. However, most of my students are V12, i.e., students who appear in Marine uniform. In September we are going to New Hampshire. When will you be taking time off?

With best greetings

Your

Aron Gurwitsch

1. "The Stranger" (S1944a) was published in *The American Journal of Sociology* and not, as was usual with lectures given in the General Seminar, in *Social Research*.
2. Originally the name for Calvinists who fled France.

3
Context as a Problem of Order
(June 11, 1945–July 17, 1949)

Is the context of the interconnections between life and world a social context? Is society as a class structure, as the totality of cognitive and behavioral models the adequate explanatory principle for dealing with the problem of human order? This question has, over and above the tautologies of merely sociological accounts, a nihilistic core which Gurwitsch attacks ("On Contemporary Nihilism," G1945). Like any cognition, the knowledge of order has to gain a "distance," that of the judging and valuing abstraction from the social and historical situation. Nihilism rejects this, replacing abstract thinking with concrete thought and closing any distance. Social behavior is reduced to natural behavior. The freedom of the actor is lost in the mechanisms of manipulable orders. Thus, context [*Zusammenhang*] itself has to be taken as a problem.

The phenomenological approach to this problem brought with it a surprising agreement, which almost amounted to a division of labor, between Schutz and Gurwitsch. Context was understood as the order of consciousness and life-world whereby the accent of the investigation could lie on consciousness (as the field of consciousness: Gurwitsch) or on the life-world (Schutz). When Gurwitsch read Schutz's essay "On Multiple Realities" (S1945), he suddenly saw this inner connection between their approaches: "Myself digging a tunnel, I hear the knocking which announces the worker on the other side" (GS 9.3.45). He defined his own understanding of the two perspectives very precisely: Schutz investigated the existence of multiple realities (such as that of dreams, of fantasy, of theoretical thought) and ran into the paramount reality of the everyday world of work. Gurwitsch was also concerned with such multiple realities, but now as a constitutional problem. His question: what constitutes the "context" or "configuration" [*Zusammenhang*] of an order of being as order?

For reading the letters and understanding such claims it is important that one take the metaphor of digging a tunnel literally and seriously in the tectonic sense. Such definitions of the two positions ("What you call X is called Y in my work") cast light on one's own position, but are necessarily vague as definitions of the probable position of the other. Thus, Schutz immediately rejected such claims and Gurwitsch did the same a few letters later.

The nihilism discussion of these first post-war years had a wider horizon: it manifested itself in the correspondence in the clash with Marvin Farber, in which not only Schutz and Gurwitsch but also Helmut Kuhn was involved (SG 2.4.48). This controversy was carried out much more sharply and with broader consequences between Sartre and Merleau-Ponty, who however are not mentioned. Schutz and Gurwitsch would surely have discussed them with their European friends when they made their first visits to France following the war: Schutz took a business trip as early as September 1946; the Gurwitsches, who had no permanent position and were thus in a very precarious financial position in these years, returned to Paris for the first time in July 1949. Aron Gurwitsch was undecided about accepting the offer of a position in Paris.

Schutz: *As soon as sociology claims to explain the riddle of the world, it has already*
          fallen prey to the nihilistic devil
          (NEW YORK, JUNE 11, 1945)

Dear Mr. Gurwitsch,[1]

My most sincere thanks for sending me the off-print of your essay on nihilism[2] which, if I am not mistaken, is a slight revision of the French essay which I
was able to see some time ago. I have now read the work very thoroughly and
conscientiously, and it may surprise you that I heartily and unrestrictedly agree
with everything you say. From a formal point of view as well, the whole thing is
very well done and of great clarity and beauty of language.

I now have a better understanding of the train of thought on the basis of
which you criticize what you call "formal sociology." I think that this critique is
rooted in the fact that you legitimately reject sociologism *in philosophicis,* but you
throw the baby out with the bath water in this critique in attributing to all
sociology the nihilistic tendencies which, e.g., are without doubt exhibited by
the currently so modern sociology of knowledge. As soon as sociology claims to
explain the riddle of the world, to deal with the definition of man, to trace
epistemological categories back to social existence, etc., it has already fallen prey
to the nihilistic devil.

But there is an intermediate sphere—that of the relatively natural *Weltan-*
schauung—for whose description and analysis philosophical categories are just as
inadequate as sociological categories for the explanation of the most modest
philosophical problem. Even if, e.g., "adjustment"—by all unclarity of this
term—is not allowed a warrant of any kind in the sphere that you deal with in
your paper, there are certain processes within everyday life that the sociologist
uses this term to signify and that can and, I think, should be described and
interrogated as to their implications.

I hope that you and your wife are doing well and that your path will lead to
New York sometime. With best greetings

Your

Alfred Schutz

1. The gap of almost a full year in the correspondence and Schutz's formal salutation
indicate some kind of interruption in the friendship. Whatever coolness might have
developed, it is gone by the time of Gurwitsch's letter of September 3, 1945.
2. "On Contemporary Nihilism" (G1945). The translation from the French (by Dr.
Anna Hatcher) was instigated by Hannah Arendt (communication from Mrs. Alice
Gurwitsch).

Gurwitsch: *Myself digging a tunnel, I hear the knocking which announces the*
             worker on the other side
             (CAMBRIDGE, SEPTEMBER 3, 1945)

Dear Friend Schutz,

When we departed you gave us some reason to hope for a visit in Cambridge. We have kept up this hope. But yesterday I met Mr. Winternitz in the library and heard that you are in Pennsylvania. So the mountain does not come to the prophet.

For general and many special reasons I would have been glad to see you. Also in order to talk with you about your new essay.[1] I have read it once more in print very carefully. My congratulations: they refer to the whole as well as the individual parts. The Don Quixote analysis, as short as it is, belongs to the most reasonable things that have been written on this subject. Your essay is really at a crossroads of all possible lines of investigation; e.g., it throws light on the historical problematic of understanding "other worlds." Most excellent the last part on the theory of science.

But I also have my personal reasons to take pleasure in your work. Myself digging a tunnel, I hear the knocking which announces the worker from the other side. What you call "multiple realities" is called "orders of being"[2] in the chapter of my book which you—for very good reasons—do not want to read. To be sure, my way of posing the question is different: you use a few paradigmatic examples to demonstrate the existence of multiple realities; I ask what constitutes the context [Zusammenhang] of an "order of being" qua order. My answer is relevance, and this phenomenon is the object of investigation. We are not really as far from one another as it often appears to us, the half-undressed ones, in the heat of the debate and of the New York summer. You have my complete agreement with your exposition of the "daily life world" as world of work. Once again, we come to the same result working from completely different ways of posing the problem.

My question concerns the constitution of the sciences, especially the mathematical. The deeper I go, the clearer three points become to me: 1) The entire problematic cannot be dealt with adequately if the treatment remains unhistorical; and history has to be underestood in the sense of a "positive" treatment of history which follows out the sedimentations. 2) It is hopeless to start from any place other than from the "life-world." The whole question of the existence of the sciences must be posed as a question of the transition from the order of the "life-world" to the "Pythagorean" order. 3) The most important motif and vehicle in this transition is what Brunschvieg called "conversion."[3]

Thus: rational, mathematical, and finally purely functional interconnections [Zusammenhänge] take the place of the regularities and normal sequences of the "life-world." (E.g.: in the life-world we know that many things are heavier than others. We experience this in carrying, shoving, etc. Formulated rationally this yields the concept of specific weight.) The problems of physics are to be formulated on this level, and a theory of science which does not begin here, at the genuine beginning, is hopeless, as hopeless as everything which goes under the title "philosophy of science."

Bringing to light the operations of consciousness that come into play in this "conversion," discovering their connection [*Zusammenhang*] with perceptual experience, but also showing the sense in which the structures of these operations of reason lie veiled in perceptual experience, the sense in which "perception" is a *pensée confuse:* these are all themes that I would like to have time to elaborate as themes in this life. All of this became plastic for me again as I, reading your work, clearly heard the knocking sounds. How good it is to hear these tones in the unarticulated racket which surrounds us.

There was one thing about your essay which quite displeased me: its neighbor.[4] *Quousque tandem* . . . If things go on like this, the journal could better be named: *Stalinism and Canine Research.* And recently, as the two *specimens* of militarily tested philosophy appeared, I asked myself what my name is doing on the title page. You told me that you had similar thoughts. I haven't written Farber about this yet; I too think that we should bring up this matter at the *business-meeting* which will hopefully take place in the near future. But then we must build a phalanx of those who do not consider it to be in Husserl's spirit to orient philosophy according to the demands of the *post-war* majesties and put it in the service of a certain kind of *mutual understanding.* Opportunism of this kind is just what we needed.

I hope that you have had a good holiday. It is possible that I will be coming to New York for two days some time in September. I will let you know in good time so that we can have an evening for us.

Best greeetings from house to house

Your

Aron Gurwitsch

1. "On Multiple Realities" (S1945c).
2. "Orders of Existence" in the published version (G1964a, part VI).
3. Leon Brunschvieg, *De la connaissance de soi* (Paris, 1931).
4. E. Airapetyantz and B. Bykow (Leningrad University), "Physiological Experiments and the Psychology of the Subconscious," *PPR* 5 (1944–45): 577–593.

Schutz: *I have devoted seven (lean) years to this essay*
          (NEW YORK, SEPTEMBER 19, 1945)

Dear Friend Gurwitsch,

Your letter of the 3rd gave me a great deal of pleasure. You know how much I value your judgment, not only because you are one of the very few whom I hold to be genuinely competent in such questions, but also because I know that you cannot bring yourself to say something that you don't mean.

I have devoted seven (lean) years to this essay.[1] I don't know if it is good, but I do know that I can't improve it. You know what our master Husserl has said about the "good philosophical conscience." As you know better than anyone, in such work one never has a good conscience. It remains to be seen whether the solutions offered stand up. But I am firmly convinced *that these are genuine and up to now unsolved, indeed unnoticed problems* on which we, each in his way and according to his talents, are working. Above and beyond differences in your treatment—and in my opinion these differences are by no means divisive or fundamental—we two have in common that we see these problems, and see them in their full importance. That is a comfort to me, as is obviously the case for you. It is a "verification" of a better kind than the verificationists can hope to achieve.

I still don't want to read your chapter on relevance, as much as it interests me. During my vacation I have continued work on completing the theory which I call by this name (I know, you do not—with good reason—understand the same thing by relevance, but perhaps the relation between the two is merely that between universal and specific). Actually, I have now finished rough drafts of three essays that deal with this problem: One is the "Tiresias," which I have already told you about. Another is sociological; it deals with a theory of the distribution of knowledge in the social world and will probably be called "The Well-Informed Citizen." The third and longest investigates the problem of choice and decision.[2] It discusses critically the relevant theories of Leibniz, Bergson, Husserl ("problematic and open possibilities" in *Experience and Judgment*) and aims at a clarification of the concept of preferred action [*Vorzugshandeln*] in economics, also coming up with interesting things for the principle of scarcity and marginal utility.

I had a kind letter from Kuhn. By the way, have you read his Cassirer review in the *Journal of Philosophy*? He writes that he enjoyed himself with you very much, and I have sent him your "Nihilism."

If you really come to New York in September, I hope very much that you will be here on those days on which I am available. My lectures begin next week and my California boss is in New York and gives me a lot to do. But I will do my best to have plenty of time with you, since I have a real desire for a talk with you.

Best greetings to you and your wife

Your
Alfred Schutz

1. "On Multiple Realities" (S1945c).
2. "Choosing among Projects of Action" (S1951a).

Gurwitsch: *Lecture before the Philosophy Club at Harvard*
(CAMBRIDGE, DECEMBER 9, 1945)

Dear Friend Schutz,

I just received the page proofs of my Kelsen review[1] (for *Isis*). Since I am aware of your interest in the two authors, that of the book and that of the review, I am sending you a copy of the proofs today. With the exception of one place, involving an absurd omission, I have not corrected the proofs I am sending you. But I don't think that it matters. This review is one of those discussions on which I lay great value. As you will see, I have stuck a very substantial part of my theory of science into it. Since I know how busy you are, I don't want to press you for a review of the review. You know without my having to say anything how welcome every utterance from you is. When the work appears, you will of course receive a "real" copy.

On Friday I spoke before the Philosophy Club [at Harvard]. My lecture followed the line that I sketched to you in New York. From the phenomenon of meaning to the intentionality of primary and higher levels, exemplified in perception. Also a longer excursus on formal logic and mathematics. The place of a formal science of meanings. Since phenomenology does not have the task of constructing this science, but traces out the relation of act to meaning, there is an easy transition to perception as well as to syntheses of identification. From there to the problematic of constitution in general. Final grounding of a science dealing with consciousness. From there to the reduction and to the concept of the phenomenon.

My friends think that I did very well. Of the philosophers, only Donald Williams was there—do you know him? He asked, after I had repeatedly said that Husserl realized Hume's *intentions,* but abandoned all of his specific teachings, what the difference with Hume might be! This question (after an hour in which intentionality is presented in explicit opposition to the one-dimensional theory of consciousness of the empiricists) shows once again how well our contemporaries have learned to listen. For the rest, Mises and Frank[2] monopolized the rest of the discussion, hardly letting anyone else get a word in: the former made remarks which can only be attributed to senility of the most serious kind; the latter was "malicious," interrupted continuously, argued obviously *mala fide* and purely verbally. At any rate, the two components of contemporary discussion were well represented: 1) don't listen, 2) don't let anyone finish. But I must say that the two made a disgrace of themselves in the eyes of several listeners. The discussion gave me the opportunity to tell Mr. Frank that *scientists* too are "primitive men," instead of speaking of the "dogmatic attitude"; Mr. Mises was told that we phenomenologists are *extremely polite.* Since he was visibly irritated, he may have understood.

It doesn't look as if we will be coming to New York after Christmas. Too bad, since I would have liked to talk, really talk to you again. But, dear friend, the trains don't go only first south and then north, but also first north and then south . . . . Apropos, it occurs to me that you recently told me of your intention to sell the furniture you have in France. If my French projects are realized, couldn't we be the buyers, at least for a part? In case, of course, you haven't yet sold it. This is only an inquiry in principle. We can talk about it more the next time we see each other.

I hope that you and yours are doing well. With best greetings from house to house

Sincerely your

Aron Gurwitsch

1. Hans Kelsen, *Society and Nature* (G1946b).
2. Richard von Mises (mathematician) and Philip Frank (physicist) of Harvard. "Ludwig and Richard von Mises were as it were hostile brothers, separated by political positions" (Alice Gurwitsch).

Schutz: *It is the concept of the context itself which you have put at the center of your thinking*
(NEW YORK, DECEMBER 21, 1945)

Dear Friend,

Many thanks for your kind letter of the 9th and the Kelsen review, which I found especially interesting. Swammerdam[1] proved the omnipotence of God to his students by means of the anatomy of a louse. I don't want to go so far as to extend this comparison to my friend Kelsen's principle of retribution. You know that I have not read his book. I shall not do so in the future either, now that I have read your review. But he told me a lot about it in Vienna, Geneva, and here. In reading your review the thought came to me why doesn't a clever economist attempt to trace both, the principle of retribution and the principle of causality, back to the processes of the exchange of goods? There the true *do ut des* is to be found! Weber once spoke of the ruthless provincial patriotism of the specialist,[2] each one of which wants to explain the riddle of the world.

I fear that Levy-Bruhl's *loi de la participation*[3] is not a bit better, and the more I work with his theories the more distrustful I become. On the other hand I am once again completely in agreement with you: it is the concept of connection [*Zusammenhang*] that all of these theories try to solve from their own specialized point of view. I know that you have put this problem in the center of your thought and therefore understand only too well why this excellent and worthy review—only you can write such reviews—means so much. Again, many thanks!

Don't be disappointed by your experiences at the Philosophy Club: "Of the base and the mean let none complain. For whatever you say, it is seen, these always win!" We live in an age in which the discussion in the agora is impossible. Instead of a universal science or philosophy we have innumerable antagonistic *we-groups* and *they-groups* of scientists. After all, is Mises' antiphilosophy so far from the attitude in which better philosophers reciprocally accuse one another of—just think!—existentialism?

Let us hope that in the new year, which we hope will bring you and your wife all conceivable blessings, we shall have many opportunities to discuss seriously the genuine problems which only arise on the ground of the larger context that we have in common.

Sincerely

Your
Alfred Schutz

P.S. Kuhn writes me: "I have read Gurwitsch's nihilism-essay and find it excellent."

1. Jan Swammerdam, Dutch natural scientist (1637–1680).
2. Max Weber, "Der Sinn der Wertfreiheit," in *Gesammelte Aufsätze zur Wissenschaftslehre,* 3rd ed. (Tübingen: Mohr, 1968), 540.
3. Lucien Lévy-Bruhl, *How Natives Think* (Princeton: Princeton University Press, 1985); ch. 2, "The Law of Participation." (Cf. E. Durkheim, "Les formes élémentaires de la vie religieuse," part 2, ch. 7, par. 6.)

Schutz: *Since the catastrophe I have avoided seeing a single one of my friends* (NEW YORK, MAY 11, 1946)

Dear Friend,

Many thanks for your very kind letter. I had delayed writing these lines, since I hoped to be able to report the results of the operation, but it will be ten days before the doctors can say whether we can hope for some—without doubt limited—vision in the eye on which they operated, and three more weeks before they can say whether there is a chance that any success will be lasting, and only then will they decide whether the same operation should be performed on the other eye as a preventive measure. Thus, we are nowhere near the end of our sufferings.[1]

You surely understand that such a situation releases the spirit only for that which is absolutely necessary. One goes through life as if with an open wound, and since the catastrophe I have avoided seeing a single one of my friends. Thus, I don't have a report on the results of the *meetings,*[2] which I had to miss. (Unfortunately, phenomenology is not one of the philosophies which gives one strength in such situations!) But one participant—Arthur Goodman—told me over the telephone that only your lecture was of the expected high level.

I would like to know what your plans are. Gaston Berger said a few words before his departure. If the course of things with Georgie doesn't hinder me, I am to go to Europe at the end of August for two to two and a half months (London, Paris, Brussels, [Louvain?], Amsterdam, Zurich). Think things over, whether you have a mission for me, *should* this project be realized.

My books have arrived.[3] But you understand too much about philosophy, and your dear wife about music. So the best things are missing. But that doesn't matter now; I haven't even looked at the things.

I hope your and my circumstances will allow us a long talk soon. There is so much that I want to discuss only with you!

Many thanks for both of you for your friendship and love from Ilse and me

Your
Alfred Schutz

P.S. I just received from Sartre: *L'Etre et le Néant*—730 pages! Of course, I haven't looked at it yet.

1. Son George, born in Vienna in 1938, was almost completely blinded in an accident. He lives in New York and owns a concert agency.
2. Meeting of the Phenomenological Society, Hunter College, April 27, 1946.
3. Books which Schutz had left in Paris and which were not in the container of possessions which Gurwitsch shipped (cf. GS 8.18.42).

Gurwitsch: *We are determined to go to France*
(CAMBRIDGE, JUNE 20, 1946)

Dear Friend,

It's a curious coincidence: I tried to call you on the evening before your letter arrived, since I was disturbed by your very long silence. But you were apparently not at home, the same for your wife. At any rate, it became later and later, and I finally cancelled the call.

It is wonderful that things with your son have taken a turn for the good. I hope it will continue in this direction. But I can only too well imagine what it means to have to wait for months. Please keep us informed regularly concerning the develoments. And we hope that your child is in a position *de brûler des étapes* and will soon reach a welcome balance.

You were too preoccupied with worries about your son for me to come with my problems. According to the Harvard regulations (three-year-limit), my time is up there. All attempts to keep me there have failed. All attempts to find another position elsewhere run into four arguments, singly or in arbitrary combination: 1) Jew, 2) not born in this country, 3) too old, 4) too good ("too high and specific flavor"; "too brilliant mind to fit into our institution"; etc.). Finally, a tiny grant came from the Philosophical Association, which along with a bit of *tutoring* will get us through the summer. Aside from the fact that these experiences provide me with material for a novel, I have learned from them that if I have any possibility in this country, this will be exclusively at the Jewish university which is to be founded (on the outskirts of Boston). But this institution, whose founding has already been decided (do you know about it?), will first begin to function in Fall of 1947.[1]

Confidentially, I can report to you that according to private letters from Koyré, Berger, and others, the *Caisse Nationale* has appointed me a *Chargé de Recherche,* with the prospect of being promoted to *Maître* in one or two years. What an irony! Poor, plundered France, with cares of all kinds, in contrast to America which swims in money! The appointment is not yet official. We are almost determined to go to France, although there is no lack of problems in this respect. The salary which they have offered is equivalent to that of a president of a *Cour d'Appel,* but you know how things look at the moment. If, as you recently wrote, you go to France in August, I would ask you to make some arrangements for me with Berger, whom you will certainly see. But there is plenty of time for me to explain to you what it is all about; and it is better said personally.

You can well imagine how much I would like to come to New York in July. The prospect of talking philosophy with you again is truly tempting enough. All the more tempting since I haven't been able to talk to a single person since February, when Berger was here; with the exception of you, I don't know of a single person with whom I could or would want to speak. My book has made good progress, I hope to finish the first draft in the course of the summer. I would have a lot to tell you about it. On the other hand, you will understand that in our precarious situation I shy away from every expenditure. But if you do go to France I shall come in any case; that is too important.

Enclosed an off-print of my first publication in physics.[2] In the hope of receiving good news from you concerning your son in the very near future, with best greetings from both of us to all of you

Your
Aron Gurwitsch

P.S. Won't Voegelin be coming to Cambridge again in the near future?

1. Brandeis University.
2. "Algebraic Discussion of Lenses" (G1946a).

Schutz: *I will go to France at the end of August*
                 (NEW YORK, JULY 10, 1946)

Dear Friend,

I still have to thank you for your letter of June 20. I didn't answer it before yesterday, when he was medically examined again and I can happily tell you that the doctor is satisfied with the healing process and pretty optimistic that some of the disturbances which the boy complains of, namely that he sees things double and blurred, will slowly disappear. Unfortunately, it remains completely open whether he will ever be able to use the eye for normal reading. At any rate, there is improvement, and we can hope that it will continue.

Thank you very much for the information which you gave me concerning Mr. S. It was precisely the answer which I expected from you.

As to the news from France concerning your position, my most sincere congratulations. Of course I would prefer it if you could remain here in this country. I don't need to tell you that I am at your service for everything you need in France. I will go to France at the end of August, but certainly not to Marseille, only to Paris, and I wonder if I will have an opportunity to see Berger. I would of course be very happy to see you again before my departure. On the other hand, you will understand that what with all of the preparations for the trip to Europe I have to budget my time, especially since I still plan to spend 10 days with my family, which leaves for Lake Placid tomorrow, and in addition I still have to take a trip to Canada this month.

Under these conditions I would prefer that you come to New York if possible on the weekend of July 27–28, which is in fact the only weekend prior to my departure which is still free. Merely a couple of hours in the evening during the week are not enough to discuss everything. If you will accept lodging without service, you can stay in my home, since I am currently without family, and if Frau Gurwitsch wants to keep us company under the given circumstances, she is heartily invited.

Please give me your answer as soon as possible.

With best greetings

Your
Alfred Schutz

Gurwitsch: *I am well informed concerning the Jewish university*
             (CAMBRIDGE, AUGUST 19, 1946)

Dear Friend,

The confirmation from Paris came two days ago. But that is not why I am writing you. I would like to request something from you, in the hope that you can fulfill my request in spite of the pressures on your time.

I am now once again well informed concerning the matter of the Jewish university. It is probable that a Mr. Nathan will play a certain role. Mr. Nathan is in the Department of National Economics of New York University, thus a colleague of Ludwig von Mises. It is possible that I will have an interview with Mr. Nathan while you are still in Europe. For this reason I would like to ask you to have Mr. Mises speak with Nathan and tell him who I am. Of course, my call to Paris must be used and it must be so arranged that when I am with Mr. Nathan it does not appear that I am looking for a position, but rather that the university has an interest in getting me.

I am sorry that I have to bother you with this so close to your departure. I hope you will be able to deal with Mises on the telephone, since he did hear me at the congress.

We haven't yet thanked you for the wonderful days with you. It was wonderful to be able to talk with you about real matters again.

We hope that you and yours are doing well, and that especially with Georgie everything develops as wished.

With greetings from both of us to all of you

Your
Aron Gurwitsch

Schutz: *The French have their old shortcoming: "très interessé," the whole thing a breezy washout and a lackadaisical end of the world*
(AMSTERDAM, OCTOBER 18, 1946)

Dear Friend,

This is the first free minute I have had in Amsterdam to report to you concerning my various conferences concerning your affairs. I spoke with Raymond Aron, Jean Wahl, Merleau-Ponty and Gaston Berger, with each separately and with the latter three also together! Unanimous opinion of all, without any influence from me: stay in the U.S.A. and do not return to Paris.

Reasons: a) The position is only for one year and its renewal will depend on the (bad) budgetary situation in France. b) Even if you do your Thesis, a non-Frenchman has no chance for an academic career; *young Frenchmen* will always be given priority. c) The salary is absolutely too small for living in Paris (which I have to confirm) and there is no prospect of earning some extra money as Berger's secretary or in Louvain (which pays its full-time employees 1000 Belgian francs per month). d) Danger of becoming stateless again, in which case one can expect great difficulties in France. e) The absolute unclarity of the internal political situation (Communism, anti-Semitism). That is the opinion of the French—unfortunately.

I myself have understood Voegelin's advice better: it is still the case in France

Alfred Schutz at New York harbor.

that one can consider oneself lucky if one does not have to work with the French. Prices, even measured in dollars at black market exchange rates (290 fr. compared to 120 officially) are terribly high. Your salary alone would be a miserable existence. The French have their old shortcoming: "très interessé," the whole thing a breezy washout and a lackadaisical end of the world. Philosophy must be "engagé": see Sartre. Politics smothers philosophy too. You would be happy with Paris and unhappy with the Parisians, as I am.

I was also in Louvain, more about that verbally, it is a chapter for itself. From there I had Sartre's *L'Etre et le Néant* sent to you. Since this book is very hard to come by, I want to let it circulate among my friends (you, Voegelin, Philipp Merlan). If you have time to read it, begin and keep it as long as you want. If you have no time, offer it to Voegelin as first reader; if he isn't interested, to Merlan.

My visit stands under the sign of my great worry about Georgie, whose right eye has gotten so much worse that it will have to be operated on right after my return, although the left one isn't yet able to read. The real woe begins now, since the child will notice his defect subjectively for the first time. Under these circumstances it is a real blessing that my work doesn't leave me time to catch my breath. I will fly back to New York on October 30. All the best to you and your dear wife.

Your

Alfred Schutz

Gurwitsch: *Tomorrow I will finish "The Field of Consciousness"*
              (CAMBRIDGE, NOVEMBER 2, 1946)

Dear Friend Schutz,

Many thanks for the kind letter which you wrote me from Amsterdam. This letter was to have been a letter of welcome. But in view of what awaits you in New York—the second operation—I don't dare to speak of welcome. Please keep us informed on developments to the extent that internal and external constraints make this possible. You yourself know, without my telling you again, with what anxiety we are following things, what wishes we have for all of you, and just how much we share your fears. Everything else is terribly insignificant in comparison with what you now have weighing on your soul.

So I hardly dare speak of my cares. Only this much: In the past few days I saw the people from the Albert Einstein Foundation. It may be that the opening of the university will be postponed for one to two years. Other informed persons deny that. Be that as it may, I will probably come to New York in the course of November in order 1) to meet Mr. Nathan, who is Einstein's commuter train to the Board of Trustees, 2) to speak with the people at Queens. Will it be possible to see you? A small pleasure for you: tomorrow I will finish the first draft of *The Field of Consciousness*.[1] I can only say "Uff."

What you had to write from France is very distressing. You are probably right; *mais le coeur a ses raisons que la raison ne connaît pas* . . . . Sartre's book hasn't arrived yet; many thanks in advance.

Frau Rosenberg was recently here. It seems that Schocken is prepared to publish a couple of manuscripts by Husserl. I tried to talk her into it. It seems however that one part of the family—especially Frau Husserl—has reservations about letting the manuscripts be published by a publishing house that is so obviously Jewish. She (Frau H) immediately wrote to Louvain, and from there came a warning to be careful. If at all possible I would like to see you and hear about Louvain.

For the moment sincere greetings to you all, and all of those wishes which need not be formulated.

Your

Aron Gurwitsch

1. In the *Nachlaß* there is a book-length manuscript (C25) of *The Field of Consciousness* (509 pages), which does not mention any post-war literature (other than a few works by Schutz and Gurwitsch), and which is thus probably the version finished on November 3, 1946. The sequence of chapters is very different from the published version. Piaget does not yet play a central role (cf. GS 8.1.51: "Piaget had consequences").

Schutz: *Jean Wahl's "The Philosopher's Way" is a major and fascinating event*
(NEW YORK, NOVEMBER 17, 1946)

Dear Friend,

Many thanks for your kind letter of the 2nd. The operation was performed on Wednesday and went without a hitch (there was much to fear). Now the week and month-long waiting period begins again. The final result will be all the more vital, since it turns out (or better: the doctors now admit) that the left eye, which was already operated on, will not see well enough for reading.

Nonetheless, I have a deep interest in how your affairs develop and what chances you have. I have by no means neglected the idea I had for you, but this plan is—at least for you—not yet ripe. It had to do with the founding of a Graduate Faculty[1] for the social sciences including philosophy and psychology. But for the time being it has been realized only on a reduced scale, namely restricted to *Economics*. But after a trial year it is to be expanded and I am of course following all developments with utmost attention. You mention Queens in your letter. I don't know what this refers to.

If you come to New York, by all means let me know as early as possible. I can't promise that we will be able to get together, everything will depend on the boy. But if it is at all possible I would like to speak to you, since I still have all kinds of things from Europe that will interest you.

And now the most important thing: My most hearty congratulations for the completion of your main business. I hope that external and internal circumstances will soon allow me to study your manuscript. —In the past few nights I have read Jean Wahl's manuscript *The Philosopher's Way*[2] (the book on metaphysics), which I brought back from Paris for Oxford Press. It is a major and fascinating event.

All the best to you and your dear wife from the two of us.

Your

Alfred Schutz

1. In Mexico City: cf. GS 3.23.47 and SG 4.20.47
2. New York: Oxford University Press, 1948. ("The book consists of lectures which Jean Wahl held in the U.S.A.": communication from Walter Biemel, March 12, 1985.)

Gurwitsch: *Merleau-Ponty's* Structure du Comportement *uses a great deal that I have said in lectures*
(CAMBRIDGE, DECEMBER 15, 1946)

Dear Friend,

Your letter with the copy of the letter that you wrote to Frau Staudinger came yesterday. Many thanks for your excellent *Testimonial*, which, I believe, will serve its purpose. You did a truly excellent job.

Now something of greater importance: Since Wednesday we have continuously thought about the new examinations of your boy. You can well imagine the anxiety with which we are following the course of these developments. I don't want to push you or in any way give you the feeling of being obligated. If you can—internally and externally can—we would be very thankful to read a few lines from you concerning this most important question which overshadows everything else. But, as I said, only if you can.

I have checked Merleau-Ponty's *Structure du Comportement* out of the library. It seems to be a very competent work. I took a look at his sections dealing with Goldstein's work. He has used a great deal that I have said about that in print as well as in lectures.[1] That I could have to some extent stimulated such a study makes me happy and sad simultaneously. Alas, how well I know that regardless of what I have the opportunity to say here, it will be scattered in the winds and cast on a sterile stony ground. I suppose that one must come to terms with one's

Fatum, but when Spinoza demands that one love it, that is certainly going too far.

Give your wife our love; tell her that many of the most important things can hardly be put into words, but they are still there and lead their extraordinary life. And that, my dear fellow, goes for you too. We join hands with both of you, and you understand what it means.

Sincerely

Your

Aron Gurwitsch

1. Merleau-Ponty attended Gurwitsch's lectures in Paris in the 1930s.

Appendix: Answer of the American Committee for Emigré Scholars, Writers and Artists, Inc. (of 1.3.1947) to Schutz. The copy of his "testimonial" has been lost.

Dear Dr. Schuetz,

I have been unable up to now to write you about the outcome of the application in behalf of Dr. Aron Gurwitsch. At our meeting shortly before Christmas the committee voted him a grant of $150 per month for a period of 6 months, and he received his first check just before Christmas.

The Committee was very impressed with Dr. Gurwitsch's record and by the recommendations they had received regarding his new book. The Committee hoped that he would be able to finish his book within 6 months.

Cordially yours

Else Staudinger

Let me add personally my very best wishes for this new year: may it be a really good one for you and all of your family.

Gurwitsch: *My dear friend, they don't want me in this country*
             (CAMBRIDGE, MARCH 23, 1947)

Dear Friend,

It has once again been a long time since we have heard from you. And we have such an ardent desire to hear how you are and how things are going.

Unfortunately, there is nothing good to report about us. A letter came from Queens recently that speaks of budgetary difficulties, so in all probability nothing will come of that. I wrote once more to inquire whether there might be something along the lines of pure mathematics or physics. But—my wife is even more pessimistic than I, and she will probably turn out to be right. Dear friend, they don't want me in this country: "one" is the *genius terrae*. You can well imagine that my Paris plans have thus been activated all over again. In spite of the great difficulties, it would appear that not only the heart but also the understanding plead for Paris. And believe me: *si mon coeur avait ses raisons, il ne les avait pas sans consulter la raison*. Even though we are almost determined to go to Paris, I don't want to do anything until I have explored the ground completely.

It goes without saying that I have not and will not speak to anyone about the hints you made to me concerning the institution that Ludwig von Mises' Mexican is founding.[1] Just between you and me: do you think that there is still the slightest chance for me in this connection, one that would justify a modification of my plans?

I would like to see you before you leave for Europe. Given the situation with ships, it could be months before we can leave. This time I would like to request some concrete things.

A letter from Benesch arrived from Paris; now they are already in Vienna. Without underestimating the problems of inflation and heating, they have written me an enticing letter. It is like an invitation to go home.

Have you heard anything about the Casablanca affair from Monsieur Dreyfus?[2]

With best greetings from both of us to all of you

Your

Aron Gurwitsch

1. Ludwig von Mises was involved in establishing a graduate faculty for social science in Mexico City. (Cf. GS 12.9.45 and SG 11.17.46.)
2. After 1931, Schutz also worked for the Gaston Dreyfus Bank in Paris.

Schutz: *The Institution which Mises planned exists in Mexico*
          (NEW YORK, APRIL 20, 1947)

Dear Friend,

There are reasons why your kind letter of the 23rd remained unanswered for so long. It arrived just after my departure for Mexico, where I had business and remained until Easter. Just after my return I had to go to Montreal, and on my return I was met with the news that George's condition has worsened to the point that an operation (with very little chance of success) cannot be delayed. The operation was day before yesterday—the third within one year—and now the usual waiting period begins, if there were anything to hope for. Luckily, the other (left) eye has made satisfactory progress now that it is being used.

But now to your letter. I still hope that your pessimism with regard to Queens is unjustified. On the other hand, the budgetary difficulties of the city of New York are only too well known.

In Mexico I had the opportunity—introduced by Ludwig v. Mises—to speak with Garcia Maynes, the head of the Cultural Institute. The institution which Mises planned exists and is very successful, but is to remain restricted to national economics for the time being. I was surprised by the high standard and scope of the philosophical work that is done under the auspices of the Cultural Institute, which however takes place exclusively in the framework of the university and in Spanish. As sorry as I am, I don't see any way for you to make your living with scholarly work in Mexico in the near future.

But is the alternative: Queens or Paris, absolute? All reports from Paris are very depressing. A pair of shoes costs 3000 fr. Mr. Gaston Dreyfus hasn't responded to my letter, but I know that he currently has many other worries. I will either sail to Europe on May 24 or fly on May 29, and as always I am at your service.

Many greetings from the two of us to you and your dear wife

Your
Alfred Schutz

Schutz: *Koyré, Wahl, and Raymond Aron are against your coming over*
(Paris, June 22, 1947)

My dear Friend,

I haven't forgotten you and your requests, but during the first weeks of my stay in Europe I was so busy that it was impossible for me to see any of my—and our—friends. I was able to do so only in the last 10 days. Koyré told me that the extension of your *bourse* has already been put through, as he has already informed you. Wahl confirms this. But both of them—as well as Raymond Aron, with whom I also spoke—are still *hanteruent* against your coming over.

You know what I think about this—not merely from the general European but also from the specifically French point of view. In the autumn the crisis here will be unavoidable, and your *bourse,* even if there isn't a real civil war, will probably have lost all buying power by December. But even if everything were to go well, all three say that after two to three years you would be without any hope here in France *vis-à-vis de rien.* And they don't merely talk this way, they act accordingly: this Fall Koyré is going to Chicago for three months; Wahl (in spite of the baby and a second child expected) for one year. Aron wants to wait for France's last chance (de Gaulle) before he decides to emigrate. Gaston Berger, whom I wrote right after my arrival, didn't get in touch with me.

I will be leaving Paris in the next few days to begin my tour, and I may be able to arrange a side trip to Louvain.

Shortly before my departure from the U.S.A. Winternitz hinted at a new possibility for you. I hope *very* much that it works out. All best wishes and greetings to you and your dear wife

Your

Alfred Schutz

I expect Mr. R. Gaston Dreyfus next week in Paris, and plan to speak with him concerning the Casablanca furniture. But where should it be sent?

Gurwitsch: *Then an offer from Wheaton College to be a lecturer in mathematics arrived*
               (Cambridge, August 11, 1947)

Dear Friend,

We were both very sorry that we couldn't see you last week. Aside from the pleasure we would have had at seeing you again we would very much have liked your personal report concerning substantive and personal matters. Mr. Winternitz[1] told us a lot, but you well know the preference that we phenomenologists give to the mode of originarity.

I would of course have liked to speak with you about your experiences in Paris and your evaluation of the tendencies and situation there. As you can well imagine, my interest is not at all academic. I will try to sketch how things stand. Shortly after your departure I received a letter from Koyré in which he informed me that the *Caisse* would renew my appointment (salary: 20,000 *francs par mois*). The official notification still has not come; I expect it in September or October.

In the meantime there have been various developments here. I was in Middletown (Wesleyan University), where they are looking for someone to replace the philosopher Krusé for one year. Although I was prepared to take the risk that the engagement would not be renewed after one year, they informed me weeks later that they had decided to appoint someone else. Next there came a very unpleasant experience with a 7th class college on Long Island (physics). The one concrete thing was an offer from Wheaton College (near here: Norton, Mass.) to become lecturer in mathematics with miserably poor pay. I have to thank, *of all people,* you will say, Mr. Richard v. Mises for this: his wife is Head of the Department of Mathematics there and was able to do away with the competition of *graduate students* with great cunning. But this position too is only for one year, and it is very questionable whether an extension will be possible, even if there should be vacancies. Since the French notification was not yet there, I have accepted the position in order to be prepared for all eventualities. I can always resign after one term.

So the problem is this: As time goes on it will not only become more and more difficult for me here, but, I believe, impossible even to find something from one year to the next. Sooner or later the veterans will have their Ph.D.'s ("all young nice American boys") and I won't be able to handle the competition, since I already have to thank accidents and personal contacts for the fact that I can survive the competition with *graduate students*. My competitor at Wheaton as I was negotiating with them was a graduate student *in spe*.

On the other hand you write me from Paris that nothing can be expected there after a couple of years. What is the basis of this pessimism? I have a very strong impression that my French friends advise me against coming because they think I am well situated here. Of course it is precisely in view of my French efforts that I cannot tell them how things look in reality. But I wonder if they would give the same advice if they knew the truth? I would like to hear your opinion on this, dear friend, *sans ignorer*, regardless of how difficult it is in general, and especially for a person of conscience like you, to give advice.

I am currently reading Merleau-Ponty's *Perception*.[2] I hear an enormous amount from my lectures in the book. He has learned a lot from me and taken over a great deal. Not only in details, where he has carried many things further. I doubt that he would have had the idea of interpreting the psycho-pathological material phenomenologically without my influence. My reaction to the reading is a mixture of pleasure and melancholy. Honest pleasure over the excellent book, which is truly a fine achievement; and also pleasure over the fact that my influence in a sense was the godfather. It is a great feeling to know that my years in Paris were not for nothing, and that my lectures had results. And the melancholy refers to the *modus präteritus*. Here I will never have such a fine influence. One can become very sad when one looks back at one's life and the effects of one's life as if one were dead. For everything that I now do in America goes into the void and is gone with the wind. I have realized so terribly clearly how totally superfluous and *useless* I am here that I often ask myself if all the cleverness that advises me not to take the French insecurity upon myself isn't in the final analysis a great stupidity.

We were away for a couple of days in the White Mountains. There we met a Mr. Ludwig Bendix:[3] an elderly man who has been here a long time already, earlier a banker and expert on public finance, knew Max Weber personally. You might know him from your daytime life; he would also fit into your nighttime life.

We wish you a good vacation and a relaxing time. How is Georgie? Best greetings from both of us to you and your wife

Your

Aron Gurwitsch

1. Emanuel Winternitz, a friend of Schutz from Vienna, was at the Fogg Museum at Harvard from 1938 to 1941, then director of the Department of the History of Music at the Metropolitan Museum in New York.

2. *Phénoménologie de la perception* (Paris: Gallimard, 1945).
3. Father of Reinhard Bendix (Berkeley).

Schutz: *During the vacation I began a systematic investigation of the problem of relevance*
        (LAKE PLACID, SEPTEMBER 3, 1947)

Dear Friend,

After a three-fold tour, your kind letter arrived in Lake Placid only yesterday—on the day of my return. I am so sorry that its content is so unpleasant, but the main thing is that you have found something at least for a short time. You must use this year to look around for something else.

The sad prognosis that there is nothing to hope for after a couple of years in France is not at all the expression of my personal pessimism, but the *unanimous,* independently given judgments of Aron, Koyré, and Wahl. During my next to last visit—since I did not see him during the last—also of Berger. Reasons? The same as here: not French, no *Aggrégation* (Berger's career is an exception), the well-known budgetary situation, in addition the political direction (the philosopher has to be *engagé!*) and the sad general outlook for Europe and France in particular.

Don't you think that there is good reason for it if Wahl (who has done truly excellent work)—with baby and second unborn child—and Koyré return to the U.S.A. (if only provisionally?) And if Aron tells me confidentially that he is only waiting to see if the great financial and political catastrophe which he expects in October/November will find the solution he expects in de Gaulle, before he decides to emigrate to the U.S.A.? I don't allow myself any judgment concerning French academic conditions, but I have the impression that the advice of all friends was informed and objective. I mentioned your difficulties here in correct form. (By the way, Wahl will pass through New York on the way to Chicago between the 18th and the 20th: c/o Colins, 142 East 49th Street). But I have a very univocal and pessimistic judgment concerning France's economic situation. *Right now* 20,000 francs are $80 at the *black market* rate and in terms of buying power! You have surely read in the newspaper that the French government, which was always too optimistic, now speaks of a ten-year period of difficulties.

I haven't read Merleau-Ponty yet, but I have been studying the Stoics and Sceptics a great deal. It has all been said and done before! And much better and seen more clearly than these days. I am getting more and more interested in Maine de Biran. During the vacation I began a systematic investigation of the problem of relevance. You know the adventures that one has in this jungle. I am very curious whether we will once more meet in the tunnels being dug from both sides. However, I still have a lot of digging ahead of me. And where is your book?

Rebus sic stantibus I am not unsatisfied with Georgie's vision, and have a slight, shy hope that *if* things continue in this way he can keep up with his normal class. Subjectively he is cheerful and very happy. But I am still scared of the medical investigation which is coming soon. I have a real desire to see you again! Best greetings to you and your dear wife and best wishes from both of us!

Your

Alfred Schutz

P.S. Do you have any news from Casablanca? In Paris Gaston Dreyfus gave me a solemn promise to get things moving. I am very disappointed in him.

Gurwitsch: *My work at Wheaton is very satisfying*
                (Cambridge, October 3, 1947)

Dear Friend,

The furniture movers just unloaded our things from Casablanca! I have opened *one* box in order to see what condition the books are in. I discovered that everything was repacked in Casablanca, so that your and my books are all mixed up. The books of yours which I found in this box, e.g., a volume of Schopenhauer (Deussen edition), seem to have survived war, water, warehouse, trip, etc., very well; a couple of mine make a rather sad impression.

I shall send you your books in one or two weeks. I can't open the crates until I have my book shelves, since the apartment is too small to stack everything on the floor. As soon as I have the shelves, I will unpack the crates and sort out your books. I had hoped to find the crates which belong to you by taking samples; but as I said, it's all mixed up.

I have of course been very happy as the framework of my "existence" has reappeared. Does that mean that I have settled down here?

My work at Wheaton is very satisfying. The college has excellent academic standards. It likes to see its graduates go to Graduate Schools. Mrs. Geiringer (wife of Richard v. Mises) gives me absolute freedom. She expressly asked me not to go lightly with occasional historical and philosophical remarks in dealing with analytic geometry and differential calculus *à propos* the interpretation of these things, although she knows very well the reasons and chasms [*Gründe und Abgründe*] that separate me from the philosophy of Mises. I don't go lightly, either. The girls are very *responsive* to my presentation, which presents mathematical technique and methods as the realization of mathematical ideas, concerning whose origin I also inform them to some extent. It is a good sign that I feel a certain emptiness when the courses end and that I already look forward to the next lecture. *Pourvu que cela dure* . . . But I am after all only *remplaçant* for one year.

How are you getting along? Above all, how is Georgie? We have gotten together with the Voegelins often. It is such a pleasure to see a person of substance *as to both character and intelligence.*

Greet your family from both of us and best greetings to you

from your

A. Gurwitsch

Gurwitsch: *Kuhn's critique of Farber's editorial policy*
              (CAMBRIDGE, FEBRUARY 2, 1948)

Dear Friend,

I received a letter from Kuhn about a week ago, which asked me to let him know what I think of his critique of Farber's editorial policy. Then I received from Farber a copy of the letter that Krusé wrote to Kuhn as well as a copy of the letter from Farber to Kuhn. You have probably also been given copies of these pieces. I can only say that I am deeply disgusted by the correspondence of each. By whom more is hard to decide. A copy of my answer to Kuhn is enclosed.

I am in a hurry. Thus only a brief inquiry as to how you and yours are getting along. It was wonderful to see you again. Unfortunately, such an event is as seldom as it is wonderful.

With many greetings from house to house

Your

Aron Gurwitsch

Note: The letters between Helmut Kuhn and Aron Gurwitsch are not available for this edition. The "critique of Farber's editorial policy" refers to the article by P. S. Popov, "The Logic of Aristotle and Formal Logic," *PPR* 8 (1947–48): 1–22.

Schutz: *Whether Russian articles should be published (in* PPR*) at all*
           (NEW YORK, FEBRUARY 4, 1948)

Dear Friend,

Many thanks for your kind letter. I too have received letters from Kuhn and Farber in this boring affair. They are obviously the documents in question. Enclosed a copy of my answer to Kuhn. Sometimes I don't understand the world any more.

I too enjoyed myself with you and your wife. I would so like to have you closer to me.

I would like to call your attention to Hammerschmidt, *Whitehead's Philosophy of Time* (King's Crown Press). This very solid work contains a great deal that is new for me, but I don't know Whitehead very well. A new booklet, "Plato's Theory of Truth" by Heidegger, has appeared. Strauss[1] says it is the most brazen thing he has run into.

There is nothing new to report about us. George is doing quite well in school. I am not making progress in any respect and am often rather downcast.

All the best to you and your dear wife

Your
Alfred Schutz

1. Probably Leo Strauss of the New School.

Appendix: Schutz's letter to Kuhn of 1.25.1948.

Dear Friend Kuhn!

I want to answer your letter of January 16 in German, which up to now has been a unifying bond between us. I am actually very sorry that the first sign of life I have received from you in almost two years is not a personal report concerning your work and your family—I have only learned from public announcements that you have left North Carolina—but deals with the disagreeable polemic with Farber. I would have much preferred to hear how you, your wife and children are doing, how you have gotten settled at the new university, and what you are working on. As it is I will have to restrict myself to the matter you deal with in your letter.

It is not entirely new to me, since Farber has told me about your correspondence and asked for my opinion as to how he should react to it. Since you know how close I feel to you, it is surely not necessary to tell you that I have done my best (and I believe with success) to cool down Farber's strong reaction as much as possible. But you surely didn't write only to me, but also to other members of the editorial committee, and have thus given the exchange of letters a turn which will have to have consequences on which I will have no influence and on which I, as I openly admit, do not want to have an influence.

If I had made use of the postcard you sent me and had to tell you whether I agree with you, I would have answered with a simple "no." I prefer to give a detailed account of why I believe that you are wrong. The problem has many aspects.

The first question is whether an international philosophical journal of *standing* is to reject an article on Aristotle's logic by a member of the Russian Academy of the Sciences because it does not exhibit the requisite philosophical qualifications. I surely need not assure you that I read Aristotle differently from Mr. Popov. I also don't hesitate to tell you that right after the appearance of the Russian article I told Farber that we needed to pay more attention to the quality of the Russian articles. I have studied modern Russian philosophy intensively in the last few years in connection with my teaching, and I can bear witness to the fact that the article by Mr. Popov is of especially high quality when measured against Russian standards. I said: "when measured against Russian standards," and with that I think I have said all that I need to say concerning what I as a philosopher think about the quality of the article when measured against international standards. Thus we are left with the choice of either publishing no Russian articles or publishing articles like Popov's. And in that case I have to say that I am for publishing. The readers of our journal surely have the good judgment to assess this kind of thing, and it seems to me that for products like those of modern Russian philosophy, publication is the best critique.

There remains the question whether Russian articles should be published at all. I don't know why you assume that our journal does so in order to bring about a better understanding with Russia. Whether we are friends or opponents of Russia: in the contemporary situation it is more important than ever to get to know Russia, and for my part I can only say that I first came to a clear understanding of the tragedy of our situation from the study of Russian philosophy. (In a used book store in London I found an English translation of the textbook in Marxist philosophy for *graduate students* of the philosophical institute in Leningrad!)

Another problem is the selection of the papers to be printed. You complain that the acceptance of these papers did not occur in the normal manner, namely through the readers of the committee. This isn't possible because only a very few members know Russian. But as far as I know the selection is made before they are translated into English by Farber himself and by McGill, both of whom know Russian. I have no evidence that these two have not chosen the best out of the material at hand.

But the main problem seems to me to be the extent to which we European members of the board are justified in interfering with Farber in his basic policy. I don't believe that you have ever been in Buffalo and seen Farber at work. I have had this opportunity repeatedly. You can believe me when I say that the journal stands and falls with Farber, that its whole existence and dissemination, the respect that it enjoys and justifiably enjoys, are the exclusive result of his incredible devotion to this undertaking. In spite of all my reservations concerning the Russian article, I agreed with Farber when he set the policy that the journal was to have as broad a base as possible. After all, the South American articles didn't generally measure up to the *standing* of *Kantstudien*. But in America you can't have a journal with European philosophy alone, and I think that we all have to be more than thankful to Farber for creating a forum in which what you and I and many others of our circle understand to be genuine philosophy can be heard. Surely you will have no objections to an issue like the last one.

Thus, I regret that I cannot agree with you, and I sincerely look forward to future discussions with you as soon as possible concerning philosophical problems.

With best greetings also to your dear wife

Your

(Alfred Schutz)

Gurwitsch: *I have the contract from Wheaton which appoints me Associate
             Professor*
             (CAMBRIDGE, MAY 4, 1948)

Dear Friend,

You have always shared the miserable things in my life with me, so it is my duty not to withhold the good things. I have just received from Wheaton the contract which names me Associate Professor of Physics, for two years to start, with possible extension in case of mutual desire and reciprocal satisfaction. I will continue to live in Cambridge and *commute* three times per week. Teaching duties involve two courses in the first semester, three in the second: the normal load at Wheaton.

When I consider that it is a very Christian college, that the president is anything but friendly to foreigners, I cannot but count it as a real achievement. To be sure, the impossibility of finding physics teachers these days did a lot to help the things along. But aside from that, a whole series of colleagues and especially women colleagues undertook very decisive steps toward my being named. All in all I have the feeling of being somewhere where they know who I am. Curiously enough, some of the unmarried women, of a type which I will have to describe *viva voce* sometime, have taken a liking to me: probably the natural reaction of these women to a man, where they otherwise only know *boys*.

Last week I spoke at Wheaton in French on *l'existentialisme français* (good thing that Farber wasn't there). I was not satisfied by the reception. I had the feeling that the students (*seniors* from the Department of Romantic Languages) turned everything that I said to them into textbook materials. These eternal school girls turn the most vital problems and phenomena into textbook paper. They are unapproachable, something remains dead; in the best—or one might also say, worst—case it is pubertary excitability, that sterile nervousness which Max Weber has taught us to distinguish from passion. The thing that seemed to impress the four (women) professors who were present seemed to be the fact that I didn't have a single note card before me and still found my way back to the main theme after various necessary digressions.

I am currently separating out a section of my book which is to be a birthday article for Goldstein.[1] Hopefully Farber will print it very quickly, i.e., in less than a year.

Kahn spent a night here recently and mentioned that you are going to Europe again. We are going over next summer. I want to look things over and see what can be done there.

What's new with you? I hope that the status quo will stabilize with your boy. We spent one day in New York in order to have my wife examined by a gynecologist, after a doctor here had put us in a panic that gave us the worst weeks of our lives. In comparison with these worries all other things were simply insignificant. I needn't tell you that. In New York everything was explained. My wife will have to be seen by the New York doctor regularly; she has every chance of avoiding an operation. We were very happy after this visit to one of the foremost gynecologists. I have to rack my memory to come up with a situation in which I have been so happy. But I don't want to be presented with such a memento again so soon. Write to us about your summer plans so we can see how we can get together again. It's high time.

With best wishes to both of you

from your
Aron Gurwitsch

1. "Gelb-Goldstein's Concept of the 'Concrete' and 'Categorical' Attitude" (G1949).

Schutz: *I have managed to finish an essay on Sartre*
           (NEW YORK, MAY 19, 1948)

Dear Friend,

I still have to thank you for your so kind letter of the 4th, which was a real joy to me. I congratulate you wholeheartedly for the satisfying contract which you have made with your college, and I can well imagine that this is a load off your shoulders. I am also very happy that the scare that you had with your wife was obviously ungrounded. My wife, who did speak with you during your brief stay in New York, did not have the impression that there were any serious fears of the kind your letter hints at. But if your wife has to come to New York from time to time, I hope that she will get in touch with my wife and visit her occasionally.

Unfortunately, I myself must go to Europe again; in fact, I am leaving next week, so an enormous amount of work is piling up here. I will be visiting the same countries as on my earlier trips, and if you want to write to me direct, your messages will reach me with some reliability between mid-June and mid-July c/o Gaston-Dreyfus & Cie . . . . If you should need something from Paris, I am naturally at your service. According to plan I am to be back at the beginning of August, but I fear that my return will be delayed until the middle of August. I shall not go on vacation or even take a few days off in September. After my return I shall get in touch with you immediately, and it would be wonderful if we could once again share a *weekend* together here or meet somewhere.

I have a request: I did in fact manage to finish an essay for Farber, on Sartre and the problem of the alter-ego, before my departure.[1] I am sending him the essay today and will send you a copy separately tomorrow—to you not in your office as a member of the editorial board, but because in my eyes you and Wahl are the only competent readers of this essay. I would like to hear from you above all whether in your opinion my presentation of the Sartre theory is correct and what you have to say about my critical remarks. Farber, who encouraged this essay, will probably reject it, since it is too long, but in that case I intend to submit it to another journal. I would of course be especially delighted, should your schedule allow it, to receive your comments before my departure, which will be on Friday the 28th.

With all best greetings

                                              Your
                                              Alfred Schutz

---

1. "Sartre's Theory of the Alter Ego" (S1948).

Gurwitsch: *The displacement of consciousness to the body in Sartre and also in*
            Merleau-Ponty seems to me to turn things upside down
            (Cambridge, May 22, 1948)

Dear Friend,

Before you leave you should receive at least a *couple* of words about your article, for which I would like to begin by congratulating you. It is absolutely splendid, although excessively condensed, so that reading it is quite difficult.

When we get together I would like to discuss a few points with you. Now, with the rush of deadlines, only one or two remarks. Your Sartre presentation is, as far as I see, correct; I accept your critical remarks both with regard to the subject-object dialectic as well as with regard to the lack of intramundane inter-personal relations. Only one question: why didn't you dig into the question of the pre-ontological understanding? The problem seems to me to lie in *this* stratum, to the extent that it is a transcendental problem. It is to this alone that Sartre's discussion of the change in the world through the appearance of the other should relate. If the pre-ontological understanding is accepted, then his discussions have a rather scurrilous effect. I don't have the Sartre text so exactly in my memory any more, and thus cannot at the moment decide just how much of what you discuss relates to the pre-ontological understanding.

The whole circle, including Merleau-Ponty, is working on the subject-object dialectic. The relevant discussions of the latter have given me a whole series of indirect confirmations for my idea of unthematized implications.

I would suggest that we discuss the whole area undisturbed and extensively after your return, on the basis of Gaston Berger's second book.[1] His position builds a bridge from yours to mine. In spite of all my commitments with regard to questions concerning the transcendental ego, I must admit that his work has caused me to make certain revisions in a certain respect. But precisely for this reason I cannot accept such sentences as *"je suis ma main"* and the like. And the whole displacement of consciousness to the body in Sartre and also in Merleau-Ponty seems to me to turn things upside down. The correct question is of course: what does consciousness of my body look like?

Please excuse these rather disordered aphoristic remarks, about which I real-ize that they are more day-dreams *en marge* of your fine essay than that they genuinely engage it. Concerning the latter more in person. Also more in person about the fact that I shall probably accept the offer that Brandeis University has made to me. I don't recall whether I have written to you about it. For a variety of reasons it would seem to deserve preference to Wheaton. Among other reasons, because while I will go there initially in mathematics, I have reason to believe that in a few years I could join the philosophy department which is to be established, and even have a more or less decisive word to say concerning its establishment. It is also significantly better financially, and in addition it would save me the rather considerable efforts of commuting back and forth. We have devoted much of the last few days to this problem. Basically, all of my acquaintances advise me to accept Brandeis. The exception is Richard v. Mises and his circle. And there the Jewish complex seems to bear pretty grotesque fruits.

If the pressures of your business in Paris should leave you enough time to discover a usable Leibniz edition, I would be very thankful if you would buy it for me. If possible also Brunschvieg, *La connaissance physique et l'expérience humaine.*

Thanks to Brandeis we will probably spend the summer of next year in France. For me it is really quite important to have personal contact with persons who work in our area once again. I often ask myself if I won't go crazy in this total isolation here. Berger wrote some time ago and once again warned against returning. The old insoluble problem, almost as insoluble as in your opinion the plurality of transcendental egos in phenomenology.

I wish you a good trip and not another disappointing one. Please give my greetings to everyone who thinks of me in Paris. If your time allows, why not get in touch with Mme. Monique Picard . . . . She is a student of mine who awaits my return just as impatiently as I await such students. It would appear that her wish has a greater chance of being fulfilled before mine, at least in America.

Best greetings and wishes. Till we meet again, all the best from house to house

Your

Aron Gurwitsch

P.S.: How right you are with "magic power" *du regard!* What level does that refer to? On the transcendental level it would make sense, though very different from Sartre's. On the mundane level it is unintelligible: if the other relates to me intentionally, that makes me his object in the same sense in which my hand becomes an object for me when I contemplate it, or one of my acts if I reflect on it. Where is the limitation of my freedom?

What an idea, to freeze interpersonal relations on the level of being caught in the act! *That* is what is behind the *regard!* And so it goes, if I objectivate the other and he becomes my tool. You are *so* right!

1. *Recherches sur les conditions de la connaissance* (Paris, 1941).

Gurwitsch: *My dear friend, I am enclosing a biographical sketch*
                   (CAMBRIDGE, NOVEMBER 9, 1948)

Dear Friend,

I think that the enclosed letter *will do.* As I told you on the telephone: it never hurts to receive an *offer.* After having slept on it one night, I still think so, *only more so.* When the *offer* is there, one can see how things are and act in the way that seems advantageous from all possible points of view. Even if I should decide to stay here, the offer will only raise my prestige and could have all sorts of other good consequences: much faster promotion, for example, and more definitive commitments with reference to the future *graduate school,* etc. Since I am so little the "glamour boy," the confirmation of my academic prestige through an offer from another school can only raise my standing. Thus, I think that one can pursue the matter in peace, all the more since, it would appear, I do not at all appear as an applicant and as one looking for a position. *Wenn* the *offer* comes (*wenn* = *if* and also = *when*), I will see how things look and decide. Since I am writing that to *you,* that is just what I mean.

I have a bad conscience concerning one point. I know the problems you are burdened with and just what your work load is. That you receive additional work from me—especially since it doesn't concern "vital" matters—that, dear friend, is a bit of a weight on my soul. I only hope that it isn't too much work for you.

Aside from all else, I am very thankful to you for my acquaintance with Albert Salomon. We were able to exchange only a few words, that is just the way things are at such gatherings. The celebration was fine but very tiring. First, to stand for almost two hours, not knowing when to talk, and then having to speak English, and the crowd—all that can make one nervous. But I am happy that things were as they were. The tenor of all the talks fit Goldstein, who—say what you will—is a great stimulus.

We were so happy to have seen you, if only so briefly, and even though what you had to tell us was so sad. Keep us informed, also concerning unpleasant developments, should they come. It is much more than the interest of friends that we take in everything that concerns you. Both of us always have the feeling *mea res agitur.* And what would things be worth if your *res* were not *nostra res.*

We will let you know about our next visit in advance, so that we can have more time with each other.

With sincere greetings and all wishes

Your

Aron Gurwitsch

Supplement: The official letter (I) which Schutz requested for the New School for Social Research, including Gurwitsch's *curriculum vitae* (II) and list of publications (III).
The original is in English.

I. Gurwitsch's letter (November 9, 1948)

My dear friend Schütz,

Thanking you again for your kind cable, I am enclosing a biographical sketch and a list of publications.

As you know, an article entitled "Gelb-Goldstein's concept of 'categorical' and 'concrete' attitude and the phenomenology of ideation" has been accepted by *Philosophy and Phenomenological Research*. I have the intention to write in a not too distant future an article on "Qualitative multiplicities" and one on 'James' concept of the object of thought and Husserl's concept of the noema." The latter article would be an amplification of No. 22[1] in the enclosed list.

All the mentioned articles are more or less closely connected with the book to be entitled "The Field of Consciousness" on which I am working now. About one half of this book is already in its final state. In my estimation it will comprise about 300–400 printed pages.

May I also mention that, while still living in France, I began to write a book on the phenomenology of perception. A certain part of the material has been absorbed in the book on the "Field of Consciousness." There is, however, still enough material left, which I could use for a book on the constitution of the perceptual world. After having finished the book on which I am working now, I have the intention to take up again my studies on perception proper.

Finally I call your attention to Nos. 5 and 6 in the list. Especially No. 5 is in some connection with the studies on Max Weber, which I pursued when I was preparing my "Habilitation" at the University of Berlin. The studies in question concerned the phenomenological clarification of some of Weber's fundamental concepts and of the phenomenon of human *"Miteinandersein."*[2] When in 1933 I came to France, it appeared to me quite inopportune to pursue my studies on Weber any longer, because, in the first place, there was at that time no interest whatever in France for studies of that sort and, in the second place, even the groundwork for phenomenology had to be laid. The *"Meditations Cartésiennes"* notwithstanding, Husserl was almost unknown in France. To find some contact with French academic life, I had to choose topics for which some interest could be expected.

Thanking you once more for your kindness and hoping that everything is well with you, I am with best regards to you and your wife

Yours
Aron Gurwitsch

1. No. 22: "On the Object of Thought" (G1947). The topics mentioned later become chapters in *The Field of Consciousness:* Bergson's concept of "qualitative multiplicities" (p. 140) and the James-Husserl comparison (p. 184).

2. No. 5: "Zur Bedeutung der Prädestinationslehre für die Ausbildung des kapitalistischen Geistes" (G1933a). No. 6: Review of Leo Strauss, *Spinoza's Critique of Religion* (G1933b). This is the only mention of the unpublished habilitation, "Die mitmenschliche Begegnung in der Milieuwelt" (G1976/G1979).

II. *Curriculum vitae*

I was born January 17, 1901 in Wilna. Since 1946 I have been a citizen of the United States.

My family left Wilna in 1906 and moved to Danzig. There I attended the Humanistic Gymnasium from which I graduated in 1919.

From 1919 to 1928 I studied in the universities of Berlin, Frankfurt, and Göttingen. My studies concentrated upon philosophy including psychology, mathematics and physics. Very soon I came in contact with Husserl's phenomenology which since then has been in the center of my interests. In 1928 I passed the doctoral examination *summa cum laude* in Göttingen. My thesis was on philosophy; it concerned relations between phenomenology and Gestalt theory (No. 1 in the list of publications). The two other fields in which I was examined were mathematics and physics.

From 1928 to 1929 I lived in Göttingen as assistant to the late Professor M. Geiger. In 1929 I married and moved to Berlin, after the Prussian Ministry of the Sciences, the Arts and Public Instruction had granted me a research fellowship in order to enable me to prepare my admission as "Privatdozent" to the University of Berlin.

Because of the political events in 1933, I left Germany and moved to Paris. From the fall of 1933 to the spring of 1940 I was attached to, and delivered lectures at the "Institut d'Histoire des Sciences" (Sorbonne). In 1939 I was appointed Research Fellow by the "Caisse Nationale de la Recherche Scientifique," an organization belonging to the French Republic, with the understanding that I was to continue my lectures at the mentioned institute of the Sorbonne.

In 1940 I came to the United States, having been appointed Visiting Lecturer in Philosophy at the Johns Hopkins University. In 1942 I moved to Cambridge, Mass., where during the following year I lived as a Research Fellow of the American Philosophical Society. From 1943 to 1946 I was Instructor in Physics at Harvard University. For the year 1946/47 I received another grant in aid of research from the American Philosophical Society and also one from the American Committee for Displaced Scholars, Writers and Artists to enable me to advance the work on a book to be entitled "The Field of Consciousness." From 1947 to 1948 I was Lecturer in Mathematics at Wheaton College (Norton, Mass.). In 1948 Wheaton College promoted me to an Associate Professorship. At the same time Brandeis University, which was in the stage of being organized, approached me and offered me an Assistant Professorship in Mathematics. It was pointed out to me that the salaries at Brandeis University being comparatively high, the university could not afford for budgetary reasons to offer me an Associate Professorship which would have entailed a still higher salary. Still the promise was made to me that at the completion of my first three-year term I would be promoted. Because of the substantial difference in salary, I persuaded myself to resign the Associate Professorship at Wheaton College and accept the Assistant Professorship at Brandeis University. Since 1948 I have taught Mathematics at Brandeis University and have also given the following courses in Philosophy: Logic, Classics in Philosophy, Selected Advanced Texts in Modern Philosophy.

I am a member of the following learned societies:
1. American Association for the Advancement of Science.
2. American Philosophical Association
3. International Phenomenological Society. I am also a member of the council of this society.
4. Mind Association
5. History of Science Society.

I am a member of the editorial board of *Philosophy and Phenomenological Research,* a periodical edited by the International Phenomenological Society.

III. *List of Publications* [See the bibliography, G1929 through G1947.]

Schutz: *"It was Husserl who urged me in 1935 to meet Gurwitsch"*
           (NEW YORK, NOVEMBER 12, 1948)

Dear Friend,

Many thanks for your very fine letter. The enclosed lines were very carefully weighed with Salomon, in order that we do not damage through *overemphasis.* You have to know Riezler!

Best regards as always

Yours
Schutz

Supplement: Letter of 11.12.48. from Schutz to Kurt Riezler, Dean of the Graduate Faculty of the New School in 1948. The original is in English.

Dear Dr. Riezler,

Dr. Albert Salomon has asked me to inform you of the curriculum and the publications of my close friend Dr. Aron Gurwitsch.

In order to give you full particulars I invited Gurwitsch to send me complete data of his career and his past and present work. Please find here enclosed the original of his answer.

It was Edmund Husserl who urged me in 1935 to meet during my forthcoming trip to Paris Dr. Gurwitsch, whom he considered to be one of his most promising students. I was immediately fascinated by his personality, his erudition and the originality of his philosophical thought. Since then I had the privilege to follow the development of his work. I read great parts of his forthcoming book and am deeply convinced that his theory of the field of consciousness is one of the few genuine achievements in the realm of phenomenological philosophy which continues the work of Husserl.

I shall always be gladly at your disposal for additional information. With kindest personal regards,

Sincerely yours
Alfred Schutz

Schutz: *Riezler is very interested, since you were a friend of Wertheimer*
(NEW YORK, NOVEMBER 25, 1948)

Dear Friend,

Only a word to tell you that Riezler has requested "some of your writings," which he wants to study, from me via Salomon. I immediately sent him everything of yours I possess.

Salomon assures me that Riezler is very interested, especially since he told Riezler that you were a friend of Wertheimer, who thought very highly of you. Since Wertheimer was also a friend of Riezler, and his judgment has a great influence on everyone in the school, it would perhaps be good if you would write me a letter in English, which I could pass on, in which you tell the story of your relations to and memories of Wertheimer. Could I have this letter at my house on Monday? Salomon will be visiting me on Monday evening.

All the best to you and your wife

Your
Alfred Schutz

Gurwitsch: *I was introduced to Wertheimer by my teacher Adhemar Gelb*
                (CAMBRIDGE, NOVEMBER 27, 1948)

Dear Friend,

Many, many thanks for your so very kind letter. I think that the enclosed letter is roughly what you had in mind and will serve its purpose.

If I am correctly informed, there are very good and close relations between Riezler and Goldstein. But it may be that these relations are disturbed on account of an unpleasant affair at the New School concerning Goldstein. I am not sure of this; I don't even suspect it, since I have no evidence; I only assume it as "compossible" with the general situation. For this reason I haven't mentioned Goldstein. Mr. Salomon—please give him my warm and cordial greetings—might be able to tell you how things stand with Riezler and Goldstein. If the relations are good, mentioning Goldstein to Riezler would perhaps be appropriate. I of course can't judge that and leave it up to Mr. Salomon.

One more point. Do you think it is opportune to inform Felix Kaufmann? I have not done so, and would only do so if I had reason to expect that it would help our project. I have a disinclination to discuss hypothetical situations, especially hypothetical situations of a personal or half-personal nature, with other than very intimate friends.

And now "in German": How are you and yours? Evi? Georgie? It is a bit disappointing that you don't mention them.

Best regards from both of us to all of you

Yours
Aron Gurwitsch

Supplement: The letter requested by Schutz concerning Gurwitsch's relations with Wertheimer. The original is in English.

Dear Friend,

Thanking you for your letter of November 25, I should like to tell you something about my connections with the late Max Wertheimer. In 1925 or 1926, as far as I remember, I was introduced to him by my teacher, the late Adhemar Gelb. At that time, I was working on my doctoral dissertation which was later published under the title *Phänomenologie der Thematik und das reine Ego*. Wertheimer was much interested in and very sympathetic towards my endeavors to bring out and develop relationships between Gestalt theory and Phenomenology. He not only encouraged me to work along the mentioned lines but was also extremely helpful in having my dissertation published in *Psychologische Forschung*.

Our connections continued throughout the following years. Since, however, we always lived in different cities, our contact was of an occasional rather than sustained nature. Whenever I saw him, he showed interest in my work and also appreciation, especially of my presentation of Gestalt theory in the article "Quelques aspects et quelques développements de la théorie de la forme" published in the *Journal de Psychologie Normale et Pathologique*.[1] Between 1933 and 1940, when I was living in Paris, I had not seen him. When in 1940 I came to this country, I paid him a visit in New Rochelle. Wertheimer had me tell at great length about the work in which I was engaged at that time and about my projects for the future. Again I found the same vivid interest and sympathy which I had always encountered when I had had discussions with him. As usual, he raised most penetrating questions in the straightforward manner which was so characteristic of him, questions which went right to the core of the matter and were of such valuable help in clarifying the points at issue. When I came to New York from Baltimore and later from Cambridge, I seldom failed to avail myself of the opportunity to see Wertheimer and to benefit from his comments and remarks.

I should like to add that in addition to the intellectual and scientific stimulation which I derived from Wertheimer, I feel indebted to him from a personal and human point of view both for the help which he extended to me in Germany and the same efforts he made on my behalf in this country towards enabling me to establish myself.

In the hope that all is well with you and your family and that I shall hear soon again from you

Cordially yours

Aron Gurwitsch

1. G1936b.

Schutz: *The faculty has decided to name Löwith*
          (NEW YORK, DECEMBER 12, 1948)

Dear Friend,

Salomon just reported to me that the faculty has decided to name Löwith. This was preceded by an extraordinarily positive report, made by Riezler in the most friendly way, concerning you and your writings. But they decided that phenomenology is already adequately represented in the faculty by Kaufmann (I am of course in sociology) and that this direction should not be strengthened. These are Salomon's words, since I was of course not present at the meeting. I regret this decision (since I have no reason to feel sorry for the faculty) merely because, as you know, nothing would have pleased me more than having you in New York. On the other hand, you are much better off where you are now with regard to security and finances, and not in a dead end here—to say nothing of an apartment and similar problems. And in the future it can only be advantageous that your candidacy was taken seriously, thoroughly considered and discussed. If you did not have the position you now have, this letter would have been difficult, but as things are the episode can only have, if any, good consequences. We are both unfortunately accustomed to having to live with what passes for philosophical sense.

As I hear, at the last moment Fink had difficulties in coming here. Many believe that they are *self-made* and that he has gotten stage fright—which sounds like him.

As to me, my life has not become more simple. May both you and your wife sustain your friendship and affection for us in the new year.

Sincerely

Your
Alfred Schutz

Gurwitsch: *The funny thing is that precisely I have to combat this tendency to the formal*
(CAMBRIDGE, DECEMBER 17, 1948)

Dear Friend,

Many thanks for your letter and even more for your friendly efforts on my behalf. I almost expected the result: I was almost prepared to hear that phenomenology is sufficiently represented by Kaufmann. You are right in much of what you have to say about that. And yet I regret the result. If an offer had come, I would probably have accepted and not merely used it.

The reasons? Some are obvious: the prospect of συμφιλοσοφεῖν with you would have tempted me very much, just as on the other hand nothing would have held me to my intellectual isolation here. The *undergraduates* are beginning to get me down. They aren't worse here than elsewhere, indeed better. Better with regard to formal talent, at any rate. But they also have talent *only* for the formal—and nothing more. The *genre* makes its appearance in the form of intellectual cunning and slyness. If one doesn't slow them down, in a few years they will have figured out everything. The funny thing is that it is I of all people (officially mathematician and logician, unofficially and in reality intensively interested in the *formal* side of consciousness in the well-known way) should have to do something against this tendency to the formal.

In other respects too there would be a lot to say about the university, things

that can only be *said* and not written. A great deal of explication and even explicitation would be required, too much to trust to a letter and not make the letter
into a memorandum. I can take the literary scene only in small doses: I prefer the
dose "0." The good thing here is that I have a pretty fair amount of time for my
πενηλοπεῖν—to resolutely make a verb out of the πενηλοπος, as you so nicely put
it. But don't worry. Things are looking up, if only slowly. The book is beginning
to take a form that I like, the form over or under which I can put my name. I am
just now revising the chapter on perception. I am not adding much that is new,
merely supplementing some things and grouping things better.

I am sorry that your life won't become "simpler." I know only too well what
this "simple" formulation makes transparent. By God, your problems are not
self-made—so there is nothing left to do but to wish and to hope. How good it
would be if all problems were solvable! But the real problems aren't—neither in
philosophy nor otherwise.

So there is nothing to do but wish you a "simplification" in the new year, and
to wish that the wish will be fulfilled.

With best greetings to you and yours from both of us

Your
Aron Gurwitsch

Schutz: *I have chosen the sociology of language for my lecture course at the New*
          School
          (NEW YORK, FEBRUARY 4, 1949)

Dear Friend,

My life is once again in great confusion, since one of my bosses has suddenly
died.[1] The changes in operations that that has caused have taken even more of
my time than was the case, and to a certain extent make my future prospects even
more uncertain than was previously the case.

I think that I have already told you that I am engaged in quite advanced
negotiations which will put me in a closer avocational relationship with the New
School starting in the Fall, but this time it is to be paid. I will have to give two
lecture courses per semester, and have chosen the sociology of language for this.

This brings me to a request: I think that you own the French collection
Psychologie du langage, which was published by Alcan and contains some 15 to
20 essays of various kinds, including essays by Cassirer, Sapir, Goldstein, etc.,
which were originally published in the *Journal de Psychologie*.[2] If I am not mistaken, the editor is Henri Delacroix. Could you lend me this volume—it is out of
print in France and not to be found. Do you perhaps have the two books by
Otto Jespersen, 1) *Language,* 2) *Mankind, Nation and Individual?* I would be

very thankful if you could lend them to me too, since they are out of print. But their loan would only be of use to me if I could keep them until Fall.

At Albert Salomon's I recently became acquainted with your friend Goldstein, who is truly a remarkable man. He told me that his book on *"language"* appeared a few weeks ago and invited me to write a review for *Social Research,* and I have made a corresponding request.

A propos Salomon: He told me in a slightly hurt tone that a letter which he wrote to you had remained unanswered. You might drop him a line.

I hope that you and your dear wife are well; I would like to hear a bit about your personal well-being.

With best greetings from house to house

Your
Alfred Schutz

1. Schutz began working for the banking house Reitler & Co. in 1929, and continued to work for it in America.
2. Edited by Henri Delacroix. Cf. Gurwitsch's review, G1935.

Gurwitsch: *We are leaving for Europe on July 7*
                 (Cambridge, February 11, 1949)

Dear Friend,

I sent the *Psychologie du Langage* to you yesterday, and you should keep it as long as you need it. I have also enclosed my review of the book (which appeared in the *Revue Philosophique*), which might be useful to you. I don't know whether you have my review. If so, please send my copy back; otherwise keep it too as long as you can use it.

Your personal news, especially what is between the lines, is not very good. I hope that you are guilty of *par un excès de pessimisme,* and I hope for developments that are in accord with your own wishes.

There is nothing new here. How are things with you? We would like to hear how Georgie is doing.

Will you be going to Europe this year? We are leaving on July 7 and plan to stay in Paris for two months. I also want to go to Louvain.

I will write to Salomon in the near future. Actually, his letter hardly called for an answer.

I am in a hurry. So I must leave it with best greetings

Your
Aron Gurwitsch

Gurwitsch: *Unfortunately, we cannot receive you in the style you were accustomed to*
(PARIS, JULY 17, 1949)

Dear Friend,

We arrived in Paris early this morning. Our address is: Cité Universitaire, Maison de Cuba, Paris.

There is also a telephone. I haven't discovered the number yet, but don't want to hold up this letter until I have discovered it.

On about August 10 I will go to Louvain for a couple of days. The date is not firm, also depends on your plans. I might go to Cologne in order to see Fink. If I do so, then from Louvain. Otherwise we plan to stay in Paris.

We hope that your schedule will allow you to see us. Unfortunately we can't receive you in the style you were accustomed to in the Square du Port Royal.[1] The one day in Paris provides the occasion for reflecting on curious phenomena of the experience of time. But more about that personally.

Best greetings and, hopefully, until we meet again soon

Your
Aron Gurwitsch

1. The Gurwitsches lived at 2, Square du Port Royal until the outbreak of war forced them to move to Gif-sur-Yvette in Paris.

4
Oh, Holy Mannheim!
(January 26, 1950–March 16, 1951)

Gurwitsch worked on one of the "final" versions of *The Field of Consciousness;* Schutz offered the first course in sociology at the New School, "Sociology of Language" (SG 2.4.49) and, as the successor to Felix Kaufmann, a course on "The Methodology of the Social Sciences" (SG 3.16.51). This short chapter presents an extraordinarily productive phase in which one tunnel topic after another was thematized.

The problem of the nexus of life-world and consciousness was specified: what is the connection between the typicality of the life-world (as pre-predicative structures) and the eidos (the eidetic core of perceptual consciousness)? For example, the color names of the Lithuanians: they have different names for "gray" geese and "gray" horses, and lack a unitary name which encompasses the gray of all gray objects. The same is true for other colors. Is the eidos "gray" thus bound to the situative object, and eidetics, as Karl Mannheim asserted,[1] tied to situations? In his discussion of type and eidos in Husserl (S1959b), Schutz later developed more radically the question of whether one must not reject eidetics completely in questions dealing with contexts in the life-world (SG 12.20.58).

Gurwitsch viewed the decisive limitations of eidetics in terms of the Platonic theory of ideas and rejected its implicit claim that *everything* can be idealized and formalized: "contemporary research into the foundations of mathematics" has been "poisoned" by this. He devoted his attention to distinct dimensions of "purely qualitative order" and to the possibility of rationalizing them. To rationalize a region of the life-world is to "relate it to an eidetic order" (GS 2.4.50).

There still doesn't seem to be a bridge between the two positions, unless the discussion of the following theses leads to a new direction:

1. A *thesis concerning space* from Schutz (GS 7.27.50) was hinted at, but remained undeveloped: the relativity to the concrete situation, thus the problem of standpoint and the origin of life-worldly orientation, would receive a radically new formulation if originary givenness lies not in the *hic* (null point of the experiencing ego) but in the *illic* of the other.

2. Gurwitsch's *thesis concerning negation* (GS 12.17.50): Koyré's remark that the proposition "The sum of the angles in a triangle is not equal to the color red" is a true proposition caused Gurwitsch sleepless nights. Gurwitsch offered "normal negation" as the solution. Schutz wanted to remove the problem from the context of predication and refer it to the relevance structures of the pre-predicative life-world. Whitehead's problematic realms of incompatibility (SG 1.15.51) could thus be reformulated.[2]

Parallel to this discovery of long-term research perspectives ("tunnel themes"), the institutional ties between the two friends were clarified: Gurwitsch moved from mathematics to philosophy at Brandeis, where he was chairman of the philosophy department until he went to the New School. Schutz spoke of "our school" (SG 3.16.51): his colleagues in sociology were Carl Mayer and Albert Salomon, in philosophy Dorion Cairns and, after 1953, Hans Jonas. Alvin Johnson gave Schutz the job of building up both departments, but the always precarious financial position of the "school" was topped only by the capriciousness of some colleagues. This chapter sketches a colorful picture of this academic landscape.

1. "We always seem confronted with a continual transition from empirical facts to the intuition of essences." Karl Mannheim, "Die Soziologie des Wissens vom Standorte der modernen Phänomenologie" (1925), in *Wissenssoziologie,* ed. K. Wolff (Berlin-Neuwied, 1964), 362.
2. Cf. in this context the editor's dissertation, *The Structure of Social Inconsistencies* (The Hague: Martinus Nijhoff, 1970), which relates the constitution of social types to social "realms of incompatibility."

Schutz: *Would even eidetics be tied to situations? Oh, holy Mannheim!*
          (NEW YORK, JANUARY 26, 1950)

Dear Friend,

I am just now reading in Jespersen's *Language*[1] (p. 429): "The Lithuanians like many primitive tribes have many special, but no common names for various colors: one word for gray in speaking about wool and geese, one about horses, one about cattle, one about the hair of men and some animals, and in the same way for other colors. (J. Schmidt, *Kritik der Sonantentheorie,*[2] 37)."

At this point a whole series of questions arise: a) Is that true? I believe that you speak Lithuanian. b) If so, are all Lithuanians "Schus" or was Goldstein's "Schu" a Lithuanian?[3] c) Doesn't this resolve our difference of opinion concerning the special eidetic character of color names? Or would even eidetics be tied to situations[4] and therefore be explained in a "sociology of knowledge" manner? Oh, holy Mannheim!

Or: Are Lithuanian color names—I don't know anything else in the literature which deals with colors—like Arabian camel names?

You see that our discussion continues to stimulate me. How nice it would be to speak with you! But the prospects that Felix Kaufmann's position will be filled at all are minimal!

Sincerely

Your
Alfred Schutz

1. Otto Jespersen, *Language: Its Nature, Development and Origin* (London: G. Allen, 1968[2]; first ed. 1922).
2. Johannes Schmidt, *Kritik der Sonantentheorie* (Weimar, 1855). Dr. Dogil [Bielefeld] reports: "The *Sonantentheorie* concerns the discovery of reduced vowels in Indo-European languages, mainly in Greek."
3. Schutz probably meant to write "Schn," a reference to Schneider, one of Gold-

stein's famous patients who is mentioned repeatedly by Merleau-Ponty in his *Phenomenology of Perception*.

4. Cf. "Type and Eidos in Husserl's Late Philosophy" (S1959b) and Charles Hartshorne, "Husserl and the Social Structure of Immediacy," in Marvin Farber, ed. 219–230.

Gurwitsch: *Along with the problem of thematization, the Platonic problem is poisoning contemporary research into the foundations of mathematics* (CAMBRIDGE, FEBRUARY 4, 1950)

Dear Friend,

Many thanks for your letter. No, I don't speak Lithuanian, and know very little about this language other than that it is one of the oldest languages spoken in Europe and is the closest to Sanskrit of all existing Indo-European languages. Up to 1918 it was pretty much restricted to the peasantry, moving closer and closer to extinction, until it became the official language with the founding of the state. One of the last to be familiar with it as a living language and to know its folk literature was Herder. Since then it has been little more than an object for linguists. Much the same is true of Lettic, which is fairly closely related to Lithuanian, and of Estonian, which is related to Finnish and belongs to the Ugro-Altaic (Mongolian) family.

I am prepared to grant the claims made by Jespersen and J. Schmidt. But it seems to me that even these claims fail to prove what is inferred from them. What they do prove is one of my theses: that colors are originally bound to objects—very plausible in light of the great age of the language. They also prove that the categorical attitude is not necessary for the purposes of everyday life and poetry (Lithuanian folk poetry is quite beautiful). One can say that at the time when their language was fixed there was no necessity for the Lithuanians to reserve words for color categories as such. There is an analogy to this in Western languages: even for us, the signs for odors are by and large tied to the objects which have these odors. This does not prove that we cannot assume the categorical attitude with respect to odors, just as the unique aspects of the Lithuanian language do not prove that the Lithuanians can't assume the categorical attitude with respect to colors. ·

As I write this it occurs to me that it wouldn't be an altogether simple matter for me to have explained to one of my father's raftsmen, whom I knew in my childhood, just what I wanted were I to ask him to assume the categorical attitude with respect to colors. To this extent the "holy Mannheim" is in a certain sense right.

When I speak of the eidetic character of color names, I mean such names as have a genuinely general meaning. The behavior of those suffering from amnesia of color names is characteristically different from that of patients suffering from amnesia of names of objects. In the latter case, reciting the correct names along with other names is a great help to the patient. He picks out the correct name without fail and rejects all false names. A person suffering from amnesia of color names, on the other hand, doesn't react to the correct name at all, repeats the word and can't get any hint at all from it. In the one case, the word is "forgotten" (i.e., forgotten in certain circumstances; in others it is used promptly), but it has a sense. In the other case the word doesn't mean anything any more. Thus, there must be a difference in principle between "red" and "clock" applied to pocket, wrist, wall clocks, etc.

It seems to me that the reason is that there is an eidetic order among colors, i.e., a *purely qualitative order* (independent of the object which is colored): this is, if you leave out the black-white series, the color circle given by E. Hering.[1] Similarly, there is an eidetic order among musical tones too (I would also mention the difference between musical tones and noise; the history of the theory of noise is very interesting): the scale series, which is repeated in the various octaves. But there is no such order among clocks, tables, pocket watches, etc. But there is one among numbers, in geometry.

This brings us to the problems which are behind my theory. There are the problems of the Platonic *Parmenides,* which are taken up again in the discussions of the first books of the *Metaphysics.* The question whether there are Ideas of any and everything runs through the entire history of Platonism. Husserl stirred it up again with his "definite manifold."[2] Without knowing it, he renewed Malebranche's problem, who as a *Cartesian* asserted that the soul is *plus familière* to us than the body, but that there is only a science of body (geometry), but not of the soul. Eidetic psychology and phenomenology is an answer to that. Along with the problem of thematization, the Platonic problem mentioned above is poisoning all of contemporary research into the foundations of mathematics (Gödel's proposition, according to which the completeness of a mathematical system cannot be proven with the means of the system for which it holds).

I cannot yet speak of these backgrounds in what I publish, since I am not yet far enough along. I cannot talk about it except to you and Voegelin, since everything is still much too vague and preliminary for myself. If only I have enough time left to get that far; or if I had a student who could continue where I have to stop. But in this country this last wish is very "Platonic." In the final analysis it is a matter of clarifying the *ratio.* When and to what extent is a realm to be rationalized, i.e., to be referred to an eidetic order? If you want to speak metaphysically, I am prepared to do so and simply ask: where does the world begin to be rational? The astonishing thing is that the Parmenides problem has reappeared in neurology, without Gelb and Goldstein knowing anything about it.

It would really be nicer if we could get together more often. I once again have a great desire to see you. How are things otherwise?

Best greetings from all of us to you and yours

Your
Aron Gurwitsch

P.S. Your obituary for Kaufmann, for which many thanks, gives a clear picture of the man, of the framework in which he worked, and of the manner in which he filled it. The clean contours of his thought and the integrity of his will speak out of your lines. Within the limits which he set for himself or which were set for him, he proved himself. Can one say more than this as the last word concerning his life?[3]

1. E. Hering, *Grundzüge der Lehre vom Lichtsinn* (Berlin, 1920).
2. Cf. the classical studies by Julius Stenzel, *Zahl und Gestalt bei Plato und Aristoteles* (1924). Concerning Husserl: cf. §131 in *Formal and Transcendental Logic*.
3. "Felix Kaufmann: 1895–1949," S1950b.

Gurwitsch: *The* hic-illic *problem goes round and round in my head*
(Los Angeles, July 27, 1950)

Dear Friend,

Please excuse the curious paper which I am using and the even more curious envelope: it is all that I have here.

Ever since we parted, the *hic-illic* problem has gone round and round in my head. I think that I have now understood it. You think: all positions in space which are originarily given are *illic*. *Hic,* on the other hand, is not originarily given, at least not in the same manner as *illic*.[1] That means: the origin of all spatial orientation is "disadvantaged" [*benachteiligt*]—in contrast to "privileged" [*ausgezeichnet*]. Every originary *illic* is referred to a non-originary *hic*. Is that how you understand the problem? (On Saturday I understood it in a different, *probably* false manner.)

If that is your problem, I believe that my "theory of marginal awareness" provides an answer, at least attempts to. After all, this is my thesis: whatever might be my theme, marginally I am aware of 1) the flow of my experiences, or better, of a certain segment surrounding the "actual now"; 2) my body; 3) a certain sector of the outer world. 2) and 3) together yield: my situation in the external world. It seems to me that the solution to the *hic* problem lies here. You are right: the *hic* is given in a different manner than is any *illic*, "privileged" *and* "disadvantaged," "privileged" on account of the continual awareness of the body as situated in the world.

We must talk about all this. The sooner, the better. Please excuse these scribbled remarks. You see how preoccupied with this I am, because of the "marginal awareness" if for no other reason. (This will be the topic of a small book.[2]) Your problem is *very* important. One of the criteria for my theory is whether it can deal with your problem.

I hope we can get together soon and talk about this in peace, in peace and at length. For now

  Best greetings

Your

Aron

1. Cf. the discussion of this problem between Schutz and Fink in the appendix to "The Problem of Transcendental Intersubjectivity in Husserl" (in S1964a). Schutz only mentions this "thesis about space" here, and it is not developed further. But cf. Husserl's fragment "Grundlegende Untersuchungen zum Phänomenologischen Ursprung der Räumlichkeit der Natur" in Farber, 307–325.

2. Cf. *Marginal Consciousness* (G1985).

Schutz: *Why do we still say "Sie" to one another? I won't go along with this nonsense any longer*
          (NEW YORK, OCTOBER 4, 1950)

Dear Friend,

I hope that you and your dear wife had a good summer and have returned home rejuvenated and strengthened. Actually, I had hoped to see you here in September as you came through New York, but I heard from Salomon that you had returned home much earlier than I. Salomon told me that you are finished with your book.[1] Before I wholeheartedly congratulate you I need your confirmation that this doesn't signify a new beginning of the absolutely last, once-and-for-all final revision ("all I have to do is re-work two chapters"). At any rate, you seem to have had a fruitful summer and I am glad for that.

We had a fine time, and after four years the five and a half weeks have shown me that one has to have a vacation. I too got a lot of work done. The essay "Making Music Together" is finished, as well as an 11,000-word monster, "Choosing among Projects of Action," which surely has no chance of being published in light of its length, although I believe that some of the things in it are pretty good. It deals with Husserl's problematic and open possibilities, and related themes in Bergson and Leibniz, as well as a theory of "ability" [*Theorie der "Vermöglichkeit"*] (*Potestativität*).[2]

And one more thing happened to me, something which shouldn't happen at my age and which one can only blushingly whisper to a good friend as a sweet secret: "I am with book." I have two chapters finished, roughly 27,000 words, perhaps a fifth of the whole, which given my way of life will need six or seven years for completion. One deals with the types of relevance, based on Carneades (Sextus Empiricus),[3] the other with the grasp of time, space, and body in the natural attitude. The whole thing is to have the title "The World beyond Question" or "The World as Taken for Granted" and be a phenomenology of the natural attitude (and simultaneously of the "relatively natural view of the world").[4] As soon as Ilse has time, she will type this first draft—and it is no more than that—and then it is to be submitted to you in all of its imperfection with the request that you tell me whether I should continue with my efforts. Such things, my dear friend, I write only for you as the only ideal reader, who knows not only the problems but also my personal circumstances, since I don't know anyone else who is so close to me in this double respect: philosophically *and* humanly. But I will only show you what I have written so far when your manuscript has gone to the printer. It is here that the tunnels which are our slogan should meet, and if they don't meet precisely, this would once again require a "new paragraph."

In light of all this you will understand how much I would like to see you. Unfortunately, I have to fly to Amsterdam and Paris on October 14 for three to four weeks, which is completely undesirable for me—and not merely because of the school. But when I return we *have* to meet, even if I have to come to Cambridge. But perhaps Raymond Aron's presence in New York (he will arrive on October 29, will do some traveling and be back in New York in the first half of December before he returns home) will tempt you to come to New York.

Social Research finally appeared with the Goldstein essay a few days ago.[5] You will receive your copy by separate post. I didn't have any *reprints* made, since they demanded the scandalous price of 52 dollars from me. Goldstein wrote me and thanked me for the trouble I took with his book. He said he would have been very interested in the way Husserl would have viewed the problems which so preoccupy him. His reaction was very kind and convinced me that he has read neither the manuscript nor the published essay. But that is what you predicted.

Have you already taken a look at the German *Meditationen*? I think the edition is exemplary.[6] I have written a couple of friendly, non-committal words for the "1,000-word" review which Farber wanted for our (no: his) journal. I would like to hear your opinion about the remarks on the *alter-ego* problem that are in the section of variant readings, pp. 238–241: the passage seems to me of the greatest significance and to open up new aspects.[7]

In addition: what do you say about Cairns's article "Phenomenology" in the newest collection of the Philosophical Library—I don't know the exact title, since I am not writing at home—and about Farber's contribution to the French-American collection?[8]

This has been a long and rambling letter. Let me hear from you soon. To you and your so dear wife as always all the best!

Sincerely yours
Alfred Schutz

Why do we still say *"Sie"*[9] to one another? I won't go along with this nonsense any longer!

1. *The Field of Consciousness* (G1964a).
2. S1951b, S1951c, and S1952. Concerning Husserl's analysis of possibilities, cf. *Experience and Judgment*, §21. "*Potestativität*," which is an unusual word in German, comes from Roman law: "the possibility of ruling," thus in the sociological sense "power."
3. *Reflections on the Problem of Relevance* (S1970b).
4. Later: *The Structures of the Life-World* (S1973).
5. "Language, Language Disturbances and the Texture of Consciousness" (S1950a).
6. E. Husserl, *Cartesianische Meditationen* (1950), edited by Stephan Strasser (*Husserliana*, vol. I).
7. S1951c.
8. Cairns (1950). The "French-American collection": Marvin Farber, ed., *Philosophic Thought in France and the United States* (Buffalo: University of Buffalo Publications in Philosophy, 1950).
9. The German "*Sie*" is the polite form. Schutz and Gurwitsch now switch to the familiar "*Du*" form.

Gurwitsch: *"The Field of Consciousness" is finished*
             (CAMBRIDGE, OCTOBER 9, 1950)

Dear Friend,

I too have decided not to go along with the nonsense (that we say "*Sie*" to one another) any longer. If you hadn't beat me to it with your kind letter, I would have made the same suggestion at our next meeting in connection with a request that I will make in what follows.

Salomon informed you correctly: *The Field of Consciousness* is finished. There are small additions to be made here and there, putting in a reference, dividing up a paragraph, etc. But that is neither "revision" nor "reworking," but in the best (or more correctly: worst) case a *mise au point*. The monster, which I estimate to be 700 typewritten pages, will now be typed, then to the corrector (for the English) and then immediately to France to the translator and then to the publisher (which one in America?).

Since about a year ago, as the book took on its definitive form, the wish has solidified in me to dedicate it to the two persons in this world to whom I feel the most "in debt" in the sense of "what one is, one owes to others" [*Was man ist, das bleibt man andern schuldig*]. The first of these two persons is *la compagne de ma vie*, who in the years of battles, of exile, of bitterness and increasing solitude made it possible for me to work. I don't have to ask her for permission. The other person is *le camarade de mes pensées*, the only person whose verification is important to me, and who, if he refuses me the verification, forces me to think through and justify my positions again and again. But he will give me permission, if I request it. It is somehow proper to dedicate it to the two of you: the one makes it possible for me to write, and it is written for the other.

When I now survey the whole thing, I can say that it is a book that I can put my name on. It is actually four books in one; I took the fifth out and will publish it later, i.e., immediately after the *Field* appears, under the title "Les trois do-maines du réel."[1] But it still has to be revised. The *Field* contains a) a complete historical-theoretical foundation of Gestalt theory. I think it is not unoriginal, in that the entire theoretical content of the Köhler-Wertheimer school is deduced from the analysis of a single phenomenon. The phenomenon is called *Gestalt-coherence.* b) There is a roughly 70–80-page-long presentation of some main concepts of phenomenology (reduction, noema, etc.), and of phenomenological idealism, a phenomenological interpretation of the abandonment of the con-stancy hypothesis, and of the concepts "object" and "topic of thought" accord-ing to James. c) My theory of perceptual implications is presented, though essentially only from the point of view of organizational problems and as an application of my theory of *Gestalt-coherence.* d) I have attempted to develop a theory of relevance and to work it out to some extent in the form of anticipatory hints. Your multiple realities have forced me to venture the step into constituted ontology. The next to last paragraph has the title "On the Concept of Exis-tence": that is an enterprise! When I look back on the last six or seven years, I have written a large book twice and a small one once.

Also in Los Angeles I finished an essay, i.e., except for the final polishing which is being done now, which will be called "Présuppositions philosophique de la logique" [G1951]. At first, the essay was to deal with numbers. But the introduction to the essay on numbers became so long and substantive that I thought about publishing the introduction itself as an article. But finally one part of the introduction has become the essay. (Please, don't be angry!) To this end I had to descend into the morass of logical literature. In so doing I made the discovery that Russell, from whom the whole Carnapism comes, has the same attitude towards these disciples as Marx to the Marxists, and that says some-thing. Recently I had a long talk with Quine here, a Russellian and one of the best, in spite of his perhaps not incurable nominalism. He said that the whole line of thought is at a dead end (better late than never) and only psychology can help. Seeing my astonishment, he quoted Piaget and my Goldstein essay.[2] To vary the master: even if I should be granted the age of Methuselah, I will only find a very restricted audience in America. But that age won't be granted to me.

Concerning the disclosure of the "sweet secret," my congratulations, in which there is mixed a certain nuance of regret. In wishing you a successful delivery I know only too well what a period you will go through. Oh yes, I know what it means, "to be with book." Women are finished with it in nine months; we labor—and it is not even yet the *labors* in the gynecological sense—years. You know as well as I do that the phenomenology of the natural attitude is still a desideratum. Neither Heidegger nor Sartre has done it. And I don't need to assure you that there is no one who can do it like you. This world of the natural attitude is a social world, a world of living-with-one-another and action. It is *à fonds* a human world, and that means a social world. You have the tie to social phenomena without which this task cannot be solved. Perhaps the reason why this task is still waiting for the person who can do justice to it is that no one has such a relation to and such a knowledge of the social.[3]

I will ask you to show me the first draft. But I must ask you, as you yourself say, to wait until my book has been sent to the corrector, if not to the printer. That is a rule which I have to apply in order to protect me from myself. I have treated relevance as a formal-noematic problem.

I am the last one to believe that this is the last word, and not to see that my theory is open to objections, indeed to objections of principle. If it is worth something, it will be corrected and thus make its contribution. But in order that the matters themselves, which alone are of importance to me, move forward, and move forward by means of reciprocal critique, my theory must first appear as I have developed it.

We will absolutely have to get together as soon as you are back from Europe. Perhaps you can come to Cambridge for a *week-end*. Since there are no distractions here, you will perhaps have more peace here than in New York. A propos, one request. I ordered the *Meditationen* in May, but haven't heard anything; now the announcement of a second publication has arrived. The publisher[4] always sends me two brochures, one to Dr. G., one to Prof. G. But when I order, nothing comes; they probably don't know to which of the two gentlemen they should send things. If your time allows, could you buy me the two books and bring them back? I will reimburse you here. That would be simpler than beginning a long correspondence, which would probably only be successful if I sign as Prof. G.

I would like to see the two essays of yours that you mentioned. As soon as you are back, I hope to send you a finished copy of the French essay: *au fur et à mesure* that parts of my book are typed and corrected by me, you will get them. One copy is planned for you, *à toute fin utile*. This is without any obligation for immediate reading.

Have a good trip and a good return home. All the best from the two of us to you and yours

Sincerely

Aron

1. The (unrevised) draft was published posthumously by Lester Embree in G1985. Cf. GS 12.4.51 and GS 2.17.52.

2. G1949.

3. But see Gurwitsch's own treatment of this "task" in his habilitation (G1976), which Schutz never had the opportunity to read.

4. Martinus Nijhoff (The Hague) published Husserl's *Cartesianische Meditationen*.

Schutz: *I have invited people to meet Raymond Aron*
            (NEW YORK, DECEMBER 2, 1950)

Dear Friend,

The trip to Europe and the two and one half weeks since then were such a strenuous rat-race that I didn't get around to writing to you or sending you the two Husserl volumes which I brought from Amsterdam. The latter should by all means happen on Monday. In the meantime, the tumult in the world has become much louder and once again its continued existence is put in question.[1]

I hear from Albert Salomon (who by the way is awaiting your answer) that he had invited you for Saturday the 9th, in order to meet a curator of Brandeis at his house. I am not invited for this occasion, but if you come, which would of course be a great pleasure for me, I would ask you to arrange things so that you can come to tea with us on Saturday the 9th between 4:00 and 7:00 (naturally with your dear wife, should she accompany you). I have invited a lot of people, also from the New School (including Riezler, Löwith, Löwe, White), to meet with Raymond Aron. I also hope that you, if you come, will have time for me on Sunday. That would be a nice occasion for us to see each other again, since during the Christmas vacation I have to take a business trip to Mexico, and I won't have a semester break since I have to make up the lectures that I missed during the trip to Europe.

So I am counting on hearing from you. In these times one has more of a need than ever for a heart-to-heart talk.

I hope that you and your dear wife are doing well, and that you already have a manuscript of your book ready for the printer.

With all best wishes also from Ilse

Your
Alfred

1. The Korean War, which began on June 25, 1950, entered a critical phase in late November.

Gurwitsch: *The theory of negation must be redone with reference to the phenomena of relevance*
(CAMBRIDGE, DECEMBER 17, 1950)

Dear Friend,

The two Husserl volumes arrived a couple of days ago. Many thanks. The first presentation of the reduction is indeed important and interesting.

You will hardly have found time to read my French article.[1] Koyré wrote from Paris that he has passed the article on to the *Comité,* and he raised an objection: Koyré claims that the sentence "The sum of the angles in a triangle is not equal to the color red" is a true sentence. This objection has made me very agitated, since on the basis of the concepts of truth which are accepted in contemporary logic it is completely justified. In my article I had called the sentence "The sum of the angles in a triangle is equal to the color red" meaningless [*sinnlos*], since there is no relation of relevance between the terms.

After receiving the letter from Koyré I walked the streets of Cambridge for two hours and made the discovery that K.'s sentence is true in the sense that there is no relation of relevance between "red" and the sum of the angles. K.'s sentence is thus true in a completely different sense from, e.g., the following sentences: 1) "2 + 3 is not equal to 7"; 2) "Portugal is not on the Black Sea." In other words, the theory of negation has to be completely redone with reference to the phenomena of relevance, and the concept of truth must be refined in the same orientation. There is a paragraph on relevance and logic in my book.[2] The French essay grew out of this paragraph. I shall resist the truly powerful temptation to rewrite this entire paragraph or to draw conclusions from it with respect to negation and truth. You can well imagine that I am very excited; for at least to some extent the validity of my theory of relevance depends on what is to be found in this newly-opened-up horizon. If only I weren't so isolated here!

It was so nice to have talked with you again. We must get together again before another six months have passed. In the meantime you have presumably spoken with Kallen; did you talk about me?

Have a good trip to Mexico. Many greetings to you and yours.

Sincerely

Your

Aron

1. *"Présuppositions philosophiques de la logique"* (G1951). Cf. the later revisions in GS 6.24.51 and GS 8.1.51.
2. "Context in Logic" (G1964c), 325–335.

Schutz: *Formal logic has forgotten that it is based on the life-world*
              (New York, December 24, 1950)

Dear Friend,

You are right, I haven't been able to read your French essay and have already told you that I will be able to do so tomorrow on my trip to Mexico at the earliest. Precisely because I haven't read it, I would like to make some remarks concerning your controversy with Koyré. I think I know my way around a bit

The Schutz family on a hike in the Rocky Mountains, Estes Park, Colorado, 1950.

with the "concept of truth" of modern logic. But it is always a matter of formal logic, which has forgotten that it is based on the life-world. In it of course there can be virtuous triangles (I need only view it as an iconographic symbol for the trinity), as well as "gray theories." For here the golden trees of life are still green.

Let us briefly analyze the sentence: "The sum of the angles of a triangle is equal to the color red." What does "is equal to" mean here? Does it mean functional equality in the purely mathematical sense, thus the substitutability of one expression by the other? Then we must say that neither "color" nor "color red" belongs to the vocabulary of mathematics. —To vary the example: "A vibrating string with 435 oscillations per second yields the color green." For George, with his *audition coloré*, this sentence is not only meaningful but true, since he simply experiences the tone "a´" as green, and does so regularly.[1] —But if "is equal to" in the example of the sum of the angles means nothing more than "having to do with," "is based on," then it is easy to come up with an example from the life-world which allows the sentence to appear meaningful and doxically sufficiently plausible, thus "subjectively true."

Let us assume that Piaget wants to explain the theorem concerning the sum of the angles to a child. To entertain it he sketches the following figures:[2]

He then runs through the proof using the *red* triangles with the help of the dotted lines, but not using the blue ones. Can't Piaget's child come to the conviction that the theorem is true for red, but not for blue triangles, the latter perhaps yielding very different results? That the "180°-quality" of the sum of the angles is thus connected with the color red? Piaget's books are full of similar examples, and Lévy-Bruhl, Cassirer, Mauss demonstrate similar things for magical-mystical thought. Would there be such a thing as ritual if sentences similar to your example were not held to be meaningful and true?

In parenthesis: While George has learned that the sum of the angles of a triangle is 180°, he doesn't yet have a proof, since he hasn't yet had systematic geometry in school. I asked him, stimulated by your letter, why this is the case. He said that there can't be a triangle with two right angles. He understood my objection that this is correct but only proves that the sum of the angles of a triangle can be at most 180, but not that it must always be 180 and not also 179, 160, etc.; but he didn't know where to go from there. When asked whether in his opinion the sentence "The sum of the angles is equal to the color red" is true, he answered literally: "Red doesn't have anything to do with mathematics unless *it means x, an unknown quantity.*" I asked him why it doesn't have anything to do with mathematics and he said that this is *human nature*. I reminded him of his identification of "a´" with green. He said that this is *unexplained*, but that perhaps there are mathematicians for whom red is connected with 180° just as green with a´ for him.

I think that George has discovered an important problem here: Why can't the *x* in an arbitrary algebraic expression be replaced by "red"?

To return to our problem. —What kind of relation is there between negation and the relation of relevance? I fear, dear friend, that in this and many other discussions we are getting more and more caught up in the terminological confusion which arises from our varying use of the expression "relevance." I have things relatively easy with my concept of relevance. The proposition: "A cord is not a snake" is true for formal logic, but not for the man in the Carneades example as long as he stands between problematic possibilities in the situation of doubt.[3] But the fact that he is in this situation of doubt shows that there are relations of relevance (in my sense) between the terms which give rise to doubt.

In other words: Every negative judgment presupposes such a situation of doubt in everyday life with the relevance structures (always in my sense) which belong to it. Negative propositions are after all *motivated;* someone (I or someone else) must have believed, wished, or asserted that Portugal is on the Black Sea if I am to have occasion to assert that this is not the case. In other words: *Every* negative proposition is an answer to an assertion, question, *belief,* etc., which temporally precedes it in the context—or it is meaningless, because fragmentary. Thus, it gets its sense from the situation of doubt of the prepredicative sphere. To put it differently: Negative sentences are essentially elliptical and get their sense first from the context of the discourse or from the "situation" in general. Husserlian: they contain an essentially occasional element.

The only difference between your "color red" and "Portugal" examples, as I see it, is that in the "color red" case the relevance relation of the life-world, which leads to the development of problematic possibilities within the framework of the "weightless" open possibilities, is harder to discover, probably also rarer. But one might be able to think of sentences which overlap Husserl's spheres of incompatibility (if there are such) and thus burst the framework of open possibilities. But then there are no problematic possibilities for such sentences and the doubt itself would be senseless—and thus also its negation by means of a decision "is not."

But here we come to ontological questions, and George is right when he refers to *human nature.* But truth requires intersubjective rectification and justification in the sphere of the open possibilities of the life-world. On your return please let me know what you think about all this. By that time I will have read your article. You may have already answered all of these questions; perhaps they don't have anything to do with your essay: but they are questions which must be answered.

Concerning Kallen[4]: Not much happened, otherwise I would have informed you immediately. The main thing: as a *personality* you have made a great impression on him. Everything else is a matter of year-long development. He would like to have you as a replacement for Felix, if we have money, since he wants a phenomenologist; as *his* successor (though I don't for a moment believe that they will allow him to go when he reaches the age limit; they will rather change the statutes) he is thinking—in strict confidence—in the first place of M. (Cornell), in the second of Koyré. Löwith is staying. Thus everything is still at the stage of the *long run*. But it is good that he thinks of you, that he likes you, and also that you have met the others. After all, no one can know whether the school and all of us will survive the next two years.

All the best to you and your wife for 1951.

Sincerely yours

Alfred

1. George Schutz described this ability somewhat differently to the editor: the specific tones are connected with colors for him, C major with white, a´ (in Schutz's example; a´ has 435 vibrations per second) with the color green. This changes nothing in Schutz's argument. George Schutz adds that this capability is not very unusual, but that the connection between colors and tones is completely arbitrary; he has never met anyone who shares his particular *audition coloré*.

2. In the original letter the triangles are drawn in color.

3. Cf. "The Problem of Carneades" in *The Problem of Relevance* (S1971a).

4. Horace M. Kallen was Professor of Philosophy and Psychology at the New School beginning in 1919. The discussion concerns the successor of Felix Kaufmann.

Schutz: *The tunnels seem to meet once again*
            (NEW YORK, JANUARY 8, 1951)

Dear Friend,

I got back from Mexico two days ago and am still completely exhausted from the strenuous work. I read parts of your essay[1] on the trip to Mexico; I say parts, since pages 3 and 19 are missing from my copy, and I would be grateful if you would send them to me. It is a very excellent work, whose value will remain regardless of how your controversy with Koyré might be decided. With regard to that, I really don't have anything to add to my remarks in my last letter, except for the observation that the tunnels seem to meet once again, since we are both completely aware of fact that all intensional logic [*Inhaltslogik*] is referred back to the prepredicative sphere. Thus, the whole problem is a constitutional problem of the relevance schema in this sphere. Be that as it may, your essay is eminently important, especially for France, completely successful in the choice, treatment, and presentation of the interconnections. My congratulations.

Farber has accepted my essay "Choosing among Projects of Action." Were you the *reader*? I just received the new edition of the *Ideen*.[2] Some of the "Supplements" are quite interesting. I might write you about it in the near future. But correspondence is so cumbersome and meetings so rare!

Let me hear from you soon; I am eager to hear not only what you have to say to my last letter, but also how the new year has begun for you and your dear wife.

Alles Liebe
Alfred

1. G1951.
2. Edmund Husserl, *Ideen zu einer reinen Phänomenologie und phänomenologischen Philosophie,* vol. I, ed. Walter Biemel (The Hague: Martinus Nijhoff, 1950).

Gurwitsch: *Here lies one of the decisive problems for the logic of mathematics*
(CAMBRIDGE, JANUARY 13, 1951)

Dear Friend,

Many thanks for your two letters. On the basis of your intimations, the trip to Mexico appears to have been more than strenuous. Given the combination of your daytime life and your nighttime life, it is unfortunately to be feared that you haven't found peace and quiet after your return either. And if that weren't enough, the vulture of high politics is circling over us. The situation appears to be dreadfully hopeless. If they want to avoid war with China, then they must leave Korea. But then they should have done so earlier or, even better, they shouldn't have even begun.

But the word *appeasement* has taken on very curious meanings: *no appeasement* now seems to mean that one joins in every Sicilian expedition. I read about that recently in Thucydides, something that can be recommended to all "statesmen."

In my hurry I must have given Koyré two copies of pages 3 and 19: your copies. Please forgive this carelessness. The missing pages are enclosed.

There is a lot to say to your letter. I hope we can talk about it soon. We are by and large in agreement; only the points of departure are different to the extent that I consciously attack the problem in terms of the problems of the foundations of mathematics and logic. A new result is a term: normal negation. "This book is not bound in black," *but rather [sondern]* green. "14 is not an odd number," *but rather* has the factor two. The "but rather" defines the negation as normal. In the case of the angles of a triangle and the color red, the negation too lacks the "but rather." If the sum of the angles is not = the color red, then most certainly not because it is = the color yellow. What is being negated here is that the terms are relevant to one another, and thus it is denied that the sentence has a sense. Thus, the negation is true in a different sense from normal negation.[1]

Thus far my provisional answer to Koyré. The whole problem requires much more work. It is intimately connected with substitution, on the basis of which according to Russell propositions arise from propositional functions. Russell deals with this in a couple of words: it is just obvious that the realm of variability can be restricted. In reality one of the decisive problems for the logic of mathematics lies here—Cassirer saw that very well—and perhaps the fundamental problem of the philosophy of logic.

There was never any question in my mind that Farber would accept your essay. But I was not the *"reader."*

All best wishes

Your

Aron

1. Cf. GS 12.17.50 and SG 12.24.50. Here Gurwitsch rediscovers the "infinite judgment" of traditional logic. As Kant notes, general logic (i.e., formal logic, Husserl's formal apophantics) "rightly" refuses to distinguish the infinite judgment from the affirmative judgment, but transcendental logic can and must make the distinction (cf. *Critique of Pure Reason,* A71–2/B97). According to Solomon Maimon, "infinite judgments are negative judgments—but they are not grounded on the fact that there is already a predicate that is opposed to the given one included in the subject (as is the case with the judgment properly called 'negative'), but on the fact that neither the [given] predicate nor its opposite can yield a possible *real* determination" (*Essay towards a New Logic or Theory of Thought, Together with Letters of Philalethes to Aenesidemus* (1794), in *Between Kant and Hegel,* ed. George di Giovanni and H. S. Harris [Albany: SUNY Press, 1985], 198). Maimon's examples are very similar to Gurwitsch's. The infinite judgment also played a crucial role in Hermann Cohen's Neo-Kantianism. Cf. Jakob Gordin, *Untersuchung zur Theorie des unendlichen Urteils* (Berlin: Akademie Verlag, 1929).

Schutz: *Whitehead too takes realms of incompatibility to be simply given*
(NEW YORK, JANUARY 15, 1951)

Dear Friend,

Many thanks for your kind letter and the two forgotten pages of the manuscript. With reference to the problem itself, I would like to draw your attention (although you surely already know the essay) to Whitehead's "The Organization of Thought," in which he says that the proposition "The specific heat of virtue is 0.033" is not a proposition at all and thus can be neither true nor false. In discussing the concept of a "propositional function $f(x)$," and with reference to Russell, Whitehead says:

> There is a range of values for x for which $f(x)$ is a proposition, true or false. For values of x outside the range, $f(x)$ is not a proposition and is neither true nor false.

It may have vague suggestions for us, but it has no unit meaning of definite assertation. . . . The range of values for which $f(x)$ has sense is called the 'type' of the argument x. But there is also a range of values of x for which $f(x)$ is a true proposition. This is the class of those values of the argument which *satisfy* $f(x)$. . . . We thus conceive two general propositions respecting the indefinite number of propositions which share in the same logical form, that is, which are values of the same propositional function. One of these propositions is "$f(x)$ yields a true proposition for each value of x *of the proper type*." The other proposition is "There is a value of x for which $f(x)$ is true."

As far as I can see, Whitehead too takes the realm of incompatibility to be simply given. You are certainly right that one of the fundamental problems of the philosophy of logic lies here.

Whitehead's essay is in his book *The Organization of Thought* (1917) and is printed in the collection *The Aims of Education* (Mentor Book M41), which is also worth reading in other respects (but with whose last chapter I have serious problems). In the "Mentor" edition the passage above is on page 114f.

Love to you and your wife

Your

Alfred

Gurwitsch: *Why may mathematicians do something which would lead to absurdity in logic?*
                  (Cambridge, January 21, 1951)

Dear Friend,

Many thanks for your kind letter. I am very thankful to you for the reference to the article by Whitehead. In fact, I didn't know it at all. One of the many gaps in my knowledge. I am much more familiar with the work of the Whitehead-Russell family, who *à propos* bitterly hated one another, from the Russell side. It is a shame that I have only now read the article, since I could have made good use of it. As it is I will do so in later articles.

I have spent months searching for just one single literary statement dealing with the question of the restrictions on the realm within which the x can vary with regard to substitution in propositional functions. I haven't found a single thing. As far as I can see Whitehead too fails to pose the fundamental question concerning what such a restriction depends on, although he senses something.

This whole question also exists in mathematics, indeed even on the elementary level of analytic geometry and the primitive theory of equations. The mathematicians have not accepted such restrictions, and that leads to complex and hypercomplex numbers. Every circle and every line, e.g., cross, if not in real then in ideal points. Finally they came up with lines which are perpendicular to themselves, etc. It would be very interesting to deal with the whole question in such a context. Why may the mathematician do something which would lead to absurdity in logic? If one really goes into it I suspect that one will come upon things which are intimately connected to the problem of the Platonic *Parmenides*.

Goldstein was here for two hours yesterday. He told me about the long telephone conversation with you. He would like the three of us to meet some time. But between you and me, that would only make sense if it were at your house. At the Goldsteins one finds a *party* of 25 people; it is of course really impossible to talk. When winter is over there is more of a possibility for me to come to New York for a *weekend* more often. My assistant drives down in his car often. But he doesn't do so as long as there is a danger of snow. I have asked him to let me know when he plans to drive early enough for me to make plans and inform you.

I hope that everything is in order with you. With best greetings

Your
Aron

Schutz: *My course on the Methodology of the Social Sciences gives me more work*
(NEW YORK, MARCH 16, 1951)

My dear Friend,

I hardly find time to write to you and I apologize for dictating this letter in English. I just wanted to tell you that there seems to be increasing interest in our school for you.

About a fortnight ago Dr. Kallen asked me to send him a selection of your papers. I picked out the most suitable ones and forwarded them immediately to him. So far, I have not received his reaction. I got, however, a call from Reizler asking me whether I could tell him your age. I told him that I believe you are three or four years younger than I am and therefore born around 1903, but that I am willing, of course, to ask you immediately for your exact age. He said literally that this is not necessary now because if he can do something for Gurwitsch, he can do so only for the school year 1952/1953.

He wanted, moreover, indications when your several papers were published in Farber's Journal, which I gave him. He said that he will not find time to read them before his departure to Europe in about a fortnight and thanked me for the information. All this looks very interesting and promising and I suggest that you should make for me a complete bibliography of your publications and send them to me with several copies. Also, I do not have a curriculum of yours and it might be a good idea that I have one, or a copy of what you sent formerly to our school, so that I am better placed to give detailed information if needed.

For months Goldstein and I have tried to get together but our mutual schedule never did coincide. Now we are finally invited Saturday evening to his home and I think you will agree that I ask him at this occasion to give several people his opinion of your personality and scholarship.

I have nothing special to report so far as we are concerned. I am, as usual, overworked and my course on Methodology of the Social Sciences gives me more work than I had presumed. I have, however, 31 intelligent students which is rather a success in our graduate classes for such a topic. Of course, it is impossible to do any writing during the school year.

All my love to you and Mrs. Gurwitsch.

Sincerely,
Alfred

5
The Field of Consciousness
(*June 24, 1951–March 17, 1952*)

Aron Gurwitsch's main work, which Schutz compares to Husserl's *Experience and Judgment,* has a colorful history, of importance to the reader interested in the details of the text. Other readers may prefer to skip this part.

Gurwitsch mentioned his work on the "field theory" for the first time in 1942, but "the essentials are already there in my dissertation" (GS 5.30.42). A first "Outline of a Field Theory of Consciousness" was finished by the end of the year (GS 12.21.42); a "first draft" required four more years (GS 11.2.46). This *Urtext* of 1946 (Archives C25) has a completely different structure from the later versions; most important, the final chapter, "Les trois domaines du réel" (GS 10.9.50) was taken out. This chapter offers an alternative theory to Schutz's "finite provinces of meaning." It has now been published by Lester Embree as *Marginal Consciousness* (G 1985).

The "corrector's version" which is discussed in these letters ("which I have prepared for the corrector": GS 9.4.51) was sent to Schutz chapter by chapter beginning in May 1951. Schutz replied with a running commentary. Gurwitsch accepted some of the objections, but obviously fewer than Schutz's often quite energetic remonstrances would lead one to suspect. This corrector's version could not be found; a French translation of the table of contents, which was enclosed with GS 6.26.51, makes it possible to reconstruct it.

The "Harvard version" is in the archives; it was revised for the Harvard University Press (which wanted a different order in the footnotes), only to be so battered by the "expert evaluations" that Gurwitsch withdrew it (GS 2.6.53). The following summer Gurwitsch spoke with Désclée de Brouwer in Paris and came to terms (GS 6.24.53); Michel Butor prepared the French translation. The English text appeared in 1964, the German translation posthumously in 1975.

The structure of these versions underwent only minor changes while the text itself "grew" from one version to the next. This is especially true for the translations into French and German: one should remember that Gurwitsch had taught in all three languages. In addition, the dates of publication are years apart. Not only was each translation authorized by Gurwitsch, but he continued to work: even philosophical concepts have very different semantic horizons in the three languages.

This can be seen most clearly in the concluding chapter, which hints at the theory of the three spheres of being (*les trois dimensions du réel:* GS 1.25.52). The German text can distinguish between *Wirklichkeit* and *Realität,* whereas English offers only the term "reality" (since Gurwitsch chose not to make use of the term "actuality," which is now used in translations of Hegel). Gurwitsch can thus distinguish *Wirklichkeit* ("Phantasieprodukte gehören nicht zur Wirklichkeit," *Bewußtseinsfeld,* 313; "Excluded from reality are the products of imagination," *Field,* 388) and *Realität* ("In jedem Augenblick des bewußten Lebens haben wir . . . Bewußtsein von der Realität," *Bewußtseinsfeld,* 341; "At every moment of conscious life, we are aware of reality," *Field,* 418), with apparently contradictory results in the English text. When dealing with such decisive points, it is advantageous to make use of all three versions of *The Field of Consciousness.*

Gurwitsch: *You are working on the structures of behavior of persons existing in the life-world. My interest is the structure of this world itself*
(Cambridge, June 24, 1951)

Dear Friend,

I am finally getting around to writing to you, now that the end of the semester period is over with. As always, it was full of a tremendous amount of messy odds and ends which had to be done.

I have read, "Choosing among Projects of Action" several times, each time with profit and pleasure. Mixed in with the pleasure was the feeling of satisfaction that comes from the confirmation of my own theses through your work. I was very happy and in this sense amused to find, in your discussion of "open" possibilities, condensations of page-long analyses of the same topic that I have in my book. You aren't familiar with the passages in my book; sooner or later I will have this chapter far enough along that I can send it to you. You can well imagine how much such an "endorsement" means to me. It is much more important than those verifications in which *A* confirms to *B* that there is a piece of paper on the stairs.

It is a great idea to demonstrate the convergence of the theories of Leibniz, Bergson, and Husserl. This idea is not at all obvious, since these theories are developed in such different contexts. I think that you are right about the convergence. I read your remarks concerning Bergson with great pleasure. You are absolutely right: what occurs in the *durée* is a modeling of what is represented in *modo futuri exacti*, perhaps future states of affairs that result from one's own actions. Precisely this view makes it clear what the transformation of open into problematic possibilities signifies. With reference to the further applications you make of Husserl's concept, I would suggest the term "alternatives" here. It contains both elements, the Husserlian and your own.

All in all this essay is one of the most important ones you have written, just as important as the "Multiple Realities."[1] I have always envied you for the directness of your presentations, which is such a pleasant contrast to my spiraling style. In directness this essay is superior to almost all of your earlier ones. It once again makes clear to me that our differences lie essentially in the direction of interest, and that for this reason the construction of the tunnel can work. You are working on the structure of behavior of persons existing in the life-world. My interest is in the structure and constitution of this world itself.

One can sum it up in this way; and this is the way I put it in my critical discussion of the "*Realities*" under the title "The psychological and the constitutive point of view."[2] If this is correct, then we have to meet; we are as it were extending our work in different directions. If I may be a bit arrogant, I would say: I provide you with the foundation. But this arrogance is the hubris of the phenomenologist, if it is hubris and not the path which our intellectual ancestors discovered in the Greece of the sixth century.

Your discussions of "because" and "in-order-to" reminded me of certain ideas, as did your seminar, in which I went straight to this point. Since I read my paper at Hunter College on "Objects of Thought,"[3]—as I remember, you weren't there—I have in me *potentialiter* a theory of the sciences of man in contrast to the natural sciences. This takes possession of me periodically. I wish that we lived in the same city; then we could work together. With such an arrangement, our differences could not even appear! I could learn a whole lot from you concerning the human sciences [*Geisteswissenschaften*] (history of law, national economics, etc.). The idea is or sounds very simple. The investigator in the sciences of man has to take notice of the fact that his object has a world and interprets this world, and does so in a manner different from that of the observer. But molecules have no world, and don't interpret it. An especially interesting case is biology with all of the Goldstein problems: all of these problems are world-problems.

Enclosed is a copy of my French translation of the table of contents,[4] which I recently sent to Jean Wahl. If my wife can do the 10 drawings which belong to part II this week, this part will immediately be sent to you. That will be another 100 pages. I am now finished with some 300 *out of* 570.

Kahn recently wrote about a *rendez-vous* with you in Aspen. I am consumed with jealousy that I can't be the third party. When are you leaving?

I am now studying Piaget's *Epistémologie génétique: Cela nous regarde grandement*. My interest is largely in volumes I and II (basic concepts of mathematics and physics). If we in phenomenology don't pay very careful attention to these things, we can be punished with sterility. One can unroll the entire question of sedimentation and of intentional history in terms of Piaget's presentation. In addition to completing my book, I will spend the entire summer and longer on these volumes, whose study is anything but a simple matter. From child psychology to the foundations of mathematics and back, several times per day, is a real *navette*.

We hope that you will have a good summer. Let us hear from you soon. Is everything in *status quo*?

With all best wishes and with great desire to see you.

Your
Aron

1. S1945c.
2. *The Field of Consciousness* (G1964a), 399f.
3. Cf. SG 5.11.46.
4. Of *The Field of Consciousness*. The reader should refer to the table of contents of the English edition.

Schutz: *With your book one has the feeling of having entered a very bright room*
          (NEW YORK, JULY 16, 1951)

Dear Friend,

You may have wondered about my long silence, but I have a rather unpleasant four weeks behind me: my boss from California was here, and in addition to tremendous amounts of work I had a lot of trouble and unpleasant encounters. During this period the study of your manuscript was a great pleasure. I am really in agreement with everything and am happy to see how many of your ideas with which I have long been familiar now appear in perfect formulations striving for a center, and how many significant details which are new even to me indicate deeper contexts—thematic and marginal. I have made a lot of notes, but in my current state of total exhaustion I am a bit distrustful of my abilities as a reader, and for this reason I want to work through the whole thing once more after I return from vacation, which begins day after tomorrow—thus in the last third of August, before I put my remarks on paper. Or is there any chance of seeing you in New York before school begins?

So for today I only want to speak of the first global impression, which is in every respect excellent. I have the same experience with your book as did Goethe with Kant: one has the feeling of having entered a very bright room. The style and organization of both parts are exemplary. A very good idea to set the "tonic" by James, also very good to prepare the figural moments by using Piaget and the Graz school. The way you present Gestalt theory is simply masterful. I don't believe that any of the Gestalt psychologists was or would be capable of achieving anything comparable. Köhler may have seen these things, but he is and remains philsophically simply a coward. Wertheimer was under-articulate and Koffka over-articulate and too elegant. I assume that the third and fourth parts will bring a systematic presentation of your critical position. What I have is in any case a "beginning" in the first sense in which Husserl used this word. (By the way, are you familiar with the magnificent exchange between Husserl and Karl Bühler following Husserl's lecture in Vienna? Husserl: "All that I have achieved in phenomenology thus far is only a beginning in the proper sense." Bühler [patting him on the shoulder]: "But a worthy one, *Herr Geheimrat!*")

And I must thank you for your kind and for me so important letter with remarks on the "Projects of Action." You often complain that you have no one to talk to: I quit trying long ago. It often leads to the depressing suspicion that one has lost the right path. Remarks like yours, or Kahn's applause for my music essay, are a great encouragement for me. One as schizophrenic as I lives with the continual fear of falling prey to dilettantism.

I would like to have gone into many details of your letter, but it is 3:00 in the morning and that is too late for me too. I hope that your dear wife and you are safely back in your home after a fine summer. Many thanks for everything and best wishes from us all.

Always your
Alfred

Gurwitsch: *I continue to drift on the boundless and foggy sea of the pre-categorical*
(CAMBRIDGE, AUGUST 1, 1951)

My Dear Alfred,

You gave me a real pleasure with your last kind letter. These conventional words are naturally completely inadequate to express what I mean. You know better than anyone that I haven't made life (read: work on the field theory) easy for myself. To think it all through again from the beginning and to systematize it in a milieu in which there is not a single person with whom one can talk, even about questions of detail, and in which one never even encounters something which looks like circumstantial evidence for a tiny idea, is not only difficult but often brings one to ask if one isn't going in circles—falling prey to dilettantism, as you put it.

Aside from the trip to Paris two years ago and from occasional visitors here (Berger, for example), your occasional communications—verbally, written, and printed—were all that belonged to my world. In addition, to formulate in a foreign language, which one somehow feels to be a hostile obstacle, and in which the people whose language it is will most likely not take the slightest notice of my word—that borders on Don Quixote.

I need not assure you that words such as "applause" and "success" do not exist in my lexicon. But when an *endorsement* such as your letter comes, and when it comes from one of the few persons in the world, the only one in this country, whom I consider competent in these matters and who has the authority to make a judgment—then you can well imagine how happy it makes me, since it gives me proof that I haven't been talking nonsense. As long as there is such "confirmation and correction" between us, everything can be borne one way or another. I am very thankful for the first global impression which my book made on you—not really to you, at least not in the everyday sense, for since you are the person you are, you tell me what you think; this openness and the discussion and controversy are a very important element in our relationship. I am very thankful for the circumstances, thanks to which I haven't withered away in this intellectual Siberia.

There are now another 100 pages waiting for you. Part III and the first chapter of part IV. Your judgment of part III is especially important to me. There the framework of phenomenology is demarcated. It is very important that just this part be distinguished by its precision. From there on the book begins to become *phenomenological*. Parts IV and V bring the utilization of the Gestalt-theoretical concepts, set forth in the first parts, now into the genuinely phenomenological realm. I can't spare you one disappointment. The philosophical critique of Gestalt theory, which can only be carried through within the framework of a total philosophical discussion of modern psychology, is only given in a few very brief intimations, and the intimations are *consciously* not pursued further. Something of this sort would have transcended the limits of the book. This discussion is only possible in a broad framework of the history and theory of science. The entire problematic of modern psychology, what in my Descartes seminar I call the *matrix of all psychological problems* at the most elementary level, can only be comprehended with reference to the specific character of the rising physics. Only from this perspective can one make clear the constancy hypothesis and Helmholtz's representative position. If everything goes well and according to wish, I would like to present some of this in two years in Louvain (before or after the congress in Brussels)—on the assumption, of course, that Van Breda invites me.

You didn't give me an address in the mountains. So I am sending this letter—*please forward*—to New York. I don't want to do this with the manuscript. Should I keep it here until you are back in New York? I can do that or, if you wish, send it to you in Estes Park. In any case you should not view the fact that I have sent it to you as an expression of any expectation on my part that you will read it any time soon. I know very well just how busy you are. I don't want to have the consciousness of an additional burden. By the way, we will be out of town once more. From August 5 to 19 we will have the following address: General Delivery, Tannersville, N.Y. We will live in a *cabin* and I plan to work all day long. Partially on additional corrections—two-thirds are finished—partially on Piaget.

Piaget has had consequences. It turns out that the entire basis on which I— luckily only privately—had constructed my reflections concerning the constitution of number requires a complete revision. What luck that I have published only the Goldstein essay and not the essay on number.[1] Otherwise I could now solemnly recant. There is also a lot that is false in the Goldstein essay: there is no "collective and"; the categorical set [*Menge*] is not the correlate of a "synthesis." Your critique is justified in an even deeper sense. I will have to rethink all of this on a completely new basis in the coming years. For me, mathematics is "the land of the Greeks." "Searching for it with the soul," I believed that I could already see its outlines. It was a *fata morgana;* I continue to drift on the boundless and foggy sea of the precategorial.

Good vacation and relaxation in the name of both of us.

Affectionately yours

Aron

1. "Gelb-Goldstein's Concept of 'Concrete' and 'Categorial' Attitude": G1949. The essay on number is probably the manuscript *"Essai sur les problèmes phénoménologique du nombre,"* which is in the archives (Ms C44 and C46). Cf. "Reflections on Mathematics and Logic," published posthumously by Lester Embree in G1974b.

Schutz: *I want to file a formal protest. This sentence buries the founding of the life-world in intersubjectivity*
(New York, August 29, 1951)

Dearest Friend,

Your kind letter and shipment came the day before yesterday, and I spent my last two nights studying the third part. I had already read the first two parts again for the third or fourth time. The first global impression is now strengthened: this is going to be something wonderful.

I am in complete agreement with everything you say in the fourth part—with the exception of one sentence on Ms page 243 [*Field*, 177],[1] which has nothing to do with the main argument but which, if it isn't a matter of a poor formulation, will throw us into great conflicts. It is a tremendous and true pleasure to see such a thing grow and come to a happy ending. Congratulations!

Since you lay such weight on my opinion, I have made some notes on the third part on the enclosed pages: they are reactions to a first reading (written as I read) and may contain a great deal which I will no longer hold to after a second reading. But you may welcome my first impressions. With the exception of the point concerning page 243, they mostly contain recommendations concerning style and formulations. With regard to the language, the entire third part should be looked through by the editor one more time: I really wish that you would precede your first paragraph by an introduction of, let's say, two pages, in which you prepare the reader for the problems he will find here, explaining why he finds them *here,* and laying out the inner organization of the whole part.[2] It is going to be hard work for the reader anyway, and you should at least say why you expect this of him and where the path leads. For the same reason I would also suggest a *résumé* at the end of the part.

Upon rereading the second part, it was often difficult for me to discover when you are only *reporting* and when you are giving your own formulations, since I am not all that familiar with the Gestalt psychological literature (although I have read Koffka, Köhler, Wertheimer, I have never studied them like Hume or Bergson or Leibniz). Look through the first two parts again: with small additions such as "always according to Koffka" you could easily clear up such doubts.

On the basis of your presentation I have understood clearly for the first time what Gestalt psychology is all about. You do a superb job of elaborating the full significance of the elimination of the constancy hypothesis. But I am becoming more and more distrustful of what the gentlemen assert positively. You will surely have a lot to say about that in the parts to come. I am only surprised that all Gestalt psychologists—even a man like Stumpf—have so little understanding of everything concerning music. Every time they move from the visual to the acoustic it ends in some absurdity, and there are good internal reasons for this. Every sketchbook by Beethoven, indeed every variation and every development, proves Koffka's theory[3] [cf. *Field*, 152–153] to be sheer *nonsense*. Sure, if we assume *figure* and *ground*, Gestalt *coherence* and *good continuation*, whole and part as givens ("that's just the way things are"), then life is easy and the phenomenologists will starve. Do these people really not see that with concepts such as "external and internal interval," "contour," "enclosed areas," etc., etc., they have, like poor lackeys, swept the dust of the entire room under the rug of the "figure-ground"? Of course, that doesn't diminish their merits, especially the fact that they have given you the possibility of telling them what they really should have done and what they really mean.

As much as I am looking forward to reading chapter 1 of part IV, I don't know if I will get to it before September 15, when I hope to see you. I simply have to write an essay over the *Labor Day Weekend,* and then I am unfortunately going to have foreign business visitors.

Once again, congratulations and looking forward to seeing you soon. Love to your dear wife.

Always your
Alfred

Should I continue to make such notations? Or are such things undesirable to you?

Supplement: Schutz's notes on part III of *The Field of Consciousness* (with references to the English edition, pp. 157–197). Comments dealing merely with stylistic considerations are not included.

1. [p. 168 and elsewhere] As Husserl wrote in the margins of his own *Meditations,* shouldn't the "misleading talk of we" be carefully avoided in this entire part? I, e.g., need to be able to cite you and I can't use the "we"!

2. [p. 171f.] I would suggest that the words "a natural science, i.e." be dropped. The rest suffices and the Gestaltists won't misunderstand anything. (Line 11: drop "as a natural science" too.) But if you want to keep the expression (Wertheimer would be in a rage), then an explanatory footnote must deal with the possible misunderstanding (namely, that you mean not natural science, but rather a science of the natural attitude). The comparison with physics on p. 172 increases the danger.

3. [p. 177] Although there are such things in Husserl, I want to file a formal protest against the sentence "It is of no importance . . . ."[4] This sentence buries entire levels of problems: namely, the founding of the life-world in intersubjectivity. *Quid juris* am I simply to accept an assertion of such import, which is asserted dogmatically? An eminent problem: can there be intersubjective noemata? I claim that this is wooden iron. If this is more than a *lapsus calami* (namely, that the thesis is to hold not merely for judgmental sense, for which it is appropriate, but also for noemata), then there is a critical difference of opinion between us at a very important point.

4. [p. 183: "All philosophical problems must, consequently, be formulated or reformulated in terms of sense and meaning."] Shouldn't—also precisely with respect to the following paragraph—the *endorsement* of Berger's theory be re-

stricted to phenomenology in the reduced sphere? Does the reformulation postulate hold unrestrictedly also for the phenomenological psychology of the natural attitude?

5. [p. 189: "Phenomenology concerns itself with consciousness as an eidetic, not an empirical science."] The first sentence is surely too strong. There are after all also non-eidetic findings in phenomenology. Perhaps "chiefly concerned"?

6.[p. 194] The horse's head[5] is of course quite correctly presented following Husserl. But I have never understood this example; how does Husserl know that it is the head of a *horse*, if the horse is not thought too? Or better: How can the head ever be "independent of and separable from its context"? It is "separable" from the body, but not from the context. (This is only a note for future discussion.)

7.[p. 197] Doesn't the musical algebraic number belong in the second group of examples? My substantive reservations are well known to you from the correspondence concerning Koyré's objection [cf. SG 12.24.1950]. "This house is equal": bad example, could be an ellipse: ". . . to many others."

Remark (1) [Footnote No. 119, page 196: "the difference between non-sense and absurdity"]: Isn't the *standard* translation "non-sense and counter-sense"? I had a long discussion with Koyré as he was writing the "Liar."

Concerning the substitution "S is p" for "tree is green," it should be pointed out to the reader trained in Dewey that eidetic variation is no substitute for induction. I know my men!—A good word for the Carnap people would also be appropriate.

1. Concerning the references to the manuscript (Ms 243) and to the English edition (p. 177), see the editorial remarks above.

2. The published version contains a paragraph entitled "The Psychological and the Phenomenological Approach to Consciousness" (*Field*, 157f.).

3. Cf. also Koffka's "law of good continuation" in his *Principles of Gestalt Psychology* (New York: Harcourt, Brace & World, Inc., 1935, 1963), 434ff.

4. The sentence "It is of no importance . . ." is in neither the English nor the German editions, which vary considerably from one another. The point at issue: Gurwitsch here defines his concept of meaning with the aid of the concept of the noema, which itself involves a generalization of the concept of linguistic meaning (cf. *Ideas*, vol. 1, §124). He asserts: "When to distinguish between perceptual noema and perceived thing, we pointed out a plurality of perceptual noemata which all refer to the same thing (namely, the different presentations of the thing, when it is seen from different standpoints" (p. 177). Schutz claims that this argument presupposes intersubjective noemata, a "wooden iron."

5. Husserl discusses the separated "horse's head" under the title "The Objective Determination of the Concept of Inseparability" (*Logical Investigations*, vol. II, 442f.).

Gurwitsch: *The development from the constancy hypothesis to the reduction was then taken up by Merleau-Ponty*
            (CAMBRIDGE, SEPTEMBER 4, 1951)

Dear Friend,

As always, your kind letter was a great pleasure for me. What you say to me is the only compensation meaning anything to me for the great labor I have done. You think along with me in a much greater measure than I could hope and expect. You can imagine what a pleasure and confirmation that is.

I am very thankful for your remarks. But please keep the following in mind: the copy which you receive hasn't been looked through by the corrector, since it is the copy which I am preparing for the corrector. He will take care of many of the linguistic problems. Then I will take all of your remarks into account and probably follow most of them. When I asked you to pay particular attention to part III, this was because it does in fact hang in the air. It was originally part of II and IV, but there it severely disturbed the flow of the argument. I finally decided to present the fundamental phenomenological concepts which are used in what follows in a special part—namely III. I am not at all satisfied with this solution—but there hardly seems to be another. The reason lies in the character of the book, which is phenomenological, but uses much psychological material precisely with a phenomenological intent. The best thing is, as you suggest, to precede it with a couple of introductory pages (concerning psychology as a "natural science," for example) and to tell the reader in the introduction that the journey enters a new sphere with part III. Given your work load I hesitate to ask you for further remarks. I can only say that I would be infinitely thankful for them, as thankful as for a gift that means a great deal and that one has absolutely no right to expect.

We will have to come to terms about Gestalt theory in person. That is a long chapter. It is naturally true that they haven't said the last word. But they have opened up the possibility of an approach to the phenomenological question—without themselves having made the journey—and, this I truly believe, they have developed concepts which we *must* integrate into phenomenology: in their place and in *their relative* justification.

As I read your suggestion that I distinguish between report and my own formulations, I had to laugh a bit. My dear, best friend, I can tell you: the whole discussion is from me, to some extent even the terminology (*Gestalt-coherence*, for example), above all the whole part-whole dialectic with reference to phenomenal identity and modification; you will look in vain for the terms "functional significance," "functionalistic conception of whole and part," etc. in Koffka, Wertheimer, and Köhler. Their discussions have served only as illustrating material. I had to create the entire conceptual apparatus myself. What I had in the way of stimulation came from Gelb's seminar. That is now 30 years ago, and back then I was a young student. The further development of the constancy hypothesis to the reduction is also from me, and Merleau-Ponty then took it up. What you have read there is *la Gestalttheorie vue par G. en vue de son insertion dans la phénoménologie.* Köhler was always and is increasingly interested in the physics of the brain; Koffka speaks the language of behaviorism; take a look at what he has to say about the *"meaning of Gestalt"* on p. 682/3 of his book.[1] I alone am responsible for the conceptual interpretation and the phenomenological reading of its descriptive results. I will change the language of the sentence on p. 243 [of the Ms]. In this context it is only a matter of an analogy between the multiplicity of acts and something identical, whatever the identical something may be. Whether there is a substantive difference between us we will have to discover in personal conversations. I think that certain noematic levels are intersubjective; the judgmental sense, for which you indeed accept my claim, is also always something noematic. We will have to see if there is an abyss here.

Enclosed are *part IV, chap. II and III*. I hope that the use of *Gestalt-coherence* in the phenomenology of perception will make you a bit more conciliatory. It is only a matter of an "analogy" [*Sinngemäßheit*]. As you will see, the concept is fundamental for the analysis of the inner horizon as well as for the perceptual process.

We have had to change our travel plans after all. We will be coming to New York either on the *weekend* of Sept. 30 or, more likely, on that of October 14. I will then have several days free on account of the holidays. It is possible that one of my colleagues will drive to New York by car and will take us along. Although my salary is rising, we are trying to keep our expenses down, especially since I want to go to Europe again next year.

Best wishes from both of us to you and yours

As always your
Aron

1. Koffka, *Principles of Gestalt Psychology*.

Gurwitsch: *I have written Farber. I am not prepared to pray to fetishes*
(CAMBRIDGE, OCTOBER 16, 1951)

Dear Friend,

A few words in great haste. Enclosed is a copy of a letter that I wrote to Farber today. Now we must see how he will answer. I also received a letter from Kaufmann[1]—not very informative. He seems to have hardly any relation to Farber any more. He writes of a "somber calamity" and of "personal tragedies." Mrs. Rosenberg thinks that one of the reasons is Louvain's success[2] and Farber's failure to awaken interest in the *Foundations* here. If that is the case—and it is surely to some extent true—then we have another "American tragedy."

I don't know what you will do. If Farber interprets that as a presidential statement, then there is no place for me on the board any more. I am not prepared to pray to fetishes, not even if they are given a *scientific* dressing. The right to pose fundamental questions is only denied one in a Siberian work camp.

I am too familiar with the fanaticism of the (from Farber's point of view) other side to have any wish to fall into an opposing fanaticism. Scylla is no salvation from Charybdis.

It was so fine visiting you. I hope we can get together again soon, either at your home or (why not?) here.

Love and all the best

Your
Aron

1. Fritz Kaufmann. "For years he was in the Philosophy Department (Buffalo) with Farber, and didn't have a very fruitful time there. His papers are in Louvain." (Information from Mrs. Alice Gurwitsch.)

2. A reference to the First International Phenomenological Symposium, which Van Breda organized in Louvain in 1951. Schutz and Gurwitsch did not participate.

Enclosure: Gurwitsch's letter questions two of Farber's editorials: "Remarks about the Phenomenological Program" (*PPR* 6 (1945–46): 1–10), and here especially "Experience and Transcendence" (*PPR* 12 (1951–52): 1–23). The original is in English.

Dear Marvin,

The article which you published in the first issue of the new volume impels me to put a question before you: Is this article of yours to be taken as a definition and formulation of your position—and you have every right in the world to define your position—or is it to be understood as a formulation of the policy of the periodical, more precisely as indicating a change in that policy? If I raise the question—to my regret—it is because your article, which reads like an attack upon the very idea of phenomenology and upon the whole work of Husserl, appears not only in a phenomenological journal but also on the opening pages of a new volume. Thus it might easily be understood as a programmatic utterance of the editor-in-chief.

In 1945 you published (also on the opening pages of vol. VI) the "Remarks about a phenomenological program." There you also expressed reservations with regard to transcendental phenomenology or, if I may express it with some looseness, with regard to Husserl's development since *Ideen*. As far as Husserl is concerned, your reservations formulated in 1945 are substantially much the same as those which you express now. Nobody in his senses, whether he agrees with you or not, will deny your right to have such reservations and publicly to state them. All this is or might be a matter of scholarly discussion and controversy. Still, in 1945 you recalled (p. 6) that Husserl "stood for an extremely earnest conception of philosophy, deriving from a tradition going back as far as Plato and Aristotle, and that he always upheld the ideal of philosophy as the ultimate science." Throughout that early article you showed sympathetic understanding for phenomenological endeavor and for the different phases and aspects of Husserl's work—that sympathetic understanding which is also apparent in your *Foundations*. That sympathetic understanding did not prevent you from expressing your reservations. But now you write of Husserl's anti-scientific feelings and bias, you speak of anti-rationalism and anti-intellectualism with regard to a philosopher who, strangely enough, had been decried in his life-time in Germany because of his rationalism and intellectualism. The present article of yours makes the impression of a repudiation and complete rejection of the whole of phenomenology and of the whole of Husserl's life work. I cannot help asking you: is this the voice of the philosophical author Marvin Farber or that of the President of the International Phenomenological Society and the editor-in-chief of *Philosophy and Phenomenological Research*?

To put this question before you is not easy for me. Dear Marvin, I am too well aware of your merits for the phenomenological movement and its members. I have not forgotten the terrible years 1939–1941 and what you did at that time. I know very well that you have been much more than the principal editor of the periodical. You appear as *primus inter pares*. But without your personal zeal and energy, without your devotion and energy, your skill and resourcefulness, the periodical would never have come into existence— especially under those circumstances which prevailed 12 years ago—and it would never have developed into one of the most respected philosophical publications in the English language. All this has been the work of your mind and of your hands. Are you now turning against your own creation? What you are writing now is very different from the "Remarks" of 1945 when you formulated a broad editorial policy, when you advocated (p. 10) "an attitude of constructive tolerance toward all serious interests in philosophy" and extended a "standing invitation to all who do conscientious work in philosophy."

Believe me, please, very sincerely yours

Aron Gurwitsch

Schutz: *Your letter to Farber says everything essential*
                (NEW YORK, OCTOBER 30, 1951)

Dear Friend,

Many thanks for your letter of the 16th with the enclosed letter to Farber. After some thought I haven't done anything, since I have come more and more to the conclusion that the only counter-measure would be to write an answering essay. I am in less of a position than every other person to assume a change in the editorial program, since after all my essay, which you are familiar with, is to appear in the next number. Your letter is very judiciously formulated and says everything essential.

I don't know what Fritz Kaufmann means by his insinuations. I think that Mrs. Rosenberg's interpretation is pure nonsense.

Natanson[1] is busily studying the first two chapters of your book and is very enthusiastic about it. He tells me that he wrote to you and received a very kind answer from you. I think that you will like the man when you meet him.

Write soon and don't forget to write how your wife is getting along.

With all best wishes

Your
Alfred

1. One year after finishing his dissertation (published as *A Critique of Jean-Paul Sartre's Ontology,* University of Nebraska, 1951), Maurice Natanson did post-doctoral work with Schutz at the New School (1951–53). He now teaches at Yale University.

Gurwitsch: *You represent the monad and I the* raison universelle
                 (CAMBRIDGE, NOVEMBER 6, 1951)

Dear Friend,

Here is the fifth part and with this, if only "unofficially," the critical discussions between us begin. The official critical discussions will be in the sixth part. But I believe that all differences between us in the final analysis are only apparent; in reality it is a matter of differences in the spheres in which we work. This is also true for the egological question. My thesis only holds for the reduced sphere: there the ego becomes a *constitutum,* whereas in the natural attitude it can be assumed just like the existence of the world.

One consequence would be that the problem of the alter ego simply doesn't exist in the reduced sphere, or exists only in a very modified form. I don't want to commit myself on this yet. But I can say this today: This disposes of the constitution of a *transcendental* alter ego. If we two knew more about the internal history of the Aristotelian traditions (e.g., Averroes and his opponents), we might be able to discuss the entire question initially in a more simple form. This is also behind the differences between Malebranche-Leibniz. You represent the monad and I the *raison universelle.* You should come up here sometime and we could see how far we can come in this final point of difference.

Enclosed the original of Farber's answer. Perhaps someone should write an answering article. I have *so* little desire to do so. My distaste for purely "world-view" polemics grows with the years. One can define positions and defend them dialectically against other positions *ad infinitum et indefinitum.* It does not and cannot yield any results. Shouldn't one rather use the time and energy one has for positive work? What one does there might have the chance of falling on ears ready to hear, as happened with the two of us. But today the world-view polemic is just like political speeches: one convinces only one's own followers. . . .

My wife is fine and sends her best wishes.

When can we get together again? Sincerely, your

Aron

Enclosure: Farber's answer (October 22, 1951) to Gurwitsch's letter of October 16.

Dear Aron,

(1) *Naturally* (obviously!) I wrote as an individual.
(2) You misquoted me when saying I accused Edmund Husserl of irrationalism. The Existentialists were referred to.

(3) My fidelity to E. H. remains—*after my own fashion* which is now no different than when I was his admiring personal student. Numerous unpublished phenomenological materials are to appear in our journal, incidentally, quite some existential material.—How then is our policy changed?

Aron, we must have a talk before too long. Can you read this paper for us? With best regards, as always yours,

Marvin

Gurwitsch   *An ocean of problems is breaking over my head*
             (Cambridge, December 4, 1951)

Dear Friend,

Enclosed please find part VI and the conclusion. The introduction is still lacking. That will take some time; I still have to make a few additions which refer to Merleau-Ponty. As you have noticed, I have hardly mentioned him. I did that intentionally, so that my book won't appear to be a paraphrase of his: now he will receive a paragraph[1] and a couple of footnotes. The real critical discussion of him and Sartre is to come later, in a book which I would like to entitle *Les trois dimensions du réel*. This is to be an expanded version of the part I have taken out of the book.[2]

I am full of understanding for your battle with time and against time. Consider the enclosed pages the way they are meant. I am sending you the manuscript *à toute fin utile:* No expectations or anything of that sort are implied. Read it whenever you have time. Please, don't consider yourself to be under any obligation *whatsoever.* . . .

He [Kurt Goldstein] was here last Saturday. Once again we had a long talk. It would appear that he, you, and I will have to have a *conclave* for the three of us sometime. The topic would be: pre-predicative experience and the concrete attitude. Our mutual understanding is complicated by the fact that he takes pre-predicative experience to be concrete behavior, whereas it seems to me that the categorial exists in pre-predicative experience in the form of *"petites perceptions."*

And that brings me to the other *conclave* which the two of us ought to have, and whose goal would be that you give me private lessons in Leibniz. I recently read the *Nouveaux Essais*—after very many years.[3] Scales dropped from my eyes, but other scales grew in their place. Isn't my thematization the transition from the *petites perceptions* to the *apperceptions*? On the other hand, doesn't Leibniz mean mathematical idealization?[4] For example, the transition from the seen movement to the concept of velocity, from the finished given curve to its differential generation? My studies of Piaget, which I am pursuing in addition to the work on my book, have put me into a state of wild confusion. A sea of problems is breaking over my head. I ask myself if I haven't taken on too much, if I am at all equal to these difficulties.

I hope that we can get together soon. In the meantime all the best; and greet your dear wife from both of us.

Your
Aron

1. Added at the end of part IV, ch. 3: "The Organization of Perception According to Merleau-Ponty."
2. Published in G1985. "... those 150 pages were not revised to include critical discussions of the French phenomenologists" (Lester Embree, Editor's Introduction, G1985, xii). Cf. GS 10.9.50 and GS 2.17.52.
3. Cf. SG 8.19.39 and the discussions which ensue.
4. On the matter of *apperception* in Leibniz, cf. Joseph Claude Evans, *The Metaphysics of Transcendental Subjectivity: Descartes, Kant, and W. Sellars* (Amsterdam: Verlag B. R. Grüner, 1984), ch. 3.

Schutz: *Doesn't your Chronos noema devour its children, the noeses?*
          (NEW YORK, JANUARY 19, 1952)

Dear Friend,

I am very disappointed that you obviously didn't stop in New York on your return from Christmas vacation, since I had very much hoped to see you again . . . .

Unfortunately, our faculty is shrinking because of the lack of money. Not only were the contracts of two sociologists (including Brodersen) not renewed, but also Löwith's. The latter responded by immediately accepting a call as *Ordinarius* in Heidelberg, where he will take over Rickert's chair as a colleague of Jaspers. He is going over on March 7. Riezler will be 70 in February, and Kallen in April. With that the philosophy department has practically disappeared. You have no business being here as long as we don't have any money.

I have put business first because I want to dedicate the rest of this letter exclusively to your book, which I began to study immediately after finishing my Princeton work,[1] which is now being typed. To date I have only worked through the fifth part, but I have done that very thoroughly. Your work, dear friend, is a very excellent, very significant achievement, of which you can be proud. Although I considered myself rather familiar with your thoughts, a whole series of things are new to me, all of them deeply stimulating and important. I still have a lot of work to do to assimilate and understand it all, but I don't really see any opposition at all between us in substantive matters. Again and again there are reciprocal confirmations of the central ideas and many supplementations in the deeper levels of the problem which have been reached at a given stage.

But still, many of your formulations are still foreign and questionable to me.

I must first look for a transformation formula, in order to translate them into my language. There is nothing I would rather have than to be able to discuss the book systematically with you for a couple of weeks. The *face-to-face relationship* is indispensable for συμφιλοσοφεῖν. When I read your book it is just like Husserl with Kant's *Critique of Pure Reason:* I always land in my own meditations and so the manuscript becomes covered with lots of "marginalia" (in the typographical and phenomenological sense). To my joy it repeatedly happened that the remarks which I made during my reading were dealt with a couple of paragraphs or pages later, or were at least intimated. We will have to spend a lot of time talking about all this, and I am noting some of the more important points here with an eye to future discussions. Please, don't take this as a critique of the *book* as it stands—it should and must remain as it is (perhaps with the exception of a sharper formulation on Ms p. 459f.; see below). My catalogue deals with questions which refer not to the book but to the problems themselves, whether they belong to the book thematically or to its margin:

1) Relation of thematic field and horizon, margin and horizon.

2) Temporality and context [*Kontext*]. In what sense can one say that objective or phenomenal temporality plays a role in the constitution of the context? Where can polythetic and monothetic graspings of sense be accommodated in this connection?

3) In "productive thinking," is the "proposition" really the theme? Isn't the theme and its field pregiven to the proposition, the (predicative) proposition being only the polythetic *reconstitution* [*Nachkonstitution*] of the predicative theme in its field? Isn't it necessary to distinguish here between the context of the prepredicative theme *of* the proposition (which remains unchanged in its field-context with *other states of affairs* after the proposition has been formulated) and the proposition *as* theme (namely in the context-field with other *propositions,* not "states of affairs")? There is after all for example a state of affairs "Columbus—America—1492—having discovered" or "America—1492—through—Columbus—discovered—having been" or "Discovery—of America by—Columbus—1492" or "1492—year—discovery—of America—through—Columbus" (all four formulations point to the same state of affairs, but each—in my usage—throwing another aspect of relevance into relief), and this state of affairs remains untouched, regardless of whether the proposition founded on it stands in the context of a line of thought which has the history of the great discovery, or another, the hegemony of Spain, as context [*Field,* 318ff.].

4) Ms p. 450 (against Berger,[2] *not* against you): The statement "A sentence like 'Portugal is not diatonic' is devoid of meaning" is itself negative, but meaningful. Therefore there is always the possibility that the question whether the statement "Portugal is not diatonic" is meaningful can be posed, if only for example, for purposes of exemplification [*Field,* 334].

5) Is there nothing at all in the thematic field which (in your language) would be non-relevant? And in the margin nothing which would be relevant? Are the three sentences Ms p. 459: "Relevancy proves to underly the phenome-

non of pointing reference or context" and "Unity of context is unity by relevance" and "Context may be said to be *based* upon relevance" (in connection
with the *leitmotif:* "unity by relevancy") to be understood to be identical in
meaning? I have some difficulties here, especially when I read on Ms p. 460:
"context *founded* upon relevancy," "relevancy and context are *correlated* concepts," "context *denoting* unity of a specific nature," "relevancy denoting the
principle which underlies that unity." Is this a founding in the technical sense?
Or which is the essence of this correlation? [*Field*, 341].

   6) Your and my concept of relevance. (Since mine contains yours as a component concept, but is broader, I shall from now on call your *relevancy* "pertinence"
in order to avoid confusions *between us*). I believe that there is no opposition at
all between us. The difference lies in the fact that you obviously do not accept
the division into *topical, interpretational,* and *motivational* relevance, which is
important for my approach but, as I admit, in the *framework of this work* is less
important. But I am not entirely certain, and I want to reflect on this much more
before I make a definitive statement. It may be that your postulate of the "co-
presence" of the pertinent, which is still rather unclear to me, is the reason why
you in principle stick to noematic analyses in your investigation of the pertinent.
You say on Ms p. 463: "The only relationship which obtains between such data
(of the second class) and the theme consists in their being experienced simultaneously." Simultaneously in which temporal dimension? This doesn't agree with
my theory of the multiple realities and of the temporal dimension which
uniquely belongs to each of them. In addition: It is true that the *non-pertinent*
(irrelevant) is *co-present*. But is it also true that only that which is *co-present* can be
pertinent? [*Field*, 346].

   7) I have reservations about the formulation (Ms p. 467) "In this awareness
consists the temporal continuity of the stream of consciousness" [*Field*, 346]. I
believe that to be an "over-statement." The continuity of consciousness is doubtlessly founded on this "awareness." (And by the way, in my opinion it must
necessarily be an egological awareness: "which must be able to accompany all of
my thought.") But this *awareness* is only *one* factor among many others. In other
words: it is surely correct, as you describe it, that themes and fields flow into one
another, but it is not correct that temporality is only experienceable through this
flowing-to-one-another. It seems to me that you need this assumption because
you construe the thematic field to be non-egological.

   And how does it come to the constitution of this "awareness," if not through
the egological "temporalizing of time" which Husserl liked to speak of so
much?[3] And how about the "steered" shifts of the themes, for example the
change of perspectives, but also of the themes themselves, that are the result of
our actions? Just think for example of Husserl's investigations of being-driven in
contrast to walking-around. Aren't your investigations too restricted to the
former? Of course, the phenomenology of the body comes in here along with
our old egological dispute. But isn't the "awareness" of the limits of the body as
a permanent element in all thematic shifts [*Themenüberschiebungen*], something
which you too recognize, sufficient for the constitution of (at least one basic

form of) temporality? Perhaps the sixth, still unread part contains things which are pertinent and relevant to this. The proposition which is simply asserted on Ms page 473, "Phenomenal time flows according to rigid laws, independently of any egological activity" I consider to be a *non-sequitur* as it stands [*Field*, 351].

8) To p. 435 [*Field*, 351, line 24]: "it follows that . . . ." Why shouldn't the material relations constitute the *framework* within which the activities of the ego undertake the analysis into field and margin? And does your theory recognize "transmarginal" conscious experiences? Examples: a) the stock of knowledge which is totally irrelevant to the theme, which is at the moment dormant, but can be reawakened; b) neutralized *cogitationes;* c) *petites perceptions* and every form of that which is "unconscious"; d) the reproducible and anticipatable; e) the forgotten in Bergson's sense; and many other things. Why do you restrict the margin to the simultaneous, retentions, protentions, and exclude reproduction and anticipation? *Quid juris* does only the *immediately* successive belong to the margin? *Ex definitione?*

9) *Gestalt coherence and pertinence:* We read on Ms p. 481 that *figure-ground* relations are specializations of the general theme-field relations. That is completely clear. But on Ms p. 483 we read that Gestalt coherence is a *prerequisite* for unity through pertinence. In which direction does the founding run? (*Field*, 356–358).

10) Doesn't your Chronos (or better: A-Chronos) noema devour its own children, the noeses? If on Ms p. 491 the positional index belongs to the noema, what is left for the noeses?[4] Is the positional index not "instituted" [*gestiftet*]?

11) Ms p. 498: The thesis that everything that is marginal is confused appears very questionable to me. After all, as your example shows, what I call "stored-away knowledge," as well as Husserl's habitualities, belongs to the margin. All degrees of *clarity* and *distinctness* are represented here. It would surely be correct that they are not polythetically reproducible without themselves becoming a new theme [*Field*, 368f.].

12) Ms p. 499, next to last line: Is the word "material" an intentional qualification? Doesn't what you say also hold for ideal objects? If not, why? [*Field*, 369 bottom].

13) *Again and again and again:* (Ms p. 500 top) "We are aware of ourselves as existing within the world" etc. Is such a statement meaningful if one simultaneously denies the ego-reference of consciousness? [*Field*, p. 370].

14) Same page, bottom: "free choice." This is of course only defensible if one leaves the intersubjective dimension out of consideration, as indeed the entire book does. If one brings it into consideration, there are "*imposed* relevances." This seems certain to me. I am not so certain whether there are not already such "imposed relevances," which restrict "free choice," in the spheres you are investigating as well. What about the Maine de Biran problem of resistance and "effort"?[5]

15) The relation "noetic modification = intra-thematic possibilities/abilities [(*Ver-*)*Möglichkeiten*]; noematic modification = field potentiality" seems questionable to me. Why shouldn't, for example, drawing the margin into the field,

JUNE 24, 1951–MARCH 17, 1952

or the elements of the field into the nucleus, also indicate noetic modifications? Or a noematic intertwining turn out to be an intra-thematic possibility?

All of this, dear friend, is very provisional; please don't hold me to these hurried remarks. Stimulated by you, my thoughts are in movement, and it will be a long time before they crystallize again. The notes above serve only to mark the main themes which I want to discuss with you.

I must now read four theses by poor doctoral candidates, and as soon as I am finished with that I will begin the sixth part. I am giving the fifth to Natanson.

I am sending you under separate cover an off-print of "Choosing among Projects of Action" and a manuscript on Santayana ("Dominations and Powers") which I read in our General Seminar. It is not for publication.[6]

Love to you and your wife

Sincerely

Your

Alfred Schutz

1. "Common Sense and Scientific Interpretation of Human Action," S1953c.
2. Gaston Berger, *Recherches sur les conditions de la connaissance* (Paris, 1941).
3. Is Schutz referring to conversations with Husserl? (Cf. the footnote to SG 8.19.39.)
4. "What we call positional index proves to have noematic status: it concerns what is experienced rather than the fact of its actually being experienced" (*Field*, p. 363).
5. Maine de Biran (1766–1824) developed a theory of the "*effort voulu*," the deliberate bodily movement, which was an object of ridicule in the 19th century. (Cf. Waldenfels.)
6. Lecture on 1.9.52. Later published: "Santayana on Society and Government" (S1952).

Schutz: *Your book is the finest achievement in phenomenology since Husserl's*
            Experience and Judgment
            (NEW YORK, JANUARY 25, 1952)

My dear friend and robber of my sleep!

Since I last wrote you I have literally spent my nights with your sixth part. You can be very proud of your book; it is the finest achievement in phenomenology since Husserl's *Experience and Judgment*. I am very enthusiastic and wish you luck and success. Such a work must and will gain deserved recognition.

Needless to say I have my questions, doubts, objections. To make them properly clear to myself will take months, perhaps years: my very first, tentative comments upon a first reading are on the enclosed pages.

In addition there are various desiderata, but you can't press your future collected works between the covers of a single book. On to the printer, that is the most important thing! I would have wished that you would show how an element from the margin shifts into the field, from there into the core; how you view the modification of one theme into another, or from one existential order to another; how it happens that figure [*Gestalt*] can become ground [*Grund*] and ground figure; what the relation between "pertinence" (your relevance) and Gestalt coherence is; why the noematic predominates over noetic analyses in your work, etc.: I mention all this only because it would be desirable if you would make reference to these open horizons of problems—I believe that they are much more than marginal intruders—in the introduction which you still plan to write.

Many thanks that you have allowed me to participate in the marvelous growth of this work through all these years. Scheler is right when he says that one can only philosophize with friends.

God bless you and love

Alfred Schutz

Supplement: Schutz's comments on the concluding sixth part ("Ontological Problems") of *The Field of Consciousness,* with which the "official critical discussions" (according to GS 11.6.51) begin. The titles and numbering of the following points (some have been condensed, some left out for stylistic reasons) are by the editor.

1. *Reality of everyday life.* I can't see that the reality of the world of everyday life can be grounded in its character as perceptual world. Why then isn't the world of hallucination a real one, the proceedings on the film screen not real? I believe that the reality of the world of everyday life is based on its structure as the world of work [*Wirkwelt*] [*Field,* 382–387].

2. *Spheres of life in modern civilization: professional spheres, etc.* Are these investigations really of an ontological nature? Can they be perceived immediately from the phenomenological theme-field analysis without clarification of phenomenological and mundane intersubjectivity?

3. *Foundation of social roles.* The content of this remark (concerning me)[1] makes a silent presupposition: 1) the sphere of intersubjectivity, which you don't analyze; 2) connected with that the "socialization of knowledge." My Princeton paper [S1953c] will make clear to you what that means.

My thesis is that "roles" (a concept which is used more and more in modern sociology: see, e.g., the two volumes by Parsons which just appeared[2]) are founded on the we-relation and its derivatives, and must be explained in terms of them. The other [*Nebenmensch*] in his roles, I in mine, we are perhaps πρός ἡὑμὰς, certainly not φυσεῖ simply "given."

The opposition which you claim between us simply doesn't exist in reality. It disappears immediately if the intermediate levels which you leave unanalyzed are worked through. In addition, it is confusing to find these problems treated under the category of ontological problems ("orders of existence," "order of reality") in a study which according to its program is restricted to the study of the topical contexts of relevance in the noematic structure. They all belong to the realm of interpretational relevancies in the mundane sphere, just like most social problems. I am quite familiar with the problem you are concerned with.

The main difficulty however is the change of roles, e.g., between my daytime and nighttime life. In my opinion this fact makes the explanation of roles as the expression of an existential order pretty much impossible. On the other hand, the fact that there are, e.g., two sexes, age groups, etc. would be accounted for existentially.[3] I admit that my presentation in "Multiple Realities" is fragmentary and inadequate. The parts of my book which are sketched out contain whole chapters on these questions. I admit that your interpretation of my concept of ideal types also finds support in the spotty presentation of "Multiple Realities." But my *Princeton paper* [S1953c] will show you *how much* agreement there is between us concerning the relation between "common sense" and type formation in the sciences.

The fact that we have come to the same result via such different lines of thought is a real joy and confirmation. Just for this reason, we shouldn't mislead the reader with oppositions which do not exist.

4. *"Typical situations."* I have great difficulties here, which have to do with the basic problem of all sociologists: *Who* defines the situation? Who confers the "definite existential index"? "Alien system" for whom? Perhaps it isn't the "intruder" who is *out of place*, but we? [*Field*, 383].

5. *The unity of the world of work.* Couldn't the "togetherness" [*Zusammenhang*[4]] be found in subjective duration and its noetic-noematic structures? The role of the unity of the objective context in the world of work [*Wirkwelt*] lies in the fact that it presents the framework in which projects can be "realized"—here we encounter the problem of "ability" [*Vermöglichkeit*] or potestivity. Next paragraph: "a continuous and coherent sequence." What makes these segments "coherent and continuous"? [*Field*, 384].

6. *Husserl's theory of the objects of fantasy.* "Only such objects, events, and actions as have endured together in *objective* time belong to the same segment of our past": Here you follow Husserl in his assertion that fantasized objects are distinguished from real ones by the fact that they have no determinate temporal position. I hold this theory to be false. After all, when awake I can remember coherent segments of fantasies and dreams, etc. [*Field*, 385; concerning Husserl, cf. *Experience and Judgment*, §40].

7. *Biography and objective time.* My life history takes place in objective time only for the biographer, not for my autobiography. (And historical time is a modification of objective time.) For me, my past life takes place in my duration, not in objective time. This could not be otherwise, since after all this past life of mine cannot be dissected into homogeneous units. You yourself have shown this marvellously in the essay on "transient phases and resting places" [G1942]. But it is correct that communication is only possible in objective time, but that is no

contradiction, since "standard time" is only the "intersection" of inner durations, synchronized by the course of events in the external world which institutes communication [*Field,* p. 386f.].

8. *Time and the imagined event.* This isn't clear to me: "The time in which imagined events occur is not an imagined time"—really?

I also don't understand the claim that it is meaningless to ask whether an imagined event is simultaneous with a real one.[5] E.g., while I was drunk, lay under anesthesia, smoked hashish, slept, I had these and those fantasies.

9. *Phantasy world and reality.* Are fantasies *really* a matter of neutrality modifications? What is neutralized in the fantasy of a flute-playing Pan? Further: aren't the heard voices real for the schizophrenic?

Further: The thesis that no fantasy world can be a sub-order of reality silently presupposes that reality is the *intersubjective world of work.* But hasn't everyone who participates in a *séance* "seen" the "materializations" at such and such time of day in the same room?

Finally: "No imagined event requires insertion into a wider context." Doesn't the context of a dream have its theme, field, margin? [*Field,* 390].

10. *Spheres of incompatibility.* "The imagining subject has complete freedom" is surely an *overstatement:* There are also spheres of incompatibility in fantasy. "Each one with its own quasi-time: all disconnected from one another"? I would assert to the contrary: *but unified in the durée,* to which they all belong. Concerning the footnote: a) does the interpretation in the text give a correct presentation of Husserl's thoughts? b) Is Husserl right? [*Field,* 390].

11. *Uninvolved in an imagined world.* The second example ["Let there be a world of imagination . . . ," *Field,* 392] of the uninvolved person in an imagined world is incomprehensible to me. I tried in vain to make the situation clear to myself by means of the first appearance of the ghost in *Hamlet.*

12. *Schutz's Theory of "Finite Provinces of Meaning"* [*Field,* 394ff.]. Now we come to the chapter which deals with my "Multiple Realities." To begin with, many thanks for the loving care in the presentation. Here I would have only two wishes: a) When you say . . . that "the system of relevancies governing life in the world of working originates from the basic experience of the fundamental anxiety," this is quite correct, but surely remains incomprehensible if you don't add that the system of various plans, which are integrated in the life plan which is dominated by *anxiety,* lies between them; b) I would be thankful if you would put in the word "intentionally" on Ms page 399, line 9, following "Schutz abides"; similarly on Ms p. 400: "The sense of their existence is intentionally no more made by Schutz etc. . . ."[6] [*Field,* 394ff.].

With this addition I only want to bring out the fact that you are not suggesting that I am unaware of the transcendental-phenomenological aspects you deal with, that in this piece you are dealing with—as in all of my work—I am, in accordance with my program and in principle, only dealing with the natural attitude.

By the way, we ought to have a discussion about the sense of the reduction sometime. Only recently I found, in a posthumously published essay by Scheler, the claim that the transcendental reduction was initially a technique for bringing the philosophizing spirit to philosophize, just as there are various "psychic" and "vital techniques" in the religious sphere or in the Orient, a problem which preoccupied Scheler more and more.[7] There may be a great deal of truth in this sentence, which is just tossed off.

But that is only an aside: now, a few first and very superficial reactions concerning substantive issues.

13. *Relevance and reduction.* Footnote: "Natural attitude is here understood in Husserl's sense as opposed to the phenomenological attitude . . ." [*Field*, 399]; I am not so entirely sure whether Husserl's ἐποχή is not precisely just a special case of the series of possible ἐποχης that I have worked out. It might above all be a matter of gaining the transformation equation that makes it possible to put *anything at all* in brackets or leave it outside the brackets. That is a problem with which I am currently deeply occupied. We would then come to the possibility of viewing every expression that stands outside the brackets as a "system of reference" for those that remain within the brackets, and what we take to require the bracket and what not would in turn be a function of what I would call "relevance" in my terminology.

Here we encounter a discrepancy between your and my use of this word, one that is deeper than a merely terminological one: For in spite of the differing use of the brackets, thus in spite of variations of relevance, your "pertinences" remain, everything is stiill bound up with everything, is in a context with it, just as before.

To put it metaphorically, it is a matter of whether I write "a + b + c + d" or "a + (b + c + d)" or "a + b + (c + d)," etc., etc. I hope that you understand me, but this is a tremendous problem, one that is not dealt with in "Multiple Realities," and in your book, too, is it neither made thematic nor does it have a place in the field. It is merely an *intrusion.* But that's what every individual case is, thank God.

For the problem of "finding a first ground of presuppositionlessness," thus for Husserl's problem, the transcendental reduction is of course the only "relevant" ἐποχή. But I believe that Carneades[8] would have been on my side.

14. *Non-real existential orders* [*Field*, 398, n. 46: "Schutz' theory gives rise to two questions: . . . from which experiences do systems of relevancy other than that prevailing in the world of daily life originate? . . . the second question concerns their very derivation."]. Here of course you are completely right. This is a great problem, which I haven't solved: my book[9] attempts to give a partial solution, starting from what is unquestionably given. I merely believe that your justified critique also hits you. To be sure, you say on [*Field*, 409][10] that non-real existential orders are subject to specific relevance principles, but you too fail to carry through their derivation and do not show in what their specificity consists. Here a great task lies ahead of both of us, which each of us will have to master in his sphere of labor. It appears to me that with your analyses you have come closer to indicating a possible derivation than I, though perhaps my theory of the modified *epochés* and of the growing tensions of consciousness (which you,

by the way, seem to implicitly reject) comes closer to a solution to the problem of specificity.

15. *Time and intersubjectivity* [*Field*, p. 397, n. 41: "Imagining, and even dreaming, . . . refers to phenomenal time . . . rather than to the time which pertains to a world of imagination. . . . The latter time is to be characterized as 'objectivated quasi-time.' "]. As I have already mentioned, I can't accept your interpretation of imagined time as quasi-objective time. What is "objective" or "quasi-objective" to mean here other than "intersubjective"? But precisely intersubjectivity can be lacking in the imagination. All of these various times grow out of and fuse in inner duration, thus in phenomenal time and out of its irreversibility.

But that doesn't change the fact that I expressed myself very sloppily in "Multiple Realities"; such things are not to be avoided in the American system of counting words for an article which is really already too long. At the place you justifiably criticize I should have referred to the fact that *standard time* is nothing but an "intersection" of individual durations and that its *irreversibility* is a result of this.

But I don't understand, especially from the standpoint of your theory, what is to be the significance in connection with the problem of time of the distinction between the time of fantasizing and the time that is attributed to the fantasized object in fantasizing. We will have to talk about this at length, since the state of affairs is different in the various existential orders summarized there under the name "imagination." From the standpoint of *my* theory there is a problem here whose solution in my opinion is not given but merely hinted in "Multiple Realities."

Section (b)[11] will have to be the object of long discussions between us, and perhaps I will find an opportunity to answer you publicly once your book has appeared. I will have to think all of this through very carefully and "take it to heart" in the truest sense of the word. Don't hold me to this, but it seems to me at first glance that the tunnels have met. Taking off from the natural attitude, the problem of the constitution of the sense structure of other "provinces" or orders of course remains open, and can only be solved by analyses such as yours. And here you have gone very far.

16. *On the concept of existence* [*Field*, 404–413]. A most excellent section, which I must still think through often and exactly. Two places are not clear to me, if they are more than stylistic carelessness:

1) Ms p. 548 (in the italicized part): *For any object to exist, means that the object under consideration pertains to a* specific *systematic order.* Why "specific"? Can't one and the same object, viewed existentially, belong to various existential orders simultaneously? Or is the word "specific" not to be interpreted as meaning that it can only belong to *one* order? [*Field*, 404].

2) Ms p. 549 (in the italicized part): *Accounting for the apprehension, perceptual* or other *of a material thing we are led towards the phenomenon of the world.*[12] What do you mean with "or other"?

The assertion that validity for propositions means the same thing as mundane existence for things is very surprising and stimulating [*Field,* 406].

Unfortunately, I don't understand the paragraph on mathematical existence. You will have to explain it to this non-mathematician [*Field,* 407].

In the very illuminating Goldstein illustration: isn't his concept of relevance rather my concept than yours? [*Field,* 407–409].

The Aristotle compilation is very valuable. I didn't have time to look at the places you quote [*Field,* 410–411, n. 84].

What you have to say about predication of reality and of existence is excellent.

17. *Conclusion* [*Field,* 414–420]. The *coda* contains an overture: I thought that the very important constants of marginal consciousness would be developed in their own chapter of the book. You do things like Mozart, who saved his most beautiful themes, out of which others would make whole movements, for the coda. The theory of the three constants is very significant.[13] But there are still more. Let me mention two of them: one, the knowledge of my own death (and its correlate, my being-thrown-into-the-world by my birth) may find a place in the concept of "embodied existence." But the other creates a large problem for you, not for me: we always have a third intersubjectivity, i.e., our knowledge of the existence of others, in the margin (which of course also involves communication with the others).

1. (Ms p. 517; *Field,* 383): "Fellowmen encountered within the sphere of professional activity appear in . . . their roles." A remark concerning Schutz was deleted at this point. (Cf. Gurwitsch, "Role-Encounter," in G1979, par. 19.)

2. *Towards a General Theory of Action* and *The Social System.* Schutz developed the thesis concerning founding in his correspondence with Parsons (S1977b and 1978).

3. The analyses of role in Gurwitsch's habilitation (G1979), with which Schutz was obviously not familiar, are not mentioned.

4. The word *Zusammenhang* does not appear in the English edition. Gurwitsch speaks of a "unity of objective togetherness" = "*Einheit des objektiven Zusammen*" (*Field,* 384).

5. "To ask whether some imagined event is contemporaneous with some real happening or which of the two precedes the other, is obviously meaningless" (*Field,* 389).

6. In the published version: "deliberately" instead of "intentionally" (*Field,* 400).

7. Cf. the similar "Remark concerning the sociological origin of high cultures and the origin of the sciences" in Scheler, *Die Wissenformen und die Gesellschaft* (1960), 438–443.

8. Schutz begins *The Problem of Relevance* (S1971a, published posthumously) with the "Problem of Carneades," a sceptical "reserve" (*epoché*) concerning the probable.

9. *Structures of the Life-World,* ch. II (S1975).

10. *Field,* 409: "Differences between orders of existence, therefore, must be accounted for in terms of the differences between the relevancy principles involved."

11. "The Psychological and the Constitutive Point of View" (*Field,* 339–404).

12. Here Gurwitsch refers to Ludwig Landgrebe, "The World as a Phenomenological Problem," *PPR* 1 (1941): 38–58; reprinted in Ludwig Landgrebe, *The Phenomenology of Edmund Husserl: Six Essays,* ed. and intro. by Donn Welton (Ithaca: Cornell University Press, 1981), ch. 4. Cf. L. Landgrebe, "The World-Concept," in *Contemporary European Philosophy* (New York: Frederick Ungar Publishing Co., 1966), ch. II.

13. The three "constants": "1) The stream of our conscious life; 2) our embodied existence; 3) the perceptual world" (*Field*, 415). Cf. G1985.

Gurwitsch: *"One is always indebted to others for what one is"*
(CAMBRIDGE, FEBRUARY 17, 1952)

My dearest Friend,

It is really scandalous: not only have I robbed you of your time, your peace, and your sleep, but on top of it all I don't even answer your last two letters. You have put me deeply in your debt with the care with which you have approached my theses. Actually, you have thought through the problems I am dealing with all over again. Since I know a thing or two about the difficulty of these things, I know what an enormous labor you have taken on. If one of us has to thank the other, it is I who am in debt to you in Goethe's sense: "One is always indebted to others for what one is." (This is one of his expressions that I love very much.) The form which this thanks will take is also given with the nature of things: the book will be dedicated to you and my wife, and then we will continue our συμφιλοσοφεῖν, in which, as we discover to our great joy, we tend rather to confirm rather than correct one another.

My thanks for all of your notes to parts III, V, VI. They will all be taken into account (especially those which refer to you) *au fur et à mesure* that I enter the improvements of my corrector into the final copy. I will begin with that as soon as the introduction is written. I hope to be able to begin with the introduction in the next few days. An entire paragraph on Merleau-Ponty has been added. I left that until the end in order to avoid the impression that my book is a variation on his themes.

You are completely right that the modifications of the thematic fields deserve a more adequate treatment. But I have already written enough about just that in the "Phenomenology of Thematics."[1] At any rate, the direction in which these things are to be dealt with is indicated there. I would see and say a great deal differently today: but I didn't want to make the book even more voluminous, and one has to stop somewhere. This act of stopping is always violent in these matters, since all scientific labor is fragmentary, in this and still other respects.

You are also right that the *Conclusion* is an *Introduction*. The theory of the three constants constitutes the content of some 150 pages which you read some years ago and about which you provided me with very important notes.[2] That was originally to be an additional part. But I took it out with the intention of making another small book out of it, which I want to start working on as soon as the large one is wrapped up. As I wrote these 150 pages it was still war-time, and neither Sartre nor Merleau-Ponty was accessible to me. I plan to write the new book directly in French and entitle it "Les trois dimensions du réel." That is the place for explicit critical discussions with Sartre and Merleau-Ponty. . . .

I hope that you and yours are well. I am playing with the thought of coming to New York for a *weekend* sometime in order to discuss a couple of your notes with you. I don't yet know when that can be arranged.

Love and best wishes

Your

Aron

1. Gurwitsch's dissertation (G1929; English translation in G1966a).
2. The "150 pages" are published in G1985. Cf. GS 10.9.50 and GS 12.4.51.

Schutz: *Kallen has asked me to switch from sociology to philosophy*
(NEW YORK, FEBRUARY 23, 1952)

Dear Friend,

Many thanks for your kind letter of the 17th and especially for your kind words. If my remarks are really interesting to you, they have achieved their goal. You don't write anything about my remarks on part IV. I have a lot of remarks about it too, but I believe I didn't send them to you because I had hoped to see you in New York during the Christmas vacation. They are of course available to you if you can use them, but they mostly deal with questions I want to discuss with you (by the way, E. now has the manuscript).

That you want to dedicate the book to me as well as your wife is undeserved, but just the intention is a great joy for me. I am very thankful to you that you have allowed me to participate in the growth and development of this book.

My Princeton paper[1] is now mimeographed and I am sending you a copy under separate cover. For various reasons it is very important to me, and I am curious what you will have to say. The conference, which was to have taken place on March 1 and 2, has been postponed (to March 15 and 16) because the papers of various participants were not finished. On the basis of what I have gathered from the *papers* which are finished, I fear the worst. My *paper* has cost me 16 hours every Saturday and Sunday since September, and has kept me, for example, from studying your work immediately. But I don't regret it, since I believe that I have made some progress.

Our philosophy department is in a state of dissolution. Kallen has asked me to change from sociology to philosophy. But I will decline. First, I have now with great effort worked up a three-year program of twelve sociology courses and seminars, and I don't have the energy and time to do the same for philosophy. Second, I would be the only one who came into question for work with theses in philosophy, whereas there are four of us in sociology. Third, if I at some time really had to live *from* "science," I would find it easier as a sociologist. But from next year on I may give two courses in sociology and two in philosophy.

Since E. won't have anything to eat starting in June if he doesn't get the grant from the Social Research Council (and up to now I haven't even been asked for a letter of recommendation), Kallen wants to let him give a course at the Graduate Faculty on modern French philosophy. This leads me to the problem of E. and Salomon's behavior in this matter, about which I don't want to say anything. However, I would like you to come to your own judgment. For this reason, I am sending under separate cover along with my essay:

1) E.'s program for his course.

2) His *term paper* on Heidegger's concept of time for the Löwith-Riezler seminar (Löwith was very satisfied, and only regretted that it is based on Waelhens.[2] [It is possible not to] know enough German to read Heidegger—just as we know too much German to read him).

So much to this theme. Please return the enclosures to me at your convenience. . . .

If you can realize your intention of coming to New York, I would be very happy, but I would have to know ahead of time when you are coming. As I said, March 15 and 16 are out.

With best wishes and greetings

Your
Alfred

1. "Common Sense and Scientific Interpretation of Human Action" (S1953c). Read to the Princeton colloquium on "Model Constructs in the Social Sciences" on March 15 and 16, 1952.
2. Alphonse de Waelhens, *La philosophie de Martin Heidegger* (Louvain, 1942).

Gurwitsch: *The entire formalistic theory of mathematics has been on the wrong track since roughly 1880*
               (CAMBRIDGE, MARCH 9, 1952)

Dear Friend,

Many thanks for your letter and all of the enclosures. To begin with, your Princeton paper. I read it immediately and have seen with pleasure just how precisely our tunnels meet. From the standpoint of the methodology of science in general this is a highly significant contribution. There are a couple of points in which I see or would say things a bit differently. But with regard to the main point (e.g., the necessity of a subjective interpretation, taking into account the fact that the objects of the *social scientist* are "engaged" subjects), you have brought it out very pregnantly and clearly, and one can only hope that the others understand it. Before I come to details and to those subtleties where differentiations rather than differences between us begin, I want to study the *paper* once more at leisure. I will have this leisure in roughly two weeks, when I am finished with my introduction. Do you want to wait so long for my more detailed remarks? May I keep the copy?

I will send you back E.'s Heidegger *paper* in a couple of days. My impressions: he should make a couple of modifications, a few condensations here, a few elaborations there, and then publish it. There is no discussion of these things in English, and his is extraordinarily well done. The fact that I personally don't have all too much sympathy for Heidegger's way of doing philosophy is *beside the point*. My opinion is that Sartre and Merleau-Ponty have done these things better, and that you, taking off from Husserl's late work, can and will go much further, precisely because of your much more concrete approach and your orientation toward the questions of social science. But that has nothing to do with E. and the quality of his work. On the basis of this *paper* my wish to have him here has become even more intense.

The realization of this wish now depends on some machinations behind the scenes, about which I know very little and on which I have even less influence; it is all so infinitely disgusting. With regard to Salomon, things are roughly the way I had thought them to be a priori. (Two enclosures accompany this letter.) Salomon is either not able or not willing to go into someone else's ideas. He reacts in a completely subjective manner and makes a personal affair out of things which are not even substantive differences, but rather merely come from a difference in interest. . . .

You didn't send me your remarks on part IV. I would be very thankful to you if you would give them to me. I will soon begin to check the corrections of my corrector, and that will be the best opportunity to take your remarks into account. Do you also have notes to parts I and II?

I recently read Cassirer's presentation of Leibniz while preparing lectures.[1] I was amazed how much my theory of perceptual implications in part IV, ch. II seems to be of Leibnizian inspiration. Aside from that, a new approach to the problems of movement in the physicalistic sense is opened up from the theory of perception. This is all very exciting. The two of us should spend many years studying Leibniz together. Supplementing one another, we would get something out of it. In my excitement I ran right to Maimon and to his concept of the differential of consciousness. I was once again dependent on Cassirer. Aren't my perceptual implications something like the differential of consciousness? If all this holds up—the coming years will have to demonstrate it—then there is only one approach to the problems of the continuum—the Leibnizian—and the entire formalistic theory of mathematics has been on the wrong track since roughly 1880. If so, the fantasts (like Cantor) were right, and the exact people fundamentally wrong.

I wish you success in Princeton. One needn't be a prophet to predict that you will surely be the only scientific speaker, precisely because you don't stare at *science*, but rather look at the things. But in this age of *science* we are further from that than ever. *Intelligibilité*, which we both believe in and which we want, counts as a sign of superstition. A *scientist* recently told me that quite openly. May the Lord God keep us healthy in this superstition for many years.

With all best greetings to you and yours

Your
Aron

Please excuse the many mistakes. I am more nervous than usual these days.

1. Ernst Cassirer, *Leibniz's System in seinen wissenschaftlichen Grundlagen* (Marburg, 1902). Cf. Gurwitsch's later book *Leibniz: Philosophie des Panlogismus*, G1974a.

Schutz: *When it comes to objects other than material objects, we can't get anywhere without intersubjectivity*
(NEW YORK, MARCH 17, 1952)

Dearest Friend,

Many thanks for your kind letter. Princeton was interesting and, I can say, successful. More about this when we get together. Here in all haste a copy of my marginalia to your fourth part, which E. gave back to me for this purpose. It is, as you will see, a matter of ideas that came to me *during* my reading (thus, before I was familiar with the following parts; but I am copying what I noted down, since I cannot now rethink the whole thing carefully enough), and less of critical remarks. I had hoped to be able to talk it all over with you during your Christmas stay in New York, so I didn't send you a copy of the remarks immediately. *Take them for what they are worth.*

Love to you and your wife

Alfred

Enclosure: Remarks on part IV, "Phenomenological Theory of Perception" [*Field*, 201–295]. Bracketed quotations from *The Field of Consciousness* are added by the editor. Other quotations are from the draft under discussion and may not appear in *Field* in precisely this form.

1. [*Field*, 207: "For a presentation in imagination to be of a material thing, it must, therefore, contain references to further presentations through which the thing may be imagined to appear from different sides and under different aspects."][1] But there is a curious phenomenon of imagined perception: the fantasizing projection of that which is to be formed. What if one wanted to apply the entire argument to the ποιεῦ? Is what is to be brought forth in the *pragma*[2] eidetically, also as well as essentially incomplete?

THE UNITY OF THE PERCEPTUAL PROCESS

2. [*Field*, 208: "Suppose that in trying to contrive the appearance of the thing when seen from below, we imagine a mountainous country, or that when we recede, in imagination, from the thing in order to see how it looks at a greater distance, we imagine a flat wall."] *Alice in Wonderland* experiences such things; indeed, in dreams it is *taken for granted*. Does the dream perhaps escape eidetics? Where then are the limits? Everything depends on the context in which the fantasy objects stand. There is always a point from which everything is compatible with everything else: incompatibility as a function of relevance (in my sense).

3. [*Field*, 209: "The identity of the thing imagined as possibly perceivable depends upon the organization of the multiple perceptions into the unity of one sustained process."] How does the "thing" come in here if not as the reality of the world of working breaking into the "reality" of fantasy? The same with Husserl's "witches" in two different fairy tales.[3]

4. [*Field*, 210: "Throughout the perceptual process the noemata corresponding to the various phases of the process must agree with one another."] This is all quite right and the best Husserl. But is "harmony and agreement" more than a reference back to life-worldly experience? Is agreement ontologically grounded? Can I also fantasy *cogitationes caecae* and, if so, what would this mean?

5. [*Field*, 211: "By virtue of complementing and continuing one another, the single perceptual noemata organize themselves into a coherent, systematic group."] Could just as well be an abrupt jump as a continuous change.

6. [*Field*, 211: "The corresponding appearances and presentations are . . . organized into a coherent noematic system."] What really happens with the noeses? It seems that for Aron everything is only a noematic variation. But perhaps that comes in a later chapter. (P.S. It came, if not completely satisfying.)

7. [*Field*, 212] "A perceptual process . . . may be . . . interrupted. . . . Phases of the process which occur after the interruption will be unified with those which occurred before": That isn't entirely correct, I think; cf. my analysis of interruption (in a chapter of my book which you haven't yet seen).[4]

8. (Same page) "Unification . . . does not concern the acts as real psychological events occuring in phenomenal time": Is it really phenomenal time?

9. [*Field*, 212: "From the noetic point of view . . . these references will appear as anticipations and expectancies."] Let's wait and see what ch. II will bring; but "expectations and anticipations" are not yet noeses, they are themselves intentional acts with their own noematic accessories; to the extent that the

word "modalization" has any meaning at all, there would have to be noematic-noetic modalizations, and only such.

10. [*Field*, 215] "The process of perception and perceptual determination of a material thing is an infinite process": That is why we need a system of relevances which determines how *far* we have to penetrate into the horizon for a given task. One could speak of a "pragmatistic" function of relevances.

OPEN INFINITY OF THE PERCEPTUAL PROCESS

11. [*Field*, 221] "What holds for material things is correspondingly true for objects of every class": That is too fast for me. Whose acts are in question here? When it is a matter of objects other than material things, we can't get anywhere without intersubjectivity. I believe that even the perception of material objects presupposes intersubjectivity; but social or political institutions are after all performances of consciousness of *others*. What about "socially derived knowledge"?

12. [*Field*, 223–227: "The Presumptive Existence of the Perceptual World."] A new form of the theodicy; perhaps rather a *confessio fidei*. The temporal dimension of anticipation is lacking here. What is emptily anticipated is necessarily anticipated (fantasied) as in harmony with the stock of experience that is at hand at the time of the anticipating. But is it really meaningful to speak of a fulfillment of the anticipation? Can this in any sense be possible except via an exchange of temporal dimensions?

SENSE EXPERIENCE AND PERCEPTION

13. [*Field*, 230] "We may assume when we hear a sound that we have no other experience, especially no visual experience, of the source of the sound": This is surely incorrect. Every *radio sound-effect* is a counter-example. ["Normally and as a rule, auditory data sounds and noises alike, are experienced as referring to their sources":] "Auditory experience" refers to a source only by means of prior experience.

14. [*Field*, 231: "Any tool presents itself as a tool, even when encountered outside a situation of concrete action . . . owing to the implied functional characters, that object is perceived under the aspect of its instrumentality."] The fact that all of this is learned and socially conditioned, and represents an explication of the noematic content, but isn't "given," proves a) that a primitive tribe which doesn't know a hammer is quite thinkable, b) that we do not perceive the functional character and indeed the machine character of many machines (machines "unknown" to us).

DESCRIPTIVE ORIENTATION OF PHENOMENOLOGICAL ANALYSES

15. [*Field*, 232] "The phenomenological reduction . . . makes (it) possible . . . to account for objects as they really are in terms of objects taken for what they are experienced as": Excellent!

16. [*Field*, 233: "Let us assume . . . we trace the origin of a sound seemingly emitted by a human voice . . . produced by a phonograph."] The "apparent"

inclusion of the source by the tone in the perception of the tone is only a special form of the fact of prepredicative experience of the world: in it we have "seen a house," "heard a human voice."

17. [*Field*, 234, n. 9: "This is another case (of) . . . James' . . . psychologist's fallacy."] Correct, but the example doesn't seem to be well chosen. There are experiences of tones that are typical from the very beginning: human voices over the radio or gramophone, etc. *Typicality conditioned by the situation.*

THE INNER HORIZON

18. [*Field*, 236: "The less familiar the thing, the higher the degree of indeterminateness."] The concept "familiar" must be analyzed. But up to now "horizon" has only been dealt with in connection with "actual perceptions." Question: can "horizon" be dealt with purely noematically? Doesn't it refer back to earlier noeses? (This is partially answered on [*Field*, 244].[5])

19. [*Field*, 237f.] "Despite . . . an almost complete lack of determinacy (of the inner horizon)": But it is of course a determinate indeterminacy. End: Superb!

20. [*Field*, 238: "Perceptions of material things, as a rule, are experienced in what Goldstein calls the concrete attitude."] I don't know whether Goldstein's "concrete attitude" has a typical character. The "apple parer" is still a type, but so is "knife."

21. [*Field*, 240] All of this is excellent, but it presupposes a typical familiarity with the social world which is "given without question." *Ibid.:* "The indeterminateness which, in the case of the perception of an unfamiliar object affects the inner horizon . . . , concerns only the . . . manner in which a certain type is realized." This isn't clear, since the "familiar object" too has its unfamiliar, because *until now* irrelevant, inner horizon.

22. [*Field*, 240f.: "An illustrative example . . . a navigator who discovers land. He does not know whether it is a continent or an island."] More precisely: under two alternative points of view that can be chosen; why: island *or* mainland? The example isn't instructive for the static concept of the inner horizon; the horizon of the coastline consists in the alteration of perspectives.

23. [*Field*, 242] "Indeterminateness of the inner horizon rather means *ambiguity* concerning the *special and particular manner* in which a *certain style and type* is realized": What does that mean? What is the difference between "manner" and "type"? "Indefinite and vague—as the contents to be comprised by a certain pattern or framework may be . . . they must fit into the pattern": Is it not merely relative what is a "framework" and a "pattern" and what a special "content"? *My Rover: Irish setter = Irish setter: dog.*

24. [*Field*, 243] "Suppose that we perceive a familiar house and that we are interested in its architectural form . . ." Sorry, but I don't understand this at all. In a certain sense the inner horizon is dependent on "interest," but the whole problem of selection lies in between. It is not the inner horizon that contributes to the formation of perception in actually present qualification. Both, as you

correctly note above, are functions of interest. I don't understand purely grammatically what "perception in the first case and in the second case" refers to. To the two house examples? Obviously!

OPEN POSSIBILITIES

25. [*Field*, 247] "The realm itself is defined by this discrimination. On the other hand the inner horizon yields no motive whatsoever to support belief in any one of the 'open possibilities.' " Is that true? The inner horizon can very well also contain problematic possibilities! "A distinction between those questions which may be raised and those which are *beside the point*" anticipates the whole problematic of relevance.

THE THEORIES OF WARD AND STOUT

26. [*Field*, 247] "To explain the phenomenon of inner horizon, allowance must obviously be made for the influence of past experience upon present perception": I believe rather that the inner horizon is constituted exclusively through previous experience rather than the unquestioned, but questionable, pregivens.

27. [*Field*, 254] "Sense impressions may come to mean what they did not originally mean": problem of historicism.

28. [*Field*, 256] "Rhythmic repetition of an identical stimulus." How does one recognize that a note is the last one? And what is a melody? "O say can you see"—or the entire verse of the *Star Spangled Banner*—or all verses?

29. [*Field*, 258f.: "Koffka's Criticism of Stout's Theory":] Musically indefensible. [Two pages later:] The same: the entire analogy is false.

30. [*Field*, 260: "We ask, how . . . it is possible to account for the phenomenon of marredness which . . . occurs when a wrong note is played."] This too isn't entirely correct, since no distinction is made between the first hearing of a melody and hearing a melody with which one is already familiar (recognized, noted). In the first case, what do "false note" and "marred" mean? See *alternation,* false conclusion (in music) etc. The "correctness" of a melody is an historical stylistic *habit* of *expectations*. The history of empty *Printfolgen* would be an example.

31. [*Field*, 263] "When we are reading a report . . . , the words, whether taken as to their mere physical existence or as symbols . . . play no role within the context of . . . meaning." In my terminology: the "product" of the action "falls out" ["*fällt aus*"].

32. [*Field*, 264] "As to such cases we maintain that the carrier of meaning can, on principle, never be a constituent of the meaning it carries." Is this correct? What about the melody or the ornament? "When the melody is heard, there is no carrier of meaning at all." I don't think this is correct. "The same" melody sung, played on the violin, flute, etc., transposed into another octave or scale, used in a composition [*ankomponiert*], varied, etc.

HUSSERL'S DUALISTIC THEORY OF PERCEPTION

33. [*Field*, 265ff.: "In the account Husserl gives . . . of the inner horizon, we must first discuss his distinction between *Hyle* and *Morphe*."] But unfortunately μορφή remains unexplained.—Is for Aron perhaps μορφή the same as *noetic form*? That would be quite noteworthy, surely also problematic. Or do we perhaps not need μορφή at all? The ὕλη has bothered me more and more: why doesn't it fall to the annihilation of the world? It only belongs to the mundane sphere. A split between noema and noesis, on the one hand, ὕλη and μορφή, on the other is a *reduplicatio sine necessitate*.

34. [*Field*, 270] "The same complex of hyletic data, Husserl maintains, may receive various apperceptions and interpretations": This is a central question. Is it the hyletic data or the noemata that allow doubt to arise?

35. [*Field*, 270: "In Husserl's analysis, the conflict is presented as a competition between two apperceptual interpretations for the same complex of sense data."] "Sense-data"? No! "Meanings"?!!

36. [*Field*, 272] "This something is identical, is a definite localisation in perceptual space." I think that this is too narrow. Localization is restricted to merely visual perception. It already ceases to hold for the tone, still less for data of the life of feeling, etc. (pain).

NOETIC ANALYSIS OF PERCEPTION

37. [*Field*, 281: "Future apperceptions are anticipated to fill in the structural pattern of the present perception."] What about the perception of the back side of a house facade in a painting? The decoy birds [*die Vögel des Appelles*⁶]. Here is a central problem of noematic—noetic structure. Since all anticipations refer to what is preexperienced in its typicality and to its experiential style, according to Aron's interpretation the noema is merely a sediment of prior noeses and so there is after all nothing but noematic—noetic data. But doesn't inner horizon mean more?

38. [*Field*, 289] "The existence of a material thing depends upon the perceptual process related to that thing proving throughout to be a process of fulfillment of anticipations." That is an *overstatement*, since the anticipated red ball can be green and dented on the back side, and yet it is a material thing. (In contrast, the formulation ["As long as the perceptual process progresses without disturbance . . . , the multiple perceptions . . . corroborate one another"] (Ms 401) with the restriction "as long as," is correct. But this restriction is dropped here.

---

1. The introductory quotations from the English edition of *The Field of Consciousness* (G1964a) have been added by the editor in order to clarify the context. The original references to the manuscript page numbers have been changed by the translator to refer to the corresponding passages of the *Field*.

2. Schutz uses the word *pragma* to refer to projected action, which is distinguished from mere reaction. Cf. "Projects of Action" (S1951a).

3. In Section 40 of *Experience and Judgment,* Husserl's example is Gretchen, not the witch.

4. *Structures of the Lifeworld* (S1973), Section IIIA2d.

5. Concerning the analysis of the concept "familiar," which Gurwitsch translated into German sometimes as *vertraut* and sometimes as *bekannt,* cf. Schutz (*CP,* 1 [S1962], 134): "the categories of *familiarity* and *strangeness* and the very important category of *accessibility.* . . ." In Husserl, cf. also the careful distinction between "the known or familiar [*Bekanntheit*]" and "trustworthiness [*Vertrautheit*]":

> In the continuous validation of its being, the world, present to consciousness as horizon, has the subjective general character of trustworthiness as a horizon of existents known in general but, on that account, still not known as regards individual particularities. This indeterminate general trustworthiness is allotted to all things which attain separate validity as existent. Accordingly, each thing, as a familiar form, has its own degree of familiarity, ranging from the known to the unknown." (*Experience and Judgment,* 37)

6. A French phrase, *"appeler des oiseaux"*: using live birds as decoys.

6
From the Theory of Action to the Theory of Science
(April 4, 1952–September 5, 1953)

A central problem in the theory of action, namely the choice between projects of action and their realization in actual behavior, had already been discussed by Schutz in his *The Phenomenology of the Social World.* He now found a solution which takes up James's conception of multiple provinces of meaning (S1951a): action is tied to the everyday world of work by the hand, body, and head of the actor, but with the aid of the multiple provinces of meaning (such as that of dreaming or theorizing), an analysis of action can also come to terms with the transcendences and symbolic worlds of "other" realities. He worked on his major study of "Don Quixote and the Problem of Reality," which presents his analysis of the transcendences of everyday experience in their life-worldly immanence.

Theorizing is one such province of meaning: in two major essays on theory formation in the sciences of action, Schutz presented the difference between everyday and scientific types and constructs. The "Princeton paper" (S1953c) was followed by a summary written for a conference at Columbia University, "On Methods in Philosophy and the Sciences" (May 3, 1953), to which Nagel, Hempel, and Schutz were invited. Schutz read "Concept and Theory Formation in the Social Sciences" (S1954a), invited Gurwitsch to the expected confrontation ("don't you want to watch your old friend Schutz be thrown to the lions?" SG 4.9.53), and was angry that "Nagel, Hempel, & Co." did not appear.

Gurwitsch drew perhaps the sharpest conclusions from these two works: the process of verification within the internal process of science exhibits the structures of social actions, and this is also true for the process of thinking through mathematical proofs (GS 5.15.53). The process of scientific research itself is grounded in the structures of action of the everyday world of work; the concept of the empirical cannot be abstracted from the context of everyday experience (as occurs in the logic of research developed by Nagel and Hempel); even a theory of science cannot be grounded without remainder in other theories if it looks for its intersubjective verification in empirical research. Theories of action and the theory of science remain in a precarious relationship with one another.

A discussion with Eric Voegelin, a common friend of Schutz and Gurwitsch, concerning his book *The New Science of Politics* illuminated the political and historical background of this situation. Voegelin searched for a "science of order" which could also provide a theory of history. Can there be an eidos of history? The original eidos of an ultimate expectation, of a goal of the historical process, is a characteristic of gnosticism which according to Voegelin is the victim of a fallacy. On the one hand, the radical separation of the transcendence of God from the world is essential to gnosticism; understood in this manner, history is a transmundane process. On the other hand, gnosticism claims that the transcendences of Christian eschatology are to be mundanized, are to become immanent. Gurwitsch argued against Voegelin's conclusion from the position of an "arch heretic" (GS 11.2.52); Schutz had an "ice-cold" reaction (SG 11.10.52) to the suspicion that he was a gnostic himself. The question of a gnostic understanding of theory and research in the social sciences stands in the background.

Gurwitsch: *I think that the Princeton paper is an achievement of the first rank in the theory of science*
             (CAMBRIDGE, APRIL 4, 1952)

My dear Friend,

You won't be angry with me for the fact that my answer to your Princeton paper[1] has taken longer than you or I had expected. A number of things came up, the main one being a real pleasure. One of my students is doing a thesis on the theories of abstraction in British empiricism from Hobbes to J. S. Mill. She got into the general theories of consciousness of this school and went deeper and deeper. I had to apply a bit of gentle force to keep her out of the maelstroms which exist in these waters. She doesn't know all too much phenomenology. What can one teach beginners in an *undergraduate school* aside from some hints in connection with Descartes, Hume, and Leibniz? (She has never heard of the reduction.) She is to learn phenomenology from you next year; I will write to you about that. At any rate, I had a great deal of preventive work to do in the last few weeks, and was very, very happy.

I have now studied the Princeton paper four or five times. The first impression has been totally eclipsed. I think that your bringing out the problems of rationality (in connection with which there is a problem which I shall mention below) and insisting on a certain continuity between *common-sense*-thought and science is an achievement of the first rank in the theory of science, since it opens up problem-dimensions which are of significance far beyond *social science*. (The life-world and physics!) In this context the postulate of subjective interpretation is given its full significance. To bring it up in connection with the mentioned continuity is indeed a stroke of genius [*ein Ei des Columbus*]. Now one can say that *because* real human beings understand themselves in a certain way, "interpret" the world and themselves, that for this reason in all sciences which treat of human beings, the object, just as it is understood by the engaged subject or subjects, must come into its own. And this gives rise to the distinction between the object as it is understood by the subject and the object as the *scientist* understands it. Here the tunnels meet once again, for in my "Object of Thought" of 1947 I came up with this distinction in a different context. All in all I can only most sincerely congratulate you for this achievement. Where will it appear?

I recently spoke with the historian Karl Deutsch [earlier of Prague] from the Massachusetts Institute of Technology. He told me that your *paper* was received with the utmost respect and that your thesis that rationality itself is a problem was very stimulating. Deutsch himself is a highly educated man who unfortunately lives too close to the calculating machine, a fact which comes to expression in his essay in *Philosophy*. It is very curious how it is precisely the non-natural scientists who fall prey to the fascination of the mechanisms.

A host of marginal notes covers the edges of your paper. There is a lot we will have to talk about. For today I only want to ask that you clear up a misunderstanding and to discuss one point.

In spite of repeated readings I consistently fail to understand your discussion of rationality at one point. On p. 30 you define *rational action* as "clear and distinct insight. . . ." This is entirely in agreement with what you write on pp. 48 and 52.[2] Accordingly, the rationality which is conferred upon the *homunculus* is an idealization of the always only partial rationality of *daily life*. On p. 36 you bring in a new theme: it is always only plausible that the other has the rational knowledge I impute to him. Why is the *homunculus,* as you say on p. 48 top, in a better position? Mustn't one make a distinction between the knowledge the *homunculus* has, a knowledge by the grace of the *scientist,* and the knowledge of the *scientist* himself? The *scientist* knows what he has conferred upon the *homunculus A* and upon his partner *B* (also a *homunculus*). But what does *A* know about *B*'s knowledge? At any rate, *A* doesn't know what the *scientist* has conferred upon *B.* Thus, if the *scientist* has conferred rationality upon *A* and *B,* does *A* know that *B* has acted in a fully rational manner?

The following remark belongs to the same context: on pp. 35/36 you assert that knowledge of the "origin and import of the socially approved standard" belongs to rationality, and on p. 37 you correctly say that a "pattern" is all the more "standardized," the less "the underlying elements become analyzable . . . in terms of rational insight."[3] My question: does the *homunculus* have this knowledge? It seems to me that to attribute it to him would be to fall prey to the misunderstanding you signal on p. 51. Surely only the *scientist* has this knowledge. It seems to me that the *homunculus* doesn't need it in order to fulfill all of the functions you sketch out on pp. 52ff. So I must have misunderstood something here.

It seems to me that one must distinguish two rationalities: the one, let's call it *rationality of action,* you define very excellently on p. 52[4]; the other, let us say *cognitive rationality,* refers to the procedure of the *scientist* in the construction of the *homunculi,* to the knowledge of *origin* and *import* of the *standards,* etc. One can't attribute the second to the *homunculus.* There is only the cognitive one in the natural sciences; in the social sciences also the one *of action* in idealized form. I am not entirely sure of myself in this last assertion since, as I said, I have the feeling that I am misunderstanding something. But repeated reading hasn't helped.

The point under discussion concerns the very free use you make of *constructs,* doing so on the *common-sense level.* The difference is the same as the one I have with Piaget. What you write on pp. 9–10 sounds to me (you don't say this expressly, and I am exaggerating for purposes of discussion) as if we have the things and then in addition a *texture of meaning,* whose interpretation is an addition to the perception, or, if that is too pointed, permeates the perception, but as an operation which is distinct from it. Here is the marginal note which I wrote on page 10: "embedded historicity"; "pervaded by meanings whose full explicitation discloses human activities"; "human activities sedimented in the objects and defining them"; "*significations et sédimentations inscrites dans les 'choses' qui, pour cette raison, ne sont pas des choses pures ou réformes, mais des objects essentiellement définis et constitués en tant que tels par ces inscriptions et par ces sédimentations, mêmes.*" I think you know what I mean.

By and large, what you call *construct* belongs to the *data* and *facts* themselves. It seems to me that the Whitehead quote on p. 1 about the "contribution of imagination of hypothetical sense presentations" is very ambiguous. The given is what it is thanks to these sense structures that permeate and qualify it. They are implied in the *data* themselves and are "silent." Of course, one can explicate them. The result is your description. But then one must ask, what have you described? The experience of the *common man* or the phenomenological analysis of this experience? Methodologically there is a difficulty here: We can only explicate all that by explicating it. But we must be clear about the fact that this *dégagement* [disengagement] posits a transformation. Thus, we describe transformed what is lived through untransformed.

I came to a similar difficulty or, rather, the same one, in my analyses of perception. I hope that I avoided it. Stimulated by your discussions I took a look at the methodological discussions concerning this in the manuscript of my French book[5]; I believe that there are some things there whose publication would be worthwhile. I have similar objections to pp. 12f., specifically with reference to "the idealization of the congruency of the system of relevances." Again, my marginal notes: "Isn't my experience *typified from the outset?*" "Is such a *transformation* necessary or factual?" Does the *common man* whom you describe have a *private knowledge* which is *then* replaced by "constructs of a typified knowledge of a highly socialized structure?"[6]

Isn't our experience permeated by these typifications from the very beginning, being what it is only thanks to them? Again, what do you describe? The experience itself or the analysis which the phenomenologist makes of it in that he not merely *dégagiert* its sense-moments but also thematizes them? We have to *dégagieren* and thematize. But mustn't we also say that what we present in this manner is contained in experience itself *undégagiert* and unthematized? The problem isn't simply: Certain sense structures permeate our experience and constitute it as such—basically an extension of the thesis of Gestalt theory. When we work out these structures it mustn't look as if there are two heterogeneous elements in the original experience: *data* and *operation upon data*. For this reason I am not very comfortable when you regularly speak of *selection*.

But none of this affects your main thesis, or it affects only the detailed specification. For example, I would say that everyday experience is analyzed, i.e., those constituted sense-structures are *dégagiert* and thematized. Only then does idealization set in, and here begins the realm of *constructs*. I believe that your thesis of the continuity between experience and the scientific construction is hardly affected by this. And as you know I am in full agreement with this thesis.

For me it is a highly welcome confirmation of my own reflections on other material in the theory of science.

Enclosed is the introduction to my book. I cannot write pretentiously. A propos: is Salomon mad at me? I have reason to suspect that he is.

Love to you and yours

Your
Aron

1. "Common Sense and Scientific Interpretation of Human Action" (S1953c).
2. The manuscript is quoted (cf. *Collected Papers*, I, 28ff.).
3. *Collected Papers*, I, 32f.
4. "The concept of rationality . . . is the expression for a *particular* type of constructs of *certain specific* models of the social world" (*Collected Papers*, I, 42).
5. "Les trois dimensions du réel," (cf. GS 2.17.52), published in G1985.
6. *Collected Papers*, I, 13.

Schutz: *This doesn't mean that a private experience which would not be socialized from the very beginning is possible*
(NEW YORK, APRIL 20, 1952)

Dear Friend,

Many thanks for your kind letter of April 4, 1952, especially for your remarks about my Princeton paper, which were a real pleasure for me. You are truly the only person to whose judgment I attach importance and who I can assume understands what I am doing. Of course you are completely correct when you say that the most important problem which is dealt with in my *paper* is the question of how the sciences that deal with human beings are related back to the life-world. I know that you have dealt with this idea from another side, and I take great pleasure in our agreement. The tunnels always meet when one takes the basic thought of phenomenology, if one has understood it correctly, as the point of departure.

Your critique was also very important to me, especially the one concerning the concept of rationality. To tell the truth, I can't really see the difficulty you mention. It is completely correct that I say that the homunculus is better off than the man in the daily life-world, who interprets this world according to *common sense* principles. You ask if one mustn't make a distinction between the knowledge which the homunculus has, which is a knowledge by the grace of the *scientist*, and the knowledge of the *scientist* himself. Of course one has to make such a distinction. The *scientist*, and he alone, determines what homunculus *A* and what homunculus *B* know and can know. You ask: but what does homunculus *A* know about what the *scientist* has given his partner *B,* who is also a homunculus? I doubt that this question is really legitimate. In the final analysis, *A* doesn't know anything at all. It neither knows anything about itself nor anything about *B,* unless the scientist has constructed his consciousness such that *A*'s knowledge also includes *B*'s knowledge. But if this is the case, then I don't really see any problem in the fact that the *scientist* also gives *A* the knowledge that homunculus *B* acts rationally.

This is by no means merely an assumption which I make. It is the continual praxis of the social scientist, especially the economist. Thus, e.g., the modern theory of *oligopoly* is based on the presupposition that each of the few firms which participate in the market situation from the supply side not merely orient their behavior in terms of the fact that they themselves act strictly rationally, but also in terms of the fact that their competitors act rationally, and the conduct of this competitor is an element of their own rational action.

You have perhaps heard of the Neumann-Morgenstern theory?[1] According to their assumption, all economic action consists merely in the assumption that here, as in various games, at every moment each partner makes selections between various possible strategies, and indeed not merely from strategies which are available to the player but also from strategies which are available to the partner. Why do you assume that only the *scientist* has this knowledge? If the *scientist* gives his homunculus this kind of knowledge, then it has it by the grace of the *scientist*.

The state of affairs may become clearer if we take an example from a sphere with which you are more familiar. Take for example an ideal discussion between two scientists. This discussion is to be a prime example of strictly rational action. It would seem absurd to me to speak of a rationality of the result of thinking. Rationality can only be attributed to the process of thought, and in it only to the categories, orientations, motivations, goals, attainability, etc. involved. In other words, the operation is rational, but not the product yielded by the operation.

I don't know if I can make myself comprehensible with these brief remarks. At any rate, I am very eager to discuss the entire problem with you when we get together again. It may well be that I have a lot to improve concerning this point if the essay is to be published. Whether this will be case, however, I don't know.

You criticize my all two frequent use of "constructs." This critique is thoroughly justified. In a purely phenomenological analysis I probably would have completely avoided the word and the concept "construct." But you mustn't forget that the theme and also the concept of "constructs" was posed by Princeton. The entire panel-seminar dealt with "Model Constructs in the Social Sciences."And I was given the task of investigating the *constructs* which are implied in the concept of rationality. Even so, I have used various subterfuges to make the topic much broader than Princeton had intended. In addition, in the social sciences there is the increasing tendency to replace the concepts of type and ideal type by the concept of "construct." Thus, e.g., Howard Becker began his critique of the Weberian ideal type by suggesting that the expression "ideal type" be replaced by the expression "constructive type."

I by no means think that the sense-structure is something additional to the perception of the thing, and I completely agree with your remarks concerning page 10. What I call "construct" of course belongs to the *facts* and *data* themselves. I also believe that the Whitehead text I quote on page 1 is to be understood in no other way. In other words: there are no *facts* pure and simple, but rather only interpreted *facts*. As you put it: everything that is given is already permeated by sense-structures.

Now you ask if this explication is an explication of the natural image of the world, or is it an explication of the phenomenological analysis. You know very well that my goal in all of my works and also in this one is a phenomenological analysis of the natural *Weltanschauung*. But if such a phenomenological analysis is to succeed, it has to present and describe what it finds exactly as it finds it, and with that the analysis of the *common sense* world is phenomenologically clarified. I don't entirely understand why such an analysis would have to have a "*dégagement*" as a consequence. Does your introduction of the concept of coherence transform the Gestalt psychological findings?

Concerning your remarks on page 12: I had of course only pedagogical reasons for taking a theoretical solipsistic ego as my point of departure and only subsequently introducing the structures which are involved in the social world. But that of course doesn't mean that I believe that a private experience that is not socialized from the beginning is possible. Here I have things much easier than Husserl, since I modestly stick to the natural world view. The problem that you describe actually only comes up on the basis of transcendental phenomenology. Only here do we have the task of finding the transition from transcendental subjectivity to transcendental intersubjectivity, or even merely that of clarifying mundane intersubjectivity in terms of transcendental subjectivity. But for me, sticking to the natural world view, there is no such problem, since already through the experience of a common language the typifications are created and transmitted according to everyone's systems of congruences, which belong to us. The natural world is through and through *social,* and our knowledge of this world is also *social* precisely in the natural view.

As you have correctly sensed, the entire problematic is a matter of finding the transition from the natural world view to the results of the analyses won in the phenomenological attitude. But that doesn't mean that this natural world view is itself free from constructions, and this is precisely what I have tried to work out.

At any rate, many thanks for the very kind care with which you have studied my paper. Your remarks are of the utmost importance for me and will be of great use to me if my essay should be published. For the moment Princeton has not yet decided whether all contributions to the symposium are to be published by the Princeton University Press along with the results of the discussions or not.[2] But I hope to hear more about this in the near future.

Now to the introduction of your book: by and large I think it is excellent. I have only two remarks to make. On page 4 you define the thematic field as copresent, and you expressly mention the retentions which could be located in the thematic field. Why not also the reproductions of earlier lived experiences, on the assumption that such reproductions are copresent with the thematic experiences. This point, as you have seen from the remarks concerning various relevant texts, is a bit of a problem for your reader. If retention is singled out here in the introduction without saying anything about what happens with the copresent memories, or what its place in the thematic field is, then the reader might from the very beginning approach your book with an attitude which you will hardly welcome.

My second point refers to your attitude toward Gestalt theory. Modesty is a very fine thing, and I am most certainly always for *understatements*. But I still think that you should say more clearly that you are attempting to give Gestalt theory the philosophical foundation it has lacked up to now. The right place for this would in my opinion be page 9, paragraph 2, and page 10.[3] Given the way these texts read now, you take a much too apologetic attitude with regard to Gestalt theory. I would strongly suggest that you revise this section and say very clearly just what you have achieved.

I still have to report that Farber wrote that you had requested that your book appear under the auspices of the phenomenological society. I think that is an extraordinarily good idea and am very happy that Farber is in complete agreement. He asked what I thought about it, and you can well imagine what I had to tell him about your book.

Salomon passed on your greetings. He is very happy about the way he was received by you and your dear wife, and told me how fantastically your position at your university has developed.

I have just begun reading the second volume of Husserl's *Ideas,* which I just received, and am very excited by it. I think that I can say that much of what Husserl says has been anticipated in my work to date. As far as I can see he also confirms much of what you have discovered in your book. But I fear that his basic principle is mistaken, since he *again*[4] begins with the assumption that intersubjectivity is based on communication, and communication in turn on empathy, and I can't quite see where that will lead. But then I haven't gotten very far with my reading. Farber asked me if I would take on the review of this and of the third volume for our journal, and I have agreed to do so, but with the reservation that I still have to decide whether I will write a simple review or a small essay. From what I have seen so far, it will be a big essay. Farber hasn't responded to this yet.

I asked for a *tape recorder,* and Ilse is writing this letter from my dictation into the machine. For this reason it may well be that the thoughts are a bit disordered and the style may need improvement. But I hope that this instrument and Ilse's kind aid will allow me to work more as well as more quickly than hitherto.

With best wishes for your wife and you and in the hope that I can see you over a *weekend* before I leave on my trip to Europe, which will probably be in mid-June. Love

Your
Alfred

1. *Theory of Games and Economic Behavior* (Princeton, 1944).
2. Published in *PPR* (S1953c).
3. Roughly page 6 of the *Field;* Gurwitsch apparently didn't follow this suggestion.
4. Cf., e.g., Husserl (around 1910): "The Acts Constitutive of Sociality, the 'Communicative' Acts," in *Zur Phänomenologie der Intersubjektivität,* part I (*Husserliana* XIII), 98.

Gurwitsch: *Your review pours a lot of water on my non-egological mill*
             (CAMBRIDGE, OCTOBER 3, 1952)

Dearest Friend,

Although I, as you correctly suppose, am swimming in a sea of work (the technical details of my book are driving me crazy), I immediately began studying your review—or what you call a review.[1] It isn't a review at all, but rather a superb presentation. Its clarity and conciseness are masterful. One learns not only what it is about but also what the line of the argument is. Your presentation, with its strict concentration on its goal, is much preferable to Ricoeur's, which is a bit ragged.[2] The brevity is admirable; you have surely invested unending labor in it. Brief formulations are hard to understand: *Je n'ai pas assez de temps pour écrire des essais courts*—as someone said. It must have cost you a great deal of time. At any rate, the English reader now has the possibility of learning what this volume is about, and he should be deeply thankful to you.

Since you consider my opinion important, I am sending you the copy back—in the hope of receiving a copy of the edited manuscript. You will find some penciled remarks in the margins, which I have tried very hard to make legible. I don't know whether I have been completely successful in resisting the temptation to digress into substantive issues. I continually felt the tendency to discuss matters with you, although in the immediate context you are above all interested in hearing what I have to say about your presentation. In what follows a couple of remarks which couldn't be put in the margins.

1. You should expand and differentiate [the beginning]. You do make the distinction between a) regional ontologies and sciences (e.g., pure theory of motion and geometry of intuitive space, not or not yet geometry as pure formal multiplicity; you don't mention either example), which are eidetic but belong to the natural attitude, and b) constitutive problems in the specifically phenomenological sense. I think that this distinction should be drawn more sharply. A reader who is not familiar with these intricate relationships and is not at home with the relevant discussions in *Ideas I* will easily be confused and fail to see the contexts and differences. For myself, this complicated state of affairs only became clear slowly and with great effort when I read *Ideas I.*

2. The expression "gives unity"[3] seems objectionable. After all, in that the separate *manifolds* are in agreement with one another, they constitute an intersubjective world, the objective one. The latter thus results as identically the same for the *manifolds,* which however remain separate *manifolds!* This holds for

what is said later about *environment, personal and interpersonal,* for the distinction between *presentation* and *appresentation,* for the problems of *empathy,* and much more. Especially for the fact that the other sees the things as I would see them if I were in his position.

3. For *my* information: What is "realizing apprehension"?[4] Is it the same thing as the perceptual apprehension of an appearing quality varying in accordance with variations in the *circumstances?* If so, then the following question: Is the objective real quality the same as the total system of appearing qualities, perceptually experienced in dependence (in the sense of *co-variation*) in changing circumstances? I too would answer positively, but I am not sure how Husserl would have answered. According to what you write on pp. 7 and 12, he seems to waver.

4. What is the distinction between "the real psychological I" and the "I—the human being" [*Ich-Mensch*].[5] This distinction did not become clear to me, even after the later discussion.

5. [The conclusion] pours lots of water on my non-egological mill. As p. 28 shows, the trinity becomes a quaternity.[6] And Fink stands waiting with still another trinity: the I as phenomenological observer.[7] Please excuse me if I find all of these trinities and quaternities very unhealthy. In my theory there is only one I, the empirical one or, if you will, the person. I am quite prepared to distinguish various strata in it. The essential thing is, it is a *constitutum,* and its constitution is to be investigated; not a simple task. The I, no different from the thing, is a substance concept. If one simply accepts such entities, instead of taking them to be constituted and going into their constitution, the result is endless complications. My theory at least has the advantage of simplicity.

Finally, a double thanks. First for the long conversation in New York. We will hardly come to an agreement as to who got more out of it: I think I did. The second thanks is for the enclosed manuscript. It was a pleasure to read it. When will the Princeton paper appear? Finally, I want to remind you of your promise to come to Boston. When is it to be kept? I don't know if I will be able to come to New York any time soon; we have spent a lot of money. But since we have to get together, the prophet must sometimes go to the mountain.

Love to you, your wife, and the children.

Affectionately yours
Aron

1. "Husserl's *Ideen II*" (S1953a).

2. Paul Ricoeur, "Analyses et problèmes dans 'Ideen II' de Husserl," *Revue de métaphysique et de morale* 56 (Oct.–Dec. 1951): 357–94, and 57 (Jan.–Mar. 1952): 1–16. English trans.: "Husserl's *Ideas II*: Analyses and Problems," in *Husserl: An Analysis of His Phenomenology,* tr. E. Ballard and L. Embree (Evanston: Northwestern University Press, 1967), 35–81.

3. *Collected Papers,* III, 17 (line 4).

4. Page 19.

5. Pages 21f.
6. "This distinction of three or four I's within the same stream of consciousness" (*Collected Papers*, III, 37).
7. Cf. the discussion between Fink and Schutz: *Collected Papers*, III, 84–91.

Schutz: *I think that Husserl's theory of intersubjectivity is the desperate attempt to save transcendental phenomenology*
          (New York, October 12, 1952)

My dear Friend,

I know how disruptive my request that you look through my Husserl review was, and owe you a debt of thanks, not only because you looked through it so carefully but also because you have read and commented on it so quickly. Your comments were more than a great help to me. Each time, you have found a weak or mistaken or unclear point, and I have, to the extent that it was possible, taken into account *all* of your comments. You are and remain the only one on whose judgment I lay absolute value. For this reason, your basic agreement with it as a whole is more than encouraging for me.

To go into the details of your extensive comments, I note, concerning the relationship between regional ontologies, the sciences that result from them such as the geometry of intuitive space and phoronomy[1], and concerning the parallel problems of constitution, that these questions constitute the main content of *Ideas III* and are put aside for its review. But of course you are completely right in your critique, and I have changed the text stylistically. By the way, I have more and more doubts about the legitimacy of these distinctions, and Husserl too had great difficulty in defending controversial theories that he once presented with equal pathos (namely in *Ideas I*) as being compatible, and the distinctions on which they are based as necessary (not merely useful, which they hardly are). One characteristic of this thinker, the basis for as many merits as defects of his philosophy, is his inexorable "stubbornness" [*Eigensinn*] (in the original sense of the word as well as in its figurative sense).

With regard to my presentation, you correctly criticize the expression "gives unity" as being "improper" for characterizing the function of empathy with regard to the separated multiplicities. It may be improper, but it is from Husserl. You will find it on p. 317 of the Niemeyer edition of *Ideas,* at the end of the first paragraph. I have made this part of my presentation clearer.

By "realizing apprehension," which is my translation of *realisierende Auffassung*, Husserl means, I think, the category of apprehension which is the correlate of the object category "real thing" (in contrast to the mere phantom), and indeed in precisely the same sense that he gives the term "apprehensional category" [*Auffassungskategorie*] (in *Ideen I*, p. 296).[2] This seems to me to be correct, since according to the line of thought of *Ideas II,* the perceptual apperception of an appearing quality in variational dependence on the varying circumstances is not sufficient for the constitution of the real thing. The phantom or ghost is also perceptually apperceived in this manner. But as you have correctly recognized, Husserl did not give this problem a final formulation (at least in *Ideas II*) and vacillates in the use of various terms.

He also does this with the distinction of various *I*-forms. You ask what is the difference between the real psychological I and the I-the-human-being. I don't know. The real psychological I is often restricted to the bodily processes [*Leibesgeschichten*] of the localized *Aistheta* or "sensitiveness"; then again it encompasses all character-dispositions, abilities, talents; and it finally turns out that the personalistic or spiritual I encompasses the I-the human being, at least when it stands in communication with the others, thus in a "social union" with them and shares an intersubjective world with them. The fact that you hold the egological trinities and quaternities to be very unholy (and to be precise, it isn't four but rather six) is something that I understand all the more since I hold Husserl's entire theory of subjectivity and intersubjectivity to be a desperate attempt to save transcendental phenomenology (better: the "exuberant use" which Husserl makes of the transcendental constitutive method).

But: I still can't see why this deplorable state of affairs is water on your non-egological mill. Husserl misunderstood the I, but the fact that he attacked the problem wrongly by no means implies that the I is a *constitutum*. Only one aspect, the I *modo praeteritis,* is a *constitutum,* and this is why both Scheler and also G. H. Mead, who in this point is curiously allied with him, trace the various I-aspects back to its temporal structure (which I finally did too). Here we can see the mistake of phenomenology, which Fink in my opinion justifiably criticized in the *Problèmes actuels,*[3] of always breaking off where the great problems of traditional speculative metaphysics begin; which is why it forfeits, as Voegelin believes, the claim to be *"prima philosophica."*[4] This claim should be incompatible precisely with the postulate of a philosophy as rigorous science.

We must do a lot of talking about all this, also about the fact that you, in contrast to my critical remark, take the various "motifs" (attraction and turning to, acting, intersubjectivity) to be mere "variations." That is the only point at which I can't accept your comments on my essay.

There just *may* be an occasion for such a discussion. A friend of ours is planning to drive to Boston on the afternoon of the 31st, and will take Ilse and me along. In this case I would return on Sunday evening (11.2) on the train. Would this weekend be all right—no obligation—for you?

Once again, deep thanks and love to you and your wife,

Your

Alfred

P.S. I received Voegelin's *The New Science of Politics*[5] yesterday and plan to read it as soon as possible.

1. The purely geometric theory of movement.
2. Cf. *Ideas,* vol. 1, tr. Fred Kersten (The Hague: Martinus Nijhoff, 1982), 341.
3. Eugen Fink, *Problèmes actuels de la phénoménologie,* (Paris, 1951).
4. Cf. Voegelin's letter of Sept. 17, 1943, to Alfred Schutz, in E. Voegelin, *Anamnesis* (Munich: R. Piper & Co. Verlag, 1966). Not in the English translation.
5. Chicago: University of Chicago Press, 1952.

Gurwitsch: *The language I speak with Voegelin is that of the arch-heretic*
            (CAMBRIDGE, NOVEMBER 2, 1952)

Dear Friend,

We were very disappointed. And only the thought that postponed is not canceled, or need not be, comforts us. We really hope that you find your way here, with or without the lady who gives you a ride.

My first impression of Voegelin's book[1] is in a letter to him, of which I am sending you a copy of the first two pages having to do with the book. A great work and yet closer to us, i.e., phenomenology, than he wants to admit. What is it for the most part, if not a phenomenology of historically active societies! The entire method is phenomenological, making use of the concept of motivation, which he just doesn't call by that name. But, as you will see, I haven't written him that, or at least not emphasized it. The language which I speak with him is that of the historian and arch-heretic.[2]

An ambiguity runs through several parts: is he speaking as an historian or as a metaphysician? As to the former, I have no argument with him. But I believe that he must go the whole way; if what he calls gnosticism is responsible for the disaster, and he is right, then he has to see that the disaster already begins where mankind is promised salvation from above and the savior is granted. Whenever there is the prospect of a Messiah there is the temptation to accelerate and help along his coming or return. Thus, as you see, I have for once laid aside the phenomenological terminology and uniform, and revealed myself to him as a mere heretic—which I am. But aside from that, his way of pursuing *politics* as *science* is surely the only possible one. And the book makes a liberating impression the way it is saturated with reality.

Harvard Press now demands that all footnotes be written in a specific form.[3] We will soon be finished with that. Then the manuscript goes to their readers, and only then will the contract be signed or not signed. I suspect that Farber will be one of the readers, Köhler another, and then I plan to bring your name into the debate, though in a subtle manner. The Press must have the fiction that they have selected the reader, not that the author has appointed him, even though, as the director told me, given the small number of people who know anything about these things, both come to the same thing. It will thus be a while before the book appears in print.

I haven't yet heard from Paris whether Desclée de Brouwer wants to publish the translation. Biemel is doing his best. A propos: Jerusalem wants an essay from me.[4] Since it would be senseless to spend months on a work which will then be published in Hebrew, and thus buried, I suggested that they translate "On the Intentionality of Consciousness." What do you think? Farber has agreed; now only the Harvard Press must give its *agrément*.

With best greetings to all of you, also in the name of my wife

Your

Aron

1. *The New Science of Politics.*
2. Concerning gnosticism and heresy, cf. A. Hilgenfeld, *Die Ketzergeschichte des Urchristentums* (Leipzig, 1884).
3. Gurwitsch submitted the *Field* to the Harvard University Press. Even after all footnotes had been rewritten the press was not willing to accept the manuscript without radical revisions, and Gurwitsch withdrew it. (Cf. GS 2.6.53).
4. Cf. G1955, parts of "The Phenomenological and the Psychological Approach to Consciousness" were translated into Hebrew: *Iyyun* 4 (1953): 193–202.

Enclosure: "*Logos does not care for man*"
A section from Gurwitsch's letter of 11.2.52 to Eric Voegelin (Louisiana State University, Baton Rouge)[1]

. . . you have renewed or, perhaps, recreated the entire categorial apparatus of political science, e.g., with the distinction between representation in the *elemental* and the *existential* sense, and then again with the idea that a political society understands itself as the representative of a "truth." The general emphasis on the self-understanding and the self-interpretation of a society is a point of great importance.

It is high time that the axiom be comprehended that wherever it is a matter of human beings and their affairs of whatever kind, there are no "facta bruta" but only understood, interpreted facts which are what the human beings and groups in question understand them to be. The analysis of the forms which this self-understanding takes on and can take on is a great task of philosophy and especially of phenomenology. You are so right in saying that what belongs to this self-understanding must be distinguished from the categories and concepts of the theoretician, which becomes very complicated when elements of theorizing enter into the self-understanding. But in any case, if one is to comprehend a society one has to start with what this society takes itself to be—perhaps, and probably in the rule, in a modus of unarticulated implicitness. It is one of the real services of this book that it has carried this point through with such consequence.

What you say about the conflict between the "imperial truth" and that of the tragedian and later of the mystic philosophers is very fine. I am inclined to be completely on your side in these parts. Your thesis throws light on the opposition that runs through all of early Greek philosophy between the δόξα of the many and the ἐπιστήμη of those with wisdom, and thus on the fundamental distinction between appearance and truth in the most general sense.

I also still follow you in what you say about the essential manner in which man is defined by his orientation toward transcendence; i.e., about the completion of the anthropological principle by the theological in Plato's sense. But as soon as the "soteriological truth"[2] appears I find myself confronted with insuperable difficulties. That "transcendence" makes a counter-movement to man, that there is a reciprocity of "God" and man, and even *amicitia*[3]: where does that come from?

Along the line of Greek thought there is only man's orientation toward the λόγος, the openness of ψύχη to the sphere of transcendence, and the *onesided* adequation of man and λόγος. It is not possible for me to see a continuity between the Platonic-Aristotelian line and the soteriological truth which appears with Christianity. There seems to me to be a gap here which can only be filled if one takes the whole mass of Jewish-prophetic motifs and ideas into account.

You have your reasons not to do this. Your problematic is defined by world-historical relevance. The Jews no longer played a role in the battle over representation in the *Imperium romanum,* nor in the Middle Ages. To that extent your procedure is justified and legitimate with regard to the logic of your problematic. But is it also justified in terms of the logic of the history of ideas? The God who reveals himself (even if in your and Niebuhr's sense), who prescribes the form of life and the condition of salvation for man, *who is concerned with man's salvation*—especially the latter—that is something that breaks into the Greek cultural world from without. And this holds all the more of the Messiah in both the Christian and the Jewish understanding. Where does it come from that transcendence will appear among us to order human affairs definitively and to bring us salvation?

Please don't misunderstand me. I am not writing as an apologist, but as *adversarius revelationis.* I agree with what you say about gnosis, old and new, and about the danger which flows from it. As a layman in these things and with the qualification which this implies, I would like to risk the thesis that the gnostic elements are embedded and motivated in the idea of the Messiah. St. Augustine could separate the temporal and eternal spheres, and Thomas could too, perhaps because the Greek tradition was not yet entirely broken. When it later comes to gnostic attempts at realization, then [they occur] not in spite of but because of the soteriology. The Puritans certainly interpreted themselves as the realizers of the divine promise of salvation on earth, and all secularized messianic or pseudo-messianic movements attempt to create heaven on earth. If this ended in disaster, was that because of secularization or because of messianism? Isn't it possible that secularization brings out motifs and possibilities that already existed in the pre-secularized stage and were only held back for certain reasons?

I am writing as a layman and you will correct me. And please take these remarks for what they are: first thoughts that occur to me after a first reading. I will spend a lot of time studying your book and will learn a great deal from it. This is only a first word. Whenever I read your book, I begin to reflect—possible in the false direction. When I have read and studied more I hope to write you further thoughts for possible correction. Your book is very stimulating for me. It casts light on so much: *a science of order* is such an important desideratum. If one takes your book as an historical study, then it is something we have been awaiting for a long, very long time. I would very much like to hear what you have to say about the last remarks.

The *science of order* is also—and precisely—a problem for those who represent the autonomy of reason (reason defined in the sense of Plato-Leibniz), and who for this reason are denied the tie to an ontology. In this situation the solution is to define man in terms of the connection to the λόγος and to comprehend the cosmos as the correlate of the λόγος. But λόγος *does not care for man.* . . .

1. Eric Voegelin later taught in Munich until his retirement and lived in Stanford, California until his death in 1985. His extraordinary correspondence with Schutz finds some echoes in these letters.
2. Soteriology: theological doctrine of salvation through Christ.
3. Friendship (between God and man).

Schutz: *Do the two of us understand absolutely nothing "de anima"?*
          (NEW YORK, NOVEMBER 10, 1952—3:15 A.M.)

Dearest Friend,

Many thanks for your kind letter and the highly interesting reaction to
Voegelin's book, which has deeply impressed me too. With less time available
than ever before (in the last 10 days I have had business visitors from Mexico
and Holland whom I had to take care of socially as well; you are spared all of
that), I have dictated into my *tape recorder* my remarks on Voegelin's book and
on a very interesting letter in which he comments on some of my attempts. Since
the letter is probably some 25 pages long, Ilse, who is also very busy, won't be
able to type it immediately, but you will get a copy. You will see how close to
one another we are here too.

My main objection is much like your "heretical" one, but on another level.
The turning point of the entire critique of gnosticism is the dogma, which is
asserted without proof (*The New Science of Politics,* p. 120), that every attempt to
search for an eidos of history involves making the Christian transcendental
eschaton immanent and is *therefore* a "fallacy." That is a gigantic *non sequitur.*
Why shouldn't it be possible in gnosticism (in Voegelin's sense) too that the soul
open itself to transcendental experience. Dear old co-gnostic and co-paraclete:[1]
do we two understand absolutely nothing *de anima*?

Enough. You write that you want to suggest me as a reader to Harvard
Press. This is a great honor which I greatly appreciate. But I think that it is
completely inexpedient from the practical point of view. Who am I in the eyes of
the Harvard Press? The fact that I could accompany you on the thorny road of
this labor and feel myself very close to you philosophically gives me credit in
your eyes (and in mine: only beggars are modest, says Goethe), but not in those
of the Harvard Press. No, you need an *accredited American* who is neither a
phenomenologist nor a Gestalt psychologist as third reader. I have thought
about this for a long time and suggest [Richard] McKeon. I met him at the
Finkelstein congress. He is interested in phenomenology, attended the Louvain
congress (see the list of participants in *Problèmes actuels de la phénoménologie*),
would like to understand Husserl better, has his good European training under
Bréhier and Robin, knows his Aristotle, loves Jean Wahl, is intelligent and open.
What do you think? . . .

[Jakob Taubes] could translate your "Intentionality" into Hebrew. Congratulations for this honorable invitation. We would never have dreamed of such a
thing back then in Paris when I suggested that Farber invite you to write a
contribution[2]! If Desclée de Brouwer takes too long, offer Gallimard the book
for the *Bibliothèque de Philosophie.* You might also think about the *Presse
Universitaire.* By the way, I have a private relationship to Gabriel Marcel—his
cousin is the wife of my good friend Charles Daniel Meyer, who is in turn a
cousin of Marcel Proust: France is the land of cousins (and you have an official
relationship through your student, who has erected an altar to him). And Marcel

is a Director at Aubier! Whatever he accepts is printed, and I am sure that he is intelligent enough to recognize the value of your work immediately. It will also give him a devilish pleasure to put one to the *"salaud"* Merleau-Ponty. You should also think about His Excellency, Gaston Berger, who, as I hear, has become *full and bright* a philosophical busybody.

Love to you and your wife,

Your
Alfred

1. The Paraclete (the Comforter) is promised in the eschatology of John (John 14:16 and 26).
2. Farber's Husserl Memorial Volume (1940): cf. the first letter in this volume.

Supplement: Excerpt from a letter from Schutz to Voegelin concerning *The New Science of Politics* (November 1952; 27 pages). (A complete English translation of Schutz's letter, along with Voegelin's replies [January 1 and January 10, 1953] and his "Im memoriam Alfred Schutz," are published in *The Philosophy of Order*, ed. Peter J. Opitz and Gregor Sebba [Stuttgart: Klett-Cotta, 1981], 434ff. and 465ff.)

. . . the chapter "Representation and Existence" is of fundamental importance. Your distinction between the self-interpretation of society by means of symbols and the explication of social existence by theoreticians (what you call the Aristotelian method) is without any doubt *the* main problem in the methodology of all social sciences. You are also completely right when you say that the classical distinction between *doxa* and *episteme* has disappeared and that contemporary social science has replaced *doxa* with the concept of ideology. After what I said in the first part of this letter concerning the possibilities of an analysis of the relative natural world view, you will understand why I am of the opinion that one can and must go further in the analysis of the structure of *doxa* without making use of the concept of ideology. This must of course occur with the theoretical means of *episteme,* such that the only apparently paradoxical problem arises as to how one can theoretically clarify *doxa* with the tools of *episteme.* The situation is somewhat complicated by the fact that after a certain time, and probably only to a certain degree, the theoretical elements can become elements of *doxa,* i.e., of the dominant relative natural world view.

It seems to me that a very characteristic shift occurs in this process. What was theoretically intelligible and understood in the clarity of *episteme* now sinks, not understood, into the realm of *doxa.* This can finally lead, and your book provides various proofs of this, to a situation in which a theoretical insight can itself become a symbol of a society's self-interpretation, whereby of course the theoretical content has ceased to be understood and has become incomprehensible. It is once again accepted as a symbol of society's self-interpretation and thus as unquestionably given. It seems to me that this has been the fate of the materialist dialectic in recent Soviet Russian philosophical literature, just as in a different area Freud's theories are obviously subject to a similar shift in form and content in Western societies. . . .

You are concerned to prove that theory does not have the task of saying something about human existences in society, but must remain an attempt to make the sense of existence intelligible by demonstrating the content of a certain class of lived experiences or encounters. I also know that it is much more important to point out that social and political existence has something to do with the order of the soul, and that in addition to the anthropological there is a theological principle. But I wonder if it isn't unavoidable, in the philosophy of history as well as in a theoretical social science, to deal with the self-interpretation of this order by the concrete society itself, and by external societies and their representatives. Wouldn't this be theory, even if not *theoria* in the sense you are after? It may be that this theory is not theory in Aristotle's sense. At any rate, I think that whatever one may call this scientific enterprise, it can be carried out without having to recur to concepts such as *sophon*,[1] *kalon, agathon,* etc. These remarks may serve to clarify the opposition that I have dealt with in the first part of this letter.

The distinction between the two truths, and the treatment of philosophical truth (allow me to name what you call "theoretical" truths "philosophical") in contrast to the truth of self-interpretation is quite excellent. I find your reference to the relation between political theory in Greece and Greek drama truly wonderful, and I hope that this relation could be worked out in more detail, if this hasn't already been done in your main work. The experience of transcendence can after all be grasped not only with the tools of philosophical speculation or with soteriological religious experience or with representation in the existential sense; art too is a tool for presenting this experience of transcendence, as is myth. And here we find once again, now on a higher level, the question whether it is possible to project a general typology of these approaches, all of which have the goal of coming to terms with the transcendent, and whether it is possible to say something concerning the limits of these ways of proceeding, concerning their compatibilities and incompatibilities, their congruences and overlappings, and concerning the possibility of moving from one attitude to others. In other words, is an aporetic of the experience of transcendence possible?[2]

. . . The third chapter ends with the claim that political theology was brought to an end by orthodox Christianity. The "sphere of power" becomes dedivinized and secular. Dedivination (according to the definition on page 107) refers to the historical process in which the culture of polytheism succumbs to atrophy, and human existence in society is reordered in terms of eternal life by the experience of man's determination by the grace of a world-transcendent God. All of this is intelligible to me, and I have no objection to this concept of dedivination. My difficulty lies in the claim that the specifically modern problem of representation is tied to the redivination of society. But redivination does not refer to a revival of polytheistic culture in the Greek-Roman sense. This claim does make good sense if its point is to show that modern political mass movements don't have a pagan character, but are rather to be interpreted as a clear continuation of the heretical branch which developed within Christianity itself (thus from components that are demonstrable within the universal church).

The antithesis of eschatology in history, in contrast to an eschatology of transhistorical and supernatural perfection, lies at the root of the split. It is shown very clearly how the unitary Christian society is articulated into a spiritual and a secular order. Here the secular order is historically realized by the Roman Empire. The Medieval *imperium* has to be understood as the continuation of the Roman Empire, and the conflict between Pope and emperor[3] is a conflict between the worldly and spiritual order in an existential and transcendental sense. Now we read (on page 110) that the specifically modern problems of modern representation grew out of this society with its established system of symbols. This occurs through the resurrection of the eschatology of the Kingdom. Subsequently, this process is simply identified with that of redivination (on page 110). I have great difficulty in seeing why this is the case. It would appear to me that the process of dedivination and that of redivination take place on fundamentally different levels. This point seems to me to be no mere detail, but is rather of decisive significance, since your entire theory of gnosticism and of possible gnostic philosophy is connected with it.

As an illustration you offer Joachim's[4] very interesting application of the symbol of the trinity to the course of history. Four typical symbols arise from Joachim's theory of history: first the third realm [*Reich*], second the leader [*Führer*], third the prophet or forerunner, fourth the brotherhood of autonomous persons. In later discussions these four symbols are investigated as to their historical development with special attention to National Socialism and Russian political philosophy. At the beginning of the third part (on page 117), we learn that the new eschatology had a decisive influence on the structure of modern politics. This is demonstrated convincingly. There follows now the very interesting thought that up to this point symbolism has only been accepted on the level of self-interpretation and described as an historical[5] phenomenon, and you now move on to take up a critical analysis of the main aspects of this symbolic system. You very correctly note that Joachim's eschatology represents a speculation concerning the sense of history that is opposed to the Augustinian speculation. Joachim's new idea (we read on page 119) is an attempt to give meaning to the immanent course of history. This occurs by appealing to the sense of the transcendental course of history. But Joachim's speculation still remains tied to the idea of Christianity. The full development of the sense of history as an intra-mundane phenomenon without transcendental influences (the idea of an immanent fulfillment, which you call secularization) only occurs in the subsequent movement, which you very correctly call "From Humanism to Enlightenment."

I have summarized these trains of thought line for line here in order to clarify them for myself, since in the course of the argument I have lost the concept of redivination. Is secularization a process of redivination in your sense? I am confused, because now the question is abruptly raised whether there is an *eidos* of history. I learn that this is not the case, that while the polis did have an *eidos* for Plato and Aristotle, this was the case in a completely different sense, namely in the sense of growth and decline. The soteriological truth of Christianity breaks with the rhythm of existence which belongs to these categories. Christianity does not know an *eidos* of history because the eschatological supernatural is not a nature in the philosophical immanent sense. And now we read (page 120), "The problem of an eidos in history, hence, arises only when Christian transcendental fulfillment becomes immanentalized. Such an immanentist hypostasis of the eschaton, however, is a theoretical fallacy."

I must admit, dear friend, that for me this *statement* is a *non sequitur*. I cannot see why an immanent hypostasis of the *eschaton* should be a theoretical *fallacy* and why on this basis one should conclude that history can have no *eidos* because the course of history stretches into an unknown future. I can't see why the sense of history should for this reason prove to be an illusion. It is obviously your position that this illusionary *eidos* arises in that a symbol of faith is treated as though it were a proposition dealing with an object of immanent experience. This claim is the only one I can find in the entire book which could be taken to be a proof of such a "fallacy."

. . . I can already predict your objection: you will reply that the objection I raise is a proof of just how deeply I myself am caught up in gnostic thought. You will consider my very question a proof for the fact that I think positivistically and pragmatically *in terms* of methodologies and theories of procedure. Like another well-known gnostic, I shall coldly look the reproach of being one in the eye. I shall do this under the condition that gnosticism really is taken in the broad sense you give it. Strictly speaking, I don't know a single great metaphysician who would not have been a gnostic according to your conceptual scheme. Such diverse thinkers as Pascal, Leibniz, Hegel, Kierkegaard are guilty of the sin of gnosticism as soon as they divert from dogma, and I am not even sure that Thomas Aquinas is entirely free from this sin. It may be that what you call gnosticism is the basic category of all anthropology and all anthropodicy.[6] Perhaps I have completely misunderstood your train of thought here, but if so, it isn't for lack of good will. It seems to me that your concept of gnosticism is simultaneously too broad and too narrow. This requires some discussion.

If your analysis of the case of the Puritans in the fifth chapter is a model for the procedure of political gnosticism (and everything you say is, with one exception which I shall mention in a moment, very convincing), then I can't simultaneously consider the discussions of your sixth chapter as an example of gnostic philosophy and gnostic development, not if gnosticism is to signify the same thing in both cases. Looking back on the introduction, I am less and less able to consider Max Weber to be a case of gnosticism in the same sense in which the politics of the Puritans is shown to be gnostic. You introduce (on pages 139 and 140) two technical devices which in your opinion have become the main tools of the gnostic revolution. The first is the Koran-character of the holy text and the second the taboo on all critical endeavors. I claim that these two technical devices are of a general nature that is common to all social spheres and all forms of society, and have nothing to do with gnosticism. Both are expressions of social power, whether or not these stand in the service of Christian doctrine. If Socrates dies a martyr's death because he is charged with *asebeia,* or Christ because he doesn't respect the Koran-character of the Torah, if from the earliest times the church has killed heretics because they didn't respect the dogma of the council, if the traitors of the doctrine of dialectical materialism suffer their deserved punishment, in all of these cases we find the same thing: power of every kind creates its Koran and creates its taboos.

The heretics are always destroyed by this conflict. In one of your earlier writings you very successfully worked out the concept of the counter-idea. Every idea which attains power (or to speak your language: every idea as soon as it has come to existential representation under a symbol) needs its counter-symbol. Quite generally, I wonder if every system of symbols in your sense doesn't simultaneously presuppose a negative symbol system, every theology simultaneously a negative theology. [I wonder] whether there is not and must not be a dialectical tension between these two positive and negative poles of the symbolic systems and the theologies, and whether the *eidos* of history isn't to be found here, as in a certain sense Hegel attempted [to show].

1. Following Gregor Sebba's reading of *sophon* (cf. Opitz and Sebba, 440) instead of *apphon* (cf. the German edition of this correspondence, 296).

2. Here the leitmotif of "Symbol, Reality, and Society" (S1955), in which Voegelin's theory of symbols is taken further, sounds.

3. Following Sebba's reading of *Kaiser* (cf. Opitz and Sebba, 441) instead of *Kirche* (German edition of this correspondence, 298).

4. Joachim de Floris (Joachim of Fiore: 1145–1202) developed the metaphysics of history of a "third realm or age," which was to follow those of the Old and New Testaments.

5. Schutz wrote "philosophical." The passage under discussion reads "described as an historical phenomenon" (*New Science of Politics,* 118).

6. Schutz on this concept earlier in the letter: "to use an expression of Dempf's" (cf. A. Dempf, *Die Hauptformen der mittelalterlichen Weltanschauung* [Munich, 1925]).

Gurwitsch: *A prolegomenon to my future phenomenology of number*
                      (CAMBRIDGE, NOVEMBER 16, 1952)

My dearest Alfred,

. . . Yesterday I received the corrections for my paper to be given next year in Brussels (International Congress).[1] You will find a copy enclosed, which is for you. As you will see, it is a kind of prolegomenon to my future phenomenology of number. And you will also find the traces of your critique of my Goldstein essay, in which you were by and large right (started out on too high a level).

A misunderstanding: I don't have any right to suggest readers to Harvard Press. They choose their readers themselves, which doesn't hinder me from mentioning your name as a suggestion should the opportunity present itself. I plan to try to do that with McKeon, but don't know if I will be able to. Many thanks, at any rate, for the advice. But I don't think much of your way of eclipsing yourself. Someone once told me about a classified ad searching for a bushel basket under which a light could be hidden. Why not rather look for two bushel baskets from the very beginning? From a practical point of view you are probably right.

The "Présuppositions de la Logique" will soon appear in a volume which Colin is editing under the title "Phénoménologie et Existence." The galley proofs came about three weeks ago.

With best greetings to you and yours

Your
Aron

1. *"Sur une racine perceptive de l'abstraction"* (G1953, reprinted in G1966a, 385–389); cf. also GS 8.1.51.

Schutz: *Have you read Nagel-Hempel on methods in the social sciences? It's enough to drive one crazy*
           (NEW YORK, DECEMBER 4, 1952)

Dearest Friend,

To my great shame I still haven't answered your kind letter of the 16th, but things were (and are) a bit hectic here. I wanted to finish my overdue letter to Voegelin and the review of *Ideas III* before the arrival of my boss, which was last week and won't let me catch my breath before the middle of January. I am enclosing a copy of my letter to Voegelin, also a copy of his letter to me of October 19, without which the first pages of my answer will be incomprehensible. As soon as "Ideas III" [S1953b] is typed you will receive a copy with a request for a critique. And tell me what you think about my correspondence with Voegelin. I believe that we are once again by and large in agreement. . . .

And now many thanks for your Brussels paper.[1] (Unfortunately there is a chance that I will participate in the congress as part of the audience, since I will probably have to go to Europe during the summer. How am I to write my book?) I am well aware of the importance of the subject matter and admire your talent for saying so many important things in such a clear and concise manner in seven pages. But this time I have great difficulty in understanding you correctly. Of course I understand what you have to say about formalization and generalization in Husserl. Since I don't know Piaget, I can't make sense of the concept *abstraction à partir de l'action*. I don't know what *action* is to mean here. Is it to be translated with "action" [*Handlung*] or with "achievement (of consciousness)" [(*Bewußtseins-*) *Leistung*]? In both cases: Doesn't every activity have its object, regardless of whether it is a manipulating or a constitutive achievement of consciousness? And isn't activity itself a process of abstraction exercised on a necessarily *one-sided* object, which constitutes the object of the action? (It is the "object for" or "in order to" of the action). So how can there really be the duality of abstraction *à partir de l'objet* and *à partir de l'action*? And what does *à partir* mean here? Aren't we simply being victimized by ambiguities in the French language at this point?

These comments are purely preliminary, since they are those of a reader who has only bought and not yet opened the *Epistémologie Génétique,* although he has heartily wished to do so. As such, I am not at all surprised that the solution to the opposition turns out in the final analysis to be a matter of a differentiation within thematization. On the other hand I consider it to be a discovery of the highest order that you also trace the distinction between formalization and generalization back to a change in the thematizing attitude, and in this manner as it were can translate the formulae for the field of gravitation into those of electromagnetics. This will require a great deal of elaboration, but it is an important idea which comes to light here. But I can't see *up to now*—although this is certainly my fault—why you need Piaget for that.

But now we come to a point that makes me uneasy. This is a problem of the inner horizon. I must first formally announce that I am in full agreement with everything you say about the function of the inner horizon *in perception*. I also understand the way in which you very creatively present Piaget's schemata so to speak as sedimentations of the pre-fulfilled inner horizons, or as open-undetermined undecided inner horizons, of earlier *perceptual* experiences. But: Your presentation almost leads me to assume that you view inner horizons as a mode of givenness of perception and only of perception. Don't other lived experiences, don't even noemata and noeses, "motives" and goals of action also have their (inner and outer) horizons? I am very confused; if you really restrict horizons to perceptions, then there is a serious opposition between us here. Many parts of your book can be interpreted in this way with hindsight.

I haven't had any occasion to single out this point up to now, since your book is concerned with Gestalt psychology and, following our master Husserl, you also have the tendency to take perception as the prototype of all experiences as your model. But just this tendency of Husserl has led to the fact that it is actually only in the realm of the phenomenology of perception that we have worked-out results of investigation. Wouldn't it be very helpful for you to think through the problem of horizons in terms of lived experiences which are not perceptual? Especially if these studies are to be prolegomena to a phenomenology of number?

A difference—and I hope not an opposition between us—lies in the fact that you take perception or mathematics as the point of departure and model in all of your works, whereas I like to think through phenomenological problems in terms of the states of affairs of music and of human action in the social sphere. In all of these spheres there are certain abstractions on a non-perceptual basis, though surely of the same type of sedimented inner horizons you describe and compare to Piaget's *schème*. I would like to suggest deriving formal logic from the laws of counterpoint, which are laws of sense [*Sinngesetze*] dependent on the tone material and its perception just as much, but no more, than the content of this letter on the sheet of paper covered with ink marks. In a word: I completely agree with the thesis "All perception has its inner horizon, whose successive uncovering determines the typicality of the perceived and thereby is a root of abstraction." In contrast, I would not agree with a thesis that would read (very roughly): "All abstraction has to start from the perceptual structure which always has to refer to the typical, since in perception—and only in it—assimilated inner horizons can be demonstrated."

I assume that you will refer me to the last sentences of the first paragraph on page 6, beginning with the words: "*Tout cela s'applique également . . .*" in order to counter my doubt. But although I have read these sentences at least ten times, I understand them neither themselves nor in connection with the line of thought of the essay. This is certainly my fault—I am perhaps currently not in very good form—but I believe that a restatement would be helpful even to better readers than I.

Finally, a double congratulations: 1) for publishing the "Présuppositions" in the Colin volume (I hope unabridged); 2) for submitting the manuscript to Harvard Press, which Miss Weintraub told me about. She, who by the way hasn't yet made any use of my repeated offers to discuss your book with her, also told me that you won't be coming to New York at Christmas. I am not sorry about this, since I will have to go to Mexico and won't be able to participate in the congress. This will make me miss Farber and others. (Farber is the *chairman* of the section "Phenomenalism.") Have you read Nagel-Hempel on social-scientific methods?[2] It is enough to drive one crazy, and if I were in New York I would jump in like a thunder storm. Perhaps my absence is "a blessing in a very effective disguise," as Churchill said. Love to you and your wife.

Always your
Alfred

1. "On a Perceptual Root of Abstraction" (in G1966a, 386ff.).

2. Ernest Nagel and Carl G. Hempel's contribution to the symposium "Concept and Theory Formation in the Social Sciences" at the annual meeting of the American Philosophical Association, December 1952. (Cf. S1954a.) Cf. also Carl Hempel, *Fundamentals of Concept Formation in Empirical Science* (Chicago, 1952).

Gurwitsch: *I have lived in Russell's logic since the beginning of August*
                      (CAMBRIDGE, JANUARY 24, 1953)

Dearest Friend,

You have every right to be angry with me because of my persistent silence. And I can't even claim to be overworked in the strict sense. But for months I have been caught up in logical and mathematical matters to an unimaginable degree. This preoccupation explains my silence, although it doesn't excuse it.

I have lived in, among other things, Russell's logic since the beginning of August. I have the feeling that I have landed on a rolling ship and helplessly search along unknown corridors for a nonexistent cabin. Another image is that of a magician who brings forth the most improbably huge monsters out of a tiny, empty top hat, and then proceeds to transform these monsters into quite familiar things. Without metaphors: it seems to me that all of "logicism" is shot through with a series of the worst *petitiones principiorum,* that the genuine problems are simply thrown out, and that absolutely elementary confusions and howlers are committed.[1] I have identified some of them; heaven knows how many remain to be discovered. The whole thing receives the appearance of exactness from the formalizing symbolism, so that one becomes sick to one's stomach. I had to submit to this penance for the sake of my studies concerning the constitution of number. One can't work on such things without going into the literature, at least critically. But I have my doubts whether I am up to it. I am hardly the Hercules who can clean out this stall.

I am very grateful for your comments on my talk in Brussels. It seems to me that there aren't any essential differences between us here. Only the forced brevity of my presentation is responsible for your difficulties. If we could get together we could clear up a lot of it very easily. Just two comments: *action* in Piaget is manipulation, and then also interiorized manipulation. In contrast, the achievements of consciousness don't come off very well in his work. The *prise de conscience* is always after the fact—that is true—and it hardly achieves anything (I over-simplify). At this point the theory of thematization begins. In contrast, the *abstraction à partir de l'action* is fundamental. One needs it on account of the purely formal (in Husserl's sense) character of numbers and other mathematical structures. This theory of Piaget provides the basis for the Husserlian distinction between generalization and formalization. Phenomenology can learn a great deal at this point.

Finally, with regard to the question of the inner horizon, you are right that this phenomenon is not restricted to perception. If I concentrate on perception and exemplify [i.e., take perception as his example] in terms of it, and, it would appear, will continue to do so, this is for reasons of methodological demarcation. But the perceptual world is also the world of actions. The truly genial thing about Piaget is the fact that he explains mathematical structures in terms of what he calls *intelligence sensorimotrice.* My talk tries to bring his *schèmes* together with the inner horizon and thereby, by virtue of the primitiveness of certain *schèmes*—which contribute to mathematics—to cast light on the universality (in the sense of Husserlian formal universality) of mathematics. Here the thought you approve of has its place, since it is essentially a matter of the direction of thematization.

And now to your letter to Voegelin. We are in complete agreement here— which is hardly surprising. Especially with regard to the methodological orientation of his book. Aside from what would have to be said about the details, the orientation of his book is one of the best vindications of phenomenological thought. Historical interpretation must do justice to what the historical structures and societies have understood themselves to be. Voegelin has done this to a degree which has—so far as I know—hardly ever been reached in historical studies.

With regard to gnosticism, I am not entirely sure whether I am in full agreement with you. What you say about Spinoza is entirely correct, and perhaps you are also right in saying that he [Voegelin] understands gnosticism too narrowly and too broadly. But do all philosophers really fall under gnosticism? Leibniz? Kant? Husserl surely, to the extent that in the last phase he became a prophet in the sense that he hoped for the salvation of the world through phenomenology. I don't agree with you with regard to Voegelin's thesis concerning the "fallacy of meaning of history." Where the *entire* historical process is goal-directed there is indeed that *fallacy*. This assertion is historically-empirically gnostic, and perhaps it is so even on the basis of its inner logic. If history as a whole has a meaning, i.e., strives toward a fulfillment, transcendence reveals itself in time; the temporal is the coming-to-itself of the absolute. But I have another question, whether that isn't a part of the Messiah idea from the very beginning, in the Jewish as well as the Christian [sense]. After all, the *gesta Dei per Francos* is pre-Joachitic and quite gnostic. Christianity originally—according to Voegelin—separated the two spheres. Was this separation defensible? Did gnosticism merely "accompany" orthodox Christianity, or were the seeds in Christianity and sprouted again and again? Did Irenaeus battle the heretics from without or rather in actuality the immanent heresy, the tendency to which couldn't be rooted out since it lay deep in the essence of Messianism?[2] When will we be able to talk about all this?

By the way, have you heard anything about Voegelin's condition after the operation? I wrote him shortly before, but haven't received an answer from his wife. Please let me know if you should hear something. Please excuse my silence. Best greetings

from your
Aron

1. Roman Ingarden gave a similar evaluation of the "logistic attempt at a transformation of philosophy" in his brilliant critique of Carnap: "*L'Essai logistique d'une refonte de la philosophie*," in *Revue Philosophique de la France et de l'Etranger* 60 (1935): 137–159.
2. Cf. Hans Jonas, *Gnosis and spätantiker Geist*, 2 vols. (Göttingen, 1934 and 1954).

Gurwitsch: *One shouldn't have to take this kind of schoolmasterly treatment*
             (CAMBRIDGE, FEBRUARY 6, 1953)

Dear Friend,

The enclosed letter, which I need to have back, came today from the Harvard Press. My first reaction was to send the manuscript [*The Field of Consciousness*] to Van Breda with the request that he recommend it to Nijhoff. One really shouldn't have to take this kind of schoolmasterly treatment. But I want to try it perhaps with the Noonday Press or even before that with Oxford Press. I seem to recall that your earlier corrector works or worked for the Oxford Press. I have forgotten his name. If he is still there I could first send him the manuscript personally and hear what he has to say.

I am of course ready to make all concessions of a linguistic nature. I would also be prepared to make two books out of this single book, but not in the manner which Herr Schoolmaster wants. The first book would include only parts I and II, and would be nothing more than a presentation of Gestalt theory, although that *en vue* to its later use in the context of phenomenology. So it would be a preparation—and only that—for the second book. The second book would be *The Field of Consciousness*. My question to you is: do you think that these first two parts are worth publishing in this form? After all, as presentations of Gestalt theory the books by Koffka and Köhler are much more comprehensive. Then too, I could only accept such an arrangement if I had the assurance that both books would appear.

What the schoolmaster wants is basically a reworking of parts I–IV. But then the two last parts would hang in the air, and it would be just as if I had never written them! Quite aside from this, I won't even consider a reworking. I have dedicated nine years to this book; I won't spend another three on revisions. To say nothing of revisions that would change the tenor in a decisive manner. The *reader* apparently didn't notice, e.g., that the discussion of the structure of the noema in part IV, ch. II requires bringing in the psychological discussion, since this makes possible the Gestalt theoretical interpretation of the structure in question. I believe that the use of concepts from Gestalt theory for the advancement of phenomenological problems is only possible in the way I have attempted it: by working with these concepts concretely, and that is what the schoolmaster calls "Gestalt theoretical analyses encroach unduly upon the basic theme." Under no circumstances will I write the book that the referee wants to have.

But before I make any such suggestion to the Harvard Press I want first to explore the field to see whether there is a possibility of having the book appear *tel quel*. To tell the truth, I would prefer to make the concessions in question to another publisher than the Harvard Press, which is known for its "helpful suggestions": cf. what Farber had to suffer.

I am sorry that I have to burden you with this unpleasant affair. But you know how important your opinion is to me.

Regards, your
Aron

Schutz: *Of the base and the mean / Let none complain / For whatever you say, it is seen / These always end¹*
(NEW YORK, FEBRUARY 9, 1953)

Dear Friend:

> *Uebers Niederträchtige*
> *niemand sich beklage,*
> *denn es ist das Mächtige,*
> *was man Dir auch sage.*¹

Your letter of the 6th arrived this morning and got me very upset. It is absolutely clear that the "reader" has no idea what your book is about. I think that this is his and only his fault: as you know, I also felt that part III isn't quite integrated into the whole (or let's say is placed before the reader a bit abruptly), and for this reason I recommended that you add a transitional paragraph, which you did. One can ask whether it should be clarified or lengthened, but that is all. How can one take seriously the judgment of a man who can write—in addition to the sentence you quote—the following about this book: "I find, for example, that the space-time criterion, which plays a crucial part in his interpretation, is insufficient as a principle of relevancy for the realm of reality."

You have to let this sentence ("for example," since one can't say *etc.*) sink in slowly. It is in the best *English idiom* and by no means a *deviation from good usage*. I turn its elements around and around in my mind. Did you know that a "criterion" can be a principle of relevance, and what's more, one for the realm of reality? And that in your work, space and time are "crucial" *criteria* for this noble end? If I didn't know how far from philosophy Parsons is, I would take him to be the "reader," since "crucial" is his *trade-mark*. But what good is all this? "The reader is the measure," as Protagoras taught us. Do you have any idea who this "reader" is? It can't be Köhler; he would be incapable of making the suggestion "the use of 'etc.' should be avoided."

Substantively, I would strongly advise you not to follow his "advice" that the work be divided. If one is justified in reading the letter from a *university press* according to "business" principles, then it seems to me that they are saying that they *might* be prepared to publish the volume on Gestalt psychology, but under no circumstances the one on the field theory. Somebody else should publish it and Herr *Reader* will add that it is hardly marketable. And the Harvard Press by no means wants to commit itself to accepting even the first volume. The Harvard Press won't give you the guarantee, which you so correctly demand, that both books appear, neither now nor after the revision, and I draw the conclusion that we must try out all other paths before taking on a "revision"—which in my eyes is a euphemism for partial publication.

I know from the reaction of the Psychology Department, to whom I have shown the table of contents, that there is an enormous interest in the book on the part of Gestalt psychologists. That the phenomenological part will find fewer buyers is obvious. I would by no means be prepared to take on myself the burden of a revision on the basis of the answer from the Harvard Press—at most a linguistic revision, since I don't know whether your corrector did a good *job*. I am certainly not competent to judge that. Natanson (and it goes without saying that I won't tell him or anyone else about the position of the Harvard Press) found the version we have—which is the one *before* the correction—to be in need of improvement. On the other hand, when one reads books from the Harvard Press such as Parsons-Shills *Toward a Theory of Action,* then one has to say that the "errors of diction and idiom" about which they complain are a classic example for *Gracchin de Seditione quaerentes.*[2]

But you don't want to hear outbursts of anger from me, but practical advice. Oxford Press: my "corrector"—Arthur Goddard—edited the book by Felix Kaufmann, the one by Jean Wahl, and one or two more for the Oxford Press. He has never had any influence there and hasn't had any contact with them for years. Although he has a certain philosophical understanding, he isn't competent to make any judgment about your book, unless it concerns merely the language, where he could certainly perform good service in return for pretty high pay. We need to find another connection to Oxford Press. Among my friends only Winternitz has one, but only to the music department, which is completely independent, and I would hold such a detour to be a serious tactical error.

I don't think much at all of the Noonday Press. . . . They publish—not unintelligently—relatively thin volumes in small editions whose production costs are relatively modest.

Nijhoff doesn't seem to me to be very promising either: The "Husserliana" series is subsidized and not, I believe, a business proposition. We have to think about other solutions. Yale U. P. and Princeton U. P. are hardly worth considering, since their philosophers and psychologists, who will of course be "readers," are hardly likely to be friends of your book. Aside from that, from what I hear they are the most adventurous.

What about the following suggestions—we can talk about the order: 1) U. P. of Chicago. 2) Oxford. 3) Henri Regnier. 4) Free Press, Glencoe, Ill. 5) U. P. of Buffalo. 6) Macmillan. 7) Columbia U. P. Of course the whole problem would be much easier to deal with if we could get a subsidy from somewhere: American Philosophical Society, American Council of Learned Studies, A.A.A.S., etc. Unfortunately, I don't know my way around in these things. Or—gingerly (with the request that you don't end our friendship) suggested—privately: Paris is worth a Mass and the *Field of Consciousness* a ticket to Baltimore.[3]

I would give the Harvard Press a polite, dilatory answer which doesn't close the door, but under all circumstances offer the book, just as it is, at most edited for language and with the addition of an explanatory paragraph in the introduction or at the beginning of part III (as you know, I have handed on the manuscript), to at least two more publishers before even considering these people's suggestions (who have good reason to break VE RI TAS into three parts in their coat of arms).

It is so important to me and surely also to you that this matter be dealt with that you will forgive me if I don't come back to your earlier kind letter for the moment.

Concerning the things themselves, I would remind you of Schopenhauer's words you love so much at the end of the *Theory of Color,* where he suggests to everyone who has something new to say that he familiarize himself with the reception of Goethe's theory of colors, and speaks of that attitude "which is just native to the human race in general": "Following this consideration I will not draw back my hands, but rather complete his work, since this work is the flower of his life, which wants to yield fruit: he relinquishes it; but well knowing to whom, and prepared."

Affectionately as always

Your

Alfred

1. From J. W. von Goethe's *"West-östlicher Divan"* (1814). English translation by Stephen Spender in *The Permanent Goethe,* ed. Thomas Mann (New York: Dial Press, 1948, 1958²), 645.
2. Gracchus instigated the revolt of the peasants against the roman Senate.
3. Reference to Gurwitsch's aunt in Baltimore (cf. GS 1.26.41).

Gurwitsch: *Marx's distinction between animal and human history is a good illustration*
(CAMBRIDGE, FEBRUARY 15, 1953)

My dearest Friend.

Let me first thank you for your kind letter. Like all demonstrations of your friendship and your sentiment, this letter did me good. You chose a beautiful phrase from Goethe as motto; let me answer you with another one:

Wer nicht die Welt in seinen Freunden sieht,
Verdient nicht, daß die Welt von ihm erfahre.[1]

But if you believed that your letter had to achieve a goal, you were mistaken. This goal needn't be realized, since it has already been realized. You needn't think I have even for one minute considered "pulling back." Quite the contrary:

as long as my physical and mental powers don't abandon me, I plan to use my hands in digging tunnels. Then I will listen with intense concentration to the sounds of boring that come from the other direction. These tones and then the shining light when the last separating wall falls and the paths meet,—that is so much more important and more interesting than the carping of a "reader."

A small delicacy seems to have slipped by you in the sentence which you so correctly admire: the space-time order is not only a criterion, and not only does a criterion become a principle of relevance, but an *insufficient* one at that. *That* is what I call magic! A propos, I suspect that the "reader" is D. W., the same person with whom Richard v. Mises became embroiled in a controversy about probability years ago. Of course I can't prove it, but the style of both writing and thought points to W., who back then demonstrated just as profound an understanding of the mathematical theory of probability as now of phenomenology. Köhler isn't capable of such achievements.

Concerning practical matters: . . . With regard to your *business*-interpretation of the letter, I think that you are right. In the final analysis, Harvard will publish only the Gestalt part, in the final analysis meaning: after a half dozen reworkings. There will always be some new "reader" who has to show that he knows something about these things. But he can only do this by making "helpful suggestions." I have had the opportunity to observe this part of academic life a bit. The gentlemen all feel—with good reason—very insecure; so they have to prove themselves; this they can do only by cavilling, most especially when they are dealing with a foreigner, towards whom they already have an ambivalent attitude. So they don't read with an eye to quality, but "critically."

Some news of a more pleasant kind: Jerusalem wants an as yet unpublished article "for the beginning." I am thinking about revising part III, par. 2–4, of my book a bit and giving it to them under the title "Phenomenological Interpretation of the Dismissal of the Constancy-Hypothesis." Although both the title and the text will be translated into Hebrew, I am less than delighted by the choice of the title. Maybe I will think of something better. Ironically, the Harvard Philosophy Club has invited me to give a lecture. I will speak to them on "Psychological Approaches to Phenomenology"[2] on April 8. That is to include James and Gestalt theory as well, whereby phenomenology then appears as something meaningful and significant.

You offered to send me copies of your correspondence with Voegelin. Please do so. And please don't infer a lack of interest from the tardiness of my answers and from their brevity. I am most urgently interested in this entire question, so urgently that I could write entire monographs about it. There is, e.g., the question of the sense of history, a question with respect to which I am rather inclined to go with Voegelin. If history—as a whole—has a sense, then there must be a final phase, the phase in which the sense is fulfilled. If this phase is not exclusively situated in the transcendent, but is to be reached on earth—and this is involved in the claim of the sense of history—then we are already in gnostic thought. If mankind can or must help in the fulfillment of Providence, then we are indeed confronted with a divination of society and of history.

I would say something similar concerning p. 21 of your November letter to Voegelin. "Power of every kind creates its Koran and creates its taboos," you write. To be sure; and heretics always have a difficult time. But doesn't Voegelin mean something quite specific with "Koran"? The new revelation, which doesn't fulfill the preceding one and take it up into itself in this—Hegelian—sense, as was the case with the Old and New Testament, but rather the revelation which declares everything which came before to be a series of worthless errors, the revelation with which precisely the phase of fulfillment begins, with which the sense of history is attained and with which history is thereby brought to a close. Understood in this way, the Koran (I don't know why Voegelin chooses the term, but he will have his reasons) breaks off the historical continuity.

A good example of this is Marx's distinction between animal and human history. So if human history has begun, why should one be interested in some document of the pre-human phase? Intolerance has a point here which it doesn't have in Socrates, etc. Dangerous errors are more than mere errors if they count as the remains of a finished period, which could as it were make it appear questionable that the phase of fulfillment has begun. For that this phase has begun is a fact which carries its proof only within itself. So no other fact can be allowed. Its mere existence puts in question the facticity of the "end" of history.

The church has always known that there are errors. It has protected the believers from error for the sake of the salvation of their souls. Superficially they—as well as other powers—did this no differently from gnostically constituted groups. But we should remember that error, as the church interprets itself, doesn't threaten the truth. The fact of the existence of the heathen is insignificant for the eternal validity of true faith. The mere existence of the doubter is fatal for gnostic formations: perhaps then the "kingdom" hasn't come yet after all?

I want to talk about all of this with you. When???

With best greetings from both of us to all of you

Yours as always

Aron

1. "One who does not see the world in his friends / Does not deserve to have the world hear of him." J. W. von Goethe, *Torquato Tasso*, I:iii. English translation in *Goethe's Plays,* tr. Charles E. Passage (New York: Frederick Ungar Publishing Co., 1980), 503–504. (Our gratitude to Dirk Grathoff for the reference.)

2. Cf. GS 11.2.52.

Gurwitsch: *I have succeeded in specifying more precisely what non-mundane consciousness means*
(CAMBRIDGE, APRIL 5, 1953)

My dearest Friend,

It has been a long time since I have heard from you. I have only heard from Weintraub, who was here recently, that you continue to function normally at the New School, and that the number of your admirers there is increasing, which is as it should be. Have you read in the *Times* that my friend London had been awarded the Lorentz Medal by the Dutch Academy?[1] He is the fourth recipient; the three predecessors were Planck, Debye, and Onning—very good and for him appropriate company. One can see from this that even in these times, now and again and in different countries, things take a natural and rational course.

Enclosed is the manuscript of the essay that will be printed in Jerusalem in a language which neither you nor I can read.[2] I naively thought that I could take 20 pages from the book, write a couple of introductory sentences, add or delete something here and there, etc. If you have time to take a look at it you will find that while all of the ideas come from the book, the fact is that a new presentation has developed. The presentation in the book is good and won't be changed. But since the context is lacking here I had to create a new presentation. In this way something has taken shape with which I am satisfied. I believe that I have succeeded in saying and making more precise what psychology as a positive science is, and thereby what non-mundane consciousness means. Further: the extent to which Gestalt theory is not phenomenology and yet can legitimately be used in phenomenology within certain limits. It seems to me that the essay has also gained more nuance compared to the book. But I want to hear what my critic thinks. I plan to publish the article again later, either with Farber or in French with Thévenaz in the *Revue de Théologie et de Philosophie* in Lausanne. By the way, do you think that I could read the article (with some deletions) this Fall in your General Seminar? If you could arrange that I would be very thankful, since I can use that here for reasons of prestige.

No news from Chicago; it is probably too soon. From Paris I heard that Van Breda is putting pressure on Désclée de Brouwer on behalf of my book[3]; the decision hasn't been made yet. To tell the truth, the French edition is very important to me, perhaps more than the one here. I hope things will work out with Désclée de Brouwer; otherwise I shall try to speak with Marcel or Armand Colin this summer. I could have made things much easier for myself if I had written it in French. That is a lesson for the future.

Give me the pleasure of a few words from you, if only a very few.

Love and best wishes

Your
Aron

1. Fritz London (born 1900) discovered the quantum-mechanical calculation of the hydrogen molecule in Bonn. He taught at the Sorbonne along with Gurwitsch during their exile in Paris, 1934–1938.

2. "The Phenomenological and the Psychological Approach to Consciousness," in Hebrew translation: *Iyyun* 4 (1953) (cf. G1955).
3. Rainer Biemel (the brother of Walter Biemel) worked for Désclée de Brouwer, and was responsible for the French edition of the *Field*.

Schutz: *Don't you want to watch when your old friend Schutz is thrown to the lions?*
(NEW YORK, APRIL 9, 1953)

Dearest Friend,

I know that it is almost unforgivable that I haven't written to you for so long, but at the moment my life is wilder than ever before. My boss is here, I have three Ph.D. theses and two sociology masters theses to supervise. Natanson's "Mead"[1] has turned out excellently, but gave me lots of work (by the way, he has accepted a position as Assistant Professor at the University of Houston starting this Fall, since we don't have any money for him here). I have to fight hard battles concerning the reorganization of the Philosophy Department.

In addition I let myself agree to give a talk on May 3 at the Conference on Methods.[2] I am talking on "Concept and Theory Formation in the Social Sciences." The title is deliberately that of the symposium at the December meeting of the American Philosophical Association, to which Nagel and Hempel have contributed articles against which one simply *has* to do something. They are published in the volume from the University of Pennsylvania Press, and you are probably familiar with them.[3] If I am finished in time I will send you the manuscript for your critique. It is unfortunately a torture to write something productive under these circumstances, and I have just revised the 7th draft to an 8th. I am paired with Margenau, who will speak on the application of quantum theory to the social sciences. Don't you want to watch when your old friend Schutz is thrown to the lions? In the afternoon the English astronomer F. Hoyle and P. van den Camp will speak.

I immediately read your Jerusalem *paper,* which I received this morning, but of course I haven't yet studied it as thoroughly as the many new and stimulating details deserve. I will be able to do that only after May 3. My first impression is splendid and I believe that the article contains a great deal that is new in comparison with the book. . . .

I don't know if you have already read *Ideen III*. (By the way, have I sent you the manuscript of my review?[4]) I would very much like to hear your view as to whether the understanding of psychology as a "double science" which is contained in the book isn't an additional support for your theory. (Which of course has nothing directly to do with your book or with the present essay, and *can't* be allowed to have anything to do with them.)

What a pity that you didn't communicate your wish to speak in our General

Seminar two weeks ago! This time they decided to announce the lectures in the catalogue, and I believe that it has already gone to the printer. I shall of course see if there is anything I can do. I assume that you will come even if your travel expenses are not paid? The General Seminar meets on Wednesday evenings (during the *Fall Term* only). But as it stands, your paper is "over the head" of the participants, especially of H. I think that I would be the only one who would dare to say something in the discussion—and I would only be able to say "yes."

Best wishes for Chicago and Desclée de Brouwer. Why don't you ask Jean Wahl where one could place the book in France if D.d.B. shouldn't accept it? I think that G. Marcel is "a slippery customer," a *homo viator,* who is more concerned with *avoir* than with *être.* . . .

I think that I haven't yet reported the most important event in my life to you. George has received new glasses—the newly developed parabolic glasses—which help him very much. He can read with them and does his schoolwork without our help.

Love and all the best to both of you from Ilse and me,

Your
Alfred

1. *The Social Dynamics of George H. Mead* (new edition: The Hague: Martinus Nijhoff, 1973).
2. 33rd Semi-Annual Meeting of the Conference on Methods in Philosophy and the Sciences in New York (S1954a).
3. "Science, Language and Human Rights" (*American Philosophical Association,* vol. 1, Philadelphia, 1952).
4. S1953b, Schutz's review of Husserl's *Ideas,* vol. III.

Gurwitsch: *Last Thursday I took on Wiener's "Cybernetics"*
             (CAMBRIDGE, MAY 3, 1953)

Dear Friend,

It is truly unforgivable that I didn't congratulate you for the truly most important event. If the new parabolic glasses really emancipate George from help in doing his schoolwork and in reading in general, then we are freed of a great worry. It is a matter of complete indifference in what way he can make use of his eyes as long as he uses them. We know only too well what has happened in these years, in reality and in your fears. Just as we have shared the fear with you, we now share with you the feeling of liberation. One shouldn't despise "scientific progress" all too much; it is quite good for any number of things, as *figura* demonstrates.

So today is the methodological day. Too bad that I can't be in New York. By the way, Margenau isn't the worst. His book on the *Nature of Physical Reality* is very unpopular among the positivists, which only goes to show that he is good. You will give me a report. You haven't sent me your manuscript, so I infer that you weren't finished on time. I am not familiar with the Nagel and Hempel articles, but I can well imagine. Brandeis too has something like a General Seminar. Outsiders speak there, and a week later it is discussed by a *panel* from the faculty. . . . Last Thursday I took on "cybernetics"; the week before, Wiener was there.[1] I have waited for this opportunity to clear up some basic questions in psychology (man is, as you know, an adding machine and vice versa) and to say some things about the question of algorithms.

My *forte* is that they can't say that I don't understand anything about mathematics and logic. It was a kind of pleasure to move in the horizon of mathematics up to Goldstein-Piaget; human beings are simply vain. Our students, to the extent that they have to do with me, are used to grief. The evening was a success.

Many thanks for your efforts to get me in the catalogue.[2] I will come even if travel costs aren't paid. And don't worry: I won't read the Jerusalem *paper,* but rather a simplified version: the lecture that I recently gave at Harvard under the title "A Psychological Approach to Phenomenology" and which was received with great interest. The discussion which followed was the best one I have seen in the Philosophy Club. Basically, this lecture deals only with the question "psychology as positive science," and phenomenology appears only on the side.

When are you coming in May? We sail on June 17, but for financial reasons will be in New York only one day, namely on the 16th. Let's make a date for that evening if you can arrange it.

With best greetings

Your old
Aron

1. Norbert Wiener, *Cybernetics* (1948).
2. His lecture in the General Seminar was held on October 14, 1953 (SG 10.2.53).

Schutz: *Natural science doesn't always speak when the natural scientists speak*
          (NEW YORK, MAY 11, 1953)

Dear Friend,

Your kind letter of the 3rd was a special pleasure. I know what dear friends you are and how much understanding you have for our boy's problem. This is why I sent you such a complete report about the great event, and your reaction is just as understanding and affectionate as I expected. Many thanks for your friendship!

One can give differing evaluations of the lecture last Sunday.[1] The auditorium was filled, but Nagel, Hempel & Co. were conspicuous by their absence. Sidney Hook only appeared for the afternoon session. No one from Columbia was there; my colleagues too showed only limited interest. I still don't know my way around in the academic jungle, and praise the free competition of the *huxters,*[2] who openly slit one another's throats.

The audience received my *paper* very positively. Margenau improvised his lecture as a polemic against me, the discussion was mainly between me and him, and if my friends say that I "won on points," that was no great achievement, since the difference in niveau was considerable. Two participants in the discussion would have been a blessing. You and Felix Kaufmann, for you would have exploded the so-called arguments from the natural sciences from within. How correct Husserl was: natural science doesn't always speak when the natural scientists speak.[3]

McGill was at the lecture, but didn't participate in the discussion. But before the lecture a man wearing glasses, with a bloated face and very sparse hair, spoke to me, and since I didn't know him he had to introduce himself—as Dorion Cairns. He is in New York "this year," was very friendly, and we agreed to meet next week. I am enclosing the manuscript of the lecture and am curious what *you* have to say to it. I intend to submit it to the *Journal of Philosophy,* not because I think they will take it, but in order to see how editor Nagel reacts. Where else could I publish it? I think that it should be published, and don't want to be the house poet of Farber and *Social Research*.

Dr. Heimann,[4] our economist, who is chairman of the General Seminar Committee, tells me that he has written to you. I of course want to be in New York for this occasion: according to my business travel plans it is probable (this in confidence for you; I haven't yet told the school anything) that I will have to be in Europe for four or five weeks beginning October 15, and the Christmas trip to Mexico might be extended to the first Wednesday in January. Please choose your date accordingly. This "professional disturbance" is really bad. It forces me to remain in New York during the summer, so that I can only take a short vacation in June, and I am unfortunately by no means sure that I will still be in New York on June 16. Needless to say I will do my best to come to Cambridge before then and see you again before you go to Europe.

For the moment I have to fight my way through the five theses of my students on whose committees I unfortunately serve. Natanson, the only one who graduated this year under my personal supervision, received a well-earned *summa cum laude* for his truly excellent book on G. H. Mead. In addition to the offer from Houston, which he has, there is now a for the time being temporary offer from Bryn Mawr "in the offing."

You don't write about the fate of your book; how are things going right now?

With best greetings from Ilse and myself to both of you

Your

Alfred

Can I send you—separately—a few *re-prints* of Husserl "Ideas II" [S1953a] for distribution in Europe?

1. "Concept and Theory Formation in the Social Sciences." It was indeed published in the *Journal of Philosophy* (S1954a).
2. Huxters are costermongers and fences, also: "money used among costermongers and low sharpers." Cf. Eric Partridge, *Dictionary of the Underworld* (New York, 1949).
3. The quote could not be identified, but cf. Husserl's "The Attitude of Natural Science and the Attitude of Humanistic Science," appendix IV in the *Crisis*.
4. Eduard Heimann (professor of economics in Hamburg until 1933) wrote a superb analysis of the fascistic causes of war in the crisis of democratic institutions: *Freedom and Order: Lessons from the War* (New York, 1947).

Gurwitsch: *You recognize the process of verification in science to be social action*
(CAMBRIDGE, MAY 15, 1953)

Dearest Friend,

Many thanks for the new manuscript, which was a real pleasure. May I keep it? On the assumption that the answer will be positive I am sending you some pages which were doubles. Along with your Princeton paper,[1] this is a very important contribution to a theory of science, and not only of the social sciences. The two pieces together really lay the foundation for this very necessary undertaking. The way you make the transition in the second part from the ideal types of everyday experience to those of science, or rather indicate the necessity of this transition: that is so thoroughly instructive, especially in connection with the Princeton paper, that one really anticipates the development of a theory of science.

You are certain of my substantive agreement anyway. I only want to mention a couple of points of subsidiary importance and then to congratulate you for an important discovery that I have found at one place. One really could have made use of the distinctions in the *Feeling of Sympathy*[2] against Nagel's thesis of the identification of *observer* and *actor*. I understand very well that you didn't go into this since it would have led you too far. I only wonder if it wouldn't be appropriate to report about it in a separate essay, with more details than in your old Scheler essay.

Then, on pp. 14/15 you might perhaps have said with more emphasis that world and facts are always interpreted, even when the natural scientist manipulates them. But that is a question of the proper dose. The "motives of action" on p. 16 are obviously "in order to" motives. It would perhaps be good to say that (this is after all your terminology) and distinguish it from the "because" motive. I think that you should add that into the published version, even if it makes the essay a bit longer. You would make the sense of "understanding" clearer, especially if you could see your way clear to take into account the relevant distinctions from Jaspers (*Allgemeine Psychopathologie*).[3] After all, the basic point is that Nagel and Co. want to recognize only "because" motives. I imagine that a more extensive discussion of precisely this point would also make the other point (interpretation) more graphic.

Now we come to the main thing (pp. 6/7 sub No 2): this is really exciting; you recognize the process of verification in the internal operation of science to be social action. This process has the structures of social actions. I have thought this through in all directions and must insist that what you say is also true of verification in the natural sciences, and even of thinking through mathematical proofs. There too it is a matter of something other than the discovery of errors in reckoning. We always have: the science of a time; a specific area of problems in it; a theory or rival theories; data which support a theory; the question as to what this evidence signifies (i.e., *A*, who verifies, asks what *B* meant with his data for his [*B*'s] theory, whether he might justifiably mean that with reference to the procedural code), and what, if another theory is tried out, the hypothesis to be verified means within the totality of the available knowledge at the time (means with reference to the contested theories) and more of this sort.[4]

All of this is irrelevant to the positive scientist, who is only interested in results, and doesn't and needn't inquire into the possibility of his science and science in general. It is very relevant to the philosopher. So, at the very beginning of the theory of science, we have social processes concerning which there must be at least a rough clarity before we can cast light on the indeed central concept of verification. If we inquire into the conditions of the possibility of science, and understand this question concretely, which is unavoidable, then we run into certain structures of human working-with-one-another.

You can be very proud of this discovery. As I read this one page, "a light went on in my head." All talk about *philosophy of science* is empty if the concrete circumstances under which science is pursued are neglected. As a result: the natural world thus plays a dual role: it provides the point of departure for all science, and all pursuit of science takes place within the structures of this world, in a sector of this world. This is indeed a fundamental result.

That your opponents were absent was only to be expected. From beginning to end, science has today been superseded by the politics of science. Ignoring is a much better tactic than discussing. Only such fools as we still want to find out what is actually going on. Problems are by and large solved by the politics of hiring. If somebody finds a difficulty somewhere, the best thing is simply not to listen. Mr. Hook spoke here last year, and W. pushed him into a corner with questions about sense and meaning to such an extent that Lerner had to come to his rescue, and did so with parliamentary means (Learner was *chairman*). (I wasn't there, since I had a class; but the reports were very interesting.)

Your letter to me arrived just after I had written Dr. Heimann. Since I had no idea of your commitments, I left the date up to him. I assume that you can diplomatically arrange things with him such that I come when it fits your schedule. I myself have no preferences. A pity that you won't be in Brussels.

Jerusalem is allowing me to publish the article [G1955] in English or

French. Should I try *Mind* or the *Philosophical Review?* I am afraid that I will once again come back to Farber, so I might as well go directly to him. A propos: I don't share your house-poet reservations. Still, a Nagel experiment would be very good and interesting. My *guess* is: he will accept it in order to demonstrate his fairness, and then he will write a reply in his formalistic way, although I hardly see what he can write. With your clear and very precise manner you can make things hard for him. So let us verify.

We often talk about the ways in which the new glasses [for George] must have meant a profound transformation in your life.

On the book front: nothing new from Chicago or Paris. But lots of new developments on the Piaget-Gestalt theory front. More about this verbally and I hope soon.

With best regards

Your
Lola

"Lola" is my true, if not official name.

1. "Common Sense and Scientific Interpretation of Human Action" (S1953c).
2. "Phänomenologie und Theorie der Sympathiegefühle" by Max Scheler.
3. Reference to an early edition of the *Allgemeine Psychopathologie.* Cf. *General Psychopathology,* tr. Hoenig and Marian W. Hamilton (Chicago: University of Chicago Press, 1963). Jaspers later elaborated the distinction between "genus" and "type" in a way that developed Max Weber's ideal types.
4. This field of problems was to be brilliantly explored by Thomas Kuhn in *The Structure of Scientific Revolutions* (Chicago: University of Chicago Press, 1970[2]).

Gurwitsch: *I am not prepared to negotiate* in puncto *the autonomy of reason*
(CAMBRIDGE, JUNE 11, 1953)

Dearest Friend,

I am writing these lines in haste, since the preparations for my trip currently dominate our entire existence in this house. First I want to tell you and your dear wife how much we enjoyed your visit. It was so good to have you with us here. We very much hope that only the beginning is difficult; i.e., that once the beginning has been made *vivant sequentes* will be the watchword.[1] I at least have had a quasi-originary experience of what it is like when the Trappist monk receives a three-day dispensation from his vow of silence.

Enclosed are the two letters from Voegelin. I am sending them back, since they are originals and not copies. I assume that you gave them to me for my perusal. (The other two, the memorandum to the school and "Ideas II" are copies and thus meant for me: is that right?) The letters are very interesting. Unfortunately I can't go into them in any detail right now. But I have to point out an ambiguity: is what Voegelin writes about Mariology and Christology intended to be merely historical, or is it to have a binding significance for us over and beyond the historical?

In the first case: all right; the historians can judge the correctness. In the second case I regret that I can't go along. You can call me a gnostic, heretic, or say other nice things to me. I am not prepared to negotiate *in puncto* the autonomy of reason: "A voice from beyond—what would it have to say to us free spirits?!" (Husserl). In the final analysis this is the source of my resistance to your ontologizing inclinations: I would vary Hobbes's great maxim, that we understand nothing that we haven't ourselves created, to the effect that we can't accept anything we cannot penetrate and survey in its structure and in the inner composition of its sense [*inneren Sinnaufbau*]. But this is a broad field and—to vary Husserl once again—a title for wide-ranging investigations and discussions.

Farber rejected the Jerusalem essay, since he doesn't accept anything which has already appeared in another language.[2] So I will make inquiries to Thévenaz or Breda or Wahl in Europe. It's actually too bad, since the psychologists here would have been very interested. But the last months have made clear to me just where I belong with my work. . . .

I wish you a good summer. Love and best wishes to you all from both of us

Your
Aron

1. According to Mrs. Gurwitsch, this was their only visit from the Schutz family.
2. The "Jerusalem essay" did finally appear in expanded form in *PPR* (G1955).

Schutz: *My ontological inclinations are pretty far removed from Christology*
          (NEW YORK, JUNE 15, 1953)

Dearest Friend,

I am going on vacation after all, so we won't have seen you before your departure. I hope that these lines reach you in Paris after a pleasant cruise, and we wish you all our love for your stay in Europe.

Many thanks for your kind letter of the 11th. We were very happy visiting you, and our discussions were most important for me. They will continue to provide much food for thought. Don't be too angry with me for my "ontological inclinations," as you call them, and don't exile me from your heart on that account. I think that they are pretty far removed from Christology.

That we understand nothing we haven't ourselves created is something

Alfred and Ilse Schutz.

I gladly admit. The ontological foundation of all understanding and self-understanding is itself in principle not available to understanding. But it is describable. If you vary Hobbes's *statement* to the effect that we cannot accept anything that we cannot penetrate and survey in its structure and in the inner composition of its sense, I answer that it doesn't lie within our "ability" [*Vermöglichkeit*] to accept or not accept that which is *imposed* on us. And what is imposed on us? Our place as human beings in the cosmos. I mean no more than that this is simply ontologically there, in its incomprehensibility and that it is only this primal foundation—as life-world—that makes all understanding possible. I don't think that I am so far from Husserl and you. For with your refusal to accept what is incomprehensible you surely don't want to say that we phenomenologists have to ignore such things. But "all this suffering serves us for sweeter babble in the future."

I sent some copies of my review of *Ideas II* by surface mail to your Paris address for general distribution. If you give me your address I will send along copies of "Ideas III." Please greet all of my friends, especially Jean Wahl and Raymond Aron as well as Gaston Berger and of course Van Breda and the Biemels. If you should talk to Merleau-Ponty, I would be interested to hear if he received my book. With great effort, I got him a copy at his request and sent it to him a year and a half ago, and he didn't even confirm receiving it.[1]

Love to you and your wife

Your
Alfred

1. This can only refer to *Der Sinnhafte Aufbau* (*The Phenomenology of the Social World*), S1932a and S1967.

Gurwitsch: *The circle around Ricoeur is waiting for something which only you can give*
(PARIS, JUNE 24, 1953)

Dear Friend,

A brief greeting from Paris, where we arrived two days ago after a voyage which wasn't all too pleasant. Many thanks for your letter. I haven't driven you out of my heart and will not do so even if you become even more ontological than you are. Please send me the off-prints c/o Jean Adler. At the end of August I will distribute them among the names you gave and to others.

I made propaganda for you today with "my publisher": the fact that I speak of Désclée de Brouwer in this way should tell you that we have come to terms. The contract will come in a few days. The conditions are good. I am very happy.

I was glad that my passages dedicated to you have called you to the attention of some people there. I told them all about you. You have to do something for your fame in France; we will have to talk about it on my return. There is an interest here in work like yours; you must take advantage of this. The circle around Ricoeur is almost waiting for something of the sort that only you can give them.

Best greetings in haste.

Your
Aron

Gurwitsch: *Brussels brought the final confirmation that we needn't work in a vacuum*
(Paris, September 5, 1953)

Dear Friend,

Only now, in the relative peace of the last days in Paris, do I get around to writing you. A more or less "complete" report is of course impossible. I hope to tell you more in person, above all about Israel. What is going on there is a great and powerful thing: a hymn to human will and human ability, but a hymn that hardly any poet could formulate, regardless of the power of his language. Only reality can produce such a thing. More about this in person.

Brussels was very intersting, in spite of the absence of many of the French (there was a train strike just then). Brussels brought the final confirmation that we—you as well as I—needn't work in a vacuum. A congress[1] such as this is a great fair where one can present one's wares. Since you weren't there, I manned two stands, yours and mine. I reported your ideas in two interventions on the theme "La connaissance d'autrui" and more extensively at the *Couloirs*. The reaction, e.g., of some young Dutchmen and Italians, was such that I can recommend that you make *one* article out of the Princeton paper and the anti-Hook-Nagel-paper[2] (leaving out the polemical passages, of course) and publish it in France. They are waiting for work like yours in Europe—and this is no exaggeration.

My own communication was read to a fairly large and good audience. The discussion was very good. It went from Bernays (mathematician in Zürich) to Minkowski (doctor in Paris), and included Landgrebe and Spiegelberg. Of course, such a congress is very uneven, but some things were very good. My train from Basel was four hours late on account of the strike, so I unfortunately missed Landgrebe and Spiegelberg. But I can read that. One would do well to keep an eye on the Dutchman van Peursen (Groningen). De Walhaens didn't speak, but we had many conversations, some about you.

In conclusion: it was very important for me to perceive very palpably that I haven't wandered off into dilettantism (private philosophizing) or gone in circles. Given life in America (without confirmation and correction, aside from you alone) one worries about all kinds of things. But they are without foundation.

We are leaving on September 16. I will not stay in New York more than one or two days, but I have to see you. We are sailing on the "Queen Mary" (tourist class, cabin no. C181). Send me a *message* whether you are free on the evening of September 21 (if the ship doesn't arrive too late, which you can learn from the Cunard Line).

We hope that you had a good summer and that you all—you above all—have enjoyed a bit of peace and quiet.

Affectionately

Your
Aron

1. Eleventh International Congress for Philosophy in Brussels.
2. "Common-Sense and Scientific Interpretation of Human Action" and "Concept and Theory Formation" (S1953a and S1954a).

7
Concepts of the Life-World
(October 2, 1953–January 1, 1956)

An extraordinarily full year came to an end. Both authors had spent the summer of 1953 in Europe. Gurwitsch was very successful at the International Congress of Philosophy in Brussels (GS 9.5.53). Schutz returned from a business trip in mid-November. Schutz (then Professor of Sociology and Social Psychology at the New School) began his second attempt to bring Gurwitsch to the Philosophy Department at the New School. In 1948 the faculty had chosen Karl Löwith over Gurwitsch (SG 12.12.48), but the position was canceled after one year. Aron Gurwitsch and Hans Jonas were then the leading candidates for the position as successor to Felix Kaufmann: "We lost honorably," Schutz had to report to his friend (SG 1.21.54), and the establishment of a "Center for Phenomenological Research" was postponed for a vague future. This plan remained a continual topic of the correspondence: shortly before his death, Schutz came to an agreement with H. L. Van Breda concerning the establishment of a Husserl Archives at the New School (SG 12.20.58), which Gurwitsch was able to open some years later.

The publication of Husserl's *Crisis* by Walter Biemel in early 1954 (first mention: GS 8.7.54) led Schutz and Gurwitsch to clarify their own concepts of the life-world. Their distance with respect to Husserl was solidified once and for all, and their own tunnel positions clarified: 1) Husserl's concept of the life-world was unacceptable and "unworthy of the phenomenological method" (SG 1.1.56). It failed because it "cannot solve the problem of intersubjectivity" (SG 8.23.54). 2) Against Husserl, Schutz asserted a mundane constitution of intersubjectivity as the foundation of the life-world: he solved the difficult problem of life-worldly transcendences in terms of his rethinking of the concept of the symbol, by deriving "the structure of the life-world from the lived experience of transcendence" (SG 10.13.54). Voegelin's studies, his critique of gnosticism and of Husserl's philosophy of history, belong in this context, which has received scant attention to date. 3) For Gurwitsch, the life-world was a "polemical concept" (GS 9.10.54), which "constitutes a reality" in the tension between the world "in which we live" and the world "which science construes."

Here too one must take care not to reconcile the conceptual differences too quickly. In determining their own positions, both referred to differences which were decisive. The concept of the life-world in phenomenological research becomes many-sided, and belongs among the necessary instruments in determining their tunnel positions. As an epistemic concept, it cannot be allowed to sink back into the *doxa* (e.g., as the "common symbol" of society's self-interpretation within the framework of a so-called "phenomenological approach"), since in this case it will suffer the same fate as the conceptual constructions of other research ideologies. (Cf., in a similar vein, Schutz's letter to Voegelin: 11.10.52).

Schutz: *Wednesday is your lecture: your friends (Goldstein, Hannah Arendt,*
          Cairns, McGill) have been invited
          (NEW YORK, OCTOBER 2, 1953)

Dear Friend,
    Unfortunately, I won't be able to spend the evening of October 13 with you.
I am planning to spend the three-day Columbus Day weekend in the country
with Ilse, Wednesday is your lecture,[1] Friday my lecture course and on Saturday
the 17th I fly to Europe. I still have a great deal of preparations and have to see
my mother before I leave. I hope that you understand and will excuse me.
    But perhaps we, along with a few other people from the seminar, can have a
glass of beer together afterwards, as is the custom.
    I have told the Graduate Office to send invitations to your New York friends
(Goldstein, Hannah Arendt, Cairns, McGill, or whomever you wish). I am
doing my best to make propaganda among the students. But don't get your
hopes up concerning the discussion.
    All conceivable love to you and your dear wife (will she be coming?)

                               Your
                               Alfred

    1. On October 14, 1953: Gurwitsch's first lecture at the New School, on the concept
of consciousness in Kant and Husserl (later published G1960 and G1964b; cf. also GS
8.4.56).

Gurwitsch: *I am more and more convinced that you must make your ideas known*
             in France
             (CAMBRIDGE, NOVEMBER 22, 1953)

Dear Friend,

    I take the arrival of the off-prints of your fine essay "Common-Sense and
Scientific Interpretation of Human Action" as a sign of your return. Knowing
you, you are happy to be back in New York. These lines are to be a word of
greeting; for the reason why they come so late, see below.
    What did you do in Europe? Did you see Wahl and make any arrangements
with him about an essay in the *Métaphysique*? That would be very important. I
am more and more convinced that you have to make your ideas known in
France.
    My translator[1] is working at a speed which is simply breakneck. He has
translated the first three parts in just under three months. The translation is
acceptable, a couple of minor things [*oderzuzers*], but not too many. I have to

change a lot: *serrer le texte,*[2] and lots of terminological changes. I have to make sure that it doesn't look all too childish when he manifests an almost religious respect before every word and, e.g., translates "obviously" with *"de toute evidence,"* where a simple "or" would be sufficient. Since one so often speaks of "proves to be etc." (sic!) in English, the text bristles with *se révèle,* and I have to eliminate these emphases.

You see the style of my changes. It is a lot of work—therefore my delayed letter. Still, part I recently went back to Paris corrected, and I am now working on part II, which I hope to have done in some three weeks. The book will be entitled *Théorie du champ de la conscience;* the page following the title page reads: *à ma femme, la compagne de ma vie, et à Alfred Schütz, le camarade de mes pensées.* The book will appear in roughly a year or, what seems to me more probable, 18 months.

The New York lecture had consequences. I am to hold it at St. Johns, suggested date January 29, but haven't heard anything final. I asked Spitzer if I couldn't also give the lecture at Johns Hopkins. This brought a pleasant letter from Boas, who suggested that I speak on Santayana's "Realm of Essence" in his seminar on February 10. I declined very politely: the time isn't convenient for me and in addition I currently have absolutely no time to work on Santayana as I would have to do if I were to speak on him. My knowledge of him is less than superficial. I wrote him that it might be possible at another time, i.e., next year. By the way, Goldstein and others have told me that I made a deep impression. Staudinger wrote me a letter in superlatives. Is this usual at the New School? I ask because superlatives always make me distrustful.

Let us hear how you and yours are doing.

> Best regards as always
> Your
> ## Aron

1. Michel Butor translated *The Field of Consciousness* into French.
2. Make the text concise.

Schutz: *What it would mean to build up a genuine center of phenomenological studies together with you*
(NEW YORK, DECEMBER 3, 1953)

Dearest Friend,

I got back from my Europe trip a week ago, but returned to so much work at the office and for school that I couldn't thank you for your kind letter. I am deeply touched that you want to dedicate your beautiful book to me, and I can only say that I am proud to have been, as you put it in the dedication, "the companion of your thoughts." It is good to hear that the translator is working so fast, and I am confident that an English edition will follow very quickly.

But more about all that and about private things another time when I have more leisure. For today I have something more important to tell you:

Your appearance in the General Seminar made a very deep impression, and you are in fact one of the five candidates who are currently on the short list.[1] The others are Koyré, who surely hardly comes in question, since he doesn't want to leave France; Löwith, to whom the faculty thinks it has a moral duty, but who will hardly want to exchange Heidelberg for New York on a permanent basis; Susanne Langer; and Jonas. You are first on Kallen's list, Jonas second and Langer third, on the assumption that they don't offer the position to an American whom Kallen is pushing. Leo Strauss, who has real influence, has Jonas first and you second. That Albert Salomon and I have decided with appropriate emphasis goes without saying. The others are still vacillating and the whole situation is far from being ripe for a decision.

Various members of the committee have asked me to give them the opportunity to take a look at the manuscript of your book, and I herewith want to ask for your authorization to do so. Your immediate answer would be very desirable; it is mainly a matter of Riezler, Neisser, and the Dean, and any misuse is completely impossible.

Needless to say, this communication is in strict confidence and has no official character. You mustn't be disappointed if you don't receive an official request, since it has been decided that under no circumstances shall letters be sent to candidates for whom we haven't yet decided.

I haven't made any secret of the fact that I am biased with respect to your person, since on the one hand I am convinced that you would be the right man for the post, but on the other hand, as your good friend I am not at all sure that I am doing you a good service in advocating that you exchange your present post for a prospective one here. I have made it known that you would obviously only be prepared to consider the matter if they would give you *tenure;* in this respect you are at a disadvantage, since our *by-laws,* which were written during the period in which we gave positions to *refugee scholars,* provide that one can receive *tenure* after two years at the earliest. They would probably make an exception for a professor who already has *tenure* in America, but two of the candidates, namely Jonas and Langer, don't have *tenure* and would accept the position without it.

With regard to salary, it is inconceivable that it would be more than 8,000 dollars, and the increase compared to your current income would probably be eaten up by the difference in the cost of living in Cambridge and New York.

You are at a disadvantage in one further point, namely in the objection, which I have a hard time refuting, that your philosophical direction is already represented on our faculty, namely by me, to which I answer that for you or for me this is hardly a sufficient reason to change our philosophical convictions.

You can well imagine what it would mean for me to work with you in building up a real philosophy department, which could develop into a genuine center of phenomenological studies by bringing in Cairns and perhaps also in other ways. Nonetheless, when I consider things rationally I come to the conclusion that as a personal friend I can't advise you to exchange the security you have finally achieved for the perpetually threatening uncertainty of a position at the New School. For this reason I don't want to take on any responsibility in this matter, neither by persuading nor by dissuading.

But should you decide not to consider this post, please let me know. I don't want to get involved for no good reason in something for which there are always resistances that must be overcome and that create an atmosphere which would have to produce animosity toward another candidate. For this reason, the idea of getting you a letter of invitation even though you have no intention of coming is out of the question, since the committee has expressly decided against this widespread practice, and that at the wish of the president.

It goes without saying that I await your answer with great interest. Regardless of how you decide, I would advise you to allow me to put your manuscript in circulation.

With best wishes for you and your wife

Your
Alfred

1. For the position as successor to Felix Kaufmann.

Gurwitsch: *I won't let the opportunity to get back into an academic milieu go by* (CAMBRIDGE, DECEMBER 5, 1953)

Dearest Friend,

I want to answer your letter of December 3 immediately, if only very briefly. Of course I authorize you to circulate the manuscript among your colleagues. If you wish, you can have a second copy for this purpose; the copy which the Harvard Press had is now available. You need only drop a line.

Please consider my interest in the New School as *bona fide*. *Tenure* is an important point: you are certainly connected with a retirement plan, and these things are transferable. The salary of 8,000 dollars is satisfactory for me. All of your information is naturally in confidence and won't go beyond the ears of my wife. For your information: if I receive an offer from you, I shall accept it as long as it is materially *acceptable* in the sense of the remarks above. I would by no means use it *for purposes of bargaining*. I will tell you why I take this position when the opportunity presents itself, preferably face to face. I won't let an opportunity to get back into an academic milieu go by, as long as it is somehow financially feasible.

With many thanks, in a great rush, and with affectionate greetings to you and yours

Your

Aron

Schutz: *My head is a suitcase that won't close*
(NEW YORK, DECEMBER 20, 1953)

Dearest Friend,

Many thanks for your kind lines of the 5th. I note the fact that you would be seriously prepared to come, and Salomon and I shall act accordingly. Your manuscript is in circulation and seems to be properly appreciated. The next meeting of the committee is on January 12. For the moment it looks like the French presidential election. A series of colleagues want an American, and unfortunately there are good candidates.

With regard to your question concerning pensions: we are now connected to the Teacher Insurance on a 5 per cent basis. I assume that Brandeis is connected to this company too, so that a transfer is possible. Concerning the main question I stick to the second *Alcibiades:*[1] may Zeus send you what is good for you, even if you don't request it, and protect you from what is bad for you, even if you request it.

You long for an academic milieu? You may well roll your eyes when you get to know it! Be that as it may, I shall do my best, but for tactical reasons I have to remain somewhat in the background, since my "bias" is notorious and I have little to say against the argument, which is always repeated, that phenomenology is already represented by me. We shall see!

Unfortunately I am terribly busy. My head is a suitcase that won't close. If one pushes something in on one side, something else falls out the other side. I can't even look forward to the Christmas vacation, since I have to go to Mexico on business on the 26th, and hope to be back on January 8.

To the new year? Dearest friend, let's stay with the old one! All the best to your wife and good health to both of you.

Best wishes,

Your

Alfred

1. The *Alcibiades I* and *II* are Platonic dialogues of questionable authenticity. Cf. also the end of S1959a.

Gurwitsch: *My admiration for your translation of Husserl's "Ideas" II and III*
              (CAMBRIDGE, JANUARY 3, 1954)

Dear Friend,

I received your translation of *Ideas II* and *III* two days ago.[1] First my thanks for the honor of being one of the three persons with whom a copy will be permanently deposited. You can be sure that the copy deposited with me will not be misused.

My admiration for the truly "pains"-taking labor which is invested in it. Of course I have only read here and there, and always with an eye to the creation of an English phenomenological terminology. In view of the dances that my translator is currently performing (part III), I can appreciate your and Natanson's work. Should our wish be fulfilled that I come to the New School and we then build up a center of phenomenological studies, one of the essential presuppositions has been met in this work. It would be desirable that something similar happen with *Ideas I*. In any case, my congratulations for the completion and my thanks in the name of all who are interested in phenomenology in the English language for having done the job at all.

The Christmas vacation was a dud. Alice suffered from a viral affair, which wasn't really all that bad, but she recovered very slowly. I also had something in me, but it didn't develop. All that slowed the pace of correcting, on top of that the worsening quality of my translator. As soon as it gets phenomenological in the proper sense I have to compare word for word with Ricoeur,[2] whom he didn't consult. All of this slows things down, but it has the positive side that one learns to appreciate certain things instead of simply taking them for granted. For all that, I am finished with part III and will shortly begin with IV, i.e., I will soon have half of it behind me. The power of the French language for condensation is astonishing: it will be one-third shorter than in English. Here and there my translator has done, with my permission, what they call *serrer le texte*. To the extent that it was a matter of linguistically conditioned length, it's fine with me; where it goes beyond that I have restored the text. He has avoided some repetitions which in fact were not really necessary. I am by and large satisfied; it will be a respectable book in its new clothing.

I have won two admirers for you. One is my colleague L. Coser, who is very impressed by your last work which Farber published.[3] We often talk about it. He seems to me to be a very promising sociologist. I only hope that the "warm" climate at Brandeis won't become a "Capua of the spirit" for him. This is a danger for all young people here; one of my earlier instructors (a mathematician) has totally succumbed to it. The other is Monsieur A. Lhotellier of Désclée de Brouwer in Paris: why not send him an off-print of your most recent work? When I was in Paris I whetted his appetite for you, now it's up to you to satisfy his appetite a bit.

Spiegelberg visited us yesterday. We can be glad that we don't have to live in the Middle West. I like Spiegelberg very much, so much that I am a bit concerned by his somewhat playful way of going out for phenomenological interviews.[4]

May the new year be generally *uneventful*, and for us in type and style like the past year. To the etc.[5] of our friendship in confirming continuation of the phases already lived through!

Best wishes to you and yours

Your

Aron

1. The translation by Schutz and Natanson was never published.
2. Paul Ricoeur translated Husserl's *Ideas,* vol. 1, into French (cf. Waldenfels, *Phänomenologie in Frankreich* [Frankfurt: Suhrkamp, 1983], 267).
3. "Common Sense and Scientific Interpretation of Human Action" (S1953c).
4. Herbert Spiegelberg's interviews with phenomenologists were to play an important role in the writing of his monumental *The Phenomenological Movement* (The Hague: Martinus Nijhoff, 1959[1], 1965[2], third revised and enlarged edition 1982).
5. A reference to "the use of 'etc.' should be avoided" (SG 2.9.53).

Schutz: *May Father Zeus protect you from all evil, even if you should pray for it, and send you all blessings, even if you don't*
(NEW YORK, JANUARY 17, 1954)

Dear Friend,

In great haste just a short report of events. The discussion concerning the position is continuing. You are in the running with two others. One of the two has probably been eliminated today after a long conference which I had in my home with some influential colleagues. But the other has a powerful "pull." In addition there is a fight about Löwith, to whom a loud minority feels that the faculty has moral commitments. I don't think that Löwith is serious competition, since in my opinion he only wants an offer that he can refuse. But you know how many intrigues are at work in a faculty in questions like this search. I, of course, have to be especially careful, particularly regarding you. Everyone knows that you are my "favorite son," and too much pressure from me would only hurt. So I have to let others work in your behalf. And although Albert is absolutely on your side, he is unfortunately somewhat clumsy. On Wednesday there is another faculty meeting, preceded by a committee meeting. Perhaps we will be able to see more clearly then, in which case I will write to you again.

May Father Zeus protect you from all evil, even if you should pray for it, and send you all blessing, even if you don't.[1]

Best wishes

Your
Alfred

1. Plato, *Alcibiades II* (cf. SG 12.20.53).

Schutz: *We suffered an honorable defeat*
(NEW YORK, JANUARY 21, 1954)

Dear Friend,

Things have changed pretty drastically since my last letter to you. Yesterday we had *committee* and *faculty meetings,* and contrary to my expectations it came to a vote. I am sorry to say that we suffered an honorable defeat. In the *committee meeting* I managed to convince them that you and Jonas be recommended *pari passu* as the only candidates. Albert Salomon supported me in this *meeting* and in the faculty meeting in the most commendable manner. Jonas had the strong support of Leo Strauss and his clique. The decisive thing was that I had to point out that you are only prepared to come under the condition that you receive full *tenure,* whereas this is not the case for Jonas. After a 1½-hour discussion we came to a secret ballot, and you received seven votes, but Jonas nine. It was good to see the way every single one of the committee members and other members of the faculty who had read your writings spoke about you. You made a great impression here with your lecture. The result of the vote is in my opinion to be explained only by the mentioned circumstance.

I don't know Jonas personally and hope that it will be possible to work with him. As I remember, you yourself have spoken of him with great respect. The faculty was of the opinion that, since the field had narrowed to the two of you, we would get a good man regardless, so that we could take secondary criteria into account in making our judgment.

You will receive a letter from Dean Staudinger in which he states that you would by all means have been invited if our original plan to fill not one but two positions had been approved financially.

Of course, I could say little against the main argument, that your philosophical direction is already represented on the faculty by me, other than the declaration that neither I nor you force the standpoint we represent in our literary expressions on our students in a doctrinaire manner in our courses.

Now that we have lost a good fight in an honorable manner, I have to tell you that while I of course regret that our dream couldn't be realized, from your point of view I see absolutely no reason to be unhappy. After 25 years of insecurity you have finally found a position at a rich and well-equipped university, which will allow you to live and work until you are old, whereas we have to worry every year whether the budget for the Graduate Faculty can be met.

So it won't be necessary to invite other friends on Thursday the 28th, as I had planned, but I hope that you and your dear wife, if she comes, will spend the evening with us.

Best greetings

Your
Alfred

Gurwitsch: *As late as the beginning of the eighteenth century there was a word "relevance" in roughly our sense*
(CAMBRIDGE, JUNE 6, 1954)

My dearest Friend,

I was very sorry that I didn't get to see your wife when you were here recently. At the last minute I had one of the few *meetings* from which I can't absent myself.

In what follows I will submit to you a vocabulary of your *termini*.[1] If you should be able to say something about them in the near future, I would be very thankful. I hope to send off the last part of the book in about three weeks. I would prefer to make any changes now rather than later in the galley proofs; that costs money and delays things. Of course it is only a question of the decisive *termini*:

1. "Finite provinces of meaning" = *sphères délimitées de sens*. What you mean are closed, delimited, and distinguishable provinces of meaning [*Sinn*]; thus, "finite" is not opposed to "infinite," but rather expresses the fact that they are closed and delimited, thus *délimitée*. "Meaning" is always a problem in French; *signification* is either very narrow, and means "meaning" [*Bedeutung*] in the most technical sense ("*signification d'un mot*"), or is much too broad, in which case it can mean almost everything. The word *sens* seems the most appropriate.

2. "World of working" = *sphère de la vie pratique,* or, more briefly, *notre vie pratique*. I hear the German *Wirkungswelt* behind your English expression. Your "working" is *Wirken*. (My translator, honest and dumb, wrote *travailler,* and here one sees the potential for misunderstanding.) *Vie active* is too narrow, since it excludes plans, etc; *sphère de nos activités* is too broad, since there is also an *activité théorique*. So I have chosen *vie pratique*, alternating it with *monde de la quotidienne*. Here as always, at least at the first appearance of the term, sometimes more often, your English expression is added in ().

3. "World of phantasme [sic!]" = *mondes imaginaires,* fits with the account that precedes it in the part on "multiple realities."

4. "Self" = *moi.* The translator intelligently wrote *Je* for the "self" which experiences itself as an indivisible totality in direct work in the world of working; then wrote *moi au sens accusatif* when the "self" *modo präterito* looks back on past action and experiences itself as "taker of a rôle"; I have let that stand.

5. "Working" = *action extériorisée.* This is action which intervenes in the world and makes changes. I thought about *action au sens propre,* but I didn't like it for many reasons. Since that is "working" [*Wirken*] again, and stands opposed to "performing," I preferred the admittedly not very elegant *action extériorisée; action extérieure* was not an option, since in this context you are talking about *monde extérieur,* and the expression *l'action s'engrène dans le monde extérieur* also comes up.

6. "Performing" = *action intériorisée.* This was a hard nut to crack. *Action mentale* was not acceptable for two reasons: it is used as illustration for *action intériorisée;* and it can also be used for *imaginer.* If it is used as illustration, it is harmless, but otherwise there is the threat of misunderstandings. By the way, Piaget was the godfather for numbers 5 and 6, but only linguistically.

That's pretty much it. One more question, but one which has nothing to do with you. What do you think of *ambiance* for "life-world"? I even use *ambiance générale et commune à tous les êtres humains* and similar expressions. Since "life-world" isn't used in the *Ideas,* Ricoeur is no help; Sartre and Merleau-Ponty simply write *monde* and mean life-world, which is very comfortable; the translator of the *Crisis* makes things even easier for himself and writes *le Lebenswelt.* According to my feel for French, *ambiance* expresses what is meant; *milieu* is too narrow, since it signifies only the immediate *ambiance; milieu* is a sector of *ambiance;* e.g., *milieu s'élargissant indéfiniment* sounds strange.

"Relevance" was a special torture. I looked through the large historical dictionaries of Ducange, Darmstädter, etc., and discovered that as late as the beginning of the eighteenth century there was a word *relevance* in roughly our sense, then it went out of *usus.* One of the lexicographers mentions the word around roughly 1720, but doesn't mention it later (have the French lost their sense for what is relevant??). Be that as it may, I can write *relevance* and note in a footnote that I am borrowing it from English.

What are your summer plans? We will go to Nova Scotia around July 10. Can we perhaps get together? I seem to vaguely remember that you want to go to Maine. In that case, although going through Boston would be a detour, it wouldn't be a big one. What about it?

With best greetings to you all

Your old
Aron

1. For the French translation of part VI, §4, of *The Field of Consciousness.*

Schutz: *It has become important to me to contrast the "world of working" and the*
          "world of everyday life"
          (NEW YORK, JUNE 21, 1954)

Dear Friend,

You shouldn't be angry that I haven't answered your so kind letter of the 6th. I first wanted to think things over at length, but my last weeks were too hectic. Let me thank you above all for the fact that you are giving such care to the translation of my terminology. It goes without saying that all of your suggestions are another proof of the loving manner with which you take up this business.

1. "Finite provinces of meaning": what do you think of the translation *sphère finie de sens*? I have reservations about your suggestion of *délimité* to the extent that it refers to something or someone who has caused the delimitation.[1] And *finie* is to the best of my knowledge the mathematical expression that would perhaps be more appropriate. But if you are convinced that *délimité* is better, I have no objections.

2. "World of working": you are of course right that my expression is a surrogate for the untranslatable *Wirkwelt*. And I am sure that a lot speaks for your suggested description *sphère de la vie pratique*. My only reservation is that just in the course of a new piece of work, which I will tell you about below, it has become important to me to contrast the "world of working" and the "world of everyday life," since I have realized that the two concepts by no means have the same extension. But in the context of the purpose of your translation I believe that *sphère de la vie pratique* says everything that is necessary. My only suggestion would be to use *sphère de l'action extériorisée*, as you have suggested under (5) for "working," here too. What do you think? I accept all of your other suggestions.

I am not in favor of your using the translation *ambiance* in the context in which you follow Husserl in using the term "life-world." That gives occasion for misunderstandings. I suggest either *le monde vécu* or, probably better, *le monde comme il est vécu,* but your feel for French is certainly better than mine.

Curiously enough, there is in fact no French word which corresponds to the German *Relevanz* or the English "relevance." I have now, unfortunately much too late, found a most excellent English-French lexicon and have had it purchased for my office. Its title is *Heath's Standard French & English Dictionary,* in two volumes, unfortunately pretty expensive. There I found *pertinence* as a translation for "relevance," which could well fill your needs.

The new piece of work I mentioned above consists in the fact that I was invited to write a long paper for the Conference for Religion, Science, and Philosophy which will meet at Harvard at the end of August. The main theme is "Symbol & Society" and I took last week off from the office against my vacation and worked 15 hours per day in order to finish the first draft. I would have liked to show it to you, but under no circumstances will it be typed before you go on vacation. I am dealing with the theme "Symbol, Reality & Society," using and expanding the Husserlian concept of appresentation. You will understand what is going on when I say that both sign as well as symbolic relations are forms of appresentation, but that signs only refer to one and the same sphere of reality, whereas symbols bind together two levels of reality.

I am planning to go to Bar Harbor on July 15 for four weeks and hope to see you at the latest at the end of August when I am at Harvard.

In wishing you and your wife a very beautiful summer, I am with best greetings to both of you

Your

Alfred

1. In the later German translation (G1975, p. 318), Gurwitsch chose the concept *umschriebene Sinngebiet:* the Schutzian objection to *délimité* holds all the more for *Umschreibung* (by whom?).

Gurwitsch: *Are meaningful words symbols?*
              (CAMBRIDGE, JUNE 27, 1954)

Dearest Friend,

Since the last part of the revised translation goes into the mail tomorrow— along with my thanks to all gods of all religions—I am writing you immediately. From the couple of hints concerning your paper I have an idea what you are doing, and I believe that I am in full agreement—even emphatically in agreement *à propos* the difference between sign and symbol. This isn't telepathy, of course, but rather our familiar experience of building the tunnels.

I have spent a great deal of time on this question recently, much more than shows in the discussions of Stout and Piaget in my book. I don't know if it would be the right thing at this stage of your work for you to take note of Piaget's interpretations of associations and conditioned reflexes. He has said fundamental things about them, i.e., about the whole question of the genesis of signs and signals. One should also take into account the work of Claparède[1] from 1933 ("La genèse de l'hypothèse"), which I unfortunately discovered too late for my book.

What Husserl writes in the *Logical Investigations* about the development of the indicative sign out of association is thin stuff in comparison with Piaget. But he, just like many if not most authors, makes no distinction in principle between sign and symbol, but rather makes the symbol a special case of the sign, although a very ingenious one. So you can well imagine how stimulating your hints were for me, since they are a confirmation of many of my ideas. The symbol does indeed mediate between two levels of reality, or, in my terminology: *ordres d'existence*. One question: are meaningful words symbols? If you answer "yes," then we are in complete agreement.

Please let me know when you will speak. I would love to be there, might even participate in the discussion, which I seldom do. If possible, I shall return from Canada a bit earlier. (Just in case: From July 8 on my address is c/o Mrs. John Casey, Victoria Beach, Annapolis County, Nova Scotia, Canada.)

A propos the terminological questions: I would still prefer *délimitée* to *finie*. I don't like the idea of finitude here, and even less since such a *sphère* stands under the and-so-forth. *Délimitée* signifies delimitation, but this is a delimitation of the sense, which is surely compatible with indefinite expansion. But this is not the case with *finie:* there one sooner or later reaches the end.

Your suggestion that I speak of *sphère de l'action extériorisée* is already accepted to the extent that the mode of spontaneity which belongs to the *sphère de la vie pratique* is precisely the *action extériorisée,* such that the *sphère de la vie pratique* is a *sphère de l'action extériorisée,* even if that isn't said *ipsissimis verbis.*

In your article, "world of working" is considered to be synonymous with "world of everyday life," so the French *sphère de la vie pratique* can alternate with *monde de la vie quotidienne.* Is that so bad for the special purpose? Anyway: whenever a term appears for the first time, the English version is given in parentheses, and often again at a later point when the discussion turns decisively on this term.

In closing, a personal request. We won't be able to go to Europe next year either. This is partially because I don't want to go until the book has been out for a while, partially for financial reasons. In order to solve one of my financial problems, I would very much like to teach Summer School [at the New School] next summer. I am thinking about a course "Introduction to Phenomenology" or "Philosophical Tendencies in the Seventeenth and Eighteenth Centuries"; preferably the former, of course. Can you arrange that? It is very early, but I know that one can't get things rolling early enough in these matters in this land of planning; by December all arrangements have already been made. That is why I am writing so early.

I wish you and your wife a fine summer. My wife suffered from phlebitis for a week, which made me into a housewife. I am in general less than proud of myself, but I do believe that I fulfill my professorial duties better than these. But it was a very light and superficial attack; the strict regimen was to avoid a degeneration. I hope that she will get over it completely in Nova Scotia.

Once again best wishes

Your
Aron

---

1. Edouard Claparède (1873–1940).

Gurwitsch: *The analyses of the "life-world" are fundamental for social science*
             (VICTORIA BEACH, AUGUST 7, 1954)

Dear Friend,

I have been waiting for some word from you the whole time, and am somewhat concerned that nothing has come. I hope your silence has no serious reason in an unpleasant sense. Since I don't know your address in Bar Harbor, I am sending this letter to New York as "please, send forward."

I will unfortunately not be able to come to Cambridge at the end of August. At the last minute before our departure we had to sublet our apartment in order to help out someone. That means that I am as it were "homeless" in Cambridge until September 8. We will stay here until the end of August and then go to Bar Harbor for a couple of days. You can well imagine how sorry I am not to see you and also Van Breda, who is coming to Boston on August 25. But I am counting on your sending me a copy of your talk. This is only *the next best* in comparison to hearing you *viva voce;* but I will just have to make do with *the next best* this time.

Before my departure Farber (according to an *on dit* he has been in Boston since June; but he didn't get in touch with me, and I was in the city until July 7) sent me vol. VI (the entire *Crisis* with the treatises and lectures which belong to it, including the Vienna lecture) for a review.[1] A magnificent work; it contains many beautiful confirmations for you. He was at his best at an advanced age. How about your reviewing it for *Social Research?* The analyses of the "life-world" are fundamental for social science.

As entertainment I began to read *Experience and Judgment* once again. I had great difficulty with the analyses of receptivity[2]—at the same points as twelve years ago (as I see from my marginal and other notes), but even sharper. There are imbalances and, what is worse, incompatibilities and gaps. If I can clear things up I will have material for articles and perhaps for another book. Essential parts of the entire genealogy of predication have to be done over. The question of what is involved in "This leaf is green" literally keeps me awake at night.[3] Basically it is a matter of πρώτη οὐσία substantively but probably also from the point of view of interpretation. It's enough to drive one mad.

Let us know how you are. We hope that you aren't in New York and that you can relax.

Best wishes from both of us to you and yours

Your
Aron

---

1. *Husserliana*, vol. VI: *Die Krisis der europäischen Wissenschaften und die transzendentale Phänomenologie*, ed, Walter Biemel (The Hague: Martinus Nijhoff, 1962). English tr. by David Carr: *The Crisis of European Sciences and Transcendental*

Phenomenology (Evanston: Northwestern University Press, 1970). (Gurwitsch's review: G1956 and G1957a).

2. Par. 17: "Affection and the turning-toward of the ego. Receptivity as the lowest level of the activity of the ego."

3. Cf. the debate with Koyré (GS 12.17.50 and following); also G1972c, G1973, and G1974c.

Schutz: *It is my conviction that Husserl's phenomenology cannot solve the problem of intersubjectivity, and this is its undoing*
          (NEW YORK, AUGUST 23, 1954)

Dearest Friend,

I found your kind letter here in my home on my return from Bar Harbor last week, where I had a wonderful vacation, although it was somewhat disturbed by business and by my mother's getting sick. I didn't work this time, since the very hectic work completing my manuscript left me somewhat exhausted. I had told the conference office to send you a copy directly in Cambridge. It was returned as undeliverable, so I have sent you another copy in Nova Scotia, which I hope you will receive. I can't wait to hear your judgment.

I am not expecting much success at Harvard, but the rare possibility of having such a long paper published just couldn't be ignored. I really needed you to discuss many things in connection with this circle of problems and even more with *Husserliana* VI [Husserl's *Crisis*]. When one has to work so completely without criticism as I do, one loses one's perspective on one's own work and no longer knows what is correct and what not, and above all, what is new or trivial. But you know this situation very well out of your own experience.

Too bad that I won't see you at Harvard, and you will also be disappointed to miss Voegelin, who is there until September 7. He has revised the entire work[1] in two volumes of 1,000 pages each and submitted the first volume (Egypt to Aristotle) to Macmillan for final acceptance. (It is the seventh version of the work which he began 15 years ago; that too will sound familiar to you).

Before I left New York, I sent my symbol-manuscript to Natanson for *editing;* on the last day I bought the *Krisis* and immediately began studying it in Bar Harbor. I was deeply moved to find things in the posthumous writings similar, often down to the formulation, to things which I have said in my manuscript. (Examples: pp. 213/14, 216, 220/21, 258/9, 261/63, 266/67, 300, 303, 305, 307/9, *310/11,* 464, 470, 479–81, 492/93).[2]

On the other hand, it is more than ever my conviction that Husserl's phenomenology cannot solve the problem of intersubjectivity, especially that of transcendental intersubjectivity, and this is its undoing. I personally share your opinion that Husserl's late writings are magnificent and of the highest value for the social sciences. Cairns thinks that this book is the weakest that Husserl wrote. I am very happy that you will review it for Farber. I do not want to review it for *Social Research,* but there may one day be an essay on the "life-world."[3]

Love and best wishes to you and your wife for the rest of the summer. Hoping to see you soon!

Always yours
Alfred

1. *Order and History,* later published in three volumes by the Louisiana University Press, 1956–57.
2. The texts in the *Crisis* that Schutz indicates stake out the first framework for an as yet unwritten comparative work on the problem of the life-world in Schutz and Husserl.
3. Published posthumously: "Some Structures of the Life-World" (S1966b).

Gurwitsch: *The concept "life-world" is a polemical concept*
           (CAMBRIDGE, SEPTEMBER 10, 1954)

Dear Friend.

I am writing to you immediately under the great impression made by reading your essay,[1] which presents the manifold problems and problem-levels of your area of research in such a broad and liberal fashion. Here levels of the life-world are discussed which were hardly mentioned in your earlier writings. My congratulations for this achievement and also for the fact that this extensive work will be published. I read your work with the greatest interest, learned a great deal from it, noted many things for further reflection. I believe that it will provide a basis for many and long discussions, since it brings to light a whole series of problems.

Your thesis that appresentation is to be explained in terms of the transcendence, or better, the many transcendences of the life-world, is too astounding in its simplicity for me to make an immediate judgment about it as a general thesis. On the other hand I agree with you that appresentation is to be understood in terms of the structures of the life-world. I also agree with your distinctions between "marks," "indications," "signs," and "symbols." But I have problems with some of your specific statements. These difficulties are grouped around three points:

I. You understand appresentation in a much broader and thus more formal manner than Husserl. You understand under the word simply the *pairing* of elements, one of which is transcendent, on the most various levels of transcendence. This raises the question as to how this being paired is phenomenally expressed in the appresenting element. Which phenomenal traits does it develop out of being paired? Are black marks on a white background phenomenally changed (and how?) when they are seen as letters? With what justification can one still speak of an *apperceptual scheme,* if the objects are subject to an *appresentational scheme?*

But since you expressly say that you don't want to go into the phenomenological problems of association, I make this remark only as an aside. You will surely admit that there is more work to be done here; Piaget has said a lot under the title "signal."

II. More important are the difficulties concerning your treatment of "signs." Is the angry facial expression really a case of appresentation? I think: the anger manifests itself in the expression; I would prefer that to the formulation that the expression is a "sign" of anger. (The problem of the *alter ego* has more sides than Husserl would admit). You treat the understanding of linguistic expressions under the same title. Does one really find transcendence here? Can one draw a parallel between the understanding of linguistic expressions and the understanding of the other, not of his anger but of his motives and what Scheler calls the "private sphere"? This is indeed in a certain sense transcendent to me, but surely the meaning of what I read is not. And for understanding what I read or hear I don't need the detour through the mental life of the one who expresses himself; rather the reverse.

For this reason, I suggest that a special rank be given to the linguistic sign and things that function in a similar manner. To mention only one: When I read words, I don't live in them but in their meanings; the words are in this sense transparent. The angry expression is not; I live in it when I see my partner to be angry. We are here dealing with physiognomic characters which belong to perception. I have reservations about imputing them to appresentation (a concept with which I was never comfortable, even in the restricted Husserlian sense). And in addition: in various places you say that a "thing" is transformed into a cultural object by appresentation. I am not so sure about that, although it is good Husserl. I wonder: 1. what is appresented; 2. what is transcendent here? If I see a hammer as a tool, it seems to me that its instrumentality is a moment of the perception, exactly like or similar to a physiognomic character.

Behind all of these theories is Husserl's idea of a level of "pure experience" within the life-world, a level which is taken to be fundamental and on the basis of which other levels are built up. I have always had my doubts about this theory. If I take *socio-cultural objects,* I understand how they can become "bodies" by means of unbuilding [*Abbau*] or some similar process; but if I begin with bodies as the fundamental level, there are difficulties in getting to the cultural objects. (Here too one doesn't need the detour through the mental life of those who have made these objects or for whom they are meant.) And history confirms me: only since Galileo are there bodies; Aristotle's physics has no idea of any such thing.

III. This brings us to the problem of the symbol. Don't you think that one can first speak of symbols when the differentiation of the sacred and the profane has been drawn or is in process of being drawn? But prior to this differentiation, the sacred is not symbolized but rather manifests itself in what from our standpoint is a symbol—from ours, not that of the participant. I wouldn't even speak of transcendence here, or if so, then with many qualifications. You mention Jacob's stone: prior to the dream it was a stone, appropriate for sleeping on. After the dream it turns out that it is God's place. So the divine manifests itself in this stone, it is richer; so one can already speak of transcendence, but it is concretely engaged in reality; certain points of reality are just marked off as the point of engagement of the sacred.

Here Lévy-Bruhl's *participation* seems to me very appropriate. Certain *facts* and *events* participate in the sacred, but that determines their being, and so they precisely aren't *facts* and *events*. But we turn them into such; to us it is "obvious" that they are *facts* and *events,* and so we interpret them as symbols. But from this point of view one can't understand that there is something like a dogma of transubstantiation, much less the dispute whether *est corpus meum* means: "is" or "means" my body.

As you see, I am more radical than you: my concept of the life-world includes all of the sacred where it belongs to the reality of a group. Put a bit differently, I have my doubts whether there is something like a fundamental level of "pure experience" common to all societies, which is then interpreted differently. Husserl, whom you seem to follow here, didn't free himself from certain remnants of the natural-scientific view of the world. I now understand the distinction you hinted at between life-world and the world of everyday life (you mentioned it in your letter), but I can't agree with you.

If—and this is the case in certain societies—men, animals, demons, etc., including the dead, constitute a society, then all of that belongs to the world of daily existence or to reality. The concept "life-world," world of daily existence, etc., is after all a polemical concept. It signifies the world in which we live and which for us—or for some other group—constitutes reality in contrast to the "world" which science constructs. If we didn't have science we wouldn't need this concept. But science has Platonic-Pythagorean origins: there the differentiation of the holy and the profane is made in the form of ἐπιστήμη against δόξα; there is already symbolism there, although there is something of a remainder of *participation* in the μεθεξις.

A pity that I can't discuss all of this with you, at least not in the immediate future. Please take my remarks as they are meant: reactions which were stimulated by your essay, not a critique. It is good that it will be published; in that way it constitutes a basis on which one can discuss. As an aside: I am not as sure of myself as my formulations suggest. And you, not I, have on your side the authority of Husserl and of most of those who have had something to say about these things. I wouldn't—not yet—make these remarks in public.

Something completely different: it seems that you didn't receive a letter I wrote to you in early July.[2] In this letter I asked you to arrange a course in your *summer school* for me next year. The last two years have put a financial strain on us. If I can teach for you one summer the strain will be gone and the following year we can go to Europe again. As topic I suggested either "Central Themes of Phenomenology" or "Seventeenth-Century Philosophy." Since these things are arranged at a very early date, I wrote to you way ahead of time. It seems to me better that you suggest it rather than my directly inquiring at the New School.

My summer was very productive. I read roughly half of Husserliana VI[3] and *Experience and Judgment*. The result is some five plans for work—but it will be a long time before they crystallize. Today I only want to mention that one of these plans concerns the question of a *Donnée primaire de la perception,* and my remarks come from there.

It sounds paradoxical, I returned from vacation mentally more tired than before; I spent the whole year teaching; in Nova Scotia I began to work again. Soon I will be able to read myself in galley proofs again.

How is your mother? Best wishes from both of us to all of you

As always

your

Aron

1. "Symbol, Reality, and Society" (S1955).
2. GS 6.27.54.
3. Husserl's *Crisis.*

Schutz: *Angels have no life-world*
(NEW YORK, OCTOBER 13, 1954)

Dear Friend.

I returned a few days ago from my strenuous business trip to Europe, which was in many respects of consequence, and by no means in a favorable sense. On my return I found your kind letter of September 10th, for which many thanks.

What you have to say about the symbol essay receives of course my full attention. I think a lot of this essay and believe that it is at least as important for me as "Multiple Realities," being in a sense its continuation. So your remarks are all the more important, and I would like to discuss them in detail:

I do indeed believe that appresentation is one—but only one—of the many means for incorporating the experience of transcendence (on each of the levels of the manifold transcendences) into the situation of the now and thus. For that is what is really at issue: not the life-world as such, but rather the temporal structure which connects the instantaneously appearing phenomenon with its before and after, the "specious present" with the retentions and reproductions, the protentions and anticipations of the time of the life-world. I have, given my lack of familiarity with the manuscripts, no precise idea of what Husserl understands by the slogan which is often heard of the "temporalization of time."[1] But if there is to be a temporal structure peculiar to the life-world, then in the natural attitude it can only be won in my current bourgeois ("specious") present by incorporating the elements which transcend the now and thus—the earlier present, the anticipated now, the other's now. Something similar holds for the spatial structure of the currently given, for which of course the "world within my actual reach" is transcended by "world within past (future) reach," "world within reach of the other."

All of these are fundamental facts of human existence, i.e., of finite consciousness. St. Thomas's angels don't have a world within their reach, no time that in this sense would have to be temporalized; they do have alter-angels, but they reciprocally share their entire conscious life. Angels have no "private" world and thus no life-world. But—with the exception of that form of appresentation that I suggest calling the symbol—it is not the case that the appresented transcends the life-world. What is transcended is the instantaneous now-here-thus, and the mechanism by means of which the transcendent is appresentatively incorporated into the now-here-thus is what makes the life-world at all possible.

I believe that many parts of the "research manuscripts" published in the *Crisis* volume are to be read in this way.[2] But Whitehead and G. E. Moore ("Defense of Common Sense") seem to me to have seen this too.[3] So much concerning the general theory, which thus does not try to explain appresentation in terms of transcendence, but rather the reverse, the structure of the life-world in terms of the experience of transcendence, in this essay more specifically: in terms of appresentation. (There are also acts of willing and feeling by means of which transcendence is experienceable and which do not originate in appresentation; but here I don't yet see clearly.)

Traditional phenomenology, including Husserl, is naive in the sense that it analyzes perception as the central paradigm without taking account of the fact that perception is after all a phenomenon of the life-world and thus implicitly presupposes the appresentative structures that lead to the constitution of the life-world. I am afraid that the device of the phenomenological reduction conceals this phenomenon. Intentionality is actually only possible within the life-world as long as the latter is not reduced to a phenomenon. The world is also maintained in the reduction as "sense," but, so they say, as phenomenon, as world as it appears to me and precisely as it appears to me. But isn't perhaps the change of the "sense" of the world that is brought about by the assumption of the phenomenological attitude caused by the fact that in the place of the having of the things themselves [*Selbsthabe*], of "being with the things" [*bei den Sachen sein*] (which in terms of the life-world "naturally" presupposes the transcendences of spatial, temporal, intersubjective modes of givenness), we have "intentionality," which puts that relation of foundation out of play?—I know very well that what I have just said is still very unclearly formulated because it is not yet thought through. But I really believe that one of the main difficulties of phenomenology is to be found here.

As you see, my understanding of the relation between transcendence and appresentation is perhaps surprising, but hardly simple. And now to your three specific remarks (since you refuse to call them objections):

1) I can't see that my concept of appresentation is broader and more formal than Husserl's. For Husserl appresentation is indeed a form of pairing, and as such one of passive synthesis ("God, if he exists, have mercy on my soul, if I have one," Voltaire is supposed to have said). Now, you ask, how does being paired manifest itself phenomenally in the appresenting elements? "Seeing black marks as letters" is your example. I fear, my friend, that you are here the victim of tracing all experiences back to perception. Of course, only the black marks are *seen,* they are *interpreted* as letters, perhaps as cuneiform script, which I don't understand, perhaps as Gregg's *shorthand.* A calligraphic ornament (for example, a Persian manuscript of a verse from the Koran) is, for those of us who can't read Persian, apperceptually and only apperceptually perceived as a pattern of this and that ornamental configuration; perhaps in addition as the stylized letter of a language unknown to us, perhaps in addition as one belonging to Arabic. But no pairing to an "appresentational" or "referential scheme" has occurred.

We knew about the magnificent feather crown of Montezuma for 500 years before a Viennese expert discovered that the order of the individual feathers according to color, size, species is a representation of the Mexican calendar, of precisely the one which is found on the famous sun stone in the Museum of Mexico.

To be sure, there is still a lot of work to be done here. But I fear that there isn't much of use in Piaget's concept of the signal (to the extent that the small book *Psychologie de l'Intelligence* discusses it). For just as Husserl bases everything on perception, Piaget bases everything on action, and the signal as communication implicitly presupposes all lower levels.

2) What does this sentence of yours mean: "The anger *manifests itself* in the expression"? Manifests itself *for whom?* Aside from actors surely only for the others, for whom the anger is precisely a sign [*Zeichen*] or indicative sign [*Anzeichen*] (*sign*) of the other's experience: of course these "forms of expression" too are socially and individually conditioned. A Japanese, Englishman, Italian show other signs of anger, many become red with anger, others pale. I see no distinction from linguistic signs, once you abandon the in my opinion false identification of the linguistic meaning with the private sphere of a concrete individual (partner). Certainly you live in the word's meaning when you hear or read something, but the word's meaning is the sign for the sense which the individual acquaintance or anonymous author (speaker), but also "everyone" who actively or passively belongs to the linguistic community in question, connects with the word (see *logos* from Heraclitus to Husserl). It is secondary that anger can be a physiognomic character: the anger of the gods certainly doesn't "manifest" itself physiognomically to the Greek tragic poet; the sea monster that Poseidon sends is a sign for his anger. Here is the sea monster that appresents Poseidon's anger, which remains transcendent, and an oracle or priest provides the interpretative schema.

Concerning "cultural objects": I don't believe that we implicitly recur to the level of a "pure experience of the life-world" in distinguishing between the apperceptive perception of a thing with these and those qualities, and its appresentative perception as a tool. You make things too easy for yourself with the hammer example. The contents of the bag of a primitive witch doctor or a cyclotron is only considered to be a *cultural object* by the "expert." This is just what I tried to show—it seems without success—in the chapter concerning symbol and society: namely that all schemata contained in the appresentative state of affairs are socially conditioned, have to be learned. Granet's books on China are full of confirmation for this thesis, and I shall never forget how I had to explain the art-history museum in Vienna to Otaka, and he an exhibition of Japanese objects to me (for example the articles needed for the tea ceremony).[4]

3) Symbol: here, dear friend, I fear a double misunderstanding. A) The sacred is only one realm of the symbolic, and what you say touches only this one special realm, but not the general structure of the symbol (works of art, etiquette, dream symbol, the "queen," etc., etc.). Every "finite province of meaning," each of the multiple realities can only be evoked symbolically within the life-world and can only be communicated by means of symbols. The symbols themselves belong to the reality of daily life; what is symbolized has its reality in another "province of meaning."

I have never been able to make sense of Lévy-Bruhl's *participation:* It is a useful label for what is meant, but doesn't say anything at all about the fundamental state of affairs.

On the other hand, I don't see that there is a difference of opinion between us in the sense that you, more radical than I (as you put it), include the "sacred" in the concept of the life-world (*pars pro toto*) when it belongs to the reality of a group. Don't I do the same? See for example my discussion of the "Thomas theorem."[5]

B) Certainly science is a realm of reality in which "world" is constructed. But the same holds for all other realities: the work of art, the "world" of the mentally ill, etc. Certainly terms such as *episteme, doxa, methexis* are symbols for realities of the "philosophical province": but I don't see what they have to do with the sacred-profane distinction.

I too am very sorry that we can't talk about all of this, at least not in the near future.

Concerning the last paragraph: it wasn't your letter, but obviously my answer to Nova Scotia, in which I sent you the first copy of my manuscript, that seems to have gotten lost. I wrote to you: a) That at our school it is decided first in April/May *whether* there will be summer school; b) that one professor from the faculty and one *outsider* are invited. Jonas would be the former; c) that only topics which are not represented in the current plan can be taught. Thus, neither "Central Themes of Phenomenology" (Cairns!) nor "Seventeenth-Century Philosophy" can be considered, but most certainly "Philosophical Problems of Gestalt Psychology," which should be very popular.

I shall of course make a note of your wish and will do my best to bring you here. In light of (a) above, the decision will be made quite late, and since Jonas will possibly replace me as "head" of the Philosophy Department, which is headless anyway, I can't promise anything. As far as I know, we pay $600. If you can get something more attractive before then, I wouldn't bet everything on one card. I have a great deal to report to you (including my meeting with Van Breda), but this letter has already become too long for my situation. I hope that you and your dear wife are doing well. Best greetings as always,

Your
Alfred

1. Cf. the editor's note concerning *Zeitigung*, SG 8.19.39. On October 11, 1933, Husserl wrote to Roman Ingarden, "A first volume concerning time in constituting temporalization is . . . almost finished." He notes that the work is based on his work concerning the problem of individuation in Bernau, 1917–1918. (E. Husserl, *Briefe an Roman Ingarden*, ed. Roman Ingarden [The Hague: Martinus Nijhoff, 1968], 84.) The "Bernauer manuscripts" are currently being edited for publication by Rudolf Bernet at the Husserl Archives in Louvain.

2. Cf. the editor's introduction to the *Krisis*, xv.

3. A. N. Whitehead, "Principles of Natural Knowledge" (1919), and G. E. Moore, "A Defense of Common Sense" (1923).

4. Marcel Granet, *Etudes Sociologiques sur la Chine* (1953) and *La Pensée chinoise* (1934). Tomoo Otaka introduced phenomenology in Japan (cf. S1937) and supported the publication of Schutz's *Der Sinnhafte Aufbau* (cf. K. Washida in *Sozialität und Intersubjektivität*, ed. R. Grathoff and B. Waldenfels [Munich, 1983], 386).

5. Schutz demonstrates the connection between the "Thomas theorem" (if men define situations as real, they are real in their consequences) and Scheler's "relative natural world view" (*Collected Papers*, III, 348).

Gurwitsch: *I believe I have made the discovery that there is no transcendental consciousness*
(CAMBRIDGE, NOVEMBER 30, 1954)

Dear Friend,

I think that it is time that we get together and talk again. Will you be in New York and have time for me on December 23 and the following days? Should this be the case, I will come to New York. On the one hand I have a great desire to see you; on the other hand I am very "occupied"—one can't call trying out this and that work.

I believe that I have made the discovery that there is no transcendental consciousness, but rather only a constitutive function of consciousness. That eliminates the problematic of transcendental intersubjectivity: I and thou are mundane phenomena and pose mundane problems. It is all still very vague and obscure to me. The sixth volume[1] has stimulated this and much more, but clarity often makes one wait a long time.

Let me know what your plans are soon. I hope that you and yours are in the best of health,

Sincerely yours

Aron

1. Husserl's *Crisis* (*Husserliana*, vol. VI).

Schutz: *Your course on "The Philosophical Foundation of Gestalt Psychology" was*
          accepted
          (NEW YORK, IN JANUARY 1955)

Dear Friend,

I am happy to be able to tell you, unofficially for the moment, that the *Summer School Committee* has accepted your offer to give a course on "The Philosophical Foundations of Gestalt Theory" in Summer 1955. The decision still has to be ratified by a *Faculty Meeting* and also by the administration, but those are mere formalities. The minimum salary is $600—but in exceptional cases and with corresponding *enrollment* it can—I believe—be raised to $700. When you are in New York, which I am looking forward to, you can talk about everything with Dr. Kahler, the *chairman* of the *Summer School Committee*.

For the moment I have been instructed to communicate this to you "without obligation" and to ask you if you are prepared to accept. Should you accept I need the following as soon as possible (*deadline* for the catalog printer is February 2): a) exact title of your course; b) "outline" for the catalog (3–10 lines); c) suggestions concerning a time and hour which would be agreeable to you. Lectures meet twice a week, either Monday and Wednesday, or Tuesday and Thursday, and at either 6:30–8:00 or 8:30–10:00.

But with reference to (b) and (c) you must give me *plein pouvoir*, so that I can coordinate your wishes with those of my colleagues, taking yours into account as much as possible.

In greatest haste affectionately as always,

Your

Alfred

Gurwitsch: *Your mother's death*
             (CAMBRIDGE, APRIL 7, 1955)

Dear Friend,

Winternitz was here late last week and told me of your mother's death. As you know, it is hard to find words adequate to what one feels when as close and dear a friend as you has to suffer such a loss. So I won't even attempt to find a formulation, an attempt which could not succeed. In my thoughts I silently extend you my hand in understanding and sympathy.

I had planned to call you as I passed through New York on the way to Durham. But my train was very late; it was very late on Monday when I arrived, and I had to leave very early on Tuesday. And now here I sit, just like almost every Easter, and have written half of the "review":[1] that is, it will be two articles of some 30 pages each. That is how much the whole thing has grown. The first article will probably be entitled "Western Man and His Science," the second "Towards Transcendental Phenomenology." I will be finished with the first in a couple of days. I hope that Farber will agree to this arrangement. I can't help him: one can't deal with a book by Husserl, much less his last one, in the usual "reviewer style."

Love to you and yours, also in the name of my wife,

Best regards
Aron

1. Review of Husserl's *Crisis:* G1956, G1957a. Final title: "The Last Work of Edmund Husserl."

Schutz: *This year wasn't favorable for my work*
(NEW YORK, APRIL 14, 1955)

Dear Friend,

Many thanks for your kind letter and your sympathetic words occasioned by my mother's death. I have read a great deal in her letters recently, which I had stored closed since 1939, and in those written during the bleak days in France the names of you and your wife appear very often. I know that you did a great deal for my mother in those times, and I want to thank you once more with my whole heart.

This year wasn't favorable for my work; I haven't had a really peaceful moment since Harvard.[1] I see almost no one. I studied your essay in Farber's March issue with great interest.[2] I have a lot to ask you in this connection and a lot to discuss with you in general. I am very much looking forward to your two announced *Crisis* essays. To what extent does the book hold up?

The annual of the Mexican philosophical faculty, "Dianoia" (edited by Nicol), has finally appeared with the Spanish translation of my "Don Quixote." It looks as if it contains very interesting contributions. There are no off-prints, Mexico isn't organized for that—but you have a copy of the English original.

One more thing: Jonas told me that he has to cancel the summer school course, since he has to go back to Canada in June because of his immigration matter. So you will have a monopoly.

Love from both of us to you and your dear wife

Your
Alfred

1. Harvard lecture: "Symbol, Reality and Society", end of August, 1954 (cf. SG 8.23.54).
2. The so-called "Jerusalem essay" (cf. GS 6.11.53): G1955.

Gurwitsch: *The American reader must be told what we understand under crisis of the sciences*
(CAMBRIDGE, MAY 24, 1955)

Dear Friend,

I am enclosing the first of the two "review articles" on volume VI, Husserl's *Crisis*. In the course of writing, which as usual dragged on for weeks, it turned out that the article about the entire volume had become long out of all proportion, much too long at any rate relative to the discussions which Farber prints. So I have decided to write two articles; I hope that Farber will accept this arrangement.

The first deals, as you will see, with the Vienna Lecture and the part published in *Philosophia* and the texts belonging to it.[1] I believe that these things and especially the Galileo analysis have to be presented in some detail at some point. The American reader must be told 1) what we understand under crisis of the sciences, 2) what are philosophical questions concerning historicity, especially in Husserl's modified Hegelian form, 3) what a historical-phenomenological analysis and discussion of the constitution of physics is, or, more correctly, into what dimensions it is to lead.

If I have succeeded in doing justice to these three points, and especially in making it convincing that science in the modern style is anything but obvious, but rather is a problem, not something which is to be either worshipped or rejected, but rather to be understood, and that this understanding requires very complicated investigations of the kind Husserl began—but only began; if, as I said, these desiderata are fulfilled, then this article, which has cost me a great deal of labor, has a point. Should you have time, I would ask you to read the manuscript from this point of view (it is for you, and thus your property). The second article is to deal with the life-world, the turn to phenomenology and with psychology.[2] In the next few days I shall begin to write, and will continue work on it in New York and later. Knowing my tempo, it will be a long time.

We will arrive in New York on the evening of June 11. We will live in Kahn's home after June 12. I hope that we will see each other until you go on vacation, and that we have a large number of fruitful talks, as always. Until then with all good wishes and greetings to you and yours

Sincerely

Your

Aron

P.S. Please confirm your receipt of the manuscript with just a line.

1. The first article (G1956) presents the portions of the *Crisis* which had already been published. The Vienna lecture, "Philosophy in the Crisis of European Humanity," was held on May 7, 1935. Since Husserl was forbidden to publish in Germany following 1933, parts I and II of the *Crisis* appeared in the Belgrad journal *Philosophia* in 1936.
2. The "problem of the life-world" (*Crisis,* §33) and the "characterization of a new way to the reduction" (§43), which Husserl distinguishes from the "Cartesian way," appeared first in the *Husserliana* edition edited by Walter Biemel. Gurwitsch divides his review on this principle.

Gurwitsch: *I am working on Kant for the first time in some 25 years*
             (CAMBRIDGE, SEPTEMBER 21, 1955)

Dear Friend,

I want to answer your inquiry concerning Eric Weil immediately.[1] He is in fact a student of Ernst Cassirer. I think that he is a man of the first class. Regardless of whether one can follow him in his thinking or not, what he has to say is of a high order and demands respect. His philosophical knowledge is extremely broad: he has worked on Hegel as well as Aristotle, has a very solid understanding of both—and of much more. He is without doubt to be named in the first line among people in France today. I have to mention his smugness in personal bearing and a certain kind of condescending affability which doesn't make personal relations with him easy, and often not pleasant.

Luckily I am now at work writing the last part of the report on the *Crisis*.

Not many people can have any idea of the amount of work involved, but you are one of the few. *Never again!* In a couple of weeks I shall read your *"Equality"* paper[2] and shall write to you then. My impression at the first reading was one of almost complete agreement; the achievement is impressive as always. As I said, more a bit later.

Since I am giving a *graduate seminar* on the *Critique of Pure Reason* this semester, I am working on Kant for the first time in some 25 years, if not longer. In so doing I have made very interesting discoveries that concern the parentage of the unity of transcendental apperception in Leibniz's principle of the monad. This has turned up some points concerning our contested question of the transcendental ego. But about this later, and face to face, if possible.

Have I told you that my brother died at the end of July? He had a heart problem, but in the last year he had improved. The whole thing is a heavy burden for me.

It is possible that I will come to New York for a *weekend* in October. I will let you know in advance.

Love to you and yours

Your

Aron

1. Eric Weil wrote a review of Herbert Spiegelberg's *Phenomenological Movement* in 1962. Schutz cites his *Logique de la Philosophie* (SG 9.19.55).
2. "Equality and the Meaning Structure of the Social World" (S1957a).

Schutz: *"Do not try to teach my children phenomenology"* *(Alvin Johnson, 1943)*
        (NEW YORK, SEPTEMBER 27, 1955)

Dear Aron.

Many thanks for your prompt answer to my inquiry concerning Eric Weil, which agrees with what I hear from other sources.

I am glad to hear that your work on the *Crisis* is approaching its end. I know only too well what a plague it involves. Of course I am very glad that you liked my *"Equality"* paper at first reading. I am eagerly waiting for your detailed commentary, but it goes without saying that I have plenty of time, since it will probably be two years before the *paper* is published.

Please let me know in advance when you plan to come to New York so that I can be sure to keep that weekend open.

You were able to give me the sad report of your brother's death at our last meeting in New York, and you will recall that we talked about it at length. I know how deeply this loss has touched you.

I would also like to hear from you how your course at the New School ended and whether you were satisfied with your success.

I was very happy that five students who studied phenomenology in the Spring semester have sent a letter to the dean with the request that Cairns be allowed to continue this course in the coming Fall semester.[1] We have of course complied with the request. But times have changed since Alvin Johnson, when I introduced myself to him in 1943, said after a friendly greeting: "But don't try to teach my children phenomenology. They do not swallow this stuff!"

Love to you and your wife

Your
Alfred

1. Thomas Luckmann recalls: "There were three of us: Ursula von Eckhardt, Thomas McDonald, Thomas Luckmann. They recruited a couple of others to sign the request (no idea who). There may (or may not) have been one more continuation. Then we three met with Cairns privately and paid him ourselves" (communication to the editor).

Gurwitsch: *Husserl's idea of the social is indeed incredibly primitive*
(CAMBRIDGE, NOVEMBER 7, 1955)

Dear Friend,

Enclosed is the second—and longer—part of the report on the *Crisis*.[1] As we agreed, this signifies neither a hint nor an obligation for you. Read it if and when you have time and desire to do so. If you do get around to reading it, let me know whether you think that it does justice to the book. And don't be angry with me for writing the article I wanted to write and not the one you would have liked to see me write. It has remained a mere report: that was my original plan, and in the course of working on it I found no reason to do anything else.

There are of course some things I would have to say. It all turns on Husserl's egological conception of consciousness, which then leads to the intersubjective complications on the transcendental level. My studies of Kant and Leibniz, occasioned by my academic duties this year, have demonstrated again and again how legitimate transcendental apperception (as the derivative of the Leibnizian monad, whose sense consists in its action) is in Kant, and how deeply illegitimate in contrast the "pure phenomenological I" in Husserl. In Husserl it simply has no function any more and exists—please forgive the lack of respect in this expression—as the appendix, which can only cause trouble. But this can't be presented in four appended pages, as you will admit. So for the moment the mere report will have to suffice.

You were in a completely different situation with the *Ideas*.[2] Husserl's idea of the social is indeed incredibly primitive, and you could point that out. But the things I am dealing with are anything but primitive.

By the way, I will be speaking about some things connected with these matters before the Harvard Philosophy Club early next year under the title "Kant's and Husserl's Conceptions of Consciousness," and will suggest this among other topics for my lectures in Germany next year.[3] (What about the *General Seminar* next year?) In my Kant seminar, which is completely histori-cally oriented and has to be such for reasons of academic protocol, I am reading Kant as the successor of Leibniz with five truly excellent students, and in doing so the underground connections are much more important to me than those on the surface which are familiar to every child. In the *College* I am reading the *Nouveaux Essais* with pretty good *undergraduates*. So these are the guinea pigs on whom I am testing my theory before I let it go public in the form of lectures.

Many thanks for the reference to Farber as the desired vice-president of the Philosophical Association. I had already given him my vote last week, and will also beat the drums for him as far as I can. (Who listens to me at Harvard?) But I don't quite understand why he wants such an office. But since he does want it, I shall do what I can to give it to him. (You can hardly imagine, my friend, how much I have withdrawn from all university, faculty, philosophical, and even phenomenology *politics* in favor of my desk, where Piaget, Leibniz, and Kant interest me much more and with real passion.) I am not on a single committee this year, and that was a real favor. But it is a different question whether that was the intent. But one should take good things as they come and not ask for the reasons.

I would like to make two requests: The first concerns your colleague Brodersen, who, as you told me, knows about getting subsidies for a trip to Europe which involves giving lectures in Germany. And Staudinger gave me the name of one other person who was in Germany last summer; but I have forgot-ten the name. (It sounded like Kamener or Kaminski.)

The other matter is the following: Beacon Press has requested the English copy of my book. I have *sub rosa* floated your name and that of Cairns as possible readers. I recently heard from a not overly reliable source that they have sent the copy to Cairns. Would you be so kind as to find out whether that is true, and if it is the case to ask him not to spend several years studying the book? I don't like bothering you with this, although I hope that you can settle things with a telephone call. But there seems to me no point in writing Cairns, since he won't answer.

Thanks in advance for your friendly help.

Why don't you and your wife come to Boston for the *convention* of the Philosophical Association between Christmas and New Year? I will be here; I plan to look around the *meetings* a few times, although I am afraid of the tedium and boredom. But if you come we might arrange a private congress, which would be much more productive.

With best greetings from both of us to both of you

Your old
Aron

P.S. How does Georgie like Rochester? [Lewis White] Beck must be a most excellent teacher, if I can judge from his students who are now in my Kant seminar. And what do you hear from Eva from England?

1. "The Last Work of Edmund Husserl" (G1957a).
2. Schutz's review of Husserl's *Ideas I* and *II* (S1953a, b).
3. Lectures in Cologne (GS 8.4.56) and Paris (5.9.59): published in 1960.

Schutz: *That is beneath the dignity of the phenomenological method*
                (NEW YORK, JANUARY 1, 1956)

Dear Friend,

I had hoped to see you during the Christmas or New Year holidays, if only occasioned by Erich Kahn's sickness. Goldstein, whom I often ask about the course of this terrible matter, told me that you would probably come. Since this obviously wasn't the case, I would like to write a few lines about the second Husserl essay,[1] which I have now carefully studied.

The manuscript is full of marginal notes. But they by no means refer—aside from insignificant questions of translation—to your superb presentation and rendering of the Husserlian train of thought. But it is precisely when this is presented in such a sharp and concentrated manner as in your essay that the weaknesses of the general position make themselves appallingly apparent. The life-world as common world, as historical civilization, as special group of contemporary privy councilors, as intersubjective community, as common ground, as the product of collective activity, as spiritual acquisition (as it turns out on reflection!): all this is such a jumble that it is beneath the dignity of the phenomenological method.

A ground becomes a horizon, a historically-relative civilization a cultural [*geistig*] acquisition of reflection (but relative to a special group), in order to then become accessible, as you clearly show, in an *epoché* of objective (Galilean) science (p. 10), although earlier (pp. 8 and 9) the universe of science presents a substruction of the life-world. And granted that the life-world doubtlessly has its essential typicality, I just can't see how Husserl can hope to come to the idea of an ontology of the life-world without clarification of intersubjectivity. And I can't at all see how the phenomenological reduction can help me there.

Others will justifiably be thankful to you for your excellent work, since they will only now understand what Husserl has achieved. I am thankful to you for it because precisely your precision has made clear to me the ship-wreck of this achievement.—By the way, just the footnote[2] on *page* 13 is worth being expanded into a book. What a fantastic idea!

Love and best wishes for 1956 from all of us to both of you,

Your

Alfred

P.S.: I plan to go to Europe in June and would like to visit a philosophical congress—*if any*. Are there any?

1. Review of Husserl's *Crisis* (part 2): G1957a.
2. "It would be of considerable historical interest to examine the science of Aristotle, which Husserl does not mention at all, under the perspective of the idea of a general science of the *Lebenswelt*" (G1966a, 426, n. 18).

8

Investigation of the Life-World vs. Transcendental Constitutional Analysis

(February 22, 1956–April 25, 1957)

In spite of the sharp terms in which the critical discussion of Husserl was pursued, it always remained substantive and never amounted to wholesale rejection: investigation of matters of substance becomes investigation of the life-world. What about the objectivity of such investigations? "When Husserl speaks of objectivity, he is not thinking exclusively or even primarily of the mathematical science of his time; he is not thinking of Einstein's physics or of quantum physics," Gurwitsch wrote in his paper on the conceptions of consciousness in Kant and Husserl, which he gave in various versions during these months at Harvard (GS 2.22.56), during his first post-war visits in Cologne, Frankfurt, and Munich (GS 8.4.56), and later in Paris. Gurwitsch is concerned with broadening the problem which becomes clear in Husserl's *Crisis:*

> It turns out that scientific objectivity is objectivity of a higher level, and is founded on a very different objectivity, the objectivity of the life-world or even the objectivity of my environing world [*Umwelt*], of the world for me. Whereas Kant had a single notion of objectivity, Husserl develops a whole series of objectivities.[1]

In this paper Gurwitsch did not make clear his own distance from the Husserlian conception of the life-world, nor just how far his own studies and those of Schutz had led to insight into the multiple objectivities of cognitive style in the life-world. "In Germany not much more is known than Husserl's name," he reported later (GS 7.1.58). He saw the main task to be that of preparing the ground anew for Husserl's works and thus for phenomenological investigations. He began this way in Paris and continued on the same path in the U.S.A. Critique is only meaningful on the basis of an independent development of one's own works, once the tunnel has taken on recognizable contours. One must at least know where the other is, if one is to discuss with him common matters and their objectivity.

There are manifold objectivities in the investigation of the life-world, and Schutz and Gurwitsch investigated them in different manners. Schutz prepared his "departure from transcendental constitutional analysis": at the third International Phenomenological Colloquium in Royaumont near Paris, he distanced himself once and for all from Husserl's attempt at a transcendental foundation of intersubjectivity. Intersubjectivity, the we-relation, and sociality are founded not in structures of consciousness but in the life-world. Every cognitive style of everyday lived experience of manifold realities has its specific epoché and objectivity. Schutz was concerned with these styles of life-worldly lived experience and cognition. Gurwitsch concentrated on the "higher levels" of scientific objectivity, on the founding of the *raison universelle,* which in turn was connected with all other styles of life-worldly cognition via the "margo" (marginal consciousness). The tunnels met.

1. From the German transcript of the lecture, "Der Begriff des Bewußtseins bei Kant und Husserl," which Gurwitsch gave in Cologne on 6.28.56. The editor is indebted to Prof. Erich Christian Schröder for giving the manuscript to the archives. The passage is not contained in this precise form in the published English version: cf. G1966, 151.

Gurwitsch: *In the coming summer I will go to Germany on a lecture tour*
             (Cambridge, February 22, 1956)

Dear Friend,

It's been a long time since we have heard from one another in this dreadful winter; first the news about Kahn, then about Albert Salomon's wife. A colleague who was in New York last *weekend* brought the news. Since we hadn't heard anything from Salomon for a long time, since summer, we weren't prepared, and it came as a sudden blow. Was she sick? What happened? And what will he, with all his inhibitions, do now? We assume that at least for the time being Hannah will be with him and take care of him.

We are regularly directly and indirectly informed about Kahn through various channels—a cousin of his lives here and drives to New York pretty often. I have also spoken with Goldstein on the telephone several times. It is alarming that the situation is so static; a few weeks ago things even got worse, and after that hardly any improvement. On the other hand, one of the head surgeons at one of the Harvard clinics recently told me that in such cases they sometimes see recuperation, even *restitutio ad integrum*—after four or five years. But no one knows what that depends on, under what circumstances it happens, and so no one will dare a prognosis. Poor Mrs. Kahn can't live on except by seeing things a bit rosy. In a catastrophe of this kind each has to live on in his own way; the main thing is that they live on. But we have to take everything she says with a grain of salt. Goldstein will be here on Friday; I hope to hear something from him. Ach, dear friend, living is the hardest task one is confronted with in this life.

Might I ask you for a favor? Cairns doesn't write, and Beacon Press doesn't know what to make of it. Would you be so kind as to give him a call and ask him when he will finally send off his recommendation? Perhaps push him a bit? *Entre nous,* he didn't even bother to acknowledge receipt of the manuscript! In this way he is doing me what one can really call a *disservice*. There is no point in my writing to him, since he simply doesn't answer. He can't avoid you on the telephone. And Paris doesn't write either: I have now written to Walter Biemel and asked him to look into things. It looks as if printing the book will take as long as writing it.

Have I already told you that I am going to Germany next summer on a lecture tour?[1] I will speak in Cologne, perhaps earlier in Düsseldorf (Kant Society), perhaps also in Louvain, then in Mainz, Frankfurt, Freiburg, and Munich. The topics are: "William James as Precursor of Phenomenology" for the America Institute; "The Concept of Consciousness in Kant and Husserl" in the [philosophy] departments and before the faculty in Munich; "The Historical Roots of Modern Psychology" in the framework of the General Studies [*Studium Generale*] in Mainz. The Kant-Husserl lecture is the fruit of my Kant seminar in the History of Ideas. I have learned to read and, I hope, understand the transcendental deduction from a Leibnizian perspective. I will try out this lecture in two weeks at the Harvard Philosophy Club.

For the rest I am very busy with studies concerning ideation and the like. I have learned a great deal from Piaget's *Logique*.[2] I read a lot in the *Organon* this winter. I have made some discoveries in Aristotle; e.g., that he was familiar with the fact that we perceive things in their typicality! I hope that I will be able to begin writing in roughly a year. I can see the face you are making, but it doesn't do any good; I have to improve my spotty knowledge.

I hope that all is well with you. How does Georgie like it in Rochester? And Evi in England? Love from both of us to both of you and greetings to the children,

> As always
> Your
> ## Aron

1. Gurwitsch's first post-war visit to Germany.
2. J. Piaget, *De la logique de l'enfant* (1955).

Schutz: *We are all trying to get Albert Salomon to work on his book on the "History of Sociology"*
(NEW YORK, FEBRUARY 27, 1956)

Dear Friend,

In great haste: many thanks for your letter. You have heard about Kahn directly from Goldstein, who is also my source of information. Mrs. Salomon had an operation for a "lung abscess" in December. Albert was very happy that the operation was so short, and the oxygen apparatus could be removed on the next morning, the private nurse already on the first day. When I heard that, I feared the worst, since I have had some experience in such things. In fact, the doctor told Hannah the truth immediately, and the poor girl didn't say a word to either father or brother. During the last 14 days, Mrs. Salomon was constantly under sedation, and didn't really suffer. Albert is very composed, and we are all trying (I think with some success) to get him to work on his book on the "History of Sociology,"[1] with Hannah helping him as secretary.

I spoke with Cairns immediately: he promised to write you and the publisher right away; he isn't quite finished with the book—he hasn't read the last part yet; he finds it excellent, and also thinks that it will sell well. Substantively he is very much in agreement, but thinks that it should be revised linguistically. I hope that you will hear from him soon; if not, let me know. He and I teach on the same day, and I can thus see him easily.—Your communication concerning Biemel surprises me. Goldstein told me that you were busy with proofreading.

The lecture tour in Germany is news to me: My sincere congratulations! I haven't forgotten that you want to speak in our General Seminar, but for the moment we don't yet know whether the whole system will be remodeled. I will intervene in time. I too plan to vacation in Europe from June until mid-September: Italy—Switzerland—England. I won't be going to Germany. Is there a philosophy congress in Europe during this period? If so, please send me details concerning registration—I would like to participate for tax reasons.

What with closing the office and everything else, I am incredibly busy. More concerning plans and work another time—best in person. George is doing fine in Rochester, he is keeping up pretty well (he missed the *Dean's list* by a few tenths of a point). But he is only a C+ philosopher: but Beck really does demand an extraordinary amount. Evi has actually finished up her English studies, and is currently skiing with her uncle in Kitzbühel. Then she will look around Europe a bit. She has to begin her job here in July.

Best wishes to you and your dear wife from both of us, and best greetings,

Your
Alfred

1. The volume appeared in 1962: *In Praise of Enlightenment: Essays in the History of Ideas.*

Gurwitsch:　*Van Breda and Cologne are working on an international conference in Krefeld*
(CAMBRIDGE, APRIL 8, 1956)

Dear Friend,

Some time ago you asked me about a philosophy convention in Europe this summer, and I didn't know of any. Now I have received a letter from Van Breda in which he tells me that he and Cologne are working on the technical details for an international phenomenology conference in Krefeld for September 13–15. It seems that a number of financial problems are still awaiting a solution. As soon as they are solved the official invitations will be sent out.

The communication from van Breda came as the answer to a letter in which I asked him to look into things at Désclée de Brouwer on account of my book. He promised me to do so and asked me to tell you and Cairns about the coming conference. I shall write to Cairns immediately. Would you get in touch with him one more time (or better, several times) on account of my book? Please don't hold this request against me; fulfilling it won't be very comfortable for you.

Confidentially: I understand Cairns less and less. A student of mine, to whom I had given an introduction to him last year, learned about his translations in this manner: he even loaned her parts of *Formal and Transcendental Logic*. Knowing the difficulty of finding a publisher, she told the Yale Philosophy Club—she is now studying at Yale—about them. This *club* has the possibility of publishing; they have published Carnap and Rousseau, among other things. Now the people at Yale write me that a series of letters to Cairns remains unanswered, and they ask me to help them in making contact. This is once again a fine situation for me. But aside from that: phenomenology has it hard enough in this country without complicating things by personal eccentricities.

I hope everything is fine with you. We are recuperating, if only slowly, from the blow: I have now been to concerts twice, and both times Kahn was present. This *présence dans l'absence* is a very peculiar phenomenon; the most curious thing is that it by no means distresses, but indeed soothes; the realm which belonged to him is there and will remain, and thus in a certain sense he is there and remains.

Please let us hear from you soon. With best greetings from both of us to all of you,

Your

Aron

Gurwitsch: *"Existentialism" seems to dominate everything*
             (CAMBRIDGE, APRIL 29, 1956)

Dear Friend,

I am very sorry to have to approach you one more time with the by now very tiresome matter of my book. Now that Cairns has finally sent his *memorandum* it turns out that it is totally unsuitable for the intended purpose. As my colleague who has contacts and influence with Beacon Press told me, the *memorandum* is so full of qualifications, hedging ("on the one hand—on the other hand," etc.) that no matter how Cairns meant it, it can only raise doubts, reservations, and hesitation in the mind of the reader, who is not a professor but an editor. According to my colleague, Cairns didn't know whom he was writing for and confused the people at the publisher, who are "simple minded," with a professional group. My colleague, who wants to get the book accepted, thus intends to make no use of Cairns's letter, and plans to request another one. He thought about John Wild. I suggested you, since you know the manuscript, though I didn't tell him that, and would have less work than Wild, and because I hope that it won't cost you very much effort.

As soon as Cairns returns the manuscript they will send it to you. Please wait a decent amount of time once you have confirmed receipt. Here is what my colleague needs: It should be a "straight forward" [sic], unqualified recommendation to publish the book, without reservations or hedges, a recommendation "which borders on enthusiasm." It would also be good if you would say that the book can also be recommended from the point of view of sales, since beyond the circle of philosophers and those interested in philosophy, it is of interest to psychologists. (For your information: in the course of one year I have received some 20 postcards from psychologists who were total strangers, asking for off-prints of the "Approach."[1]

Cairns hedged so much on this point that the result was almost the opposite. If you, as you told me once, are still of the opinion that my book can serve as an introductory presentation of phenomenology, it would be good to say that. You can see the general *trend* of the letter of recommendation from these few remarks. I am not angry at Cairns and don't want you to remonstrate with him. From what my colleague told me (he didn't read the memorandum to me) I can only see that he confused the role of the reader with that of a reviewer.

Herr Strasser was here for two days and brought me your greetings. He held two lectures here, one on Heidegger and another which gave an overview of phenomenological tendencies in European philosophy. Both lectures were good, clear and to the point. Their upshot was the for me very sad result that there really isn't a school of phenomenologists any more. Strasser himself said that there are only centrifugal and no centripetal tendencies.[2] "Existentialism" seems to dominate everything.

I don't have to tell you how much I too believe that we must begin with the life-world, and how necessary it is that we investigate and describe it. But does that mean that we have to get so stuck in it that we never get to anything else? If one speaks of human beings and what belongs to them, doesn't one have to take into account that man doesn't rest content with simply being in the life-world? Can one forget the idea of knowledge, of truth, etc.? It is hard for me to convince myself that *angst*, mood [*Gestimmtheit*], hope, and such things really are the key to the characteristics, and very essential characteristics, of the world. And if we are to talk about philosophical anthropology, hasn't Cassirer seen much more about man? If we begin with the life-world, don't we do so in order on the one hand to understand its constitution out of our consciousness, and on the other hand to understand the structure of the founded and higher-level worlds?

Those are some reflections which came to me after Strasser's visit. They confirm what I have repeatedly caught myself thinking recently. I am being pulled closer and closer to Cassirer, Brunschvicg, and Piaget, who, as different as they are from one another, don't abandon and don't want to abandon the traditional—in the best sense—orientation toward ἐπιστήμη. The new blood that phenomenology needs so desperately will have to come from this side.

It is very distressing to me to see how those who are physically so close to Husserl (i.e., in terms of the manuscripts) are moving away from him intellectually. Is there anyone still there who wants to realize the program of constitutive phenomenology or even, if only with modifications, believes in it? You recently wrote me that my report on the *Crisis* had made clear to you that Husserl's project has failed once and for all. That would be a very distressing result of my report, although I don't believe that it is a result.

It is too bad that you can't go to Krefeld. Whether I go depends on whether I am able to get new berths on the Cunard Line on September 20 or 18 instead of the 13th. What about the hypothetical possibility of a *weekend* trip to Boston which you mentioned recently?

With best wishes from both of us to you and your dear wife,

As always

Your

Aron

1. "The Phenomenological and the Psychological Approach to Consciousness" (G1955).
2. Cf. Stephan Strasser, *Phenomenology and the Human Sciences* (Pittsburgh: Duquesne University Press, 1963).

Schutz: *I prefer to dedicate myself to the investigation of the life-world*
(NEW YORK, MAY 1, 1956)

Dearest Friend,

In a great rush (I literally don't know which way, if any, to turn), thanks for your letter of the 29th. It is too bad that Cairns, after waiting so long, was obviously the bumbler that he is in most practical matters: of course I am not familiar with his "letter of recommendation," but he spoke to me about your book in the highest terms and doubtless believes that he has recommended it most warmly. His only reservation was that he thought that the English needed to be revised, and you know how demanding he is in this respect. We "newcomers" have after all only a very limited understanding when it comes to English style.

You know what I think of your book, and you also know that I will know how to give my convictions the right form of expression, if I am asked. But tactically, we must consider whether even a somewhat less warm recommendation from Wild might not be more effective than a glowing one from me: 1) I am quoted extensively in the book; 2) Harvard vs. New School. But you and your colleague understand these things better than I. I am of course at your service. But in any case make sure that the book is sent to my home address. The school will be closed for renovation after May 14 and everything is a mess.

The *comité* in charge of the General Seminar has, so I hear, accepted with pleasure my suggestion that you be invited, although—perhaps correctly—some doubt has surfaced that your topic might be a bit too technical for this framework. I am not a member of the *comité*, but am glad that Jonas, with whom my relations aren't very good (I will have to tell you why sometime), is strongly in favor. You should hear from Chairman Heimann before the vacation begins.

I have been invited by Finkelstein to participate in a seminar of his "Institute on Ethics" which will meet throughout June: topic, "Equality of Opportunity in Education."[1] It is a group of 15 persons, including MacIver, McKeon, Lasswell, Plamenatz (Oxford), Charles Frankel, Hofstadter, Rabi, Hoagland (the biologist) and Clarence Faust (Ford Foundation), in addition to representatives of the religions. I couldn't decline, especially since the first half will take place at Lake Mahouk, a wonderful place in *upstate* New York, and since a very nice honorarium will be paid. So I decided not to go to Europe.

Otherwise I am terribly busy with the reorganization of my business activities, doctoral examinations, *theses defense,* foreign business visitors, imminent arrival of my boss, and Evelyn's arrival yesterday after a ten-month absence. In addition there is the fact that Merleau-Ponty talked me into a short Scheler essay for a collection on recent philosophy (Husserl: Ricoeur; Heidegger: Waelhens) being edited under his leadership,[2] which must be finished in English by June 30th. In July and August I am going on vacation to the west coast and the Canadian Rockies with Ilse.

The local musicological society has invited me to repeat my lecture from the General Seminar, "Mozart and the Philosophers." It was a great success. As soon as it is published in *Social Research* you will receive your off-print. This fall I will probably read it to the students at the Peabody Conservatory in Baltimore.

I am currently in no position to say anything reasonable concerning the problem of speculative (constitutive) phenomenology. But was there ever a phenomenological *school?* I think and have always thought that the phenomenology of the natural attitude is much more pressing and also much more fruitful. If all transcendental phenomenology is founded in the life-world (although, oh wonder of wonders, the latter is constituted by the former), then I prefer to dedicate myself to the investigation of the life-world. We now have some twenty "entrances" to the transcendental sphere, but I don't see a single "exit" from it. There is the life-world and there it remains—*etsi furea expellas*—and there it comes into the monads without windows θυραθὲν. What a transcendental architecture! Like simpletons we have to drag the *lumen naturale* into the solipsistic "*Santé*" with sacks.

My visit to Boston is out; everyone prefers to come to New York—which you should understand. Will I see you when you come through on your way to Europe?

And many thanks for your permission to show your manuscript with all reservations to my *partially sighted* student. This is a terrible case of a misled talent, which I am naturally concerned about for personal reasons. I may have to ask for your help.

Love to you and your wife from both of us

Always your
Alfred

1. The first meeting organized by Louis Finkelstein took place at Harvard: cf. "Symbol, Reality and Society" (S1955). Schutz wrote "Equality and the Meaning Structure of the Social World" (S1957a) for the meeting mentioned here.
2. *Les Philosophes célèbre* (Paris, 1956), S1956b.

Gurwitsch: *The discussion in Frankfurt was contested by Adorno, who, as is well known, hears the grass growing and thus doesn't need to listen*
(TIROL, AUGUST 4, 1956)

Dear Friend,

We have been in this beautiful village in Tirol for two weeks now and are recuperating from the life we lived for five weeks. We traveling actors went from place to place every three or four days: my poor wife was completely busy unpacking and packing; we both developed a great distaste for taxis, express trains and—above all—porters. Now that we have come back to life it is time, high time, that I report to you.

Since this letter isn't to be a monograph I shall restrict myself to personal matters, since that is what you will find most interesting. My lectures were much more of a success than I was prepared for, more than even my most daring dreams would have thought possible. 200 persons in Cologne: the Biemels had arranged everything so nicely and cordially that the feared arrival in our first German city turned into a *family reunion*. 200 in Bonn as well—for the lectures I gave in a different form at the New School three years ago.[1] The same lecture in Freiburg before an equally respectable public. Fink, by the way, is so far away from phenomenology that he doesn't even want to talk about it, and refuses to work with students in this area. He is working on the young Marx.

In Munich we had to move into a larger lecture hall (I think it was the *Auditorium Maximum*) for "Kant-Husserl"; the other lecture ("James as the Precursor of Phenomenology") took palce before a smaller public in the *Oberseminar* of the America Institute. Kuhn was very cordial and friendly. We have known him and his wife for some time now and have gained a very high opinion of them—especially of her. More about that another time, but look for a book edited by her along with two others, . . . You Have Haunted Me in the Night [. . . *Du hast mich heimgesucht in der Nacht (sic)*].[2] It is a very important book.

In Frankfurt, "James" before 150 persons; "Husserl-Kant" in the philosophy department. The discussion was contested by Adorno, who, as is well known, hears the grass growing and thus doesn't have to listen. There philosophy only exists on the side; in the foreground stands the demasking sociology of those who have seen through everything.

In Mainz they asked me to publish the Kant interpretation—which you will hear at the New School—in German. I agreed, although it disturbs my work plans a bit. In Cologne they invited me to spend my *sabbatical year* there as a guest professor supported by Fulbright; I will seriously consider that. Biemel has written several times about the echo in Cologne. It is really more than one can believe.

And Van Breda has set the date for my book's publication. I have it in writing: "*L'ordre d'exécution est donné,*" i.e., it is now at the printer; I will have the galley proofs soon, "*la sortie est prévue début janvier.*" In contrast, Beacon Press has definitively declined. Did anyone ask you?

Although it was taxing, the tour was deeply satisfying for me. The fear of succumbing to dilettantism is banned for some time.

Will you be able to read this letter? And where will it reach you? We often think of you up here in the mountains which you have certainly often climbed. In one corner I can see a snow-capped mountain with glaciers. But even individuals such as us, who keep to the lowlands, get their money's worth here.

From both of us best greetings to both of you

Your old
Aron

1. "The Concept of Consciousness in Kant and Husserl" (cf. SG 10.2.1953). The Cologne lecture (presented on 6.28.1956) is in the archive.
2. *Du hast mich heimgesucht bei Nacht,* ed. Reinhold Schneider, Helmut Gollwitzer, and Kaethe Kuhn, published by the Christian-Kaiser-Verlag.

Schutz: *I am deeply immersed in Scheler and have read a lot of Kant*
(NEW YORK, OCTOBER 1, 1956)

Dear Friend,

Yesterday I saw Voegelin, who, to my surprise, told me that you got home a week ago. I am naturally very disappointed that I couldn't see you or at least talk to you on the telephone when you came through, but according to Voegelin you went straight from the ship to the train.

Voegelin supplemented your letter from Tirol, in which you reported the wonderful success of your lectures, with quite a few details. He also told me— somewhat mysteriously—that you have a chance of being offered a chair in

Holland (?) and that your position at Brandeis has recently given you cause to be dissatisfied. I would have liked to talk about all that and many other things, also many substantive matters. Is there no chance at all of seeing you in New York before your lecture in the General Seminar?

We had spent a wonderful first half of our vacation (west coast and Canadian Rockies) when we were called back to New York because Ilse's mother, who was in the country near here, had to enter the hospital. Ilse was able to care for her for ten days, but then she died, and Ilse, who was very close to her, is still quite *down*. Your letter from Tirol was forwarded to me and reached me so late that I couldn't answer it in time.

This sad incident and the transitional difficulties caused by the reorganization of my life have meant that I have worked less than I had planned. I am deeply immersed in Scheler—for the essay for Paul Weiss[1]—and have read a great deal of Kant in this context. I have run into some very curious things in the transcendental schematism, and will have to talk about them with you.

An off-print of my Mozart paper, which I have dedicated to the memory of Erich Kahn, will be sent to you in the near future. To your dear wife and you, love from both of us

Your

Alfred

1. Special issue of the *Review of Metaphysics* (S1957d).

Gurwitsch: *On reading my book I am actually very satisfied with it*
              (CAMBRIDGE, NOVEMBER 13, 1956)

Dear Friend,

You will already have heard that my lecture at the New School has been changed from December 12 to the 5th. Mr. Heimann called me up about this some time ago. I would like to know if I can be of any use to you on December 4; if so, I would come to New York in the course of the *early* (?) afternoon. Please let me know pretty soon so that I can plan my trip accordingly.

I am writing in haste and haven't written sooner because I am deeply involved in proof reading: roughly half of it is finished. It is curious the way it dwindles in French and in print. The book will hardly exceed 340 pages (the print *is* very small). Nothing essential has been left out; but the French language allows for condensation, and some repetitions have been avoided by the translator, and more by me. I don't know if I dare say it—and if so only to you: upon reading it after so long a time I am actually quite satisfied with it, although I already know how a great deal of it should have been written.

Best greetings from the two of us to all of you. Looking forward to seeing you soon

Your
Aron

Schutz: *You have always had sound judgment. So why don't you have faith in mine?*
(NEW YORK, NOVEMBER 18, 1956)

Dear Friend,

I shall of course expect you with pleasure on December 4, and you will stay with us. The only open question concerns my time. Normally I would have the entire afternoon and evening at my disposal. But I have just been informed that my *boss,* whom I haven't seen for six months, is flying here from London on precisely the 4th. I don't yet know if he will take the morning or evening flight on the 4th. If the latter is the case, everything is all right, since that means that I will see him on Wednesday morning. Should he *suadente diabolo* take the morning flight, then I would only be able to see you briefly on Tuesday, but would be free roughly 2–5 on Wednesday. I will write as soon as I know more.

By the way, Cairns would like to see you. He was dismayed when I told him that Beacon Press had rejected your book, and assured me that he had written a very good recommendation, whose contents he sketched. His only critical remark was that it should be revised stylistically. Cairns is an honest man, and I believe him more than the people from Beacon Press, about whom I hear curious things.

I am not at all surprised that you like your book, since you have always had sound judgment. So why don't you have faith in mine?

Love to you and your wife. See you soon!

As always your
Alfred

Gurwitsch: *Our entire understanding of Kant has been muddied by H. Cohen's approach*
(CAMBRIDGE, JANUARY 27, 1957)

Dear Friend,

. . . I see from the list that you are going to Royaumont. Please give my greetings to Jean Wahl and everyone who knows me. I hope that you will tell me *orally* what goes on there. I am giving the Kant-Husserl lecture on Feb. 15 at Yale. I have begun to gather material for the essay, which is to deal only with the Kant interpretation in Leibnizian perspective. If you love me, pray with me to the gods that this thing doesn't get too big for me.

Since you are interested in the "schematism" I would like to call your attention to Malebranche (*Recherche de la Vérité,* livre III, partie II, chapt. III). There one can read (with curious reference to Augustine):

> Car les idées des sens et de l'imagination ne sont distinctes que par la conformité qu'elles ont avec les idées de la pure intellection. L'image d'un carré, par exemple, que l'imagination trace dans le cerveau, n'est juste et bien faite que par la conformité qu'elle a avec l'idée d'un carré que nous concevons par pure intellection. C'est cette idée qui règle cette image.

Kant knew Malebranche. More important than this historical-philological remark is the fact that the problem of the relation of sensibility/imagination to the understanding was an important problem in the 17th/18th centuries, and that Kant here reacts against Leibniz as well as against Malebranche, both of whom devalue sensibility as well as imagination over against the understanding (if the traditional interpretation is correct). The nice thing is to see how Kant uses this Malebranche theory, which was intended in a negative way with regard to the imagination, but redevelops it in a positive sense. Isn't that a point worth pursuing?

Our entire understanding of Kant is muddied by the approach of H. Cohen,[1] who attributed *his* philosophy to Kant, telling us what Kant *actually* meant but didn't say, since he was subject to "relapses." In this way we read Kant as a contemporary, torture ourselves with difficulties *of our own making,* and make an understanding of his greatness impossible. I plead for reading him in light of the 17th and 18th centuries, above all in light of Leibniz, and that one not reject any concern for mental processes as psychology in a philosophically objectionable sense. My essay—to be written in German—is to serve this purpose.

I am happy to be able to tell you that my doctor sent me home after my annual physical examination as being totally uninteresting. The same for my wife. We are both very proud of being quite banal in this respect.

With best greetings from both of us to you and your wife

Your, as always
Aron

---

1. Hermann Cohen (*Kants Theorie der Erfahrung,* Berlin 1871) was the founder of the Marburg school of Neo-Kantianism.

Gurwitsch: *It has become an* idée fixe *of mine to solve Kantian problems by*
viewing them from the perspective of Leibniz
(CAMBRIDGE, MARCH 10, 1957)

Dear Friend,

I have just finished a letter to Bruges concerning the *service de presse* for my
book. They have requested a list of journals to which review copies should be
sent. I have included *Social Research*. I suppose that maybe Cairns will write for
P.P.R., Natanson for the *Philosophical Review;* could you somehow see to it that
it doesn't land in the wrong hands [in *Social Research*]? The book should appear
in roughly one month, since they are working on the question of *service de presse*.
A Frenchman who is currently here told me that "they" know about its imminent publication in Paris.

I would very much like to see Winternitz:[1] for personal reasons (it has been
so long since I have seen him) and for Guggenheim reasons. Will he be in New
York during the summer? It is possible that I will come through New York on
April 12/13; will he be available then? You will presumably be in Paris then; is
your wife going with you?

I am working on Kant. It is growing and growing. I have just solved the
riddle of the "synthesis of apprehension," which no one has really understood up
to now. The solution: the multiplicity offered in sensibility is a *petite perception*
which is in addition *confusée*. The synthesis of apprehension is thus the kind of
articulation such that the multiplicity is run through and developed, but does
not thereby collapse, but is *grasped as* a multiplicity, whereas prior to that it was
only lived through [*erlebt*].

It is becoming an *idée fixe* of mine to solve Kantian problems and difficulties
by viewing them from the point of view of Leibniz. To tell the truth, I am often
scared stiff by this *idée fixe*. No doubt I am going too far. But: *soit!* One way or
another it is certainly fruitful and legitimate. My critics will take care of the
necessary corrections. This time I have a clear conscience in my "exaggerations."
When the article (it is possible that it will become a small monograph of some
100 pages, I don't know yet) is finished, I hope it will be clear to the reader that
here, just as in all of my work, I am not offering final truths and definitive
positions, but merely attempting to bring work on the problem forward. For the
rest: *vivant sequentes*.

Best wishes to both of you from my wife and your

Aron

1. Emanuel Winternitz, Schutz's friend in Vienna, taught at the Fogg Museum at
Harvard from 1938 to 1941 and then in New York.

Schutz: *My essay for Royaumont: my departure from transcendental constitutional*
          analysis
          (NEW YORK, MARCH 15, 1957)

Dear Friend,

In great haste: thanks for your letter. Hooray for the news from Bruges.
Social Research: I can't write the review myself, since according to our—perhaps
correct—practice up to now, no one who is connected with a book is allowed to
review it. Difficulty: the reviewer must know French—and how! Does Goldstein? I could perhaps get him. The right man would have been Riezler. Do you
have suggestions?

Winternitz will give a lecture on "Angel concerts" at Brandeis on Wednesday
the 20th at 8:30 in the evening. He has to go on to Boston and Yale the next
morning. Bodky, the dean of the music department at Brandeis, will know when
you can speak with him; he himself doesn't know. He will be very glad to see
you and help with the Guggenheim matter as much as he can.

I am leaving on April 18, so I will be in New York on the 12–13th, but
pretty busy; but I would like to see you, if only briefly. I am up to my neck in my
essay "Transcendental Intersubjectivity" for Royaumont, which has to be in the
mail by the end of next week. In it I analyze the impossibility of every single step
in the proof of the Fifth *Meditation:*[1] my departure from transcendental constitutional analysis. I read Cairns the rough draft and was very happy that he was
honestly impressed and thought the matter to be very important. If I had one
more week I would have come to you in order to hear your judgment. You and
Cairns are the only ones whose opinion means anything to me in this matter.
You will receive a copy of the—German—manuscript as soon as I am finished
with writing and Ilse with typing. I *had* to get twenty years of reflection off my
chest, even if the thing will be of little use for Royaumont (it is also too long).

What you write about your Kant study is tremendously exciting. I am at the
moment too deeply involved in my things to have more than a confused *petite
perception* of your theory. But it seems to be *the* solution! Long live Gurwitsch as
the founder of the neo-Leibnizian school! The synthesis of apperception as the
transition between perceptions! I hope to be able to talk about it with you soon.
Go ahead and have your fixed ideas: others have enough loose ones!

All the best to both of you from Ilse and me
As always

                                        Your
                                        Alfred

---

1. Husserl's "Fifth Cartesian Meditation" (cf. S1957b).

Schutz: *Now the path is free to repair to the fruitful Bathos of the life-world*
          (NEW YORK, MARCH 22, 1957)

Dear Friend,

Here is your copy of my Husserl paper, which I sent off to Paris today. What a pity that I had to do so without having your commentary! It is the result of twenty-five years of reflection, and of exhausting labor during five *weekends*. I still don't have any distance from the essay, but in proofreading much of it seems to me to be quite successful.[1]

Since unfortunately all of your comments came too late to be used for Paris, you have a long, long time to tell me your opinion. I am naturally very curious about your judgment. For me personally at any rate the essay signifies the end of an epoch. Now the path is free to repair to the fruitful *Bathos*[2] of the life-world:

> A fellow who speculates
> is a beast on dry heath
> led round in circles by an evil spirit
> while all around is luscious, green pasture.
>
> *[Ein Kerl, der spekuliert,*
> *ist ein Tier auf dürrer Heide*
> *von einem bösen Geist im Kreis herumgeführt*
> *und ringsherum ist fette, grüne Weide.]*

But I have things easy with you. Since there isn't a transcendental ego, but only a thematic field which isn't egological, you can't constitute me at all! I am very satisfied to be bound to you in the highest mundane intersubjectivity, on the presumption that you don't send me off permanently into the "margo," but allow me from time to time the thematic place which I, which we, deserve.

With intersubjective *love,* your primordi(n)al and egological

Alfred

1. Contribution for the Third International Phenomenological Colloquium in Royaumont (Abbey near Paris), April 27–30, 1947: "The Problem of Transcendental Intersubjectivity in Husserl" (S1957b).
2. *Bathos* = depth (from Kant's *Prolegomena*, A204: information from B. Waldenfels).

Gurwitsch: *This time we aren't working on a tunnel but against a ghost*
             (CAMBRIDGE, MARCH 28, 1957)

Alfred Schutz

Dear Friend,

Many thanks for the "Intersubjectivity," which arrived two days ago. In the next few days I will study it as it needs to be studied. For the moment I could only glance into it a couple of times, not only because of the "Kant," which has bewitched me, but because I have also had a tooth complication of the most disgusting kind, right when I can least tolerate it. If I am in New York on the 12/ 13th, I want to talk with you as extensively as possible.

Two things for now: the essay is *very important,* one of the most important works in the past years; the topic was overdue and had to be treated. And we are much closer to one another than you think, if for contrary reasons. This time we aren't working on a tunnel, but have allied ourselves, each for his own reasons, in combating a common opponent, who is also a ghost. Since the ghost will presumably continue to spook people for a long time to come, our coalition will continue for a long time to come, and, as is the case with good allies, we will also carry out our own private feuds and infinitely complicate matters.

For the rest, you are mistaken: the two of us are not fields of consciousness but quite complicated beings, and totally *mundane.* I deny that you have a transcendental ego; I am very fond of you as a mundane one, and you will occupy a preferred place in my thematic fields, just as I hope to be your theme on occasion; indeed (the height of arrogance) a not-so-irritating one.

With mundane love, your

Aron

Schutz: *The most important new acquaintances: Ingarden and Minkowski*
          (ROYAUMONT, APRIL 25, 1957)

Dear Friend,

A canceled session offers me the first opportunity to write to you. First I want to thank you very deeply for the wonderful dedication which you wrote in the copy of your book which you gave to the school. I am certain that our philosophical and human reciprocal understanding will be even more intimate in the future.

Everyone speaks of your book, has either read it or is reading it or wants to read it. Those who have seen it are very enthusiastic, e.g., Waelhens, who is halfway through it. I am introduced to strangers as the man to whom Gurwitsch dedicated his book, and I bathe in this glory. (That is not a joke, but literally true.)

It is impossible to report about this wonderful place and interesting discussions, especially delightful reunions with Fink, Jean Wahl, Gaston Berger. The most important new acquaintances: Ingarden[1] and Minkowski, who is however curiously reserved.

And now the most important: Biemel reports (and asks me to write to you) that all university officials and ministries have approved your lecture series during your sabbatical in Cologne, but that shortly before his departure he unfortunately heard that Fulbright has declined, the reason given being that you selected another country than West Germany. He can't make any sense of it. I don't understand what is going on there, but assume that this is in conformity with the law in terms of which Fulbright receives money from the so-called counter-funds of the countries that received Marshall aid. It would be a good idea for you to get in touch with the Fulbright people at once and then report to Biemel.

The conference comes to an end on Tuesday the 30th, I am leaving on the train for Vienna on that evening, and will fly back to New York from there on May 4. I will have a lot to tell you and am glad that we will spend a lot of time together in June/July.

Love to you and your wife. To close with Goethe's greeting: *"Und so fortan."*

As always, your
Alfred

1. Roman Ingarden (1893–1970) was forbidden to teach in Poland during the Stalinist years. During that period he translated Kant's *Critique of Pure Reason* into Polish. Only in 1956 was he again offered a position in Cracow. (Cf. Krasnodebski in R. Grathoff and B. Waldenfels, *Intersubjektivität und Sozialität* [Munich: Fink Verlag, 1983]).

9
Parting
(June 6, 1957–May 16, 1959)

The last two years were overshadowed by the knowledge and foreboding of Schutz's illness. It was an extraordinarily active phase of work and publishing. Especially Schutz's letters made clear—as it were in closing—just how he wants to understand the differences and commonalities of their tunnel work: The Gurwitsch problem, as he called it, lies in the span between the formation of types and typification; the Schutz problem: where does intersubjectivity and socialization begin? But perhaps such a summary, said Schutz in the end, is only "the slave rebellion of that consciousness which had been banned into the dungeons of solipsism by the invention of the Cartesian devil" (SG 12.7.1957).

One last summer in Europe: the Schutzes in the Stiermark, the Gurwitsches in upper Engadin, before traveling to the Philosophy Congress in September 1958 in Venice, their last meeting. From this meeting we have the only photograph of the two friends together; "The Dioscuri immortalized in conversation with Rotenstreich" (GS 9.24.1958). Aron Gurwitsch went to Cologne for a year as guest professor; Schutz returned to New York where he made preparations to take a year off, with Gurwitsch to take over his duties. His last letter of May 16, 1959 made these arrangements. Four days later Alfred Schutz died in New York.

Schutz: *My blood isn't red enough*
(NEW YORK, JUNE 6, 1957)

Dearest Friend,

Since my return from Europe my life is even more hectic than ever (*end of the term, make-up lectures,* foreign visitors) and on top of that I have to submit to a taxing series of injections because my blood isn't red enough. Now all of that is coming to an end and I am looking forward to [seeing] you and your dear wife. Jonas tells me that you will arrive no earlier than the first day of lectures, namely on June 17, and will temporarily live in a hotel. I will surely hear from you at that time.

Do you have off-prints of your two *Crisis* essays? If so, please bring one for me. And please send another to John Wild (c/o Van Breda). Wild, who is spending his sabbatical in Europe, read a (by the way very mediocre) paper in Royaumont dealing with the problem of a phenomenological anthropology starting from the *Crisis*. I called his attention to your two essays, which he wasn't familiar with, since the journal isn't forwarded to him. He was very interested, and I promised him to ask you to send him an off-print, should you have some.

We will have infinitely important problems to discuss, and since I won't go on vacation until the end of July we will finally have enough time to do so. Ilse will probably be with Marianne Lowe, who has rented a house on Long Island and invited her, in the second half of June.

See you soon. Love to both of you as always

Your

Alfred

Supplement: Schutz sends copies of this Royaumont report to Marvin Farber, Dorian Cairns, and Aron Gurwitsch. Date: May 9, 1957. Original in English.

Dear Marvin,

I just returned from Europe and want to report to you about the meeting in Royaumont.

It was really a highly interesting discussion and it was a pleasure to meet Fink again and to get acquainted with Ingarden. Remarkably enough both came to similar conclusions as I did concerning the problem of constitution. I have arranged that copies of the most interesting papers be sent to you, Gurwitsch, and Cairns. The three of you would have enjoyed the meeting.

You will be most interested in Van Breda's plans. Let me start with the statement that Van Breda spoke—in public as well as privately—in the nicest way of you and your work. As to the series he wants to edit under the name of "Phaenomenologica," he appointed a committee of advisors consisting of the directors of the "Archives," mentioning especially your name as director of the "Archives" in Buffalo. It seems, however, that a hitch developed. The "Archives" in Strasbourg was transferred to Paris and there is now a fight on, whether the "Archives" in Paris should be located at the Sorbonne, according to the wish of Jean Wahl and Ricoeur, or at the Ecole Normale, of which Hyppolite is now director. It seems that Van Breda is more in favor of the Ecole Normale and he asked Gaston Berger, who in the meantime made a tremendous career for himself, to be an arbiter of this issue. The editorial committee cannot be constituted before this local question has been decided upon.

Van Breda meanwhile suggested that Louvain take care of all the preparatory work. The first volume to be issued will be a book by Fink dealing with the problem of the "Phenomenon."[1] The second volume will contain the papers presented last year at the meeting in Krefeld.[2] The third and fourth volumes will be issued in 1959 as a memorial for the 100th anniversary of Husserl's birth. His former students will be invited to prepare articles with personal recollections.[3] Van Breda told me that he wants to concentrate entirely on this series and that he had no intention to publish a journal.

I took the opportunity to tell him that Cairns expects to finish a volume on Husserl's "Phenomenology"—late in 1958 or early in 1959—in English which would be suitable for this series. Van Breda was pleased to learn of this fact.

I was also invited to attend a meeting preparing the formation of a "Phenomenology" European society. The following persons were invited:

For France   Jean Wahl
    Holland   Kuypers[4]
    Belgium   Van Breda (who presided)

Hermann L. Van Breda and Aron Gurwitsch at a Husserl colloquium at the New School.

Germany   Fink and Volkmann-Schluck
Yugoslavia   Miss Micic[5]
Poland   Ingarden.

I was invited as representative of the U.S.A. mother society. Van Breda read the letters he exchanged with you and had words of high praise as to your willingness to cooperate with their plans. I read to them the message you have asked me to convey to them.

Van Breda suggested the formation of a "Société Internationale de Phénoménologie, Branche Européenne" with the purpose to promote Husserl's philosophy. He pointed out that it is not his intention to give this association a legal form. The main purpose is that he would thus be in a position to approach government agencies like UNESCO and similar organizations in the name of such a group.

He would be willing to establish cooperation with the American International Society in the form of a "Fédération" in the French meaning of the term. He read the constitution of our society and mentioned that it would not be acceptable that each member of the European Society has to pay a fee of $10 to the American Society as provided in the constitution. I replied that I was sure to speak in your name when I said that you do not expect any financial contribution from the European members, except from those who wish to receive our journal. Only if certain amounts had to be paid to the international organization of Philosophical Associations, an appropriate arrangement would have to be made how these amounts should be allocated between the American and European organizations.

At this juncture, Ingarden intervened and declared that scholars residing behind the Iron Curtain would have difficulties in joining the European Branch of an American organization domiciled in the U.S.A. and having an American president. He himself had certain troubles because of his membership in our Society. It would be impossible for people such as Patocka[6] or Miss Micic to join such an organization. He suggested, therefore, that the European organization have a separate board and a separate president and that both organizations cooperate in form of a "Federation" as suggested by Van Breda, it being understood that in such a Federation both branches should have equal rights. It was decided to proceed along these lines. I did not object because I felt that this corresponded entirely with your intentions. Incidentally, Van Breda informed me later that it is his intention to suggest several members of our Board as board members of the European Society, among them, of course, yourself; the name will be, as suggested by Van Breda, "*Société Phénoménologique Internationale, Branche Européenne*." So far, the Society has not been constituted in due form, but Louvain was charged to do the preparatory work and to send to those who might be interested to join a short memorandum containing the important points of the statutes.

I was charged to inform you of this development and to ask you whether you might be willing to add to the name of our Society the word "American Section" or something to this effect. Of course, it was explained that this is a mere suggestion and by no means a decisive point.

I have just to add that Van Breda delivered an interesting paper on "Phenomenological Reduction." After having consulted with Jean Wahl and John Wild, I suggested to Van Breda to let me have the French text of his contribution which I want to submit to you for possible publication of the English version in your Journal. The three of us felt that at this juncture it might be a nice gesture to publish a contribution by Van Breda, who so far has published nothing in our journal. Of course, you are under no commitment.

Incidentally, all the papers presented at the meeting in Royaumont will be published in French in a volume to be edited by the "Cercle Culturel de Royaumont"[7] with a Series, in which contributions of the earlier meetings concerning Pascal and Descartes have already been published. The contributors are free as to the publications of their papers in other languages.

This is all I can report by correspondence. Everyone missed you badly; we sent you a postcard with the signatures of your friends, which, I hope, you have received in the meantime.

I am sending copies of this letter to Gurwitsch and Cairns in order to keep them informed.

With kindest personal regards.

Very sincerely yours,
Alfred Schütz

1. *Sein, Wahrheit, Welt* (The Hague: Nijhoff, 1958).
2. *Husserl und das Denken der Neuzeit*, ed. L. Van Breda and J. Taminiaux (The Hague: Nijhoff, 1959).
3. *Edmund Husserl, 1958–1959*, ed. L. Van Breda and J. Taminiaux (The Hague: Nijhoff, 1959).
4. Karl Kuypers, *Der Zeichen- und Wortbegriff im Denken Augustins* (Amsterdam, 1934). Karl Kuypers was professor in Utrecht. (Information from J. Taminiaux.)
5. Zagorka Micic (1903–1982) from Yugoslavia. "She studied in Belgrad, Berlin, and in Freiburg under Husserl, a member of his inner circle of students. 1937 dissertation in Belgrad: 'The Philosophy of E. Husserl.' She later taught in Skopje." (Information from Thomas Luckmann, 1.17.1985.)
6. Jan Patocka (1907–1977) went to Freiburg to study under Husserl and Heidegger in 1933. As Secretary of the *Cercle Philosophique de Prague* he played a role in the invitation which brought Husserl first to Vienna and then to Prague in 1935.
7. *Husserl* (*Cahiers* de Royaumont, Philosophy No. III) [Paris, 1959].

Schutz: *I thank you again for all your friendship and encouragement*
        (NEW YORK, SEPTEMBER 16, 1957)

My dear Friend:

I tried in vain to get for you the French edition of Leibnitz's *Nouveaux Essais*. I am sending you, therefore, under separate cover my own copy of the Boutroux edition. Unfortunately, it contains merely the text of the preface and of the first book, but I understood that these are precisely the portions in which you are interested. You may keep this book as long as you need it but I should appreciate your returning it afterwards to me as the edition is out of print.

I wish to indicate to you that the *Oeuvres Choisis* of Leibniz which you have seen in my library were published by Garnier, Paris. Unfortunately, I learned that this edition is also out of print.

It was a great satisfaction to me to have spent this pleasant day with you both in Cambridge and I thank you again for all your friendship and encouragement.

As always, your
Afred Schutz

P.S. My German-writing secretaries at work and at home don't have any time. Therefore this English letter,[1] in which the "fringes" sound less hearty than they are meant: Winternitz, who is moving, claims that he wrote you two days prior to my visit to you and of course approves of your using his name.

1. The body of the letter is in English; the handwritten P.S. is in German.

Gurwitsch: *You haven't written a word about your health*
            (CAMBRIDGE, SEPTEMBER 30, 1957)

Dear Friend,

Just a couple of words to thank you for sending me the *Nouveaux Essais*. I found it yesterday when I returned from New Hampshire. We had two days off for the holidays, and so we went away for four days. There I sketched out my lecture for Venice: "Sur la conscience conceptuelle."[1] Nothing special, hardly more than a working program which can be formulated in eight pages. It can in no way be compared to your fine essay which you read to me in Cambridge. But quite appropriate for the purposes of this congress. I will start writing it out in about two or three weeks. You will get your copy then as always.

Villalobos, whom you will perhaps remember, wants to translate my report on the *Crisis* into Spanish. Farber has given his agreement.

You haven't written a single word about your health. But we are eager to hear about it.

Love to your wife and you,

                                        Your
                                        Aron

P.S. I shall return the *Nouveaux Essais* in about three weeks.

1. International Philosophy Congress in Venice, September 8–11, 1958. Gurwitsch spoke on conceptual consciousness (G1959b) and Schutz on the structures of the life-world (S1966b).

Schutz: *As to my health, I am a man who has seen better days*
         (NEW YORK, OCTOBER 3, 1957)

Select and inestimable Friend!

Letters such as I receive from you arouse in me a feeling which for my taste tenderly sweetens life, and seem to be a kind of foretaste of another; if I seem to read in your honest and thankful soul the comforting proof of the not totally disappointed hope that my academic life won't slip by without bearing any fruits at all . . . .

As you see, I too have acquired a bit of Kant and know how to use it in the right place to the right person. I am very glad—to continue in a more fashionable tone—that you still have good memories of the essay I read to you in Cambridge. As soon as I get around to it I plan to expand it and then you will receive your copy.

How nice that you were able to sketch out your lecture for Venice! Now that the deciphering of the "linear B" code[1] has succeeded, I assume that its title is "Sur la conscience conceptuelle"—but the "Sur" is all that I am sure of. I may write something else for Venice—I am thinking about an interpretation of Sextus' tropes with the ἐποχή that belongs to it.[2]

Van Breda writes that the "*Colloque Phénoménologique*" will meet on September 10 and 11 in Venice, and that the program hasn't yet been set. So he doesn't yet know if he will be able to use my life-world essay.[3]

Keep the Leibniz as long as you wish. With regard to my health, I am a man who, as they say, has seen better days.

Love to you and your wife from both of us

Your
Alfred

My congratulations for the Spanish translation of the "Crisis." Where will it appear? And where is Villalobos now?

1. Reference to Gurwitsch's very illegible handwriting. "Linear scripts A and B" are developmental stages of Minoan writing (Crete). Cf. Sterling Dow, "Minoan Writing," *American Journal of Archaeology* 58 (1954): 77–129.
2. The problem of relevance led Schutz to Sextus Empiricus and his tropes (metaphorical argumentation). This was worked out only posthumously: Alfred Schutz and Thomas Luckmann, *The Structures of the Life-World* (Evanston: Northwestern University Press, 1973), section 3, B, 182–228. Concerning the theory of tropes, cf. Goedeckemeyer, *Geschichte des griechischen Skeptizismus* (Leipzig, 1905), and Léon Robin, *Pyrrhon et le Scepticisme Grecque* (Paris, 1944).
3. "Some Structures of the Life-World" (S1966b).

Gurwitsch: *Your typicality, plus Husserl and Merleau-Ponty, provide the points of departure for the theory of concept formation*
(CAMBRIDGE, OCTOBER 31, 1957)

Dear Friend,

   Enclosed is your copy of my lecture for Venice, "Sur la conscience conceptuelle." As I have already written, it is actually little more than a sketch of a
work program and the formulation of a problem. I have deliberately chosen to
start with a theory that appears in almost all logic books today—and by no
means only in those in English—and that is presented as being almost self-
evident. The problem I have formulated is only one of many to which this theory
gives rise; it may not even be the most fundamental problem. But there you have
the limitations of space and time. And I am not so much concerned with this
theory as with my problem, and the theory is simply the *point of departure*. As
you will remember, I have already written about the "Présuppositions philosophique de la logique."[1] In a sense that is what I am doing here too, and once
again only fragmentarily.
   I am sorry to hear that the essay you read to me in Cambridge still belongs,
to put it in your language, to the realm of intimate relations between us.[2] For the
problem of typicality (which comes up on pages 6ff.) I couldn't have wanted
anything better than to be able to refer to this article. Since that isn't possible, I
looked for *the next best*. My choice fell on the "Common Sense" paper [S1953c],
for which I have always had a certain weakness. Should you be of the opinion
that you have formulated typicality in a way more to your taste in some other
work, let me know. I won't be sending the manuscript off all that soon, and can
still change it. The footnote speaks of "*plusieurs travaux dont nous citons en
particulier*": but we can list something else *en particulier*.
   I am anxious to know what you will say to this very preliminary note.
Listening to your essay in my room was quite decisive for the composition of my
note. Your typification, plus what Husserl says about it and the little that
Merleau-Ponty remarks, provide the point of departure for the theory of concept
formation whose elaboration I plan to begin when the Kant[3] is finished (which
won't be long). How nice that we are not only still working on our tunnels but
that now the stones which each digs up are used in the building of the other.
   Please let us know how you are doing *en général,* but with regard to health *en
particulier*. About five weeks ago they put me through a whole series of medical
investigations—laboratory, X-ray, etc. I had lost a lot of weight, which began as
early as last summer in New York and continued here. My wife went into one of
her panics and the doctor, who is terribly anxious, feared horrible things. The
results were totally negative; the X-ray doctor, a Viennese whom you may know,
Dr. Felix Fleischner, whom we also know quite well personally, searched desperately, but didn't find anything, searched on and on, went farther than all instruc-
tions, and still found nothing. He finally reassured my wife, and was even
successful in doing so. The gentlemen then agreed that I am very nervous,
something that I have known for quite some time. In the meantime I have put
on weight without taking any medicine. I haven't felt bad at all recently; I
haven't felt at all sick or in any way abnormal. But my poor wife has suffered
indescribably (in order to reassure her, I have been through four investigations);

it was one of those panics which is a foretaste of hell. When they torture victims with fear in hell, they can't produce any worse fear.

With the same mail, but as a book, I am sending you back the Leibniz. Many thanks for your kindness. It did me very good service. But now I shall begin to write the Leibniz-Hume problematic[4] as background for Kant, and for that I need other writings by Leibniz and the later parts of the *Nouveaux Essais*. The next two chapters will be the real test. Wish me luck.

Best wishes from both of us to both of you and to Evelyn, whom I have grown very fond of.

I take it that Georgie is back in Rochester.

As always your old
Aron

1. G1959b.
2. Schutz was in Cambridge in early September (SG 9.16.1957). In the last letter they speak of "my life-world essay," which was only later translated by Gurwitsch and published (S1966b). Schutz obviously didn't consider it finished.
3. "The Kantian and Husserlian Conceptions of Consciousness," G1960 and 1964b, English translation in G1966a. Cf. also GS 5.9.1959.
4. Cf. also the problem of identity in Hume, Husserl, and Leibniz: SG 8.19.1939.

Schutz: *The slave rebellion of that consciousness which was banned to the dungeons of solipsism by the Cartesian evil genius*
(NEW YORK, DECEMBER 7, 1957)

Dearest Friend,

First I want to thank you and your dear wife, also in Ilse's name, for your kind lines of the 29th. I am very happy to report to you that Ilse's recuperation has made astonishing progress—all too much progress, in the sense that I fear that she will over-do herself. She showed no trace of anything like a psychological shock either before or after the operation. That was left up to me, something which no one will understand better than your wife. If things continue in this way, Ilse should be able to return to her normal life in about two weeks.

I have found my way back to normality enough to have thoroughly thought through your *very fine* and wonderfully condensed essay.[1] *By all means* not another line: if the listeners (or readers?) take the time to consider every word very carefully, you will have an extraordinary success at the Congress. To be sure, you are completely right that in the context of our relationship the essay is merely a work program—for both of us, each in his own way—and almost every sentence is a chapter heading. In what follows some thoughts which went through my head and which by no means refer to the essay, but only to the very serious problems which it lays bare.

I wonder, namely, whether the prepredicative experience of the world, as well as the conceptual structure of the class or of the propositional function, can be given a unitary treatment at all. Mustn't one perhaps make the following distinctions:

1) Problems of the *formation* of types (in prepredicative lived experience) and concept formation; that is, the constitution of the class or of that which, once constituted, will be called class. How does a type become a "habitual acquisition"? How do the fabulous passive syntheses of coincidence, of similarity, etc., work? How does it happen that I execute the transition from the prepredicative into the conceptual? By a reflexive turning back? By explication of the implications? By elucidation [*Verdeutlichung*] and clarification? And whichever intentionalities might be at work here: does the transition occur in one fell swoop? Or polythetically? Is the concept perhaps the monothetic grasp of polythetically executed prepredicative type formation—just as the types which have become a "habitual possession" are the *monothetic* correlate (this term doesn't fit here because of its relation to the thetic, of course) of the *polythetic* perceptions?

Has the typification of the underlying perceptions—including the *petites perceptions*—already occurred in the act of apperceiving? So shouldn't one, to be precise, have to say: in prepredicative world experience we apperceive the world as typified because the mere perception is essentially current lived experience, which could never become a "habitual possession," and apperception is precisely typification of the *percepta*? Would that even throw new light on the problem of "sense-data" with which Broad, Moore, and Whitehead (each in his own way) wrestle?

And similarly the step from the apperceived type, which has become an habitual acquisition, to the concept (for example as class).

2) *Second group of problems;* The type has now become a "habitual acquisition" (the concept—the class—is constituted as extensive). The second group of problems surfaces: how is an experience ordered into the series of types that is available in the stock of experience (ordered to concepts, "subsumption" or: *quid juris* the propositional function?)? Does—with reference to the type—synthesis play [the role] of recognition?[2] What are the implied intentionalities here—or is recognition not an intentional act? Perhaps not even an "achievement" of consciousness, but rather pure passivity? Does passivity have intentionality? What about passivity in general? It isn't "governed" [*durchwaltet*] (*whatever this means*)?

And what about—predicatively—subsumption? (E.g., your excellent example of the "blue" material vs. "blue" Mediterranean). The one-time *tabula rasa* hasn't after all transformed itself into a box of little shops, each bearing a pure label. The activity of conscious life doesn't "govern" [*durchwaltet*] a "filing system": otherwise better go right to the information and storage theory of good old Norbert Wiener. A preliminary question to the Kant question of how synthetic judgments—*a priori* or *a posteriori*—are possible: how is a propositional function possible with reference to pre-formed classes? And what happens on the higher and higher levels of synthesis?

Further—for already constituted types and classes—what does positionality and neutrality relate to? Is the type (the class) already "posited" in that it is constituted? And when, when, when does the evidence of being-at-the-things-themselves turn up? What is "originarily giving" in all of this?

3) *Third circle of problems* (or apology for my, as you know, very old distrust of hoping for help from pathology): types have become a habitual possession, concepts are constituted. Both have found linguistic expressions (words, sentences, propositional functions): *Le concept est pris en comprehension, le générique est devenu le général.* (I know, you take just the opposite path.) Now—through a brain injury—the already-built-up stock is buried. The world, which was already ordered under *abstracta* and pre-experienced as thus ordered, shrinks again to the concreteness which is tied to situations. That is Goldstein's terminology. But the linguistic residues remain. What is going on when *"les malades ne sont* plus *à même de regarder un objet sous l'aspect de sa similarité à autres objets, de prendre l'objet donné pour un représentant d'autres objets* pareils *(pareils?* for whom: the patient? the doctor? in itself?) *et qui, en raison même de leur similarité,* peuvent être considerés *(quid juris?* by whom? to what end? in what total situation for whom?) *comme appartenant à une même classe."*[3]

All of this is very imprecise (not your fault, but Goldstein's). There are classes for me, for the doctor, perhaps for "us, the *ex definitione* 'normal' people" (which really already presupposes the entire life-world and its being ordered under "our" types and concepts, the ones which are valid for "us"). But for the patient there *were* perhaps earlier similar classes (we will never be able to find out), there were such for him when he was still healthy, but they don't exist any more now.

He has been shoved back out of the second level into the first, *and for this reason he thinks only concretely and in terms of situations.* He does experience the pencil as a thing for writing, but in his shriveled world he isn't interested in the way *this* pencil right here belongs to other pencils which are not present, indeed he *can't* be interested in it, since the types (classes) that were preformed and habitually available (and still are for the doctor and us "normal" persons) just don't exist for the patient any more. To use your language: *L'événement constaté s'est retransformé dans un événement à constater. Il est devenu—véritablement—un "objet en question."*

4) *Fourth group of problems*—or the Gurwitsch problem. You begin your investigations with the prepredicative life-world, which is already ordered under types—thus on the second level. You have every right to do so—especially since you announce it clearly. All (or, as you say carefully: most) objects are objects of a certain kind.

The excellently formulated distinction between the perception of an object of a certain kind on the one hand and the apperceiving of this object as a specimen (or representation or a special case) of a type on the other hand is decisive. That means: prepredicative perceptual consciousness is already typical and generic. The transition to the concept takes place in two steps: First, the object perceived in its typicality is disassembled [*zerlegt*], in that its immanent generic properties are separated from it and grasped as special specific objects of consciousness: the generic thereby becomes the general. The perceptual object has now become a representative of the concept. With that the class-concept is disclosed. Second (possible) step: going on to develop ideal and normative concepts—ideal in the Platonic sense.

All of this is excellent. But if I am right about my "first level"[4] (concerning the development of types), then we have a preliminary level in the development of types as such. How is the individual grasped as an individual in the generic? How does that happen? What makes up the generic? How is it given or constituted? There is no doubt that it doesn't come θυραθέν into consciousness. Do we have here—in your language—another form of thematization? Or a primal thematization [*Ur-thematisation*]? Or the counterpart of thematization (since after all this—according to you—is separation, *d*evelopment [*Entwicklung*])? But in this case one must ask whether the pregivenness of generic types is a condition of all thematization—or at least of thematizing perception; further, whether that which is given non-thematically can be synthesized; and whether passive synthesis isn't non-thematic perception on the way to thematic apperception.

5) *Fifth group of problems*—or the Schutz problem: Where does socialization and intersubjectivity set in? Are objects like trees and mountains for everyone? How does this come about? Are they such prepredicatively as genera, indeed as the same genera for everyone? Or is the word required, and if so, does the transition from the typically generic to the general-conceptual occur with naming? Is perhaps the use of a proper name already predication?

But isn't, on the other hand, the gesture of pointing also intersubjective? Does the typical world perhaps have a merely physiognomic character? And if this is the case: is there an intersubjective physiognomic interpretation, i.e., the same physiognomic characters for everyone? Or: viewed from your point of view: are there thematic elements which are intersubjective and, if so, how is this possible? Or: viewed from my point of view: are there relevances which are intersubjective and how is this possible? Or: common problem for you and me (which commonality really answers the just-posed question in an exemplary fashion, strangely enough): are thematization and the development of relevance teachable? What are the conditions of this teachability? And what would be the intersubjective preconditions of teachability in general?

You see what kinds of questions your essay has stimulated. Perhaps they are only the monsters of a certainly over-taxed brain and pure nonsense. Perhaps this is the slave revolt of that consciousness which has been banned to the dungeons of solipsism by the Cartesian evil genius. I am not encapsulated within myself [*bei mir selbst*], but most certainly also not with the things themselves, since there are no things before I have made them thematic. So one gets dizzy when one looks down into the unfathomable presuppositions of presuppositionlessness.

Please save this letter, of which I have no copy, as the basis for future "sweet babble," even if you think that all of my questions are nonsense. But some of them are liable to have a point.

Take a look at the quite witty presidential address by Randall Jr., whom I otherwise don't think all too much of: *in tyrannos!*

The first part of my Scheler essay has appeared in the current number of the *Review of Metaphysics.*[5] I will receive off-prints of both parts bound together as soon as the second appears—probably in March.

I have decided not to submit a paper for the philosophy congress in Venice. If Van Breda wants to have the relevance essay[6] for the phenomenology meeting, he can have it. For the moment the phenomenology program is not set. Whether we go over this summer will depend on my and Ilse's health.

Love and many thanks

As always your

Alfred

1. "Sur la pensée conceptuelle" (G1959b).
2. This sentence could also mean; "With reference to the type—does the synthesis of recognition play [a role]?"
3. "The patients are no longer capable of regarding an object under the aspect of its similitude with other objects, of taking a given object as representative of similar objects which, by reason of their similarity, can be considered as belonging to the same class." "On the Conceptual Consciousness" (G1966a), 392.
4. Cf. "Concept and Theory Formation in the Social Sciences" (S1954a), where Schutz distinguishes everyday and scientific types as constructs of the first and second order. This argument with Gurwitsch concerns a deeper-lying difference between development of types and typification.
5. S1957d.
6. This refers to the essay (*not* the book) "Some Structures of the Life-World" (S1966b).

Gurwitsch: *My claim is that there is no such thing as a non-typifying experience*
              (CAMBRIDGE, DECEMBER 12, 1957)

Dear Friend,

First, our joy that your wife is doing much better and our hope that the whole story will soon have become an episode of the past. The address of Lucien Goldmann: . . . . That was his address a year ago; since he moves quite often, it might have changed. Then my sincere thanks for the good handling of the Guggenheim matter. If everything depended on you alone, then. . . .

Your long letter concerning my Venice lecture was a very special pleasure. I will save it as a basis for future conversations. I already want to go into one point today, since it is relatively easy to answer.

When you ask *what* a certain typification determines, *for whom* objects are *pareils,* one has to go into the social surrounding world and its relevances.

Certain relevances (in your sense) rule in *my* world, so the things are typified in *this* way. I have taken over typifications from my parents, etc., and the medium of taking them over is, among others, language. (I learned all that from you.) We have to ask Piaget, Stern, Bühler, and others what a typification looks like prior to language. My claim is that there is no such thing as a non-typifying experience; at most there are some individual objects and beings in an otherwise typified world.

We have to make one distinction, and you will agree with me: on the one side typification itself and as such, i.e., as a determining structure of experience (*antéprédicative*); on the other side the specific typification which is accepted in one or another social world. Or let's put it this way: the universal and formal structure of experience, which is decisively co-determined as typifying, is specified in various ways. All change of specification takes place on the ground of the universal conditions of experience as typifying and presupposes this ground. This is precisely parallel to the phenomenon of relevance (in my sense) and the specifications of this universal phenomenon, which yields relevance in your sense.

We will have to talk about these things at great length. Your whole letter is so far from being the product of over-fatigue that on the contrary it touches on a great many problems on which I, alone and with you, have to reflect very carefully if I, which God may allow very soon, begin working on my planned third book concerning levels and stages of concept formation. Perhaps you will come to the *convention* after all and bring your wife along. Please let me know which enticement is most promising; I will then make use of it.

Love to all of you

Your old
Aron

Gurwitsch: *Kant did not succeed in doing justice to the phenomenon of connection*
(CAMBRIDGE, JANUARY 15, 1958)

Dear Friend,

Enclosed you will find yet another manuscript of mine. The Metaphysical Society is having a *meeting* at Brown University (Providence) at the end of March. Two symposia are planned: one on the *philosophy of history* or something like that; the other on *being* and *existence*. They asked (it would be more correct to say: tormented) me to make a *statement* on *existence* from the phenomenological standpoint for the second symposium. So I have once again written one of my "condensations"—as you will see, it is partially (part III) an excerpt from my book. I am curious to hear what you will have to say; I almost fear that this time I won't have your applause.[1]

Just between us: I am sick and tired of the "condensations" as well as the formulations of positions and work programs. I would like nothing better than to return to genuine phenomenological work in which one can really get down to brass tacks, realize the "programs," and not care a whit about the positions. I am most comfortable with concrete work—there one has the feeling of getting something done. But it may be a good thing that some time passes before I begin on the theory of concept formation. By considering the problem from all sides in peace and quiet, "dreaming" about it and turning myself over to my dreams, the theory ripens.

Two-thirds of the Leibniz/Kant are now written (first draft, in which *no* monographic literature is taken into account, consciously so!). I have written two chapters since October: The first deals with the *petites perceptions* in Leibniz and Kant. The other, longer and more difficult, with the concept of the soul in Leibniz. It turned out to be necessary to give a very extensive presentation of the concept of substances and monads, partially in terms of the correspondence with Arnauld and de Volder.[2]

I have finally understood what Hume signifies (the shattering of connections [or contexts: *Zusammenhänge*]): that Kant did not succeed in doing justice to the phenomenon of connection, i.e., in restituting connection, and that one can only develop a theory of connection with Leibnizian concepts.[3] I have realized just how Leibnizian my book is (for example in the theory of perception, which really is more than a recapitulation of the Husserlian). So the whole thing leads right to one of my problems all over again, and I am thankful to you that during the summer you encouraged me to write a final chapter on the "Limits of the Kantian Conception of Consciousness."

How are all of you? We hope that your wife has already forgotten the operation and all the rest. And that you have not only refound your equilibrium but find yourself in a good equilibrium.

Greetings to your wife and Evi from both of us.

Most sincerely as always
Aron

1. "The Problem of Existence in Constitutive Phenomenology" (G1961).
2. The "Kant manuscript" is in the Gurwitsch papers and is being prepared for publication by Thomas Seebohm. See the Afterword for a discussion of Gurwitsch's reasons for abandoning the project of the Kant monograph.
3. The word *Zusammenhang* can have a variety of meanings in different contexts: connection, relation, interrelation, nexus, context, coherence, etc. In metaphysical contexts such as Leibnizian philosophy, it can mean connection or relation. In a Kantian context it would refer to the problem of connection or *Verbindung*. Cf. the Afterword to this volume.

Schutz: *I spoke at Columbia. But there is no sense at all in talking to these people*
           (NEW YORK, MARCH 16, 1958)

Dearest Friend,

   It has been a long time since I have heard from you, and I hope that
everything—above all your health—is in order. Please write to me soon. I would
also like to hear how your Europe plans are coming along. Did you get the
Guggenheim, and will you have a full year in Europe? As things now stand, Ilse
and I plan to leave for Naples on June 2 on the "Constitution," then Rome,
Vienna (where I have business), then vacation in the Austrian and Swiss mountains, the Salzburg Festival, Padua, Venice.—I still haven't heard either from
Van Breda concerning the exact program for Padua, or from the congress concerning the program for Venice. Do you know any more?
   Although my last report concerning you comes from Jonas, I don't know if
he has spoken with you concerning his plans, so I will sketch out the way things
have developed (needless to say in strict confidence and only for you). As you
know, I will be on a *leave of absence* in the Spring Term 1959, which I shall
probably spend in Europe, since otherwise neither the school nor my boss will
leave me in peace. Jonas has been elected vice-dean for the school year 1958–59
(an important year, since the 25th *Anniversary* of the Graduate Faculty falls in
this period), but set as a condition that he be absent for the entire year 1959–60:
he has claim to one semester as *sabbatical,* and he wants another as *leave of
absence.* He plans to complete not only his biology book but also the third
(Plotinus) volume of his book on gnosticism, to which end he wants to be in
Europe with his wife and three children during that year. . . .
   Why do I tell you all this? Of course, we need a replacement for Jonas at least
for 1959–60. Jonas himself wondered if you would be interested in replacing
him for this year. I told him that to my knowledge you plan to be away from
Brandeis 1958/59 and that I doubt that Brandeis would give you two years *leave
of absence* in a row. But that I would ask you (which I hereby do). If my hunch is
right, it would be a matter of more than one year, and no doubt the replacement
would have a good chance of becoming the successor. The *pros and cons* of such a
possibility (*pros* for me, *cons* for you) is something we have discussed so often
that I can spare you this time, except to note (also in confidence) that our
administration hopes to drum up an *endowment* for the Graduate Faculty on the
occasion of the jubilee, and that certain persons have expressed their doubt that,
should this fail, the annual deficit of the Graduate Faculty is acceptable *à la
longue* for the New School.
   At any rate, now is the time for you and me to announce your possible
interest while you and I are here, since things could happen quickly. In order to
take no chances, I have had a confidential conversation with Cairns. He is very
successful as a teacher—the students have requested that he continue his Husserl
course in the Spring semester. Cairns, who of course knows very well that you

were one of the final candidates along with Jonas and that you would be interested in being his successor, which he would find delightful, would be prepared to take over Jonas's full *teaching load* during his absence (1959/60). (He wants to go to Europe during the summer too this year, and I believe that he would like to beef up his finances.) But he said that he wouldn't want to do this in the long run. This may open up a possibility that he "save the place" for you. But we will have to take steps in this direction very soon. I only wanted to inform you of these developments today. I would be interested in hearing your reaction.

Enclosed is your copy of the intersubjectivity essay from the *Philosophische Rundschau*.[1] I hope to receive the off-prints of my two-part Scheler essay from the *Review of Metaphysics* in the near future, and you will of course receive your copy immediately.

The Philosophy Club of Columbia (*faculty and graduate students*) invited me to give a lecture, which I gave last week. For this purpose I have revised an old manuscript (1942/43) and your copy is enclosed: "Tiresias or Our Knowledge of Future Events."[2] Much of it is of course only all too familiar to you—I have to repeat myself so often in essays; I brought in some material from the ideas which went into the relevance essay which I read to you; some of it (such as, e.g., the interpretation of the boundaries of the "specious present") is probably new. The whole problematic is rather important to me (as preliminary work toward a book). If you have time at some point, let me know what you think about it. I plan to read the essay this Fall in our General Seminar and then to offer it to the *Journal of Philosophy*.

Needless to say, I spoke at Columbia *in partibus infidelium*. The reception: *respectful bewilderment,* e.g., a long discussion of why I analyze Tiresias instead of Cassandra, since there is some difference there! And whether the difficulties are only the problems of "conditional propositions," which concern the entire past! And what about the law of entropy? It was impossible to discover what the speaker meant. But there is no point in talking to these people: since I am fed up with this level of discussion I shall repair to the "intellectual water level" [*geistigen Wasserspiegel*], which is the beautiful word with which Spann "Germanized" the level of discussion.

Ilse is fine, I have seen better times. Love to you and your wife

Your
Alfred

1. S1957b: It is the only essay Schutz published in German.
2. S1959a (cf. SG 9.19.45).

Gurwitsch: *Whether I would consider a call to Berlin*
                        (CAMBRIDGE, MARCH 22, 1958)

Dear Friend,

Many thanks for your kind letter and the "Tiresias article." What I don't really like in your letter is the statement at the end that you have "seen better times." What does that mean *in concreto*? Even if you don't believe the doctor, please perform the ἐποχή on his opinion and then let me know what this bracketed opinion is. But note that the bracketing changes nothing in the substantive content of that which is bracketed.

I shall restrict myself to business matters in my answer today. There are various considerations.

The positive response from Fulbright came yesterday. I didn't really believe in it; the surprise is all the more pleasant. Since you have helped the matter so energetically, I want to repeat my thanks to you. The success doesn't make my thanks any more sincere, but it is happier. We have shared so many bad times that we have a right to share our joy on occasion. I haven't heard anything from Guggenheim.

There has been no change in my interest in the New School. If Jonas really does leave and I should be his successor, I would welcome that on the basis of positive as well as negative grounds. I don't have to write yet another time concerning the positive. The negative ones are that I feel less and less comfortable here and positively "out of place." There are indeed reasons why I long for an at least halfway academic milieu. The one here isn't; and there are many other reasons. Should, for example, the president discover what he calls a "distinguished and prominent philosopher," and should he force him on me—which is his honest intention—that will begin a period of battle which I don't want and which I, given the local customs, am not up to.

This is all of course confidential. The next thing even more so, if only because of its vagueness. For more than a year I have been personally and unofficially asked if I would consider a call to Berlin. My first answers were negative. As the inquiries were repeated, and the situation here more and more unpleasant, I finally wrote that I wouldn't reject it *a limine*. This elicited a recent official invitation from the Rector to give a lecture which is to take place most probably in June. According to my unofficial information, they want to look me over, but they also want to look over other people. They wanted Fink; but he declined. I too want to look over people, things, and conditions. But please take this for what it is. Not only is the egg not yet laid, but the other egg, out of which the legendary hen will someday come, is also not yet laid. The whole thing is so fraught with maybes and so hypothetical that it can't be allowed to have any influence on the matter of the New School. I tell you this of course *à titre personnel;* but I would also ask you in your role as professor at the New School (do you still remember our discussion at the beginning of our friendship concerning the "schizophrenic I hypothesis"?)[1] simply to forget it.

Love from both of us to all of you

Most sincerely

Your

Aron

P.S.: Now that it is clear that I shall be gone for the entire year 1958/59, it seems to me very unlikely that Brandeis will give me a second year off the following year. Above all the dean, with whom my relations aren't bad, raises the objection that this breaks continuity. As I see it, it would be very unwise even to pose the question at this point.

Please tell Cairns that his willingness to keep the place warm for me is very touching. A propos: have you seen McGill's review of my book?

The "Tiresias" is *very important;* more about that another time. There is more in it about the genuine problems of induction than in all of the specialists on "scientific method." The absurdity of a human consciousness to which the future is known—is a *trouvaille. Félicitations.*

1. Cf. SG 7.21.58 and SG 8.19.39.

Schutz: *Whether a non-communist Jew has any business in Berlin of all places*
           (NEW YORK, MARCH 27, 1958)

Dear Friend,

Good news, for once! Most sincere congratulations for the Fulbright, which is not merely materially welcome, but also a long since deserved tribute. I share your joy and think of Nestroy's statement: "I have shared the bad days with you, it is my holy duty not to abandon you in the good ones."

So how shall we share this year? We are sailing for Naples, *weather permitting,* on June 2 on the "Constitution," then on to Rome, where we plan to remain until the end of the month; from Rome on to Vienna, where I have things to do, for two weeks, then I plan to go to an Austrian or Swiss vacation retreat for five or six weeks. We have tickets to some performances at the Salzburg Festival at the end of August, and from there we plan to travel leisurely through the Dolomites to Padua for the (for me to date mysterious) phenomenology meeting and to Venice for the philosophical congress. We will probably have to fly back before it comes to an end.

A propos Fulbright: I was also a sponsor for my colleague Dr. Ernst F., who was also invited to Cologne (as a superb musicologist). He too received a Fulbright, so you will be there at the same time. This was especially surprising, since F. is already 67 years old. He is a very educated and amusing man, and his wife will interest yours, since she is a very talented painter who has had great commercial success, as she designs wonderful Christmas cards for a large firm.

With regard to business, I completely share your view that it wouldn't be wise to ask Brandeis for a *leave of absence* for a second year in a row. We shall see how things develop with Jonas, who—obviously—takes the attitude that he will only be gone for one year. Cairns is very interested in taking over a full *teaching load* for this year (1959/60). I did not give him your thanks, since there is no reason for it. We weren't talking about "saving a place" for you: I note this in order to clear up misunderstandings. What happened was rather that I asked Cairns whether he would be interested in taking over a full load during Jonas's absence, since I didn't think that, as Jonas had suggested, you would be able to come to New York for that year (in light of your absence in 1958/59). Cairns expressly stated that he would be interested in this only for one year, but not permanently. I told him that I would like this, since in case Jonas should not return after this year, you would surely be the top candidate since, as Cairns knows, you were Jonas's closest competitor. Cairns answered that we three would without any doubt make up a wonderful department, and that he would be delighted with such a solution. I told him that one can never know what advantages his full-time teaching might bring during one year, since should you for any reason not be interested in coming to us should Jonas leave, whereas he, Cairns, wanted to continue, then the chances would be much improved.

This was an informal conversation, since I have no official mandate. But one can't speak of "saving a place," and although Cairns is one of the most loyal and honest people I know, you have no reason to be touched.

I have seen McGill's review:[1] "Where kings build, the carters have a lot to do." *Social Research* still hasn't received the review copy which Arnheim is waiting for.

Berlin is an honor. But in your place I would consider very carefully whether a non-communist Jew has any business in Berlin of all places. Sure, if it were Freiburg or Munich!—But I can only refer to the conclusion of my Tiresias: May Zeus give you everything that is good for you, even if your friends and you don't ask for it, and keep all evil from you, even if you and we pray for it!

Love and best wishes to both of you

Your
Alfred

P.S.: My James-Bergson seminar yesterday was devoted to you. The student giving the report, who is writing a thesis on Unamuno,[2] was to have dealt with your article on *transitive parts,* which, as you know, I am especially partial to, but also brought in parts of your book. Needless to say he misunderstood a lot of it, but if you are interested I will send you his paper, which gives evidence of serious work. You would have taken great pleasure in the discussion. I have 10 really good students in the seminar.

Another student, R., wants me to be his *thesis advisor* on "The Secularization of Reason" (Voltaire, Comte, S. Simon, the young Marx). He claims to have been at Brandeis for three years and to have studied under you. What do you think of him?

1. Review of *Théorie du champ de la conscience* (G1957b): PPR 18 (1957–58): 422f.

2. Miguel de Unamuno y Jugo (1864–1936) taught philosophy in Salamanca, Spain. The "article on *transitive parts*": G1943. The student was Fred Kersten, now Professor at the University of Wisconsin–Green Bay. "To this day, however, I don't think that I misunderstood Gurwitsch" (letter to the translator, October 24, 1986).

Gurwitsch: *A Marxist mentality: has seen through everything; nothing is questionable*
(CAMBRIDGE, APRIL 19, 1958)

Dear Friend,

To my astonishment and consternation I see that I haven't yet answered your very kind letter of March 27. The reason for this neglect is that I am overloaded with work to a truly fantastic degree. I haven't had anything like this for many years. I have simply taken on too much, and now I am paying the price. (And I haven't written anything on the Kant book[1] for weeks.) This overwork had the effect that I could neither sleep nor bear to look at paper. When school let out two weeks ago I was at the end of my rope, and we went to New Hampshire for four days. Then I returned to my mountains of work.

I am quite familiar with R.: he is quite capable, not without learning. The fact that he is a Marxist is only noteworthy because he has a curious—by no means rare—Marxist mentality in whose service his intelligence stands. That is, he has long since known it all, seen through everything, can't wonder at anything, problems and questionable things don't exist. The only thing left for this truly sharp intelligence to do is only to expose, to unmask, to uncover. So a great effort is wasted. It is always a sad thing for me to see how a good, even very good talent doesn't develop because its owner, instead of devoting himself to substantive issues and problems, puts his talents in the service of certain "higher" goals. As I recall, the work he did in my seminar was very good. He saw in me, as in every non-Marxist, a "class enemy" who has "power," and whom one has to somehow satisfy.

If one could cure him of his wrongheadedness, it would be a good deed, and should one succeed it would be well worth the effort.

I am touched by what you say about my role in your seminar. Of course I would like to see the paper that deals with me. (I would be thankful if I didn't have to read it in a hurry.) *A propos:* you will be interested in the fact that my book has had an echo in Italy, of all places. A Mr. Pucci refers to me in the *Archivio di Filosofia,* and another man from Turin, equally unknown to me, has asked me for a copy. Natanson wrote recently that he will review it in the *Philosophical Review.*

I recently got a negative reply from Guggenheim. I had expected just the reverse. At any rate, once again my thanks for the trouble you have gone to in this matter.

Aron Gurwitsch teaching at the New School.

To judge by your letter we will see each other first in Europe.
Love to all of you from both of us

Your

Aron

1. Cf. GS 1.15.58.

Schutz: *Van Breda has canceled the phenomenology meeting in Padua*
(NEW YORK, MAY 1, 1958)

Dear Friend,

Many thanks for your kind lines of the 19th, which bother me because I can't imagine what the "price" of your being overworked might be. Please, let me know briefly what is going on.

I hope Guggenheim isn't too great a disappointment for you, since you have the Fulbright. Winternitz told me that Guggenheim surely heard of the Fulbright being granted and turned you down for that reason. What are your plans now? As you probably know, Van Breda has canceled the phenomenology meeting for mysterious reasons. Nonetheless we will leave for Europe on June 2 on the "Constitution." I hope we will get together in Venice.

It is too bad that we can't get together earlier; I would have had a lot to tell you about, including an unpleasant exchange of letters with Farber.

I shall send you the "paper" by my student which deals with you after the end of the semester.—Many thanks for the information about R., which was important for me.

Love to both of you from both of us

Your

Alfred

Gurwitsch: *Not much more is known about Husserl in Germany than the name*
(COLOGNE, JULY 1, 1958)

Dear Friend,

We hope that this letter reaches you in Vienna and above all that it finds you all in good health. If I remember correctly, you planned to remain in Vienna until July 5.

I held my lecture in Berlin about a week ago (that is the lecture whose manuscript got into the wrong package at your house). To use a catch phrase, I can best sum up my impression of its reception as "fascination with what is foreign." In Berlin, just as in Germany in general, little more is known about Husserl than the name (a few years ago there wasn't even that). Here they are hardly accustomed to analytic work on concrete questions; every lecture, regardless of how short, contains the "whole world"; in each one the avalanche of all problems is turned loose on the listener. So my presentation had to sound strange, all the more since all philosophy exists in Heidegger's shadow. But there seems to be a fascination in precisely this foreignness.

One *Ordinarius* in Berlin is a student of Heidegger, a living relic of the youth movement (much younger than I), who feels a curious attraction to my character, i.e., the character of the sceptical Jew. We were treated like princes; and we will talk about the practical-political aspects of the lecture when we get together. The students have a hunger for philosophy the way I pursue it. In the colloquium with them it became clear that they know, as it were, nothing at all about Husserl. But they are pretty well oriented with regard to Kant. The general level is pretty good. Another characteristic of Berlin is a relatively high number of women who are working on habilitation theses.

Tomorrow we are going to Paris for some two weeks. (Address: *chez* M. Jean Adler, Paris 17ᵉ.) We will stay two weeks in the home of absent friends. Since a hotel in Sils-Maria has turned us down, we don't know where we will go. We hope to find mail on that in Paris. Please let us know in Paris what your further plans are.

Best wishes from both of us to both of you.

Yours as always
Aron

Schutz: *I have a lot of business correspondence: man lives on bread too*
(ALT-AUSSEE, STIERMARK, JULY 12, 1958)

Dear Friend,

Your letter of the 1st addressed to Vienna has just reached me here, since I unexpectedly had to go to Zürich on business. I am writing in haste so that these lines will reach you in Paris, just provisionally, in order to let you know what my program is:

We will remain here until roughly the end of the month; from August 2 to 20 our address is Hotel Kuhn-Sonnhof, Seelisberg, Switzerland. Please let me know there where I can write to you, since I found the package with your essay here and plan to read it intensively in the next few days. I also have many other things to tell you.

Berlin seems to have been a great personal and substantive success for you. You know how much pleasure it gives me that you as a human being and philosopher receive the recognition you deserve. Let your friends work for your habilitation: there will be plenty of time to consider accepting if it comes to that.

Today I have a lot of pressing business correspondence to take care of—man lives on bread too—and only write so that this letter will reach you in time. You will hear from me in more detail as soon as I hear where you will be.

Best wishes to you and your dear wife from both of us

Your
Alfred

Gurwitsch: *Berlin has placed me "primo loco" on the list for the first chair*
              (PARIS, JULY 16, 1958)

Dear Friend,

You shall receive an immediate answer to your kind lines of July 12. First concerning external matters, i.e., our travel plans. We are leaving Paris tomorrow and going to Switzerland. Starting July 20 we will again have an address: Hotel Edelweiß, Sils-Maria, Grisons, Switzerland. We don't know how long we will stay there. Should it get too cold in the middle of August, we will go on to the area around Lugano. In any case we will be in Venice on September 10: Pensione Accademia. If I am not mistaken, you are in the "Luna." Couldn't you arrange things so that you come through St. Moritz on your way from Austria to Seelisberg so we can meet for a day? I have a strong desire to see you—*sous tous les rapports concevables.*

Berlin was indeed a success, in human as in substantive terms: in terms of the latter the success, to exaggerate, of an exotic being. My way of thinking, analyzing, of keeping myself most strictly and exactly to my topic (and not, as is fashionable in Germany today, to bring down the sum total of all philosophical problems on the hearers like an avalanche) seemed strange. They didn't conceal that. On the other hand precisely the strange and unusual seems to have a great attraction for Germans. With regard to one *Ordinarius,* who was and is humanly and politically unobjectionable in every respect, I had the feeling that I, as an old sceptical Jew, was encountering a German youth (in the best sense of the word). How curious that I don't have this feeling of otherness with the French: with neither Koyré nor Minkowski (both of whom are, however, Jews) nor Hyppolite, who invited me to come from Cologne sometime in order to lead a *Colloque* with his *Normaliens.*

From Berlin came the report that the faculty has put me *primo loco* on the list of the first chair. I have declared that I would seriously consider an offer from Berlin. I haven't made any further *commitments,* and none were expected of me—

at the present stage. There are so many factors which one has to consider, e.g., the question of my retirement. And the Brandeis situation appears in its absolute absurdity in the light of the reception in Cologne, Berlin, and Paris. *Ach,* if you only knew what a burden the whole Berlin question is for both of us.

Have a good time in Alt-Aussee: until we meet again sometime soon. Love to both of you from my wife and me.

Best wishes

Your

Aron

Schutz: *Not being or mere appearance, but rather being or sense is the dilemma here*
(ALT-AUSSEE, STIERMARK, JULY 21, 1958)

Dear Friend,

Many thanks for your exciting letter of the 16th. So Sils-Maria worked out after all ("There suddenly, my friend, one became two")—a worthy place for a philosopher! Shouldn't there be something symbolic in the fact that you are living in the "Academia" in Venice, while "lunatic" tendencies assert themselves in me?

As much as I would like to see you—since I too have a lot to talk about—a glance at the map will convince you that it would only with great difficulty be possible to stop in Sils-Maria on the way to Seelisberg (near Lucerne)—aside from the fact that I want to avoid this altitude. But you might want to show your wife the Vierwaldstättersee? We will stay here until August 3, and will be in Seelisberg, Hotel Kuhn-Sonnenberg, from the 4th to about the 20th. Should you want to visit me there, you should call ahead or notify me some other way, since I will have to go to Zürich once or twice.

Heartiest congratulations for the *primo loco* call to Berlin. That is a well-earned success that you can and should be proud of. That the Berlin problem gives occasion for much serious thought is something that I can well understand. Were it a matter of Cologne, Frankfurt, Munich, Bonn, Hamburg, I would recommend accepting without any reservations, since I am more and more convinced that people like you and me are out of place in America. (For me that has nothing to do with the school, but with other scholarly things, which I shall tell you about in person.)

Berlin is, for political reasons, another matter. I am not worried about war, revolution, and such things at the moment. But I am convinced that there will have to be some kind of settlement of the German question soon, and I can't imagine that in this case the two universities will continue side by side in Berlin. Even if they should do so (to say nothing of the situation if they should not) it will by no means be comfortable for an independent philosopher who is a Jew, has no sympathy for dialectical materialism and also none for existentialism, to come into this situation of rivalry. It may be even worse there than at Brandeis.

Finally, the current generation of students in the East Zone has grown up under the Ulbricht propaganda. I read in an article here what Georg Lukacs has to go along with, and I wouldn't like to participate in the blessings of red academic freedom under a "pink dean." If Ingarden should come to Venice, you will also hear some interesting things in this respect, even with the care which he imposes upon himself. But if the "free" university retains the upper hand, it will probably have to become even more "German" than it is, i.e., even more youth-moved in the clearing of Being.[1]

I write all this to you because I have the feeling that you want to hear my opinion, although Ilse, perhaps correctly, says that it is irresponsible to interfere in such questions. In your place I would want to work at using the call to Berlin to get to another German university in the West Zone. The fact that this is altruistic advice must be clear to you, since I can only with difficulty separate myself from the idea of having you at least close by (if not at the Graduate Faculty). But we will talk about all that, at the latest in Venice.

In the last few days I have studied your article in detail.[2] It is excellent work, and the enthusiasm of the Berliners is more than understandable. Above all, your German style is much better than your English. The quiet, cautious mode of presentation makes things completely clear.

You have no idea how much I learn from you, even when you talk about things I am very famliar with. Naturally, I have no objections to your *presentation* of Husserl. But precisely because you have presented his theory of consciousness so clearly, I have solidified the suspicion I have had for many years that the theory of intentionality can never lead to the constitution of the objective world, and that it simply presupposes the life-world as its unquestioned basis. This holds even aside from the problem of intersubjectivity, which has not been solved in transcendental phenomenology and most likely cannot be.

What is lacking is precisely a worked-out ontology which doesn't remain satisfied with setting up regions or formal ontologies. E.g., p. 20 of your presentation: *quid juris* can I claim that I am conscious of the "strict identity" of the noema in separate perceptual acts?[3] How do I really know that the adumbrations and perspectives are those of one and the same perceptual object? Indeed, that this perceptual object is the same (visual thing) or that as an object of manipulation it is the same (visual thing) object of another perception (tactual thing), or that as an object of manipulation it remains identical with the perceptual object—perhaps even "strictly identical" or "numerically identical," *whatever this means!*

Assuming that the "sense" of the noema is identical, but the object changes through the intervention of a *génie malin* or by Father Malebranche's instantaneous creation? Assuming that it is the fate of the Leibnizian monad to have to move on to ever new perceptions, because the mirrored universe happens to stand always in a Heraclitean flux? And in Husserl I don't even have transcendental apperception as a guarantee of unity, but rather an I which is both mundanely and transcendentally in principle schizophrenic. As a result of these unclarities, Husserl develops neither a theory of the objective world (world for me, if you will: the *Trisselwand*[4] in front of my window is "the same" as 22 years ago and indeed, for me, unchanged), nor a defensible theory of intersubjectivity, nor— and I owe this insight to the last pages of your essay—one of causality. In addition: what does this talk about a "passive synthesis" mean? Isn't that wooden iron? Are there such things as *passive achievements* of consciousness?

The blunder comes from the fact that Husserl applied the discovered identity of ideal objects (Pythagorean Theorem: p. 31) to all noemata[5]—but again I ask: *quid juris?* And to bare my heart completely in this confession: I have become so heretical that I no longer understand how the eidetic reduction can be per- formed, if only the identity of the noematic sense and not that of the objective object is presupposed. I also no longer understand how evidence can be traced back to "being at the things themselves" if we can at most get to the identity of the noematic sense of conscious acts! Not being or mere appearance, but being or sense is the dilemma here.

Don't ban me from your heart on account of my doubt. Love from us to you and your wife

Your
Alfred

1. This phrase plays on the German youth movement of the early twentieth century, parts of which fed into the rise of the Nazis, as well as on Heidegger's "clearing of Being." Heidegger joined the Nazi party in 1933.
2. "The Kantian and Husserlian Conceptions of Consciousness"; G1964 (German), G1960 (French), G1966a (English).
3. "Acts of perception are intentional acts . . . to each of them there corresponds a perceptual noema, and—we remember—the same noema can correspond to a multiplicity of acts." (G1966a, 155–156). Cf. also the earlier version: GS 8.4.56.
4. A mountain.
5. The reference is to Husserl's critique of Locke's general triangle (*Logical Investiga- tions,* Second Investigation, §11). Cf. G1966a, 156.

Gurwitsch: *I think I have shown why Husserl can solve problems where Kant fails*
(SILS-MARIA, SWITZERLAND, AUGUST 10, 1958)

Dear Friend,

I am finally getting around to answering your kind letter of VII/21. The "finally" refers to the fact that I have been hard at work ever since we got here, after having done literally nothing for two months—travel preparations, travel- ing around Europe, Parisian noise, etc. etc. Things are going very well here—

they have rarely gone so well—thanks to the spirit of Nietzsche[1] (?), the quiet, the magnificent, massive, and spacious mountain landscape. There is a cliff opposite my window that sends me greetings and encouragement every morning. In three weeks I have written almost half of the last chapter of the Kant-Leibniz book. So the end of the first draft (*sic!* you know me) is almost in sight (let's say November–December, since there will be interruptions—such as travel, the congress). Then a lot of time will be devoted to consulting the literature, but at any rate the first version is there.

I am glad that you liked the Berlin lecture. It is by the way in press: Biemel wants to publish lectures which were held at the Husserl Archives in Cologne in the series "Phaenomenologica."[2] I gave this lecture two years ago in Cologne (and later at the New School), if in a different—much more primitive—form.

We will have to talk about your substantive remarks: I don't agree with you at all. I think that I have shown how and why Husserl can solve problems where Kant failed. (That is by the way the systematic chapter which I promised you a year ago. Since it is a part of the lecture, I will only hint at these things in the "concluding remarks" of the book.) For the rest, don't worry: if you turn your back on intentionality, you still retain your place in my heart. To lose that you would have to do things you are not capable of doing.

A propos Berlin: you are right, and not your wife. I also write that because I want to know your opinion and because I value it greatly. I have obviously forgotten to mention one aspect of the matter. If I retire in Berlin, we will have a pension of some $500 per month—at Brandeis about $300. That should not be left out of consideration. For the rest, I don't have an offer yet, but only the recommendation that an offer be made, and the faculty has put me *primo loco* on that list. The government, which has the last word, can still raise the objection that I am too close to retirement age (65 or 68?).

We will stay here about two weeks and will be near Lugano around August 25 (until the congress). Where will you be after you leave Seelisberg on VIII/20? Before we go to Lugano we want to spend three days in Soglio (an enchanting Medieval Italian mountain village).

All the best and love from us to both of you for your remaining summer stay

Your
Aron

1. Sils in Upper Engadin was the temporary residence of Nietzsche between 1881 and 1889.
2. The volume was not published (but cf. G1964b).

Gurwitsch: *Alice discovered this picture of the "Dioscuri"*
(ON THE WAY TO COLOGNE, SEPTEMBER 24, 1958)

Aron Gurwitsch (center) and Alfred Schutz (right) in conversation with Nathan Rotenstreich.

My Friend,

Alice discovered this picture, of which there was only one copy, on our last day in Padua, after you had left. I think that you will enjoy seeing the "Dioscuri" immortalized in conversation with Rotenstreich.[1] So I am sending it to you.

We are leaving tomorrow and will be in Cologne on Sunday or Monday. We stayed here for another entire week—in Ravenna, e.g., which was really worthwhile. The address in Cologne: Bensberg bei Köln, Kaule 16.

Please forgive the wrinkled page; I can't find anything else.

Love from us to both of you and Evi.

Your

Aron

1. It was to be the last meeting between the two friends; and it is the only photograph of Schutz and Gurwitsch together. They are in conversation with N. Rotenstreich, philosopher from Jerusalem. Cf. also GS 5.9.59.

Schutz: *Do you recall that the new Pope blessed us in Venice?*
          (MINNEWASKA, N.Y., NOVEMBER 1, 1958)

Dear Friend,

I hope that the two of you are now installed in your new house and feel at home. I would very much like to hear more about your decisions concerning your future activity, but above all, whether you have gotten any further along in the decision concerning the Berlin question.

Many thanks for the photograph from Venice; my wife especially takes great pleasure in it, and it is good that we are both captured in a picture. You look very imposing in it, by the way. —Do you recall that the new Pope blessed us when he spent an hour at the meeting at which McKeon presided?[1]

Since my return I have been very busy with preparations for the new book.[2] (Kurt Wolff, who by the way will be going to Brandeis permanently in Fall '59 as sociologist, speaks jokingly of this activity as *Erev Sabbatical* [Sabbatical Eve].) I can't tell you how important it is for me that the general program and the organization which I discussed with you in Venice found your agreement and that you think that the whole thing is worth the effort. In Venice I realized how important a longer time spent together would be for both of us.

Perhaps it can be arranged that we get together for a longer period of time after your return from Israel. Enclosed is a not-yet-corrected copy of the essay for Van Breda's Memorial Volume.[3] I am trying to write the essay I promised to Farber on the concept of type in Husserl, but keep running into ever greater difficulties.[4] Above all I wonder whether free variation in fantasy, which leads to the eidetic reduction, is really all that free. What is its relation to the formal and regional ontological realms, what is its connection with the spheres of incompatibility, with the frameworks of open (in contrast to the problematic) probabilities? And finally: what is the connection of the type to the Leibnizian *principium identitatis indiscernibilium*?[5] Since you are deeply involved in Leibniz, can you perhaps tell me what you think about this last point?

Our friend Cairns is a very funny person; he hasn't been in contact with me at all since Venice, and just for fun I am for once going to wait until he telephones.

The Tiresias essay will appear in *Social Research*.

Please let me hear from you from time to time. Our best regards to you and your wife

Your
Alfred

1. John XXIII was elected on 10.28.58: Angelo Guiseppe Roncalli was Cardinal and Patriarch of Venice prior to his election.
2. Schutz worked on the *Structures of the Life-World* in Seelisberg (MS II-IV), and was currently working on MS V, which was finished in New York. (Cf. Thomas Luckmann's Preface to S1973, xxiv).
3. The essay: "Husserl's Importance for the Social Sciences" (S1959c). "Van Breda's Memorial Volume": *Edmund Husserl: 1859–1959,* ed. H. L. Van Breda and J. Taminiaux (The Hague: Martinus Nijhoff, 1959).
4. "Type and Eidos in Husserl's Late Philosophy" (S1959b).
5. Cf. SG 8.19.39: The question concerning the Leibnizian principle of identity, which stood at the beginning of the correspondence, is now answered by Schutz in terms of the theory of types.

Gurwitsch: *Here they define a professor as a scholar whose profession keeps him away from his work*
                (BENSBERG BY COLOGNE, NOVEMBER 25, 1958)

Dear Friend,

It is high time that you hear from me. We have settled into a very nice and comfortable house. Unfortunately, the house is in a small town, and it takes a good hour to get to Cologne with the electric. This can be unpleasant, especially for my wife. Every time we go to a concert it means a long ride back and forth. But that is the price which one pays to have a house to oneself.

As to real life: it is really something very different to talk before grown people rather than before children. My lecture hall is quite full, all the more so in light of the fact that I am a guest professor who has nothing to do with examinations, and the German students generally only go to the ones who will examine them. The topic of the lectures is the same as those I held at the New School, but the approach is completely different. It develops from session to session and is both deeper and broader. I am basically quite satisfied with what I have done thus far, but it is a pity that I have no notes. (It would be easy to develop something written from the way in which phenomenological motifs develop behind my back from Piaget.)

With regard to the state of philosophy in general, I would refer you to the note that is in the December number of Farber's journal.[1] I don't know the situation in Freiburg first hand, but I can only confirm the rest. Aside from that, all colleagues are under a truly fantastic strain: with examinations, in comparison with which the American high school teacher function is child's play, with search commissions, with unavoidable philosophy and university politics of all kinds and with a lot of avoidable monkeyshines on the radio and more. Here they define a professor as a scholar whose profession keeps him from his work. One has to be afraid of this whole operation if one is a craftsman of philosophy and wants to remain one, and doesn't want to become its administrator and statesman.

Landgrebe is holding a colloquium every two weeks along with myself and others, in which a Husserl text (Phenomenological Psychology) is read. He knows these things very well, and Biemel knows the texts better than almost anyone. But outside of the academic context it only rarely comes to a genuine συμφιλοσοφεῖν with Landgrebe or with anybody else. They even consciously avoid it; no one asks what one is working on. Although we see each other socially every now and then, we hardly ever speak about things in a manner that even approaches our discussions in your study. The people are not only overworked: I have the suspicion that they are hardly interested in things.

I have an old theory which I learned in America, that when the *activities* begin, the substance has disappeared. I am treated with a consideration I am not used to, but still remain a bit the curiosity on the side. And the relations between the German professors themselves are hardly any different, as Landmann of Berlin recently told me. They get along more or less—pursue politics with, for, and against one another—intellectually one is blocked off.

I was in Berlin about two weeks ago for negotiations. They will let me know in about a month what they can offer me. From the negotiations I saw that the sum which I can count on after my retirement is not so significantly more than what I can expect in America. What Khrushchev's statement,[2] which was made just as I was in Berlin, means for my thinking I needn't tell you. I can well remember the time when every political crisis and announcement of one led to a nervous crisis. One could even accept that, if one had the security of intellectual congeniality—as in Paris. But just that is questionable and is becoming more and more questionable.

I have agreed to write an article for the 100th birthday for the *Zeitschrift für Philosophie*.[3]

I am working on it now, to my great displeasure, since in the article "On the Phenomenological Theory of Perception" I am again mulling over some things which are in my book. Since my book doesn't yet exist in German (Walter de Gruyter is interested) I have a number of reasons to think that this is the right thing to do. But it isn't any fun, and places demands on me in every respect which are excessive and positively ridiculous. For this reason only a brief thanks today for "Husserl's Importance for the Social Sciences."

Your remark on free variation proves that we are indeed Dioscuri. I have recently begun to suspect that there is a *petitio principii* here. Since free variation is to discover invariancies, it simply cannot be completely free; but if it is directed, one already has to have a certain knowledge of that to which it is to lead. I will speak about this doubt on December 12 in Louvain (*"Problèmes phénoménologiques de l'idéation"*).[4]

On the following day I am speaking in Brussels (*"La conception de la science chez Kant et chez Husserl"*) before the *Société Belge de Philosophie,* which is gathering for a special *Réunion* for this purpose. (They will yet succeed in making me a megalomaniac.) In Israel they want to exploit me in grand style: between March 10 and 25 I am to take over two sessions of Rotenstreich's Husserl seminar, hold a double lecture on "Perception" before a philosophical-psychological group, another on "Ideation" before the philosophy club, and finally the Kant-Husserl before still another group that is still more specialized.

How can we arrange to get together following our return from Israel? I think that it is absolutely necessary that we have eight or ten days of peace and quiet to talk to one another—without the *trappings* that belong to the congress. Aside from free variation, there is a whole series of things connected with your book about which I want to hear what you have to say. Could you come somewhere in Italy sometime around the middle of May? I have also floated the idea that we might come to Vienna, which neither of us knows, for a week to ten days. That would also have the advantage that we would have more peace in a home; but it would be a major detour and our finances aren't looking very bright. Fulbright will probably pay for my trip to Israel.

Stay healthy, with best and most sincere greetings from us

Your

Aron

1. James V. McGlynn, "A Note on Philosophy in German Universities Today," *PPR* 19 (1958–59): 248–252.

2. On November 27, 1958, Krushchev demanded that Berlin be made a "free city."

3. "Beitrag zur phänomenologischen Theorie der Wahrnehmung" ["Contribution to the Phenomenological Theory of Perception"], in *Zeitschrift für philosophische Forschung* (G1959a).

4. This lecture as well as the following one were not published.

Gurwitsch: *I wrote off Berlin recently*
             (Bensberg, December 19, 1958)

Dear Friend,

I spoke in Louvain and Brussels last week, which was once again one of my triumphs. I of course mentioned your published contributions on typification in Louvain in connection with ideation. The discussion touched on you in Brussels as well, especially in my conversations with Ch. Perelmann.[1] I told him that you are coming to Europe next Spring, and whetted his appetite for you. He would like you to speak at the *Société Belge de Philosophie*, where I lectured on Kant-Husserl. Since I couldn't tell him anything precise about your exact plans, he asked me to write to you. You should let him know when you will be in Belgium so that they can arrange something.

The main purpose of these lines is to whet your appetite for him. He has published a book this year with the telling title *Traité de l'argumentation*. The book is in two volumes with a total of some 750 pages; I haven't read it, but I did look at the table of contents very carefully and have heard about it. It is an attempt at a logic of argumentation as opposed to one of demonstration: in Aristotle's language, a dialectic and not an analytic; in our language, a logic of the life-world and not of formalized idealities. It concerns the way a lawyer argues, or a politician or a *directeur* before his *conseil d'administration*. Perelmann himself speaks of *probabilité* in contrast to *vérité démonstrable*. I can well imagine that the book will interest you—but since I haven't read it, I can't say any more. You may find confirmation, perhaps even stimulation, in it, precisely because it is written from a standpoint oriented to logic, and thus from a totally different orientation from the one in which you normally work. If you browse in it for a couple of hours, it shouldn't be a waste of time. When he told me that he considers idealized logic to be a special case of his "*argumentation*," it was very stimulating for me, since I can use just that.

I wrote off Berlin recently. Mr. Khrushchev has announced that he plans to make Berlin a chronic *point névralgique*. May—in the line of the Platonic prayer—the gods have an offer sent from Brussels! I fit into its atmosphere so much better than into that of the "Watch on Being"[2]—the title of a comedy by Gabriel Marcel which is to appear shortly.

My wife and I wish all of you love and a healthy reunion in what we hope is a very good new year.

As always,
Your
Aron

1. Chaim Perelmann, a Belgian philosopher at the Free University of Brussels, died in 1984. He devoted his career as a scholar and a teacher to what he called "New Rhetorics."

Major books: *La Nouvelle Rhétorique* (Paris, 1958); *Le champ de l'argumentation* (Brussels, 1970); *Justice et Raison* (Brussels, 1972). (Information from J. Taminiaux.)

2. *"Wacht am Sein"*: a play on the title of a very chauvinistic German song, *"Die Wacht am Rhein"* (The Watch on the Rhine).

Schutz: *My state of health is very labile*
           (NEW YORK, DECEMBER 20, 1958)

Dearest Friend,

While you have received two "official" letters from me (and will soon receive a third in which we accept your offer to give a course here, both for Fall 1959 and for Spring 1960), your kind private letter of November 25 has remained unanswered. Today too I have to restrict myself to the most important things in answering, above all because there are many interesting things to report to you—as always with complete openness and confidence for your information.

Concerning your letter: I was naturally terribly interested in everything you reported about German academic life, and you know how happy I am about your deserved success. It is so important that you found the same recognition in Belgium and Israel as in Germany, or perhaps even greater! From your acceptance of our offer (conditional on Brandeis's agreement, which I would ask you to request *immediately*), further from your remarks concerning the conditions in Berlin, and finally with reference to the whole situation in Berlin, I conclude that you will hardly be prepared to accept Berlin. I have always feared entanglements of the current kind; that they come so quickly and from Mr. Khrushchev may be a "blessing in very effective disguise" (Churchill's words).

With regard to the suggested meeting in Europe, I would in principle be very happy if we could meet in mid-April, for example in Sicily. We can hope and pray that this will be possible: it depends on the degree to which I have come along with the work on my book by then, since this is the main thing. Unfortunately, the best of plans don't help me very much, since my state of health is very labile. In the last few weeks I have had a very serious shortness of breath caused by heart asthma (the insufficient activity of the heart caused water to collect in the lungs) and I had to submit to treatment to drain them, which, although effective for my breathing, has weakened me, all the more if one is allergic to the drugs and has a blood pressure of 105 and a pulse of 110. Unfortunately I have periods in which I can't work at all, and I am behind in everything. I haven't written a single line of the "Type" article for Farber, and not a line of a symposium article for the International Sociological Congress,[1] "A Program for the Sociology of Knowledge," to which I was invited and which is very important to me. Both articles should be finished before my departure in late February, and in addition there are infinitely many things having to do with school and business that have to be dealt with before the end of the year. —So I don't want to make any definite plans for April.

It is really providence that you too have important objections to "free variation." I would have liked to hear your lecture in Louvain. I fear that the eidetic reduction will turn out to be just as indefensible as the solution to the problem of transcendental intersubjectivity. If I succeed, my type essay[2] will show why this is the case.

But now to the important events in our school, which directly concern you. To begin with I should mention that unexpectedly our Psychology Department has a lot of students. There has long been a need for a philosophy course which is designed above all for psychologists. I suggested you, but there was no money. Now I have succeeded in getting a large contribution for the Graduate Faculty, which is to pay your salary (among other things). This is important for the following reason: Jonas is going on *sabbatical* in *Fall '59*. He also wants to take a *leave of absence without pay* in *Spring '60*, since he wants to take his family to Europe for the entire year. Whether he remains away in *Spring '60* as well depends on whether or not he can get enough money from the various foundations to which he has applied. Fulbright isn't a possibility for him, since he is a *Canadian citizen*. But the others don't pay very much. Nonetheless, he and Staudinger, who is handling the negotiations with the foundations, are optimistic. The decision will be made in February. Cairns will take over two of his *Fall* courses on the same conditions as you, plus payment for student advising and thesis direction; by the same token two of his *Spring* courses, should he take *leave of absence*. A third course is to be taken over by an *outsider*. We thought of Paul Weiss, but he declined. Now Jonas has approached Walter Kaufmann for his Nietzsche course. He is in principle agreeable, but wants to give his definitive acceptance some time before Christmas. Should he accept, there wouldn't—in the absence of the money I have arranged—be any money for you. But now it is there and you are invited whether or not Walter Kaufmann accepts. You are also invited for *Spring,* whether Jonas takes a *leave of absence* or not.

Please consider under which two titles your course on the philosophical foundations of psychology can be divided over two semesters so that students can take either part independently of the other. And please prepare *outlines,* early as it is. Your appointment is to be confirmed by the faculty on January 15, and I will need the *outlines* for the catalogue right after that. I will write all of this officially in a couple of days.

But that is only a prelude to a more ambitious program. The current administration wants to have you *full time* for us, the idea being that you give three courses in the Philosophy and three in the Psychology Department (just as I divide my time between philosophy and sociology and belong to both departments). In addition to the reason mentioned above as to why they want to have you in the Psychology Department as well, there is the consideration that Kurt Goldstein will hardly be able to continue teaching after 1960. You are to replace him and represent his direction as his successor, which would hardly signify a *sacrificium intellectus.* Of course, all of this is at the moment a plan and wishful thinking, but perhaps interesting enough.

But the following two circumstances make it even more complicated and interesting: 1) I (as I believe I told you) along with Van Breda have never abandoned the idea of getting the transcribed Husserl manuscripts on *microcards* for the school. You can see from the enclosed copy of Van Breda's letter how this has developed. (This matter is strictly confidential also with respect to Cologne and Freiburg.³ I have only mentioned it to a very few colleagues here, since I have given Van Breda my word that nothing will be said or leaked before the contract is signed.) In addition, I have rounded up the sum needed for financing and brought the whole thing to Simons⁴ in gift wrapping on a silver platter. But he poured cold water on it and may be right: the school isn't the right place for something like this; we (Cairns and I) don't have any trainees; we would be taking on a great deal of responsibility; what is the content of the contract; etc., etc., etc. Result: he wants to go slowly and wants a report from a faculty committee (a president always brings in a committee when he doesn't know what is going on, and he has no idea of phenomenology). Instead, I have constituted a one-man committee which consists of me, and after long meetings and discussions it arrived at the unanimous decision to drop the whole thing, which would only cause me trouble and loss of energy as well as work in both directions. But I have changed my attitude in view of the fact that Cairns is very much for fighting things through, and has set his heart on it. Since Cairns has to have a hernia operation in the next few days, we have put off further steps until the middle of January.

In the meantime, Staudinger let me in on his plan (or wishful thinking? One never knows for sure with friend Staudinger) for you sketched out above. This would of course change everything. For you, Cairns, and finally I would, given the certainty of Jonas's benevolent neutrality, present a fine group of competent phenomenologists which could certainly make something out of the matter.

2) In addition the following coincidence: on the basis of an act of Congress, the Department of Health and Education is granting relatively lucrative subsidies to *graduate faculties,* both to participating students and for new programs at *graduate faculties.* We are working on an *application* for one of them for a *research center* in phenomenology, in which the Philosophy, Psychology, and Sociology Departments would cooperate. (Above all, a *"joint seminar"* is to be established!) We are thinking of Cairns, you, and me, of course. Curiously enough this idea stems from the Psychology Dept., which knew nothing of the action sketched under (1), doesn't know anything, and can't be *allowed* to know anything. Unfortunately, we can't mention this in our application for the above reasons. The program as such has the enthusiastic support of Asch, Henle, Jonas, and of course Cairns and myself. I am very pessimistic that we will receive one cent from the Health and Education Dept. for such a program, good as it is, especially in view of the fact that we are simultaneously proposing a program in economics (*underdeveloped countries*). But in this country one never knows, although the enmity to *all* serious philosophy takes on terrifying dimensions.

(Read, e.g., the two symposium *papers* on humanistic education in the current *Journal of Philosophy*.)

Summing up: If even only two of the three projects (the third or rather first is your *full time job*) are realized, this could open up interesting possibilities for the three of us (Cairns, you, me), for you perhaps more interesting than Brandeis. You may feel more comfortable with us.

But: The general situation at the school has, as you know, great disadvantages, and I want to emphasize them once more in this context:

1) *Financial:* As you know we have no *endowment*. This year (1959) is our *25th Anniversary*. A large *fund-raising* action is planed. If it works out, everything is all right. If not, then in my opinion the future of the Graduate Faculty is on very weak ground. We have over-extended ourselves with our new (second) building.

2) Staudinger and Simons have reached the age limit and will leave us in 1959 and '60. I don't know who will come, but it will be Americans, and that says it all.

3) It is uncertain what they are planning with the Philosophy Department. If I get mad, I will go back to sociology when Salomon goes into *retirement* in 1960.

4) Should the new *ruler* try to tell us what courses we should teach and which not, I shall resign.

This is enough for today, and I only have enough energy left to wish you and your dear wife all imaginable good for the new year. Let us know soon what you think of the whole situation. Sincerely,

Your

Alfred

1. International Sociological Association in Stresa (Milan), September 8–15, 1959.
2. "Type and Eidos in Husserl's Late Philosophy" (S1959b).
3. In addition to the Husserl Archives at Louvain, there are branches of the Archives in Cologne and Freiburg.
4. Hans Simons was President of the New School, Hans Staudinger the Dean of the Graduate Faculty. Cf. Benita Luckmann, in Grathoff and Waldenfels (ed.).

Gurwitsch: *The idea that I should be the successor to Goldstein makes me blush*
              (BENSBERG, JANUARY 9, 1959)

Dearest Friend,

Your long letter of December 20 was here when we returned from a two-week (private) visit to Paris a couple of days ago. Your very brief remarks about your labile state of health have me very concerned. Both of us want to know much more about it: how you are doing after the draining; whether this drainage has to be repeated; what the doctor says about the whole thing and what prognoses he makes. And I have many other questions which I can't formulate, because I don't know what I can ask. But you can easily quiet our agitation if you would ask your dear wife (should it be too boring for you) to write us a very detailed report about the situation. Is it possible to attack the root of the problem, namely the inadequate heart function? Since I know how much you love us, I am counting on receiving a very extensive report in the near future.

As you correctly surmise, in light of the political development, which will make Berlin a *point névralgique,* I have refused the call. The letter which I then received from Herr Weischedel almost brought tears to my eyes. I knew that they wanted me, but I didn't know just *how much* they wanted me. But after my whole life I can't put myself in the situation of a *guerre des nerfs* again, and I was very open about this.

So now that Herr Khrushchev has kept me from going to Berlin, I am very, truly very interested in the New School. (You can of course count on my discretion in all points concerning Louvain.) If they want me at the New School *full time,* I authorize you to announce my willingness in principle. For the moment it cannot be more than a willingness in principle. There are a lot of details that are best discussed *viva voce,* indeed can hardly be discussed any other way. These include, e.g., also the modalities of my being divided between philosophy and psychology.

I am after all not a psychologist in the conventional sense, although there are a certain number of psychological themes, even in the technical sense, that I would be quite happy to treat: Gestalt theory, Piaget, psychology of language *à la* Goldstein and also *à la* Henry Head, etc. (The idea that I should in a certain sense be Goldstein's successor *makes me blush.* I can surely confide my ulterior motives, which are not for public consumption, to the *camarade de mes pensées.* As I read this part of your letter, I immediately had the thought: after all, who are you to dare reach for this crown!?)

For the rest, they can make the division such that I treat some philosophical themes of eminent psychological interest for and in both departments, such as James, Bergson and similar things, Helmholtz too. If they want a philosopher in the Psychology Department, then it is very advisable and very proper to go to those thinkers who have formulated the psychological questions in a fundamental form. And in light of my experience in Cologne it is becoming more and more clear to me that one has to teach the psychologists their own history. But those are *curae posteriores.*

My interest in the New School has also been increased by the fact that in my absence a few things have happened at Brandeis which prove to me that I am no longer up to this den of snakes. I won't bother you with details. Among other things, they terminated Dreyfus,[1] whom you know, behind my back (i.e., without asking my opinion). There was absolutely no reason to do this; the whole thing is a dirty trick. In doing this they wanted to get rid of someone whose loyalty to me is well known.

In Paris I saw, among others, Wahl and Hyppolite, both of whom send their greetings. With Hyppolite I had to play the interpreter of the book you are currently working on. I made do by speaking of your published essays, which I turned into the forerunners of your new book; I hope you have no objections. There is a plan to bring me to Paris for lectures in late April / early May. I am to speak on ideation in Wahl's *Collège,* just as I did in Louvain on Kant-Husserl before the *Société de Philosophie,* just as in Berlin, Brussels, the New School, etc. Then I should have an informal evening or afternoon with students of philosophy at the *Ecole Normale.* The lecture before the *Société* isn't certain yet; that depends on the program, which may already be set, and on the synchronization (in the negative sense) with the *Congrès Bergson.*

We have also changed our plans for Spring. The summer semester in Cologne is beginning earlier than usual—just in this year—on April 15. In addition, Fulbright is paying for the trip to Israel only by airplane. (This concerns currency agreements which I don't completely understand.) Since we want to spend some time in Greece and can only do so on the return trip, I requested that my lectures (there are five or six) begin as early as March 8. Rotenstreich hasn't been able to answer yet. Against this background I wonder if we will be able to organize our *rendezvous.* When are you leaving? Perhaps we can get together here in late February.

Please keep me informed concerning your health. Both of us wish you all—and this time you in a more special sense—love, goodness, and beauty

As always your
Aron

1. Hubert Dreyfus was an Instructor at Brandeis 1957–1959. He is now Professor of Philosophy at the University of California, Berkeley.

Gurwitsch: *Gaston Berger has invited me to speak in Paris before the "Société Française de Philosophie"*
(BENSBERG, JANUARY 20, 1959)

Dear Friend,

Enclosed the *outlines* of the two courses; they can be taken independently of one another. From the *outlines* you will see how I plan to separate the problems. This didn't cause any difficulties. My "biography" is on the same page—years ago I gave, as they assured me, a very honorable *lecture in Wellesley,* but I have forgotten the title and don't have any possibility of looking it up here. If you think it is important to mention it, please check the catalogue for summer school 1957, where I mentioned it. Please excuse this bother.

I have already requested the authorization from Brandeis, but haven't received an answer yet.

Once again not a word concerning your health. We talk about you very often, and sadly enough often about the problem of your health. Please give us a bit more detail so that we don't have to speculate. It would be even better if your reports made these conversations pointless.

I very much hope that Cairns will keep you working on the matter of the Husserl Archives at the New School. I at any rate want to do everything I can to encourage him and strengthen his influence in this matter. I am convinced that we three together could in fact constitute a kind of phenomenological center— by which I do not mean the sometimes grotesque philological meticulosity of the editors which I have seen here and in Louvain. I rather mean a substantive discussion of the substantive problems which are much more important to the three of us, but at least to us two, than the reconstruction of the nuances of Ms. 3753 to 3754.

You know me well enough to know that I generally don't manifest inclinations to megalomania. But I do believe that a trio such as ours could hold up its head before every philosophy department in the whole world. Jonas and Marx too are quite up to comparison. For me, the chance to participate in such a project would be simply enchanting, to say nothing of what the proximity to you would mean to me, both the geographical and the professional. Perhaps you understand what I mean in saying that I would like to move into an academic milieu.

Gaston Berger has invited me to speak (Kant-Husserl) in Paris before the *Société Française de Philosophie* on April 25, and I shall probably also speak on ideation in Wahl's *Collège*. For the rest, I can also report that Walter de Gruyter is interested in a German translation of my book; a translator has also been found.[1] I will read through the translation and make some additions (but only of a literary kind). E.g., when I was writing it the *Crisis* hadn't yet appeared, nor had *Ideas II* and *III*.

Best wishes from us to all of you

Your old
Aron

---

1. It was to be fifteen years before the *Bewußtseinsfeld* appeared (G1975).

Schutz: *Every attempt to clarify the basic concepts of Husserlian philosophy*
          demonstrates the indefensibility of the construction
          (New York, February 3, 1959)

Dearest Friend,

   Aside from our official correspondence, which has been taken care of now
that you have sent in the excellent *outline* for the *Fall* and *Spring Term* courses
59/60 and your biographical *statement,* I have to answer three private letters
from you. To the official business correspondence I only want to add that we
have set your courses for both the *Fall* as well as *Spring Term* on Friday evening
(8:30–10:10). The reason is that at least in the Fall, Dr. Asch wants to hold his
very popular course in Social Psychology from 6:20–8:00, and we wanted to
give the students a chance to hear you on the same evening. Asch will be giving a
seminar in Social Psychology at the same time, but it is generally attended by
only a very few students.
   You so kindly ask about my health and write that you talk about me with
your wife very often. Unfortunately, there isn't much to say. I have to reconcile
myself to the fact that I have been hit hard, and can only hope that the present
acute state, as my doctor promises, will go over into a milder permanent state. I
don't want to bother you with medical details, but things have gone so far with
me that I can't walk one block without having breathing difficulties, and I get
terribly tired as a result of my low blood pressure. My capacity to work has been
reduced to a fraction, and it is still uncertain whether the trip to Europe might
remain a pious wish. —Just between us, I am afraid that if this state doesn't
improve, I will hardly be able to continue my activity at the New School this Fall
in a responsible way. I have already reduced my business activity to a minimum.
   This state of my health also has the consequence that I don't plan to write
Perelmann concerning the invitation to Brussels. I also received an invitation
from Biemel to speak in Cologne, and also another invitation to participate in a
symposium on the sociology of knowledge at the International Sociology Congress in Milan/Stresa. I don't think that there is much chance that I will be able
to accept these invitations. If I go to Europe I shall have to devote my little bit of
energy to finishing the planned book; further, to writing the afterword to the
second edition of the *Sinnhafte Aufbau,* which Springer will publish in Vienna.
Finally, I am also negotiating with a publisher here concerning a collection of
my most important English articles, which I want to collect in one volume under
the title "The Problem of Reality of the Social World."[1]
   I will soon be 60 years old, and successes at lectures and congresses don't
mean much to me any more. But above all I have to avoid trips and exertion, and
I hardly think that we will be able to see one another in Europe, unless you can
come through Vienna. At any rate, keep me informed as to your address when
you leave Cologne.

I don't have to tell you how happy I am at your multiple successes. This year has truly been very important for you.

With regard to the New School, after much reflection I have decided to do nothing for the time being concerning the Husserl manuscripts. A main reason was the cool reception of the project on all sides, which was then joined by objections from Jonas. I would only have more work and effort and thanklessness from both sides in the whole thing. Since President Simons and Dean Staudinger will retire in the next 18 months, I also have no idea what the new administration's attitude will be to all of these philosophical endeavors I told you about. In the hope that you will come and perhaps take over the matter along with Cairns, I shall handle the negotiations with Louvain in such a way that I say that I would first like to become acquainted with the intentions of my new administration before I assume a moral obligation to Louvain.

Now, with regard to the plan of your permanent activity at the Graduate Faculty, there is the news that the *Education Committee* has sent the pressing request to the *Trustees* that a *Full Professor in Psychology* and one in *Philosophy* be named as soon as possible. Dean Staudinger, whom I informed of your letter to me of January 9, asked me confidentially to place an excerpt from it at his disposal; I did so, retouching the wording of your letter a bit. I am enclosing a copy of this letter to Staudinger.

I am having great difficulty with my essay for Farber, which is to have the title "Type and Eidos in Husserl's Late Philosophy." I may be in an especially critical mood, but every attempt at a clarification of the basic concepts of Husserlian philosophy demonstrates the indefensibility of the construction. If I should succeed in finishing the work, I shall have a copy made for you and send it to you.

With all the best

Your

Alfred

1. Later edited by Maurice Natanson: *The Problem of Social Reality* (S1962).

Gurwitsch: *At a conference in Frankfurt everyone admitted that he no longer knows what science is*
(BENSBERG, FEBRUARY 17, 1959)

Dear Friend,

The report on your state of health in your last letters didn't make me very happy. Nevertheless, if the doctor expects a stabilization at a tolerable level, that means that you will be able to function to some extent as long as you are careful. You will no longer be able to be the "Atlas" who takes on all burdens and responsibilities, but intellectually you will be able to do and achieve what is most important for you, even if you have to be careful how you expend your energy. So far as that may be from an absolutely satisfactory state, I wish you *rebus sic stantibus* that this stabilization is realized soon and that it does so at the best and highest possible level. But you have to go easy on yourself until that happens, and afterward too. I can well imagine how that goes against your grain, but now your intelligible character has to gain the causality of action, and that under the imperatives of practical reason in the hygienic understanding. (How do you like the burlesque?[1])

We are flying to Israel on March 2. I will give five or six lectures in Israel, then perhaps one more in Italy (Bari). I am invited to Paris for the end of April (*Ecole Normale, Collège* by Wahl, *Société Française* by Berger).

Two weeks ago I took part in a conference on science and pseudo-science in Frankfurt (one of the most interesting meetings in my life). Astronomers, physicists, chemists, physiologists, but also theorists of science and two philosophers all admitted that they no longer know what science really is. Szilasi and I made the attempt to interpret a piece of Hegel's philosophy of nature to them, and you should have seen how seriously for example Freundlich (Einstein's colleague) listened. *Comment les temps changent!!* That brought me an invitation to speak on Leibniz in May at Oxford, but not by the philosophers—God protect me—but in the History and Philosophy of Science.

I was very interested to see from your letter that the New School wants another psychologist and a philosopher. For very egoistical reasons I would hope that you get the philosopher's position approved very soon, and I would like to announce my claim on the position. Along with you and Cairns, I throw down the gauntlet to any other team. I have contact with South Americans here, and when they ask me about the U.S.A. I always recommend the *Philosophy Department* at the New School. From a distance one actually sees even more clearly what possibilities exist in addition to the realities at the New School. *A propos:* it is of course quite all right with me that you gave Staudinger the relevant passages from one of my letters.

I hope that things are going well. Let us hear from you. Love from house to house

Your true

Aron

---

1. A "burlesque" of Kant's practical philosophy.

Alice and Aron Gurwitsch in Israel to Ilse Schutz
(MARCH 2, 1959)

Dear Friends,

Many thanks, dear Frau Ilse, for your letter in which you report on developments, and also for informing us so promptly and exactly. We were dismayed that poor Fredi had to undergo the operations; we are so sorry that he had to suffer through all of that; and we can well imagine what you have been through. Perhaps his general condition will really improve now. What you write about heart, breathing, etc., really does give cause for hope in this direction, and the doctors too think it probable.

May it all have been a *blessing in disguise*. I am writing these lines shortly before holding a lecture—but I was anxious to write to you immediately. Please give him our best greetings and most sincere wishes for a good and total recovery. And you too will need a recuperation in your own way.

Most sincerely from both of us to all of you

Your
Aron

Many many loving greetings and above all a good recovery

Your
Alice G.

Gurwitsch: *To begin with, Israel—fascinating—but it is not a Jewish country*
(BENSBERG, MAY 9, 1959)

Dear Friend,

It has been a long time since I have had any direct news from you, not since the letter which your dear wife sent to us in Israel, in which she told us about the double operation and also about the favorable general medical prognosis. I heard indirectly from Berger in Paris that you are doing well. We would both be very happy to get word from you directly that the good prognosis has been confirmed, i.e., that you are on the way not only to a special but general recuperation.

The long trip has come to an end. There is a great deal to tell. It was as interesting as it was exhausting: 12 lectures in two months. First Israel: we saw the desert this time; that is an experience which one has to have. It doesn't consist of uniformly yellow sand on a flat surface; the sand is yellow and black and green and red, and the mountains are 1000 meters high and more; still higher in Sinai, which is not accessible. One can only understand what it means that a hermit withdraws into the desert when one has been there, where one is truly alone with God and, as it were, withdrawn from the hustle and bustle of human life.

The country as such is unique and fascinating. But it isn't a Jewish country— at least not in the sense, or in any sense, which we connect with "Jewish." To be sure, in Jerusalem you can go from the Central Europe of the twentieth century to the Persia of the fourteenth or to Buchara in the twelfth in twenty minutes. But these are enclaves which, even if they survive a long time, will remain enclaves. The essential thing is that the world is no longer in any sense questionable for the people who are growing up there, that for them problems have the sense of difficulties which are to be solved, but no longer refer to deeper uncertainties. One shouldn't make evaluative judgments, but they are different from us, and they in turn don't understand people like us and have no desire to understand us. Perhaps *tant pis pour nous* or *tant pis pour eux,* but that's the way it is.

The students at the university are quite bright and take things very seriously. It is astonishing how much they know about Husserl. This is Rotenstreich's work. No one talks just to hear himself talk and to show how clever and brilliant he is, how he has already seen through everything. This contrast to what I am used to at Brandeis has done me good.

For certain reasons I had to speak to the psychoanalysts in Tel Aviv (in German). I spoke on the principles of a phenomenologically oriented psychology, and demonstrated to begin with the theoretical and general historical roots of the Freudian conceptual framework. These are people of our generation and ten years younger. They have no idea of what is going on in the world, of the tendencies in France and Holland. The only thing they know is what is going on in psychoanalysis in the U.S.A. Binswanger, Minkowski, Buytendijk are almost unknown. It was very instructive.

After Israel came Italy: Rome, Florence, Milan. In Rome I spoke on "Ideation" at the Congress for the Philosophy of Science. A substantial part of the audience was French. Unfortunately, the discussion got off on the question of whether bees and birds have symbolic systems. As Bernays finally got to speak, his brief words and references to gaps in my presentation (these gaps were deliberate for purposes of presentation) confirmed my theory in a very desirable sense. The great confirmation came in the lecture by Fréchet, which followed mine: "L'abstrait dans les mathématiques." What Fréchet said was basically well known, but presented against his background of broad and sovereign knowledge, and his discussions were absolutely permeated by mathematical culture. You can only hear such things from old Frenchmen. His entire lecture brought me confirming examples for what I said or merely thought about formalization. You know my fear of losing touch with ongoing research, especially in the mathematical-logical realm. Fréchet exorcised this fear, but simultaneously the contrast with *Nagel e tutti quanti* and their formulations was unavoidable.

In Milan I made the discovery of a phenomenological center which Paci (the way prepared by Banfi) has brought to life in two years. Paci is a genuine Husserl missionary, and his students are infected by his zeal. I told them about you. Send him some off-prints: he is very interested in us, asked me about my bibliography. He wants to stay in contact. We will have to see what comes of it. But the whole thing looks good; he wants to create a center of phenomenological *studies,* but not *editions.* For the moment it is all in the stage of assimilation and appropriation, but it is very good that we are catching hold in Italy.

In Paris I spoke before Wahl's *Collège* at the *Ecole Normale* (the finest of the fine) and before the *Société Françise de Philosophie* under the chairmanship of Berger. With regard to Paris I can be brief: *je fus chez moi.* I am enclosing a copy of the invitation to the lecture at the *Société;* you may find it interesting.

Simultaneously, but not via air mail, I am sending you your copy of an article I have written for the *Zeitschrift für philosophische Forschung,* the occasion being the Husserl anniversary.[1] As you will see, it consists of excerpts from my book. My batteries are exhausted for the moment; I have given all that I had; it is time to read, to think for a while, and not have to produce anything. It is a good thing that I now have a longer period in which to read a part of the literature on Leibniz and Kant before I finish the book. (The French want me to write it in French; the Germans insist that it be written in German; *quoi faire???*)

Classes have started in Cologne once more: I am lecturing on the "Constitution of Philosophical Rationalism and the Mathematical Natural Sciences in the Seventeenth Century." Some of my students from last semester have made faces over this being my last semester in Cologne. They had hoped that I would stay so that they could write their dissertations under me. This lecture has 100 students, the one last semster had 70. How easy it is to be a success in Europe. And I have the feeling that I would have even more resonance in France or even Milan than in Germany.

All the best, and let us hear from you. Best wishes from us to all of you,

As always, your

Aron

1. G1959a.

Appendix: Invitation to Gurwitsch's lecture at the Sorbonne on 4.25.1959 (excerpt).

Société Française de Philosophie
C.C.P. Raymond Bayer, Paris 5693.03

Vous êtes cordialement invité à assister à la prochaine réunion de la Société Française de Philosophie, qui se tiendra le Samedi 25 Avril 1959, à 16 h. 30, à la Sorbonne, Faculté des Lettres, Salle Cavaillès, Escalier C, Ier étage (couloir de droite).

Sujet traité:

La Conception de la Conscience
chez Kant et chez Husserl

M. Aron Gurwitsch, Professeur à l'Université Brandeis, Waltham (Mass., U.S.A.) se propose de développer devant les membres de la Société les arguments suivants:

Une étude comparée de la philosophie théorique de Kant et de la phénoménologie husserlienne aurait ou être déjà tentée à la suite de la publication, en 1913, du primier volume des *Ideen zu einer reinen Phänomenologie und phänomenologischen Philosophie* (trad. par M. P. Ricoeur sous le titre *Idées directrices pour une phénoménologie*), ouvrage dont les tendances kantianisantes n'ont pas passé inaperçues. Non seulement Kant et Husserl figurent parmi les théoriciens les plus éminents de la subjectivité, mais encore, s'ils descendent dans les profondeurs de la vie subjective, ils le font en vue de rendre compte de l'objectivité. En replaçant les object à l'intérieur de la vie consciente d'où ils tirent leur origine, il devient possible de poursuivre l'objectivité jusqu'à ses racines dans cette vie et de la faire ressortir comme produit de la subjectivité. C'est en ces termes que l'on peut décrire le but de Husserl. Les mêmes termes se prêtent aussi, nous semble-t-il, à caractériser les intentions de Kant, du moins dans une certaine approximation. . . .

Prière d'adresser les observations au Pr. Gurwitsch, 12, rue Colbert, Paris 2e

Schutz: *My body doesn't function at all properly any more*
          (New York, May 16, 1959)

Dear Friend,

It was good to get a letter from you after so long. If I haven't written to you, it was because you didn't give me an address where I could reach you.

Since you ask about my health, I have to tell you that the two operations only dealt with a relatively secondary matter. My heart problems have gotten worse, and the operations did their part here, of course. I am in such bad condition that I intend, if we can find something appropriate, to go to a sanatorium in Switzerland to recuperate. My body doesn't function correctly at all any more: the major difficulty is that all available medicines cause terrible allergies in me. Work on the planned book is out of the question.

Under these circumstances you will forgive me if I am brief and don't discuss your so interesting travel report. I will restrict myself to extending my sincere congratulations for your great success. Between us I don't need to assure you how happy I am that you receive recognition everywhere.

I only want to touch on two things:

1) It seems to me to be very important that you get in contact with Voegelin as soon as possible, if you haven't already done so. He complains that he hasn't heard from you and writes that he might have the possibility of a teaching position at a major German university for you.

May 21, 1959

Dear Mrs. Schutz:

May I beg you to let me share your sorrow?
For I too loved Alfred Schutz.

I admired him as one of the greatest scholars
I have known in my life. I loved him as a man who
used his scholarship, not imperially, to subjugate
inferior men, but humanly, to help them to a higher
level of thought.

He was the good genius of the aspiring thinker.
How many I have met who acknowledged gratefully their
debt to Alfred Schutz, philosopher and teacher, but
more than that, carrier and transmitter of the intellectual light that shone in the ancient Academy and Lyceum.

A great man does not die. His spirit goes on,
working among us. It enters into the collective life
of man, bearing no name, indeed, but in the upward
movement of man it is spirit not name that signifies.

Sincerely,

Alvin Johnson

Alvin Johnson

Mrs. Alfred Schutz
25 West 81st Street
New York 24, New York

2) The second thing concerns the Graduate Faculty. I don't know if I have written to you that Jonas too considers you the first candidate for the second full-professorship which has now been given to the Philosophy Department. He only thought of Jacob Klein for personal reasons. But he turned down an offer from the Graduate Faculty. We will have a new Dean beginning in Fall 1959. I had a long conversation with him concerning the future of the Philosophy Department, and everything depends on whether the new Dean and the new President—Simons reaches retirement age in 1960—want to turn the Graduate Faculty into a general forest-and-meadow faculty, or whether they believe that it is its mission to bring European theory to America, not only in philosophy but in all disciplines. Luckily, the Dean is of the latter opinion, and that is of course a great asset [*Aktivum*] for your candidacy. Otherwise we would of course have a pressing need for a neo-positivist or a symbolic logician in order to round out our program.

Please let us hear from you soon. Best greetings to you and your dear wife.

Always your
Alfred

Aron Gurwitsch to Ilse Schutz
(COLOGNE, JULY 18, 1959)

Dear Frau Ilse,

I was very happy when I saw your handwriting. That it is difficult for you—difficult to the point of being impossible—to write letters is something we understand only too well; we know very well how you feel now and what your situation is. There is not much that one can say in such circumstances.

My wife notified you of my vacation address. I sent it to Natanson shortly before our departure from Cologne, just as you requested, and also to Dean Staudinger, who also requested it.

If my calculations are correct, Georgie has now graduated. What will he do now? Will he remain in New York so that you will be with both children at least for the near future?

We will arrive in New York on September 2. We will get in touch as soon as we have finished with the harbor formalities. You can believe us that the impossibility of seeing you was and is a great burden for us.

Best greetings to you and the children

Your
Aron Gurwitsch

Aron Gurwitsch. © Alexandre Métraux.

Supplement: Letter to Dean Staudinger, July 16, 1959

Dear Dean Staudinger:

My vacation address (from July 20 to August 20) will be Hotel Edelweiß—Sils-Maria (Engadin) Switzerland.

The catalog for the coming year already contains my biography and also the outline of two of my courses. Long ago I sent you the descriptions of four further courses, and some time later I received from the New School copies of these descriptions. However, I do not remember which office sent me the copies (carbon copies on blue paper).

I spoke with Dr. Jonas over the phone. We shall see each other in Switzerland.

Please excuse the form of this letter, which I am writing a few hours before my departure. Tomorrow I shall write to Mrs. Schutz from Basel.

With kindest personal regards.

Cordially yours,

Aron Gurwitsch

Supplement: Gurwitsch's note on the death of Alfred Schutz (*PPR* 20 (1959): 141–143).

Alfred Schuetz (1899–1959)

On May 20, 1959, Alfred Schuetz died in New York City; he is survived by his wife Ilse, his daughter Evelyn, and his son George. A native of Vienna, he lived in that city until 1938, when the occupation of Austria by the Nazis compelled him and his family to emigrate from the country of their birth. The following year they settled in New York City and in due course became naturalized American citizens.

He had studied law in Vienna, where H. Kelsen had been one of his teachers. After he had acquired his degree he joined a banking firm in which he came to hold a most responsible position and with which he remained in association throughout his life. In New York he became affiliated with the New School for Social Research and for many years combined his work in the banking firm with his academic duties. Since the foundation of the International Phenomenologial Society, he was a member of its Council, and since the inception of this journal, he belonged to its board of editors.

Alfred Schuetz was a person of an almost unique kind: he had a large variety of interests, the widest general culture, a cosmopolitan outlook. Very rarely indeed does one encounter a man of such thoroughgoing learning and perfect competence in highly diverse fields as Schuetz had in philosophy, the social sciences, music, and literature. Whatever he undertook, he did from the perspective of his broad and encompassing knowledge. His mind was as penetrating, sharp, and keen as his heart was warm and generous. There was something radiant in him. He shouldered responsibilities that often seemed to surpass the capacities of a single man. The universally respected scholar of international reputation was at the same time an urbane man of the world, a gentleman with all the nobility of character which this word connotes.

The fields to which he mainly devoted his work were philosophy and the social sciences; thus he became a philosopher of the social sciences and of social reality. His interest in philosophy was aroused at a rather early phase of his intellectual development and he felt himself drawn to thinkers such as Bergson, W. James, Husserl, Scheler, and Sartre, whose ideas he presented, interpreted, and discussed in his several writings with that independence of mind which was so characteristic of him. Among the classical philosophers of the past, it was especially Leibniz who had captured his attention and of whose work he had detailed knowledge and intimate understanding. The philosophical problems which were to him of major importance and to which he repeatedly devoted his efforts were those related to temporality and intersubjectivity in all their forms. This specific philosophical orientation of his thinking led Schuetz to view social relationships and actions under the "subjective" perspective, i.e., as they are lived and experienced by the actors involved, rather than considering them exclusively, or even primarily, from the point of view of the onlooking observer and the disinterested theoretician. In the focus of his interest was human existence in the social world which he tried to explore in all its dimensions, ramifications, and stratifications. Such an eludication was also to throw light on the fundamental concepts used in the social sciences and on the presuppositions on which these sciences rest. Schuetz's familiarity with the social sciences and social reality proved highly fruitful for his work in philosophy proper. It gave concreteness to his analyses and enabled him to bring to philosophy, especially phenomenology, original points of view and to open up new horizons. With remarkable consistency he adhered to this orientation of his work from his early book (to be reprinted) *Der sinnvolle [sic!] Aufbau der sozialen Welt*—an analysis of M. Weber's sociological concepts in the light of ideas of Bergson and Husserl—up to the numerous important articles in the English language, most of which he published in this journal and in *Social Research*. Some time ago he conceived the plan of a new book to be entitled "The World as Taken for Granted" in which he intended to work out and to complete what he had begun in his articles, and to present in a systematic and elaborated form the results at which he had arrived. Tragic events have put a premature end to his endeavors and projects.

Alfred Schuetz was esteemed, respected, and loved by his colleagues who knew that they could rely on him in all situations. He was admired and cherished by his students, some of whom are indebted to him for the decisive turn he had given to their intellectual development. To those who were privileged to be his friends, his friendship was one of the most precious gifts of their lives. His scholarly contributions will be points of departure for much research work to be done in the years to come. He will leave a lasting imprint on the work of all whose interests move along lines similar to those he followed.

Aron Gurwitsch

New School for Social Research.

Afterword

J. Claude Evans

It is a cruel irony that although as early as 1948 Alfred Schutz and Aron Gurwitsch began discussing the possibility of a position for Gurwitsch alongside Schutz at the New School for Social Research, it was Schutz's illness and then death that finally brought Gurwitsch to The Graduate Faculty of the New School. There Gurwitsch was at last able to concentrate on graduate teaching, and he found a circle of excellent students, many of whom had specifically come to study phenomenology with Schutz and Dorion Cairns. For Gurwitsch the teacher, these were to be satisfying years, after his early despair that his voice would never be heard in his new intellectual environment (cf. GS 12.15.1946).

As teachers, both Schutz and Gurwitsch had an extraordinary impact on their students. In his dedication speech for the establishment of the Husserl Archives at the New School for Social Research as a memorial to Alfred Schutz, Richard Zaner spoke about Schutz the teacher:

> A man of great personal character, bearing, and engaging warmth, Alfred Schutz gave unstintingly of himself to his many students. . . . In his teaching and his writings—in courses and in counsel with students—he constantly insisted on the necessity of serious study of the works of thinkers of every persuasion and discipline. . . . He constantly sought out what was common to the divergent currents of thought rather than what separated them.[1]

To anyone lucky enough to study with him, Gurwitsch was an impressive teacher, cut from the cloth of the German university tradition. His scope was imposing, ranging from courses on specific issues and/or figures to historical surveys. The latter invariably provided a thesis that demonstrated the unity of an historical development and had a systematic intent. Although he did not use notes, his lectures were beautifully organized and timed to fit the period available. Many of his lectures were taped and transcribed by students. His seminars on Piaget, Cassirer, Husserl's *Cartesian Meditations,* etc., and his famous two-semester seminar on the *Critique of Pure Reason* had a different structure. In the seminars, student reports on the text under discussion were subjected to a careful critique, after which Gurwitsch would open the text, glance at it, and begin speaking, pausing at times for discussion. He would then glance at the next section of the text and resume his commentary with a characteristic "Ah yes. . . ."[2]

His students learned many things from Gurwitsch above and beyond a command of the texts studied or Gurwitsch's views of them. They learned a respect for the historical tradition, which was never treated as dead history but rather as the historical background against which it becomes possible to understand our own world and our own problems. They learned a care and rigor in dealing with texts and problems, a sober fair-mindedness that preceded all questions of agreement or disagreement. Above all, Gurwitsch taught by example the Platonically erotic passion for thinking and an intense impatience with unclarity (especially one's own), a passion for pursuing questions wherever they might lead.

A measure of the impression made by Gurwitsch's teaching is reflected in the dedication of Henry Allison's *Kant's Transcendental Idealism,* which Lewis White Beck, the dean of American Kant scholars, has called "probably the most comprehensive and substantial study of the *Critique of Pure Reason* written by any American philosopher"; it reads, "To the memory of Aron Gurwitsch, with whom I began my study of Kant."[3] Allison, whose dissertation on Lessing was the first directed by Gurwitsch, so dedicated his book in spite of the fact that his own Kant interpretation differed radically from that of Gurwitsch.

Aron Gurwitsch died in Zurich on June 25, 1973. He was on his way to the first colloquium on social phenomenology in Constance/Gottlieben, West Germany, where he was to speak on "Merleau-Ponty's Phenomenology of Perception in the Light of Husserlian Critique."[4]

The reader of the correspondence is not prepared for the surprising turn that Gurwitsch's work took in the 1960s. Although one can follow, through the letters, the development of a monograph containing his "Kant interpretation in Leibnizian perspective" (GS 1.27.1957), with Gurwitsch himself announcing that "the end of the first draft . . . is almost in sight" (GS 8.10.1958), he ultimately abandoned this manuscript, which was for all practical purposes finished.[5] Instead of publishing the Kant monograph, he devoted the 1960s to working on a monumental book on Leibniz, which appeared after his death (G1974a).

This unusual abandonment of a nearly finished book requires some explanation. Gurwitsch once told Maurice Natanson that when he was unable to resolve a problem he had raised at a certain point, he stopped work on the manuscript.[6] It has generally been understood that what was at issue was an unsolved problem in Gurwitsch's Kant interpretation itself, but the text of the monograph shows no traces of an unsolved problem of interpretation. The shift from Kant to Leibniz begins to make sense if one takes into account that all of Gurwitsch's work in the history of philosophy ultimately had a systematic intent: an issue was of interest if it threw light on genuine systematic problems. Thus, it may be that the "unsolved problem" was a systematic one that Kant was unable to solve, and not a problem in Kant interpretation that Gurwitsch could not solve.[7] There are intimations of this explanation in the correspondence itself. Gurwitsch writes, "I think I have shown how and why Husserl can solve problems where Kant failed. (That is by the way the systematic chapter which I promised you a year ago . . .)" (GS 8.10.1958).

In his essay "The Kantian and Husserlian Conceptions of Consciousness" (G1960), Gurwitsch developed this point in terms of the problem of accounting for a series of perceptions of a stable thing. According to Gurwitsch, Kant can at most account for a series of sequences of *similar* sensory data in which there is, however, no identical thing that appears. Gurwitsch rejects H. J. Paton's claim that Kant "deliberately identified 'sensory data' with 'sensible qualities' as states of things,"[8] arguing rather that what Kant calls sensory data are psychical facts whose objectification cannot yield the consciousness of identical objects.

This argument is developed at some length in chapter IX (the "systematic chapter") of the monograph. Gurwitsch accuses Kant of remaining unclear about the distinction between sense data and the qualitative properties of things. Indeed, he thinks that this occurs precisely at the point at which such a distinction has to be presupposed by Kant's own argument, that is, in the "Analogies of Experience." Whereas in the essay Gurwitsch had rejected Paton's claim that Kant identifies sensory data with the sensory qualities of things, in the monograph he *appeals* to Paton:

> The important point here, namely the *identification of representations [Vorstell-ungen] or sensory data with properties or states of things,* was seen clearly by Paton. According to him it is an essential teaching of Kant's critical philosophy that "objective events are only appearances to human minds, and may even be described as ideas," as well as vice versa, "actual and possible sense-perceptions are to be regarded as states of permanent objects," such that Kant has created a "deliberate identification" of sensory data with the states or properties of things.[9]

As Gurwitsch notes, on this reading Kant turns out to be "not so different" from Locke, Berkeley, and Hume.

Now one might argue that this reading of Kant is psychologistic and misses the significance of Kant's transcendental turn. Kant does in fact employ the vocabulary of the theory of ideas found in the pre-Kantian tradition, but arguments such as the "Refutation of Idealism" require that terms such as "representation [*Vorstellung*]" and "intuition" be given what Gurwitsch would have called a *noematic* interpretation in many contexts.[10] Such a reading would lead to a very different interpretation of Kant's answer to the problem Gurwitsch poses.

Be this as it may, given Gurwitsch's interpretation of Kant he is surely correct in claiming that Kant cannot give an adequate account of the consciousness of identity. As a result of this state of affairs, Gurwitsch, I suspect, simply lost interest, not in Kant (since he continued to teach the *Critique* using his "Leibnizian" perspective) but in the Kant monograph. He had shown to his satisfaction that a "Leibnizian" reading cast great light on Kant, but from a systematic point of view this only led so far and ended in a philosophically untenable situation—untenable even from the point of view of the Kantian approach itself. Having exhausted what he took to be the resources of the Kantian position, his attention rather naturally shifted to Leibniz, since early in 1958 he had written to Schutz, "I have finally understood what Hume signifies (the shattering of connections [or contexts: *Zusammenhänge*]): that Kant did not succeed in doing justice to the phenomenon of connection [*Zusammenhang*], i.e., in restituting connection, and that one can only develop a theory of connections with Leib-nizian concepts" (GS 1.15.1958).

Leibniz is a presence throughout the correspondence, Gurwitsch expressing in 1952 his amazement at "just how much my theory of perceptual implications seems to be of Leibnizian inspiration" (GS 3.9.1952). Thus, when Gurwitsch accuses Kant of falling back into a Berkeleyan style of phenomenalism or a Humean atomism, he is pointing to a problem which not only Husserl but also Leibniz could solve, each in his own context and way, of course. The very tools which were to open the door to a more adequate understanding of Kant are now to be investigated in their own context. The result was *Leibniz: Philosophie des Panlogismus* (G1974a), which appeared after Gurwitsch's death. Gurwitsch inter-prets Leibniz's philosophy as a "panlogism," according to which "the universe presents a realized and incarnated logic," such that "order and connectedness [*Verknüpftheit*] rule in the universe as a whole as well as in all of its parts" (G1974a, 18). This places the concept of the "internal relation or connection [*innerer Zusammenhang*]" (cf. Ch. 1, §2) at the center of the interpretation of the system of substances, the inner structure of individual substances and the phenomenal realm (Chapters 5, 6 and 7 respectively). As Gurwitsch points out, the Leibnizian logic of internal relations has its contemporary counterpart in the problem of the organization of consciousness. In this context he mentions Berg-son and Merleau-Ponty, as well as his own concepts of "Gestalt coherence" and "functional significance," in *The Field of Consciousness* (G1964a). Thus, Leib-nizian panlogism finds its counterpart in Gurwitsch's theory of context and Gestalt contexture. The result of a decade of intensive work, Gurwitsch's *Leibniz* is *the* book to date on Leibniz in the sense that, more than any other work, it offers a coherent and detailed interpretation of the Leibnizian system as a whole while summarizing a century of Leibniz scholarship.

Gurwitsch continued to write essays in phenomenology while working on *Leibniz*. In the "Introduction" he announced his intention to devote the years remaining him to Husserlian phenomenology,[11] but he was unable to write the projected book on the phenomenology of logic. A number of posthumous publications appeared; these are listed in the Gurwitsch bibliography in this volume. A bibliography of secondary literature on Gurwitsch can be found in the 1981 issue of the *Journal of the British Society for Phenomenology*. This special issue, edited by Lester Embree, is dedicated to Gurwitsch.

Following Schutz's death, his friends took up the task of making his pub-lished work more easily available to a broad public. The three volumes of Schutz's *Collected Papers* appeared in 1962, 1964, and 1966, edited by Maurice Natanson, Arvid Brodersen, and Aron Gurwitsch, respectively. The only book which Schutz himself saw published, *Der sinnhafte Aufbau der sozialen Welt* (S1932a), appeared in English as *The Phenomenology of the Social World* in 1967.[12] The book on the problem of relevance on which Schutz worked be-tween 1947 and 1951 (cf. SG 10.4.1950: "I am with book") was edited by Richard Zaner (S1970b), who had studied with both Schutz and Gurwitsch. The partially written *Structures of the Life-World* (cf. SG 11.1.58) was completed by Thomas Luckmann, who had studied with Schutz at the New School (S1973 and S1984). Schutz's influence began to spread more broadly in the 1960s. Perhaps the most immediate example of his impact is the ethnomethodology founded by Harold Garfinkel,[13] but in recent years Schutz's work has become increasingly relevant to virtually every field of the human sciences.

The systematic investigation of social milieux pursued by Richard Grathoff, the editor of this correspondence, is a particularly interesting example, since he has used this correspondence itself in reconstructing the milieux in which emigrant scholars from Europe lived and worked.[14] A recent volume, *Worldly Phenomenology: The Continuing Influence of Alfred Schutz on North American Human Science,* edited by Lester Embree, contains a series of essays reviewing Schutz's influence in various fields and discussing the potential that Schutz's work has for these disciplines; it also includes a large bibliography of secondary literature on Schutz.

The following is a selected bibliography of secondary works on Aron Gurwitsch and Alfred Schutz.

Cox, Ronald R. *Schutz's Theory of Relevance: A Phenomenological Critique.* The Hague: Martinus Nijhoff, 1978.

Grathoff, Richard. *The Structure of Social Inconsistencies.* The Hague: Martinus Nijhoff, 1970.

Grathoff, Richard, and Bernhard Waldenfels, eds. *Sozialität und Intersubjektivität: Phänomenologische Perspektiven der sozialwissenschaften im Umkreis von Aron Gurwitsch und Alfred Schütz.* Munich: Wilhelm Fink Verlag, 1983.

Embree, Lester, ed. *Life-World and Consciousness: Essays for Aron Gurwitsch.* Evanston: Northwestern University Press, 1972.

———, ed. *The Phenomenology of Gurwitsch.* Special issue of the *Journal of the British Society for Phenomenology* 12 (1981). Contains a bibliography of secondary literature on Gurwitsch.

———, ed. *Worldly Phenomenology: The Continuing Influence of Alfred Schutz on North American Human Science.* Washington, D.C.: The Center for Advanced Research in Phenomenology & University Press of America, 1988. Contains a bibliography of English literature on Schutz.

Natanson, Maurice. *Anonymity: A Study in the Philosophy of Alfred Schutz.* Evanston: Northwestern University Press, 1986.

Thomason, Burke C. *Making Sense of Reification: Alfred Schutz and Constructivist Theory.* Atlantic Highlands: Humanities Press, 1982.

Wagner, Helmut. *Alfred Schutz: An Intellectual Biography.* Chicago: University of Chicago Press, 1983.

Wolff, Kurt H., and George Psathas. *Alfred Schutz: Appraisals and Developments.* The Hague: Martinus Nijhoff, 1984.

NOTES

1. Richard Zaner, "Dedication Speech: Alfred Schutz Memorial," April 2, 1969, at The Graduate Faculty of the New School for Social Research.

2. See also Lester Embree, "The Legacy of Dorion Cairns and Aron Gurwitsch: A Letter to Future Historians" in E. F. Kaelin and C. O. Schrag (eds.), *Phenomenology in America* (Dordrecht: Kluwer, 1989), 130–131.

3. Henry E. Allison, *Kant's Transcendental Idealism* (New Haven: Yale University Press, 1983), v. Beck's statement is on the dust cover.

4. Cf. R. Grathoff and W. Sprondel, *Maurice Merleau-Ponty und das Problem der Struktur in den Sozialwissenschaften* (Stuttgart: Enke, 1976).

5. The manuscript is being edited for publication by Thomas Seebohm.

6. Personal communication from Maurice Natanson. The date of this remark could not be determined.

7. This general hypothesis has been confirmed by Dr. Bethia Currie, who studied with Gurwitsch in the mid-1960s and discussed both Kant and the Kant monograph with him in some detail.

8. "The Kantian and Husserlian Conceptions of Consciousness" (G1960), trans. Richard Zaner, in *Studies in Phenomenology and Psychology* (Evanston: Northwestern University Press, 1966), 158.

9. Monograph, ch. 9. Quotations are from H. J. Paton, *Kant's Metaphysics of Experience* (London: Routledge & Kegan Paul, 1936), vol. II, 253 and 306f.

10. See Joseph Claude Evans, Jr., *The Metaphysics of Transcendental Subjectivity: Descartes, Kant and W. Sellars* (Amsterdam: Verlag B. R. Grüner, 1984), 47f., 53–55, and 72–74.

11. G1974a, 9.

12. Translated by George Walsh and Frederick Lehnert (Evanston: Northwestern University Press, 1967). The translation is unfortunately very unreliable.

13. See Harold Garfinkel, *Studies in Ethnomethodology* (Englewood Cliffs: Prentice-Hall, 1967).

14. Cf. Grathoff's Afterword to the German edition of this correspondence.

Bibliography

I. Bibliography of the Writings of Alfred Schutz[1]

1. Shorter book reviews and pieces on contemporary issues concerning economic policy (mostly in Viennese papers) have not been systematically collected. The editor and the Archives in Constance would appreciate references and copies.

Abbreviations:

CP I, II, III: *Collected Papers,* volumes I, II, III (cf. Schutz 1962, S1964a, S1966a)
PPR: *Philosophy and Phenomenological Research*

1932a Der sinnhafte Aufbau der sozialen Welt: Eine Einleitung in die verstehende Soziologie. Vienna, 1932, 1960[2]; Frankfurt, 1974[3]. (Translations into English, 1967; Spanish, 1972; Italian, 1974; Polish, in preparation.)

1932b Review: Edmund Husserl, *Méditations Cartésiennes. Deutsche Literaturzeitung* 53: 2404–2416.

1933 Review: Edmund Husserl, *Formale und transzendentale Logik. Deutsche Literaturzeitung* 54: 773–784.

1937 Review: Tomoo Otaka, *Grundlegung der Lehre vom sozialen Verband. Zeitschrift für öffentliches Recht* 17: 64–84.

1940a "Phenomenology and the Social Sciences," in *Philosophical Essays in Memory of Edmund Husserl,* ed. Marvin Farber. Cambridge: Harvard University Press, 1940: 164–186. (*CP* I, 118–139; reprinted in. Phenomenology, ed. J. Kockelmans, New York: Doubleday, 1967: 450–472.)

1940b "Editor's Preface" to Edmund Husserl, "Notizen zur Raumkonstitution." *PPR* 1: 21–23.

1941 "William James' Concept of the Stream of Thought Phenomenologically Interpreted." *PPR* 1: 442–452. (*CP* III, 1–14.)

1942 "Scheler's Theory of Intersubjectivity and the General Thesis of the Alter Ego." *PPR* 2: 323–347. (*CP* I, 150–179.)

1943 "The Problem of Rationality in the Social World." *Economica,* New Series 10: 130–149. (*CP* II, 64–88.)

1944a "The Stranger." *American Journal of Sociology* 49: 499–507. (*CP* II, 91–105.)

1944b Review: Marvin Farber, *The Foundation of Phenomenology. Philosophical Abstracts* 3: 8–9.

1945a "The Homecomer." *American Journal of Sociology* 50: 363–376. (*CP* II, 106–119.)

1945b "Some Leading Concepts of Phenomenology." *Social Research* 12: 77–97. (*CP* I, 99–117.)

1945c "On Multiple Realities." *PPR* 5: 533–576. (*CP* I, 207–259.)

1946a "The Well-Informed Citizen: An Essay on the Social Distribution of Knowledge." *Social Research* 13: 463–478. (*CP* II, 120–134.)

1946b "Editor's Preface" to Edmund Husserl, "Die Welt der legendigen Gegenwart und die Konstitution der außerleiblichen Umwelt." *PPR* 6: 323.

1948   "Sartre's Theory of the Alter Ego." *PPR* 9: 181–199. (*CP* I, 180–203.)
1950a   "Language, Language Disturbances and the Texture of Consciousness." *Social
         Research* 17: 365–394. (*CP* I, 260–286.)
1950b   "Felix Kaufmann: 1895–1949." *Social Research* 17: 1–7.
1951a   "Choosing among Projects of Action." *PPR* 12: 161–184. (*CP* I, 67–96.)
1951b   "Making Music Together: A Study in Social Relationship." *Social Research* 18:
         76–97. (*CP* II, 159–178.)
1951c   Review: Edmund Husserl, *Cartesianische Meditationen und Pariser Vorträge*.
         PPR 11: 421–423.
1952   "Santayana on Society and Government." *Social Research* 19: 220–246. (*CP* II,
         201–225.)
1953a   Review: Edmund Husserl, *Ideas*, volume II. *PPR* 13: 394–413. (*CP* III, 15–
         39.)
1953b   "Phenomenology and the Foundation of the Social Sciences (Edmund Husserl's
         Ideas, Vol. III)." *PPR* 13: 506–514. (*CP* III, 40–50.)
1953c   "Common Sense and Scientific Interpretation of Human Action." *PPR* 14: 1–
         38. (*CP* I, 3–47.)
1954a   "Concept and Theory Formation in the Social Sciences." *Journal of Philosophy*
         51: 257–273. (*CP* I, 48–66.)
1954b   "Don Quijote y el Problema de la Realidad." Tr. Marta Diaz de Leon de
         Recasens and Luis Recasens-Siches. *Dianoia* (Yearbook of the Department
         of Philosophy, The University of Mexico) 1: 312–330. (*CP* II, 135–158.)
1955   "Symbol, Reality and Society." In *Symbols and Society*, ed. Bryson, Finkelstein,
         Hoagland, and MacIver. New York, 1955: 135–204. (*CP* I, 287–356.)
1956a   "Mozart and the Philosophers." *Social Research* 23: 219–242. (*CP* II, 179–
         200.)
1956b   "La Philosophie de Max Scheler," in *Les philosophes célèbres*, ed. Maurice Merleau-
         Ponty. Paris, 1956: 330–335. (*CP* III, 133–144.)
1957a   "Equality and the Meaning Structure of the Social World," in *Aspects of Human
         Equality*, ed. Bryson, Faust, Finkelstein, and MacIver. New York, 1957:
         33–78. (*CP* II, 226–273.)
1957b   "Das Problem der transzendentalen Intersubjektivität bei Husserl." *Philo-
         sophische Rundschau* 5: 81–107. (*CP* III, 51–91.)
1957c   "Kurt Riezler" (co-authored by Horace Kallen.) *Proceedings and Addresses of the
         American Philosophical Association* 30: 114–115.
1957d   "Max Scheler's Epistemology and Ethics: Part I." *Review of Metaphysics* 11: 304–
         314. (*CP* III, 144–178.) (An initially unpublished part, "Scheler's Kritik
         an Kants Philosophie," is published as Part D in the German edition of
         Schutz's *Collected Papers*.)
1958a   Part II of 1957d: *Review of Metaphysics* 11: 486–501.
1958b   "Some Equivocations in the Notion of Responsibility," in *Determinism and
         Freedom*, ed. Sidney Hook. New York, 1958: 206–208. (*CP* II, 174–276.)
1959a   "Tiresias, or Our Knowledge of Future Events." *Social Research* 26: 71–89. (*CP*
         II, 177–293.)

Posthumous Publications

1959b   "Type and Eidos in Husserl's Late Philosophy." *PPR* 20: 147–165. (*CP* III,
         92–115.)
1959c   "Husserl's Importance for the Social Sciences," in *Edmund Husserl: 1859–1959*,
         ed. H. L. Van Breda and J. Taminiaux. The Hague: Nijhoff: 86–98. (*CP* I,
         140–149.) Volume III of the German edition of Schutz's collected papers
         contains autobiographical remarks by Schutz concerning this manuscript.

1960   "The Social World and the Theory of Action." *Social Research* 27: 203–221. (*CP* II, 3–19.) This manuscript is part of the Schutz-Parsons correspondence: see S1978.

1962   *Collected Papers*, vol. I: *The Problem of Social Reality*, ed. Maurice Natanson. The Hague: Martinus Nijhoff, 1968², 1971³, 1973⁴, 1977⁵. (German translation 1971; Spanish and Italian in preparation; Danish collection 1975.)

1964a *Collected Papers*, vol. II: *Studies in Social theory*, ed. Arvid Brodersen. The Hague: Martinus Nijhoff, 1968², 1971³, 1977⁴. (German translation 1971.) The following two essays appeared here for the first time:

1964b "The Dimensions of the Social World." (*CP* II, 20–63.) This is an English translation of Part IV: "Structural Analysis of the Social World," from *Der sinnhafte Aufbau der sozialen Welt* (1932a), tr. Thomas Luckmann.

1964c "Don Quixote and the Problem of Reality." (*CP* II, 135–158.) Original English version of S1954b.

1966a *Collected Papers*, vol. III: *Studies in Phenomenological Philosophy*, ed. Ilse Schutz. The Hague: Martinus Nijhoff, 1970², 1975³. (German translation 1971.) The following essay appeared here for the first time:

1966b "Some Structures of the Life-World." Tr. from German by Aron Gurwitsch. (*CP* III, 116–132.)

1967   *The Phenomenology of the Social World*. Evanston: Northwestern University Press. A translation of *Der sinnhafte Aufbau* (S1932a) by George Walsh and Frederick Lehnert.

1970a *On Phenomenology and Social Relations: Selected Writings*, ed. Helmut Wagner. Chicago: University of Chicago Press. This volume does not contain any previously unpublished material.

1970b *Reflections on the Problem of Relevance*, ed. Richard M. Zaner. New Haven: Yale University Press. (German translation 1971; Italian translation in preparation.)

1972   "Choice and the Social Sciences," in Lester Embree, ed., *Life World and Consciousness*. Evanston: Northwestern University Press; 565–596. The manuscript is an unpublished part of "Choosing among Projects of Action" (S1951a).

1973   (with Thomas Luckmann): *The Structures of the Life-World*, trans. Richard Zaner and Tristam Engelhardt. Evanston: Northwestern University Press, and London: Heinemann. Complete translation of S1975.

1975   (with Thomas Luckmann): *Strukturen der Lebenswelt*, vol. I. Neuwied and Darmstadt; Frankfurt: 1979².

1976   "Fragments on the Phenomenology of Music," ed. Fred Kersten. *Music and Man* 2: 5–71. (Reprinted in *Search of Musical Method*, ed. F. J. Smith. London: Gordon & Breach.)

1977   "Husserl and His Influence on Me," ed. Lester Embree. *The Annals of Phenomenological Sociology* 2: 41–44.

1978   *The Theory of Social Action: The Correspondence of Alfred Schutz and Talcott Parsons*, ed. Richard Grathoff. Bloomington: Indiana University Press.

1981   *Theorie der Lebensformen*, ed. Ilja Srubar. Frankfurt: Suhrkamp. This volume contains the first publication of the following manuscripts from 1924 to 1927: "Lebensformen und Sinnstruktur"; "Erleben, Sprache, Begriff; Sinnstruktur der Novelle (Goethe)"; "*Sinn einer Kunstform (Musik)*."

1982   *Life Forms and Meaning Structure*. Translation of S1981, ed. Helmut Wagner. London: Routledge & Kegan Paul.

II. *Bibliography of the Writings of Aron Gurwitsch*[2]

2. Smaller reviews are not listed. See the German journals which are mentioned (1929–1933), the *Recherches Philosophique* after 1933, and *PPR*.

Abbreviations:

SPP: *Studies in Phenomenology and Psychology* (G1966a)
PTS: *Phenomenology and the Theory of Science* (G1974b)
PPR: *Philosophy and Phenomenological Research*

1929   "Phänomenologie der Thematik und des reinen Ich." *Psychologische Forschung*
          12: 279–381. (English translation by F. Kersten in *SPP*, 175–286.)
1930   "Ontologische Bemerkungen zur Axiomatik der Euklidischen Geometrie." *Philo-*
          sophischer Anzeiger 4: 78–100.
1931   Review: Fritz Kaufmann, *Die Philosophie des Grafen Yorck von Wartenburg.*
          Zeitschrift für Aesthetik und allgemeine Kunstwissenschaft.
1932   Review: Edmund Husserl, "Nachwort zu meinen *Ideen zu einer reinen Phäno-*
          menologie und phänomenologischer Philosophie." *Deutsche Literaturzeitung* 28,
          February 1932. (English translation by F. Kersten in *SPP*, 107–115.)
1933a   "Zur Bedeutung der Prädestinationslehre für die Ausbildung des 'Kapi-
          talistischen Geistes.'" *Archiv für Sozialwissenschaft und Sozialpolitik* 68:
          616–622.
1933b   Review: Leo Strauss, *Die Religionskritik Spinozas als Grundlage seiner Bibel-*
          wissenschaft. Göttingische Gelehrte Anzeigen, 124–149.
1934   "La Place de la psychologie dans l'ensemble des sciences." *Revue de Synthèse* 8:
          399–439. (English translation by D. Herman in *SPP*.)
1935   Review: Henri Delacroix (ed.), *Psychologie du langage. Revue Philosophique de la*
          France et de l'Etranger 120: 399–439.
1936a   "L'Acquisition du langage d'après H. Delacroix." *Revue de Synthèse* 12: 227–
          233.
1936b   "Quelques aspects et quelques développements de la psychologie de la forme."
          Journal de Psychologie Normale et Pathologique 33: 413–470. (English transla-
          tion by R. Zaner in *SPP*, 3–55.)
1936c   "Développement historique de la Gestalt-psychologie." *Thales* 2: 167–176.
1938   "XI. Congrès International de Psychologie." *Revue de Métaphysique et de Morale*
          50: 145–160.
1939   "Le fonctionnement de l'organisme d'après K. Goldstein." *Journal de Psychologie*
          Normale et Pathologique 36: 107–138.
1940a   "La science biologique d'après K. Goldstein." *Revue Philosophique de la France et*
          de l'Etranger 129: 126–151. (English translation by R. Zaner in *SPP*, 69–
          88.)
1940b   "On the Intentionality of Consciousness," in *Philosophical Essays in Memory of*
          Edmund Husserl, ed. Marvin Farber. Cambridge: Harvard University Press;
          65–83. (Also in *SPP*, 124–140. Reprinted in *Phenomenology*, ed. J.
          Kockelmans, New York: Doubleday Anchor, 1967; 118–136.)
1941   "A Non-Egological Conception of Consciousness." *PPR* 1: 325–338. (Also in
          SPP, 287–300.)
1942   Review: James Street Fulton, *The Cartesianism of Phenomenology. PPR* 2: 551–
          558.
1943   "William James' Theory of the 'Transitive Parts' of the Stream of Conscious-
          ness." *PPR* 3: 449–477. (Also in *SPP*, 301–331.)
1945   "On Contemporary Nihilism." *Review of Politics* 7: 170–198.
1946a   "Algebraic Discussion of Lenses." *American Journal of Physics* 14: 49–50.

1946b   Review: Hans Kelsen, *Society and Nature*. *Isis* 36: 142–146.
1947   "On the Object of Thought." *PPR* 7: 347–356. (Also in *SPP*, 141–147.)
1949   "Gelb-Goldstein's Concept of 'Concrete' and 'Categorial' Attitude and the Phe-
         nomenology of Ideation." *PPR* 10: 172–196. (Also in *SPP*, 359–384.)
1951   "Présuppositions philosophique de la logique." *Revue de Métaphysique et de
         Morale* 56: 395–405. (Reprinted in a volume of essays from the *Revue de
         Métaphysique et de Morale: Phénoménologie-Existence*, Paris: Armand Colin,
         1953; English translation by A. Rosenthal in *SPP*, 350–358.)
1953   "Sur une racine perceptive de l'abstraction." *Actes du XI. Congrès International de
         Philosophie*, vol. 2. Amsterdam and Louvain: 43–47. (English translation by
         A. Rosenthal in *SPP*, 385–389.)
1955   "The Phenomenological and the Psychological Approach to Consciousness."
         PPR 15: 303–319. (Partially translated into Hebrew in *Iyyun* 4 (1953):
         193–202. Reprinted in *Essays in Phenomenology*, ed. Maurice Natanson;
         The Hague: Martinus Nijhoff, 1966. Also in *SPP*, 89–106.)
1956   "The Last Work of Edmund Husserl, Part 1." *PPR* 16: 370–398. (Spanish
         translation by E. Vera Villalobos in *Lecciones y Ensayos* 6 [1957], Buenos
         Aires. Also in *SPP*, 397–418.)
1957a   "The Last Work of Edmund Husserl, Parts 2–5." *PPR* 17: 370–398. (Spanish
         translation by E. Vera Villalobos in *Lecciones y Ensayos* 7 [1958]. Also in
         SPP, 418–447.)
1957b   *Théorie du champ de la conscience*. Bruges and Paris: Desclée de Brouwer. (En-
         glish translation, G1964a; German translation 1975.)
1958   "Preface" to Quentin Lauer, *The Triumph of Subjectivity*. New York: Fordham
         University Press.
1959a   "Beitrag zur phänomenologischen Theorie der Wahrnehmung." *Zeitschrift für
         philosophische Forschung* 13: 419–437. (English translation by F. Kersten in
         SPP, 332–349.)
1959b   "Sur la pensée conceptuelle," in *Edmund Husserl, 1859–1959*, ed. H. L. Van
         Breda and J. Taminiaux. The Hague: Martinus Nijhoff. (Reprinted in
         English translation by F. Crosson in *The Modelling of Mind*, ed. K. Sayre
         and F. Crosson; Notre Dame: University of Notre Dame Press, 1963. Also
         in *SPP*, 390–396.)
1960   "La conception de la conscience chez Kant et chez Husserl." *Bulletin de la Société
         Française de Philosophie* 54: 65–96. (English translation by R. Zaner in *SPP*,
         148–174.)
1961   "The Problem of Existence in Constitutive Phenomenology." *The Journal of
         Philosophy* 58: 625–632. (Also in *SPP*, 116–123.)
1962   "The Commonsense World of Social Reality: A Discourse on Alfred Schutz."
         Social Research 29: 50–72. (Reprinted as the Introduction to Alfred Schutz,
         Collected Papers, vol. 3, ed. Ilse Schutz; The Hague: Martinus Nijhoff,
         1966. Also in *PTS*, 113–132.)
1963   "An Apparent Paradox in the Leibnizian System." First published in Hebrew:
         Iyyun 14–15: 145–155. (English: "An Apparent Paradox in Leibni-
         zianism," *Social Research* 33: 47–64.)
1964a   *The Field of Consciousness*. Pittsburgh: Duquesne University Press. (English of
         1957b.)
1964b   "Der Begriff des Bewußtseins bei Kant und Husserl." *Kant-Studien* 55: 410–
         427.
1965a   "The Phenomenology of Perception: Perceptual Implications," in *An Invitation
         to Phenomenology*, ed. James M. Edie. Chicago: Quadrangle Books; 17–29.
         (Reprinted in: *Perception: Selected Readings in Science and Phenomenology*,
         ed. Paul Tibbets; Chicago: Quadrangle Books, 1969).

1965b   "Comment on the Paper by H. Marcuse, 'On Science and Phenomenology.' "
         Boston Studies in the Philosophy of Science, vol. 2, ed. Robert S. Cohen and
         Max W. Wartofsky. New York: Humanities Press; 291–306. (Also in *PTS,*
         33–59.)
1966a   *Studies in Phenomenology and Psychology.* Evanston: Northwestern University
         Press.
1966b   Review of *Husserliana IX:* "Edmund Husserl's Conception of Phenomenologi-
         cal Psychology." *Review of Metaphysics* 19: 698–727. (Also in *PTS,* 77–
         112.)
1967a   "Husserl's Theory of the Intentionality of Consciousness in Historical Perspec-
         tive," in *Phenomenology and Existentialism,* ed. Edward N. Lee and Maurice
         Mandelbaum. Baltimore: The Johns Hopkins Press; 388–401. (Also in
         PTS, 210–240.)
1967b   "Galilean Physics in the Light of Husserl's Phenomenology," in *Galileo, Man of
         Science,* ed. Ernan McMullin. New York: Basic Books; 388–401. (Also in
         PTS, 33–59.)
1968   "Bermerkungen zu den Referaten der Herren Patocka, Landgrebe und
         Chisholm," in *Proceedings of the XIVth International Congress of Philosophy,*
         vol. 2. Vienna: Herder Verlag; 209–215.
1969a   "Social Science and Natural Science," in *Economic Means and Social Ends,* ed.
         Robert L. Heilbronner. Englewood Cliffs: Prentice-Hall; 37–55.
1969b   "Towards a Theory of Intentionality," in *The Isenberg Memorial Lecture Series,
         1965–66.* East Lansing: Michigan State University Press. (Reprinted in
         PPR 30 [1970]: 354–367.)
1970   "Problems of the Life-World," in *Phenomenology and Social Reality: Essays in
         Memory of Alfred Schutz,* ed. Maurice Natanson. The Hague: Martinus
         Nijhoff; 35–61. (Also in *PTS,* 3–32.)
1971   "Einleitung" to Kurt Goldstein, *Selected Papers/Ausgewählte Schriften.* The
         Hague: Martinus Nijhoff; xi–xxiv.
1972a   "On the systematic Unity of the Sciences," in *Phänomenologie heute: Festschrift
         für Ludwig Landgrebe,* ed. W. Biemel. The Hague: Martinus Nijhoff: 103–
         121. (Also in *PTS,* 132–149.)
1972b   "Zwei Begriffe von Kontingenz bei Leibniz," in *Weltaspekte der Philosophie:
         Rudolph Berlinger zum 26. Oktober 1972,* ed. W. Beierswaltes and W.
         Schrader. Amsterdam: Editions Rodopi; 101–118.
1972c   "Substantiality and Perceptual Coherence: Remarks on H. B. Veatch, *Two Log-
         ics.*" *Research in Phenomenology* 2: 29–46.
1973   "Perceptual Coherence as the Foundation of the Judgment of Predication," in
         Phenomenology, Continuation and Criticism: Essays in Honor of Dorion
         Cairns, ed. F. Kersten and R. Zaner. The Hague: Martinus Nijhoff: 62–
         89. (Also in *PTS,* 241–267.)

Posthumous Publications

1974a   *Leibniz: Philosophie des Panlogismus.* Berlin: Walter de Gruyter.
1974b   *Phenomenology and the Theory of Science,* ed. Lester Embree. Evanston: Northwest-
         ern University Press. (This volume contains the previously unpublished es-
         says "Reflections on Mathematics and Logic," 60–76; "An Introduction to
         Constitutive Phenomenology," 153–189; "Some Fundamental Principles
         of Constitutive Phenomenology," 190–209.)
1974c   "On Thematization." *Research in Phenomenology* 4.
1976   *Die mitmenschlichen Begegnungen in der Milieuwelt* (Habilitation thesis of 1931),
         ed. A. Métraux. Berlin: Walter de Gruyter.

1977   "Outlines of a Theory of 'Essentially Occasional Expressions,' " in *Readings on Edmund Husserl's 'Logical Investigations,'* ed. J. N. Mohanty. The Hague: Martinus Nijhoff, 1977. (Also in G1985, 65–79.)
1979   *Human Encounters in the Social World,* translation of G1976 by Fred Kersten. Pittsburgh: Duquesne University Press.
1985   *Marginal Consciousness,* ed. Lester Embree. Athens, Ohio and London: Ohio University Press. (This volume contains the initial draft of the "Les trois domaines du réel," which is mentioned in GS 10.9.50, GS 12.4.51, and GS 2.17.52, and the text of a lecture, "The Phenomenology of Signals and Significations," delivered on April 14, 1937, at the Sorbonne in Paris.)

Index

Academia: teaching careers of correspondents, xi, 113–14; emigration and Gurwitsch, xxvi; Gurwitsch on anti-Semitism, 54; postwar France, 84; offers and academic prestige, 103; Gurwitsch and Brandeis University, 284

Action: as theme of social science, xvii; projects of and realization in actual behavior, 171

Adjustment: Gurwitsch on Evangelium of universal, 72

Albert Einstein Foundation: Brandeis University, 86

Alter ego: existence and reduced sphere, 147

Ambiance: translation of "life-world," 226

American Committee for Emigré Scholars, Writers, and Artists, Inc.: grant to Gurwitsch, 89

American Express Co.: France in 1940, 14

American International Phenomenological Society: federation with European society proposed, 270

American Philosophical Association: submission of paper by Schutz, 19, 27; grants to Gurwitsch, 56, 59, 82

Amnesia: eidetic character of color names, 115–16

Angels: life-world, 235

Anger: expression as appresentation, 232, 236

Anthropology: gnosticism, 189; life-world, 253

Anticipation: open infinity of the perceptual process, 166

Anti-Semitism: sensitivity of Gurwitsch to, 2; Gurwitsch and Johns Hopkins University, 41; Gurwitsch on Jew's place in academia, 54

Appeasement: politics and war, 129

Apprehension: Husserl's concept of, 181–82; Kant and synthesis of, 261

Appresentation: signs and symbols, 227; transcendences of life-world, 231; signs and linguistic expressions, 232; Schutz's and Husserl's concepts of, 236

Arendt, Hannah: acquaintance with Alice Gurwitsch, xxii

Argumentation: from orientation of logic, 301

Aristotle: John Wild, 65; Popov and Russian philosophical literature, 97; and general science of the *Lebenswelt*, 247; perception and typicality, 250

Aron, Raymond: postwar France and emigration, 91, 94

Atomism: Jamesian theory of fringes, 24; James and intentionality, 27

Average: contemporary interest in, 72

Awareness: continuity of consciousness, 151

Baltimore: Gurwitsch on, 63

Banking: career of Schutz, xv, xxii*n,* 26

Beacon Press: Gurwitsch and publication, 245, 252–53; Schutz on, 259

Bendix, Ludwig: acquaintance with Gurwitsch, 93

Berger, Gaston: and Gurwitsch in Paris, 14; subject-object dialectic, 101

Bergery, Gaston: *Front Populaire,* 18

Bergson, Henri: themes of correspondence, xxix; convergence of theories with Leibniz and Husserl, 135

Berlin: non-communist Jews in 1950s, 286; Gurwitsch and university, 291–92, 292–93, 299, 302; Khrushchev and political situation, 299, 301, 302

Binswanger, Ludwig: Gurwitsch on, 18

Biography: Schutz, xix, 319–20; Gurwitsch, xix–xx, 104–105; and objective time, 155–56

de Biran, Maine: resistance and "effort," 152

Board of Economic Warfare: Schutz as senior consultant, 68

Boas, George: Gurwitsch and Committee for Displaced Foreign Scholars, 32–33; Gurwitsch and publication, 50

Body: consciousness in Sartre and Merleau-Ponty, 101; awareness of and thematic shifts, 151; socio-cultural objects, 232

Brandeis University: establishment, 82; Gurwitsch and teaching position, 84, 101–102; Albert Einstein Foundation, 86; Gurwitsch as head of philosophy department, 113; general seminars, 205; intellectual climate, 221, 284; Gurwitsch and leave of absence, 285; academic politics, 306–307

Brecht, Arnold: establishment of Graduate Faculty of New School, xxiv–xxv; German occupation of France, xxv; attacked Schutz's sociological perspective of emigration, 42

Van Breda, Hermann Leo: preservation of Husserl's works, xvi; Husserl Archives, 268;

334

336

Formalization: generalization and thematizing
attitude, 192, 194
Frame: and horizon in reference to ego, 47–49
France: German occupation, xxv; internment
camps; xxxvi*n;* war and intellectual climate,
12; postwar economic conditions, 82, 94;
postwar political environment, 84, 86, 91,
94; Gurwitsch and feeling of otherness, 291
Frank, Philip: behavior during discussion, 78
Fréchet, Maurice: formalization, 313
Free choice: imposed relevance, 152
Free variation: freedom and direction, 300
French: ambiguities of language, 192;
Gurwitsch and translation, 216–17; power
of condensation, 221, 258; translation of
"relevance," 226; terminology and translation, 228
Freud, Sigmund: theories in Western societies,
187
"Fringed": use of term, 43
Fringes: Jamesian theory of and Husserl's inner
horizon, 22–23, 28
Fulbright Foundation: source of funds and
grant to Gurwitsch, 266, 284; Schutz as
sponsor, 285; and Guggenheim Foundation,
289

Garfinkel, Harold: influence of Schutz, 325
Geiger, Moritz: education of Gurwitsch, xx;
lack of references to in works of Gurwitsch,
xxxv*n*
Geiringer, Mrs.: Gurwitsch and teaching of
mathematics at Wheaton College, 95
Gelb, Adhemer: Gestalt theory and psychopathology, xx; introduced Gurwitsch and
Wertheimer, 108
Generalization: formalization and thematizing
attitude, 192, 194
Geometry: regional ontologies and science, 181
Germany: suppression of Husserl, xv–xvi, 290;
influence of Heidegger on philosophy, 290;
Gurwitsch and feeling of otherness, 291; academic conditions in East Zone, 293; recognition of Gurwitsch, 302; Gurwitsch and university tradition of teaching, 321. *See also* Berlin
Gestalt-coherence: Gurwitsch's theory of, 121;
phenomenology of perception, 144; and pertinence, 152
Gestalt theory: Jamesian object of thought, 22;
historical-theoretical foundation, 121;
Schutz on Gurwitsch's presentation of, 137;
criticized by Schutz, 140–41; phenomenology, 143, 196
Gnosticism: *eidos* of history, 171–72, 186;
Voegelin and phenomenology, 183; idea of
the Messiah, 185, 195; metaphysicians, 189,
195; Max Weber, 190
Goldstein, Kurt: Gestalt theory and psycho-

pathology, xx; relationship with Riezler,
107; meeting with Schutz, 111; reviewed by
Schutz, 119; prepredicative experience, 148
Grasped act: egological structure, 53
Grathoff, Richard: influence of Schutz, 325
Gray: Lithuanian language and color names,
113, 114
Greece: philosophy, 184–85; political theory
and drama, 188
Guggenheim Foundation: rejected Gurwitsch's
application, 53, 54, 287, 289
Gurs: internment camps, xxxvi*n*
Gurwitsch, Alice (Raja): first meeting of corre-
spondents, xv; employment in Paris, xx, xxii;
Zionist youth work, xxxv*n*; on France after
declaration of war, 2; depression during war,
30

Harvard University: fellowship and Gurwitsch,
58, 59, 81; philosophy department in 1942,
65–66; Schutz on Gurwitsch's teaching at,
68
Harvard University Press: Gurwitsch and publication, 183, 191, 196, 197–98, 200
Heidegger, Martin: persecution of Husserl, xvi;
relationship with Husserl, xxxii–xxxiii*n*;
Leo Strauss on, 97; Gurwitsch on philosophy of, 163; influence on German philosophy, 290; Nazi party, 294*n*
Herder, Johann G.: Lithuanian language, 115
Heresy: Gurwitsch and Voegelin, 183; gnosticism, 190
Hic-illic problem: Gurwitsch's theory of marginal awareness, 117
Historicism: Lévy-Bruhl's theory, 43
History: context of correspondence, vii; refugee scholars, viii; nihilism and social sciences
in Europe, xvi–xvii; Gurwitsch on refugees,
70; constitution of sciences, 75; Voegelin
and *eidos* of, 171–72; Voegelin and phenomenology, 183; philosophy of and self-
interpretation of society, 188; eschatology,
188; Joachim's theory of, 188–89; *eidos* and
Christianity, 189, 195; sense of and
Voegelin, 200; Marx, 201; Gurwitsch and
teaching, 321–22
Hodgson, Shadworth Holloway: discussed by
Gurwitsch and Perry, 63
Horizons: Jamesian theory of fringes, 22–23,
28; and frame in reference to ego, 47–49;
indeterminacy and perception, 167–68;
open possibilities, 168; inner horizons and
perception, 192, 194–95
Human nature: truth and relevance, 126, 127
Hume, David: terminology and translation, 12;
and Husserl, 78
Husserl, Edmund: influence on Gurwitsch and
Schutz, vii; interpretation as theme of correspondence, viii–ix, xxviii; criticism of and